Analytical Peace Economics

The Middle East is at an unprecedented crossroads between the established Euro-centric system and the emerging Asian powerhouses like India and China. Their economies, policies and social structures are a halfway house between these two dominant groups and are an important case study to examine in order to highlight future prospects and problems of the global system. The Middle East is an important missing piece in a huge global puzzle. This book takes a significant step towards understanding that puzzle and offers solutions for how to fully integrate this missing jigsaw piece into the global economic system.

Analytical Peace Economics: the illusion of war for peace focuses on three critical issues in the Middle East that dominate discussions about their place in the global political economy: conflict, oil and (regional) development. Examining economic and social development in juxtaposition with conflict and peace, this book adapts, develops and applies historical, geographical, economic and psychological methods, creating a nuanced approach to the collective understanding of the economic and social dynamics in the region. By developing theoretical models and analysing empirical research, this book offers an economic analysis of the attempt to find peace through war and seeks to find alternative solutions.

This book will be of interest to researchers, policymakers and doctoral students of economics, finance and social sciences as well as advanced undergraduate students of peace economics and development studies.

Partha Gangopadhyay is a Professor of Economics and Director of the Centre for Economic Policy and Modeling at the University of the South Pacific, Fiji, and Associate Professor of Economics, Western Sydney University, Australia.

Nasser Elkanj is an Associate Professor of Finance at the American University of the Middle East, Kuwait.

Routledge Studies in Defence and Peace Economics
Edited by Keith Hartley, University of York, UK and
Jurgen Brauer, Augusta State University, USA

For a full list of titles in this series, please visit www.routledge.com/series/
SE0637

Analytical Peace Economics
The illusion of war for peace

Partha Gangopadhyay and Nasser Elkanj

LONDON AND NEW YORK

First published 2017 by Routledge

2 Park Square, Milton Park, Abingdon, Oxfordshire OX14 4RN

52 Vanderbilt Avenue, New York, NY 10017

Routledge is an imprint of the Taylor & Francis Group, an informa business

First issued in paperback 2019

British Library Cataloguing in Publication Data
A catalogue record for this book is available from the British Library

Library of Congress Cataloguing in Publication Data
Names: Gangopadhyay, Partha, author. | Elkanj, Nasser, author.
Title: Analytical peace economics : the illusion of war for peace /
Partha Gangopadhyay and Nasser Elkanj.
Description: Abingdon, Oxon; New York, NY: Routledge, 2017. |
Includes bibliographical references.
Identifiers: LCCN 2016017517 | ISBN 9781138935457 (hardback) |
ISBN 9781315677439 (ebook)
Subjects: LCSH: War–Economic aspects. | Peace–Economic
aspects. | Middle East–Politics and government. |
Africa, North–Politics and government.
Classification: LCC HB195. G36 2017 | DDC 303.6/6–dc23
LC record available at https://lccn.loc.gov/2016017517

ISBN: 978-1-138-93545-7 (hbk)
ISBN: 978-0-367-87410-0 (pbk)

Typeset in Times New Roman
by Out of House Publishing

Partha Gangopadhyay dedicates the book to his son Karno Gangopadhyay

and

Nasser Elkanj dedicates the book to his parents and his three sisters

Contents

Figures

Tables

Foreword

The most important article I read as an undergraduate in the early 1950s was KW Rothschild's classic in the *Economic Journal*, 'Price theory and oligopoly'. In it, he argued that Clausewitz's principles of war contained the most appropriate structure within which to study the market behaviour of oligopolists. His arguments have had a major and sustained influence on my research ever after.

Now Partha Gangopadhyay and Nasser Elkanj, in this remarkable original book, *Analytical Peace Economics: the illusion of war for peace*, have gone in exactly the opposite direction to Rothschild. They use the technical advances on the frontier of economics and management science to illuminate the causes and consequences of conflict. Using a variety of approaches and much empirical and experimental work, Gangopadhyay and Elkanj analyse conflicts in the Middle East, the 'war on terror', the worldwide arms race, and the differential impacts of conflict on developing and developed nations, and on regions within them both.

The analysis is an enlightening combination of deep economic intuition, common sense, and high-powered economic and econometric analysis. The authors are careful to point out limitations of the analysis and the findings, and to suggest topics and areas for further research. Nevertheless, the book is a major step forward in our understanding of some of the most important and frightening issues facing the modern world, illustrating the strengths of clear thinking and evidence-based findings in modern economic analysis.

G.C. Harcourt,
School of Economics, UNSW Australia and the former
President of Jesus College, University of Cambridge,
1988–1989 and 1990–1992

Foreword

We are in an epoch different to any other in human history. The problems we face are global in nature and require cooperation on a scale unprecedented in human history. To solve these urgent challenges – over-population, climate change, ever-decreasing bio-diversity, and migration crises – we need to bring about peace. Because without peace humankind will never be able to achieve the levels of cooperation, trust, inclusiveness and social equity needed to bring about solutions to global challenges.

I am a strong proponent of the need to study, advocate and act on peace and focus on bringing a strategic approach to raising the world's attention and awareness around its importance to humanity's survival in the twenty-first century. This is why I am fascinated by the revelations unearthed in *Analytical Peace Economics: the illusion of war for peace*. Through the intellectual endeavours of Partha Gangopadhyay and Nasser Elkanj, we are brought closer to an understanding of how to bring peace about. We learn about the influence of politics on conflicts, the causes and consequences of terrorism in the Middle East and North Africa, the use of participatory conflict management procedures, and the role of economic inequality in conflicts.

Certainly, I agree with the authors when they say that, 'Before the 1950s, work in the area of conflict was performed in the main by political scientists. This has changed with the growing awareness of economists about the impacts of conflicts on the economy.'

Although societies that are peaceful, socially cohesive, stable and safe are undeniably worthwhile in and of themselves, they also make economic sense. Research by the Institute for Economics and Peace consistently finds that more peaceful societies are also more prosperous. In fact, when the economic impact of violence and the fear of violence are considered on a global scale they are equivalent to at least US$ 14.3 trillion. Basically, 13.4% of GDP is lost to violence every year. Then, of course, the pivotal role of peace in encouraging prosperity extends to broader social outcomes, such as education, health and overall well-being.

Peace is more than the absence of violence. In truly peaceful societies, there are high levels of what I refer to as 'Positive Peace', this is the attitudes, institutions and structures that promote resilience in society, enabling nations to overcome adversity and resolve internal economic, cultural, and political conflict through peaceful means. Compare the way in which two European countries have dealt with their economic crises over the past few years to demonstrate how a country with strong Positive Peace manages; Iceland was much more resilient than Greece, which is lagging behind in Positive Peace. Or in the case of natural disasters, compare the resilience of Japan in the face of the 2011 tsunami, to that of Haiti after the 2010 earthquake.

What creates peaceful societies also creates the optimum environment for many other conditions considered beneficial: strong business environments, superior ecological management, better gender rights.

Positive Peace also builds the capacity for resilience and the possibility and incentives for non-violent alternatives to conflict resolution. Stronger Positive Peace reduces the level of violence within a society in two ways. First, it removes the source of grievances that could generate violence, and second it means that legitimate and effective non-violent resolution avenues are on offer. A decrease in violence will also lead to a virtuous cycle. Less is spent on violence containment, allowing more funds to be invested in other growth expanding opportunities, thereby helping to further improve peace.

Personally, I find the study of peace most rewarding and have been surprised by how little we actually know about peace. That is why the ambitious research contained within this book is a vital contribution to our understanding of the most crucial issue of our time. I commend the inquiry and determination of Gangopadhyay and Elkanj in seeking to find an answer to one of humanity's most enduring and consequential of questions: What is the solution to war?

Steve Killelea, Executive Chairman and Founder,
Institute for Economics and Peace, Sydney, Australia

Acknowledgements

To write an acknowledgement is usually a pleasant surprise. It is a surprise because it means that the writing process for this research monograph is coming to a grinding halt – finally, indeed. It is pleasant for the very reason that the process of writing, just like any other long journey, is critically anchored to an optimal stoppage point where the extrinsic motivation for seeing the outcome of research is in perfect balance with the intrinsic motivation behind plugging away at the monograph. Predictable though this may have been, just like life itself, the fact that it was a priori predicted, does not make it easy to live it post-hoc, or a posteriori. What remains to be seen in future days is whether the pleasure from having seen the final product will be followed by enjoying concrete, critical, rational and constructive criticisms of our collective, often lop-sided, efforts in writing this monograph. During the long incubation period many people have contributed to this product. We are going to hand-pick a few lest the emphasis is misplaced. We would like to thank, for both accepted and rejected advice, Jurgen Brauer, Manas Chatterji, Mansoob Murshed, Steve Killelea, Raja Junankar, John Lodewijks, Alex Mintz, Raul Caruso, Rahul Nilakantan, Daniel Hyslop, Camilla Schippa, Biswa Bhattacharya, Oscar Hauptman, Bobby Banerjee, Yanis Varoufakis and Sriram Shankar. The book would not have reached its current form without detailed comments from anonymous referees and Keith Hartley. It is an opportunity for us to humbly express our deep gratitude to the late Michael Intriligator and the late Walter Isard, two Goliaths in our field, for their active and unflinching support to our research from the very first day of this project.

1 Conflicts, development and progress

Introduction

Wars and conflicts, in the opinion of many European philosophers like Baron d'Holbach, are nothing but a 'remnant of savage customs'. In 1788 George Washington, a contemporary of d'Holbach from the other side of the Atlantic, issued a stern warning that it was time for agriculture and commerce 'to supersede the waste of war and the rage of conquest.' Yet time and again, the wild rage of war has pivoted on the calculating and often a rational belief that a brief and momentary madness of war can smother many future and catastrophic wars. This belief offers the rational foundation to wars as a war for peace as the globe witnesses wars – unfolding with an unfailing regularity – in the Balkans, in the Gulf, and then the unleashing of wars on terror after 9/11. This sentiment is nothing new as in 1790 the new French Revolutionary State enunciated the 'declaration of peace to the world', which rather prematurely announced to have ended the savage wars in Europe forever. The declaration of peace after the French revolution assumed 'a single society, whose object is the peace and happiness of each and all of its members'. It took less than two years after the declaration of peace for Europe to be dragged into a series of bloody wars that continued for 23 more years. It temporarily halted with the defeat of France in 1815. In other words, many wars are fought with the forlorn hope of a perpetual peace at the end of this final war, yet wars and conflicts bedevil our human history with unfailing repetitions. Nation states often direct every possible political, social and economic resource towards the 'just' war for an utter defeat of the enemy – one last time. This is the war for peace – the abiding theme of our work in this monograph.

When one objectively looks at the Middle East and North Africa – one sees oil. Our vision is also partly frosted by oil that is a potential source of conflicts in the region. A major focus of the US foreign policy has been to ensure access to foreign oil supplies especially since 1971. Since 1971 the US has wilfully chosen to reduce its domestic oil production. By the year 1996, the United States started importing half of its use of oil. The major vulnerability of the US economy is that the country has 21 billion barrels of known crude oil reserves. Against this backdrop of non-renewable stock of oil reserve, the appetite for oil in the US economy is colossal, about 17 million barrels daily. In terms of simple stocktaking, the US oil reserves would disappear in a period of less than four years if the US did not secure oil from other countries. The US has failed to shift away from oil as the primary source of its energy as the annual demand for oil is projected to grow at 1.2% per year in the 2020s.

The heavy dependence on oil and limited known stocks of oil reserves made the US government overzealous in its efforts to control the global supply of oil. In strategic terms, the US government has a keen interest in geographical locations of our globe that have large stocks of oil. If one looks at the Middle East one notes Saudi Arabia, the world's largest producer of oil, with the world's largest reserve, and Iraq, with the world's second biggest reserve. It is more than a coincidence that we see the US naval facilities and troops stationed in these two countries with a constant vigil over most of the gulf region. At the same time, the history of the post (Second World) war has noted that many nationalist leaders in the Middle East and North Africa – most of which had been corrupt regimes for a long time – started getting their horns locked with the US government over diverse issues. Somewhat uncomfortable feelings in the Middle East and North Africa centre around the suspicion that the US often seeks to control the world's oil price: as an example, if the oil price increases by $1 a barrel then the US will be forced to increase its annual expenditure on oil by $4 billion. To stabilise the price of oil, the US seeks to increase the production of oil in Iraq from 4 million barrels daily to 6 million barrels daily in the mid-term and to more than 12 million barrels daily in the long term. Despite the recent US interests in oil, the history of bloodshed has been a sticky problem for the region. Let us have a cursory glance at the unfortunate history of bloodshed in the region.

1.1   Conflict in the Middle East: history of bloodshed

The 'War for Peace' refers to our collective efforts, or their failure, to find a long-term cure for costly and violent conflicts. At least for the last 60 years, the Middle East and parts of North Africa[1] have remained the most unstable region in the entire world as a result of political, ethnic and religious conflicts in the region.[2] The heart of the crisis is the Arab–Israeli conflict, which has been the focus of international diplomacy and worldwide media for decades. The hostility between Arabs and Israelis has filled our globe with collective violence leading to acts of terrorism, counterterrorism and interstate armed conflicts (Bailey, 1990). The Arab–Israeli conflict has included at least 26 crises and five major wars: 1948 Arab–Israeli War, 1956 Suez War, 1967 Six Day War, 1973 Yom Kippur War, 1982 Lebanon War, and 2006 Lebanon War.[3] In addition, the region has experienced two wars in Iraq (1991 and 2003), and the Iran–Iraq War between 1980 and 1988. The civil wars in Libya and Syria saw unprecedented depths of horrors in the recent years. The Middle East is the most militarised region in the world with one-third of the world's arm imports flocking to the region (Bureau of Verification and Compliance, 2000).

It is conventional, before starting any discussion about the term 'conflict', to define it. There has been no generally accepted definition of 'conflict' in the literature until now. The word derives from the Latin *conflictus*, meaning 'striking together with force'. Pondy (1967) suggests other definitions, stating,

> The term conflict has been used at one time or another in the literature to describe: (1) *antecedent conditions* (for example, scarcity of resources, policy differences) of conflictful behaviour, (2) *affective states* (e.g. stress, tension, hostility, anxiety, etc.) of the individuals involved, (3) *cognitive states* of individuals, i.e. their perception or awareness of conflictful situations, and (4) *conflictful behaviour*, ranging from passive resistance to overt aggression.

Conflict has a wide range of activities such as: civil wars, coups d'état, crime, riots, strikes ... and so on.

Burton (1997) defines conflict as 'a relationship in which each party perceives the others' goals, values, interests or behaviour as antithetical to its own'. Deutsch (1973) distinguishes between conflict and competition. He assumes that although competition produces conflict, not all conflict reflects competition. Folberg and Taylor (1984) distinguish between conflict and dispute, where conflict is interpersonal and unknown except to the individual, and dispute is interpersonal and manifested or communicated.

The Stockholm International Peace Research Institute (SIPRI) defines conflict as

> the use of armed force between the military forces of two or more governments, or of one government and at least one organised armed group, resulting in battle-related deaths of at least 1,000 people in any single calendar year and in which the incompatibility concerns control of government and/or territory.
>
> (Dwan and Holmqvist, 2005)

Another useful definition comes from the Uppsala Conflict Data Program (UCDP):

> a contested incompatibility that concerns government or territory or both, where the use of armed force between two parties results in at least 25 battle-related deaths. The requirement is that one of these two warring parties must be the 'government of a state'.
>
> (Wallensteen and Sollenberg, 1997 and 2005)

Our research on conflict is divided into five interrelated blocks. First we explain how economic inequality can cause intra-state conflicts. In the existing literature econometric studies have not convincingly established such causality (see Humphreys, 2003), though qualitative studies clearly point to inequality as a major source of conflict. The main problem in the existing literature is that econometric research has used an overall measure of inequality instead of group inequality (see Humphreys, 2003). Our research will develop theoretical models and offer empirical findings based on alternative measures and indices to explain the role of economic inequality in conflicts. In this very context, we will introduce and highlight the role of *justice* for impacting on collective violence in the region.

Second, our research also intends to explain how politics can precipitate, fuel and perpetuate conflicts. The politics of conflict is based on the idea that the choice of government policies plays a significant role in determining the possibilities of conflict. The research in this monograph will examine how government policies, market mechanisms and global shocks like global warming can feed on each other to create exchange *entitlement failures*, which can in turn drive collective violence and inter-group conflicts leading to a complete collapse of security for the region. For explaining conflicts we will adapt and apply the models of entitlement failures to collective violence for the very first time. We will also create an index of long-term vulnerability to assess various existing models and explain new models of conflicts and peace in the context of entitlement failures.

Third, considerable attention will be devoted to model, explore and explain the causes and consequences of terrorism in the region. In the existing literature, two formal and widely circulated models by Eckstein and Tsiddon (2004) and Abadie and Gardeazabal (2008) are proposed, to study impacts of terrorism on the economy, each focusing on particular factors and channels through which terrorism affects an economy. Eckstein and Tsiddon (2004) choose a closed economy model to argue that terrorism raises the death rate and the *discount rate*, which in turns translates into a reduction of income and other macroeconomic variables. On the other hand, Abadie and Gardeazabal (2008), by exploiting an open economy model, take capital outflows as a consequence of terrorism to explain effects of terrorism on the economy. In our work, in contrast, we posit terrorism impacts on the *vulnerability* of a nation and just not the death rates and discount rates. We will develop an index of vulnerability from eight factors and the death rate is one of them. Based on the new index we will offer new empirical insights. We also develop a new theoretical model of terrorism that proposes that terror groups create and own terror-specific assets, which are financed and 'owned in some sense' by global/international decision-makers. Like any asset we postulate a quasi-market for each terror asset and explore how market equilibrium and equilibrium asset price dynamics will evolve in the contest of terror assets. Our theoretical model explains how some very complex behaviour of terrorism can arise from simple models of equilibrium asset prices in quasi-markets. In our quasi-market, for each asset there is a group of buyers and a group of sellers. We posit that both buyers and sellers of an asset face a gamble regarding the future value of an asset, related to the unknown element of law enforcement and counterterrorism activities. At any point in time, terrorists can only make honest guesses. In reality, the value of the asset may go up or decline. We derive the asset price dynamics associated with terror activities based on the expected value of this gamble. The outcome is, in its context, structurally stable although the underlying dynamics are not straightforward. We find that the dynamics of this model are represented by a quadratic map of the type that is well recognised in the literature on chaos. Although asset price dynamics are completely deterministic, we show that these dynamics can evolve in a chaotic fashion under a set of usual parametric restrictions. As a consequence, terrorist organisations and counterterrorism agencies will fail to converge on an *ex ante* derivable equilibrium outcome. Our main intuition in the theoretical model is as follows: building on the work of Chai (1993) and Shapiro and Siegel (2007), we dichotomise a terrorist organisation into two interdependent cells. First, we have the terrorist leaders and political representatives. Terrorist leaders recruit a network of operators who undertake terrorist-related activities. The leaders are responsible for financial and other resources and delegate the task of terrorism to the operators. Thus, funds flow from leaders to operators. In return terror-related activities are undertaken by operators, which will benefit leaders. As we know from the literature, the terrorist operators may engage in rent seeking by usurping funds and resources from the operatives' cell. Resources can also flow from the operatives' cell to the counterterrorism authority as bribes. The terrorist leaders can also bribe the counterterrorism authority directly. From Bloom (2005), Siqueira (2005) and Bueno de Mesquita (2008) we know that the success of terrorism will critically depend on screening, brainwashing, rent seeking and factionalisation among terror operatives. These problems will also be predicated on the degree of cooperation among operatives, due to imperfect group cohesion within the terrorist organisation as highlighted by Berman (2003); Iannaccone and Berman (2006). Finally, both terrorist leaders and their operatives strategically respond to the counterterrorism strategies, and counterterrorism in turn depends on terrorist activities. We formally model this complex web of terrorism in Chapter 4. We then test the implications of the theoretical model from our newly created data set to explain how terrorism impacts on and gets impacted by various socio-economic factors and counterterrorism policies in the region. From our modelling we are able to explain how a virtuous dynamics can be created in the region to reduce the bane of terrorism and conflicts in the Middle East and North Africa.

Fourth, we propose that a possible participatory conflict management procedure (CMP) can be the harbinger of peace in the region. The findings are based on a field study and field experiments undertaken in Israel and Lebanon, funded and sponsored by the University of Western Sydney in 2010. From the CMP we aspire to discover 'stable points' for collaboration between Arabs and Israelis. We note that stable points are mutual joint cooperative arrangements that diminish the probability of conflict *re-escalation*. There are clear examples of joint actions that have brought peace, as in Europe where a small joint action between four countries to form a coal and steel community was the initial step that led to the formation of the European Union. The formation of the European Union ended a century-old conflict and brought peace between Germany and France. The CMP in our work consists of four phases: the first phase identifies the crucial actors, the objectives of each actor, and the relative importance of each objective for the different actors. The second phase detects the local 'stable' positions. The third phase embraces a certain process with the different actors about what sort of joint projects would be coherent with the most satisfying outcome. In the fourth phase, the CMP reaches several crucial objectives for both parties, and a MATLAB program (version 7, release 14) is used to verify the stability of all possible joint actions among all conflicting parties.

Finally, we will develop a comprehensive model to understand the determination of military spending. We will develop the theoretical model to explain why military spending is not based on a rational foundation and outline their consequences for the region and the globe. We will also provide detailed insights into the causes and consequences of such irrational decisions. Further details will be available in Section 1.5 of this chapter.

1.2   Research problems

This research seeks to offer tentative answers for the following research questions – on the basis of a detailed data set that we have created – by also developing appropriate econometric, theoretical and economic models for seven nations from the Middle East and North Africa.

a.   What are the dynamics of conflicts and potentials for peace in the Middle East and North Africa before and after 1948? What are the most important peace attempts during this period? This segment is a historical study that will concentrate on the Arab–Israeli conflict and be available in the Appendix of this book.

b.   How are local conflicts created in the region along with democratisation and the spread of market principles? What are the constraints on and incentives for conflicts? Why do conflicts recur in some societies while other societies retain a peaceful composition? Can we explain collective violence as a product of exchange entitlement failures? What causes such failures? What is the relationship between inequality and conflict? Is conflict a product of justice? Does justice deter conflicts? We will examine the source and dynamics of conflicts (such as poverty) in a set-up in which democratic principles and market ethos are introduced into a traditional and developing economy/society of the Middle East and North Africa.

c.   Is collective violence rooted to the long-term vulnerability of a nation, or its region? How do we define and operationalise the long-term vulnerability of a nation? What are the impacts of changes in long-run vulnerability on conflicts and terrorism? We will develop an index of long-term vulnerability for seven nations in the region and use the index to answer the above questions.

d. Can we coordinate military spending to reduce the long-run vulnerability and risks of terrorism? What are the causes and consequences of terrorism? We will develop comprehensive models and utilise a newly created data set to answer the questions.

e. What roles do arms markets have on the long-term vulnerability and terrorism in the region? Do arms imports exacerbate the vulnerability of the region? What are the determinants of arms spending? What are their consequences for the region? We will develop several economic and econometric models to test the effects of different variables on the probability of conflict, terrorism and their impacts on the economic variables in the Middle East and North Africa.

f. Are there any links between local conflicts and rebellions vis-à-vis global factors? Do global warming and the global oil market shape collective violence and terrorism in the region? We will offer new insights to explain how global warming and oil markets have impacted on the regional conflicts through the channel of entitlement failures.

g. Finally, we devote considerable energy to model a conflict management procedure (CMP) for explaining how to create peace in the region. What are the 'stable positions' for cooperation amongst belligerent groups in the region? What are the possible CMPs that aspire to discover stable points for collaboration between confrontational parties? This is an experimental/questionnaire-based field study using a feasible participatory conflict management procedure. To gather data for this experiment we have used a questionnaire to elicit the sensitivity of each policy objective for each actor from the region.

1.3 A brief literature review

Before the 1950s, work in the area of conflict was performed in the main by political scientists. This has changed with the growing awareness of economists about the impacts of conflicts on the economy. Moreover, an increasing number of academics and policymakers have been focusing on the economic dimensions and causes of armed conflicts. More efforts have been directed at understanding the dynamics of conflicts and, at the same time, developing more effective policies for conflict resolution.

The initial motivation for violent conflict between two groups (or even between two individuals) may be related to the 'rage of the rich'. On the other hand, Baron and Greenberg (1990) state that 'opposing interests lie at the core of conflicts'. They note that there is substantial indication that conflicts in work settings often derive from the relations between individuals and are based on personal characteristics, a view endorsed by Forsyth (1990). Forsyth (1990) indicates three main mechanisms that lead to conflict: personal characteristics, competition over scarce resources, and the use of threatening and contentious influence strategies.

Since World War II, we have seen civil wars, regional crises, international tensions and threats of global war, especially in the Middle East. Azar et al. (1978) classify conflicts into three categories: 'clearly international conflicts and wars', 'clearly civil wars', and 'a mixture of international and civil wars'. They find that most conflicts occur in the third world, and that the intervention of the Big Powers (USA and former USSR) in these conflicts adds to their severity and leads to dreadful consequences. Isard and Chung (2000) go further, arguing that such interference from a third party introduces complexities which prevent the evolution of cooperation between the two original parties.

Most of the new literature on conflict has focused on what belligerents might gain during the course of conflict (see Jean and Rufin, 1996; Keen, 1998; and Kaldor, 1999); this offers a perspective from which conflict is not seen as something that interrupts economic activity. The motivations for conflict are tied to the opportunities they offer individuals or states. An interesting study by Mwanasali (2000), in the context of the Democratic Republic of Congo, notes that various states benefit from the war. In this research we will try to explore whether these opportunities, in which some groups benefit at the expense of others, can result in regional inequality – propelled by bad economics and partisan politics – that leads to more violent conflicts.

1.3.1   *General message from political economy*

In 1527 Niccolo Machiavelli in *The Prince* suggests that conflicts within a society are justified if and only if they can engender a collective good, '*publica utilita*' in his words. In other words, the Abrahamic religions and the Machiavellian statecrafts came to share the concept of a 'just' war/conflict as a pathway to peace – including wars against its own citizens. Though he cautioned the prince/government about using its power against its own people, it is the Machiavellian idea of 'one last and just war' for lasting peace that is a continuing theme behind most conflicts in the modern world (see Machiavelli, 1961). On the other hand, for classical thinkers in India (mainly Kautilya) and China (mainly Sun Tzu), there is no 'just' war within an empire/state and their stark reminder to the political power is to achieve and embrace intra-state peace by every feasible means (see Brekke, 2009). The classical thinkers from India and China urge the political power to *export* violence overseas – not as a just, or moral, war but as a *strategic* ploy to weaken rival empires! A perpetual question for ancient scholars, especially in India, is about the mechanics of statecraft to create and maintain peace within the empire. Kautilya ascribes a direct role for the political economy for achieving peace: the only vehicle for achieving intra-state peace, according to Kautilya, is by sharing the opulence and thereby reducing inequality within an empire. In the ancient societies of China and India, wars thus came to be viewed as the '*public bad*'. Since war is a collective bad, the advice from the ancient thinkers to the political power is to choose all means – just, unjust and *devious* – for avoiding and mitigating the probability and effects of wars within an empire. Now let us turn to modern economics for understanding the role of wars and peace.

Marshall defines economics on p. 1 of the *Principles of Economics*:

> Economics is a study of mankind in the ordinary business of life; it examines that part of individual and social action which is most closely connected with the attainment and with the use of the material requisites of well-being.
>
> (Marshall, 1961, [1890], p. 1)

The words 'conflicts', 'crime', 'war', and 'politics' do not appear in the index to Marshall's *Principles of Economics*. With regard to the power of love and chivalry as organising principles of social life, Adam Smith said:

> In civilised society [man] stands at all times in need of the cooperation and assistance of great multitudes, while his whole life is scarce sufficient to gain the friendship of a few persons.
>
> (Smith, 1993)

Love and friendship may sustain cooperation among a few partners, but the elaborate division of labour essential for modern life has to rely on the force of self-interest. Hayek introduces a similar definition:

> These habits [of generosity] had to be shed ... to make the transition to the ... open society possible ... [The] mores [of the market economy] involve withholding from the known needy neighbours what they might require, in order to serve the unknown needs of the thousands of unknown others.
>
> (Hayek, 1979, epilogue)

Hayek thinks that economists are civilising students through teaching them selfishness. Vilfredo Pareto offers another definition, as we know from Hirshleifer (1994, quoted on p. 2):

> The efforts of men are utilized in two different ways: they are directed to the production or transformation of economic goods, or else to the appropriation of goods produced by others.
>
> (Pareto, 1966)

Pareto suggests that, yes, one can produce goods for mutual beneficial exchange with other parties; but also that one can acquire wealth in other ways through grabbing and looting goods that someone else has produced.

The main storyline of human history is to maintain the balance between these modes of economic activity (the one leading to greater aggregate wealth, and the other to conflict over who gets the wealth) (Hirshleifer, 1994). From Hirshleifer (1994) we also know that Karl Marx did stress the importance of conflict as an option. This image appeared when Marx noted that all forms of conflict, including wars among nations and even the battle of the sexes, could be squeezed into the ill-fitting mould of the class struggle:

> The history of all hitherto society is the history of class struggles.
>
> (Bartlett, 1968, p. 686)

According to Bartlett, Niccolo Machiavelli had a clearer thought:

> It is not gold, but good soldiers that insure success … for it is impossible that good soldiers should not be able to procure gold.
>
> (Bartlett, 1968, p. 687)

This is Machiavelli's version of the much-celebrated golden rule: *he who gets to rule, will get the gold.*

Human history is a record of the compromise between the way of Niccolo Machiavelli and what might be called Coase's Theorem. According to Coase's Theorem, people will never waste 'an opportunity to cooperate' mediated by a mutually beneficial exchange. What might be expressed in Machiavelli's Theorem is that no one will ever miss an opportunity to gain a one-sided advantage by exploiting another party (Hirshleifer, 1994). Machiavelli's Theorem on its own is only a partial truth, but so is Coase's Theorem standing alone. With regard to international conflict, Carl von Clausewitz offered a definition (see Rothfels, 1941):

> For achieving the political aims that are the end of war, the decision by arms is what cash settlement is in trade.
>
> (p. 154)

Clausewitz's view of a state remains influential in peacetime only because it dumps serious damages on its people in the event of war.

This takes us to the generally accepted view that the social arrangements, laws, and judicial systems that humans have devised will mitigate the power struggle. It is widely held when people cooperate they do so as a conspiracy for aggression against others. At a softer level, cooperation is a response to such aggression. A nation whose institutions can create favourable circumstances for Coasian cooperation, which will propel the 'ordinary' business activity of Marshall and the society, will become prosperous. What will happen then? Adam Smith has warned us:

> An industrious, and upon that account a wealthy nation, is of all nations the most likely to be attacked.
>
> (Smith, 1993, p. 659)

If the gains from group aggression are big enough, invaders can get their act together. Sigmund Freud said:

> It is always possible to bind together a considerable number of people … so long as there are other people left over to receive the manifestations of their aggressiveness.
>
> (Tripp, 1970, quoted on p. 668)

And on the defensive side, invasion cements the unity and fighting power of the group attacked. The bottom line is that nations with wealth-enhancing laws and institutions will not be able to enjoy the fruits thereof unless, when challenged, they can put up a tough fight. And the same holds for political parties, clubs, families and business firms.

The book of Niccolo Machiavelli, *The Prince*, came as an immoral shock to many of his contemporaries and he came to be dubbed as 'evil' or a more sobering expression 'a teacher of evil' by Leo Strauss in the twenty-first century. Machiavelli offered his famous advice that a prince 'must acquire the power to be not good, and understand when to use it and when not to use it, in accord with necessity'. It is Max Weber, in his famous lecture 'Politics as a Vocation', who argued that *The Prince* is a moderate book when compared with the *Arthashastra* of Kautilya, since Kautilya recommends that peace within the empire be embraced at any cost including the exports of horrific violence to rival empires. Sun Tzu of ancient China went a step further,

> To win one hundred victories in one hundred battles is not the acme of skill. To subdue the enemy without fighting is the acme of skill.
>
> (Sun Tzu, quoted in Brekke, 2009, p. 131)

For the role of political economy in creating and perpetuating peace, the shared view of two ancient civilisations from China and India is that peace is the ultimate goal of a society and the means to achieve peace is through the preservation of the empire and wars are the last resort. The advice to the political power is to use all sorts of ploys to soften the need for bloodshed, violence and wars – before dirtying one's hand. The road to peace is portrayed very clearly in the work of Kautilya: promoting social justice and prosperity for his people is usually in the king's self-interest as it eliminates bloodshed, conflicts and violence (see Waldauer et al., 1996).

> If a king favours the wicked and banishes the good, acts in an impious manner, punishes the good and rewards the evil, steals from and oppresses ordinary people, harms 'principled men and [dishonours] those worthy of honour', then he will create only greed and disaffection among the people. ... Subjects, when impoverished, become greedy; when greedy they become disaffected; when disaffected they either go over to the enemy or themselves kill the master.
>
> (Kautilya, quoted in Spengler, 1971, p. 72)

1.3.2 *Economic models of conflict: a cursory glance*

The main inputs for conflicts from an economic perspective are the military manpower. In the past, it was volunteers who answered the call to arms; but for the all-consuming and large-scale conflicts of the nineteenth and twentieth centuries, reliance on volunteers was deemed inadequate. Conscription became the norm. Conscription is the compulsory enlistment of young men citizens for military service. Beyond conscription and volunteer forces lies another potential source of manpower: mercenaries, or employees of private military and security companies (Brauer and Van Tuyll, 2008).

Other main inputs of conflict from an economic perspective are the use of weapons: swords, cannons, guns, bombs, missiles, and so on. However, these are not used to produce useful output, as in the case of ordinary economic production: each party gathers the inputs as a means of an offensive/ self-defence against counter parties. These inputs, called by Hirshleifer (1989) 'technologies of conflict', result in wins or losses for the parties involved in the conflict. These technologies of conflict have been introduced to the literature as a contest-success function as Tullock (1980) did for rent-seeking activities.

Consider two opposing parties 1 and 2 with a choice of weapons G_1 and G_2 (for guns). For any combination of guns we could expect the probability of winning or losing for each party using the following model:

$$p_1(G_1, G_2) = \begin{cases} \dfrac{f(G_1)}{f(G_1) + f(G_2)} & \text{If } \sum_{i=1}^{2} f(G_i) > 0; \\ \dfrac{1}{2} & \text{otherwise.} \end{cases} \quad (1)$$

For $p_i(G_1, G_2)$, $i = 1$, 2, to be probabilities, they need to take on values between 0 and 1 and add up to 1, or equivalently they must satisfy the following: $0 \leq p_2(G_1, G_2) = 1 - p_1(G_1, G_2) \leq 1$. Moreover, we can expect an increase in one party's guns to increase her own winning probability and reduce the winning probability of her opponent; that is, $p_1(G_1, G_2)$ should be increasing in G_1 and decreasing in G_2. This model has been employed by scholars in different fields, such as Schmalensee (1972) in the economics of advertising, Szymanski (2003) in sports economics, Konard (2005) in contests, and Tullock (1980) and Nitzan (1994) in rent seeking. Luce (1959) axiomatises such probabilistic choice functions in relation to utility theory, while Skaperdas (1996) provides an axiomatisation in relation to contests. Key to both axiomatisations is an *independence of irrelevant alternatives* property. In the context of conflict, thus, property requires that the outcomes of conflict between two parties depend on the amount of guns held by these two parties and not on the amount of guns held by third parties to the conflict.

The most commonly used model is the one employed by Tullock (1980), now used in the economics of conflict:

$$p_1(G_1, G_2) = \frac{G_1^m}{G_1^m + G_2^m} \quad (2)$$

Where $m > 0$ and $f(G_i) = G_i^m$

Hirshleifer (1989) argues that the probability of winning in this case depends on the ratio $\dfrac{G_1}{G_2}$.

Another functional form model is:

$$p_1(G_1,G_2) = \frac{e^{kG_1}}{e^{kG_1} + e^{kG_2}} = \frac{1}{1 + e^{k(G_2 - G_1)}} \tag{3}$$

where $f(G_i) = e^{kG_i}$ and $k > 0$.

All three models assume that the sum of winning probabilities for all parties concerned equal 1. There are circumstances, however, where the result of war may be a draw or an impasse. Blavatsky (2004) assumes a new model, which takes into consideration such a possibility:

$$p_1(G_1,G_2) = \frac{f_1(G_1)}{1 + f_1(G_1) + f_2(G_2)} \tag{4}$$

In this research, those models will be developed to reach:

- economic and social models of irrational conflicts
- a model of the evolution of conflicts in developing nations along with democratisation and spread of market principles
- a combination of the probabilistic voting model and the conjectural variations model in order to endogenise the nature of competition and government policy.

1.3.3   *The economic origin of conflicts*

Though the economic origin of conflicts is a complex topic, we will provide a brief synopsis of it.

1.3.3.1   *Wealth and conflicts*

At first glance one might say that rich nations would be more violent because they have more to fight over. However, a number of researchers have shown that wealth reduces the likelihood of civil war. This negative correlation between wealth and conflict is found in many studies such as Collier and Hoeffler (2002a) and Fearon and Laitin (2003). Humphreys (2003) finds that a country with a GDP per capita equal to $250 has a predicted probability of war onset of 15%. This probability is reduced by half if the GDP per capita rises to $600, and to 4% if the GDP reaches $1,250. Fearon and Laitin (2003) predict that countries with a GDP per capita of approximately $600 have an 18% probability of engaging in conflict over the next decade, dropping to 11% once the GDP per capita rises to $2,000, and to less than 1% at $10,000. How can this be explained? Homer-Dixon (1994) and Fearon and Laitin (2003) suggest that wealthier countries are more capable of protecting their assets against rebels. Homer-Dixon (1994) theorises that poverty causes violence, and indicates scarcity as a cause of migration, which results in conflict between identity groups over resources.

The motivation to use violence may increase if the value of assets increases. Evidence for this is found in Bates' (2001) historical literature on European development. A study by Keen (2000) mentions that if there is a rise in the value of assets of a country, then this may lead to a rise in the value of controlling the state.

Mack (2002) raises a doubt, wondering why, if increasing wealth leads to decrease in conflicts, we are seeing the opposite. An explanation is offered by Humphreys (2003): perhaps there are other variables that outweigh the mitigating effects of increased wealth, such as population size. Another reason is the uneven spread of economic growth across different regions (Humphreys, 2003).

Given all this, what is the relationship between wealth and interstate conflict? Some scholars argue that as states get richer they look abroad for invasions. For example, a study by Choucri and North (1975) notes that increased wealth in a country leads to an increase in their needs for goods and resources; any shortage in goods and resources may encourage a country to satisfy their needs through direct control over resources of poorer countries.[4] In contrast, a study by Zuk (1985) argues that conflict-oriented states during the period 1870–1914 were able to fill their needs through trade with sovereign states. Certainly, the statistical evidence for this relation is varied, and the majority of current research suggests that there is no strong relationship between wealth and conflict. Moreover, there is no strong relation between the business cycle and the onset of conflict, as a study by Thompson (1982) involving France, Britain, Germany and America over the period 1792–1973 argues. These studies, though valuable, do not address the question of belligerence between equally wealthy states, or the role of governmental decisions in inciting conflict. In this research we will try to fill this gap by studying the relation between wealth and interstate conflict in the Middle East countries.

1.3.3.2   Inequality and conflicts

Does economic inequality breed conflict in nations? It is widely agreed that 'good things', such as money income, have to be more or less evenly distributed. In the real world good things are not equally distributed, which may increase the risk or the cause of conflicts (as is assumed by political scientists and some Marxist theorists). The relation between inequality and conflict has been of interest to several economists (Lichbach, 1987; Cramer, 2003). There are two kinds of inequality: 'horizontal inequality' and 'overall inequality'. 'Horizontal inequality' refers to the differences in income between regional or ethnic groups while 'overall inequality' considers the differences between incomes of all individuals in an economy. The most common, widely used measure of income inequality is the Gini coefficient.[5]

If one group benefits more than another from economic growth, this may increase inequality, and in turn may increase dissatisfaction among some sectors of the population. This may result in an outbreak of conflict or intensify a current conflict (Alesina and Perotti, 1996; Stewart, 1998). Alesina and Perotti (1996) argue that inequality is correlated with a greater incidence of political instability. The worst effect of these conflicts may be additional economic disruption, which deepens existing inequalities.

Recent empirical and theoretical studies have suggested that inequality is strongly implicated in the emergence of conflicts. In recent years many developing countries have faced processes of industrialisation and urbanisation that brought with them institutional changes and market uncertainties. Often the results were that some people became fairly wealthy while others received a lower income. One reason is that strategies for income growth do not include any method that ensures that lower income earners will gain an advantage from it. There is a sizeable literature dedicated to an analysis of the relationships between different forms of inequality and political and social conflicts (for example, Gurr, 1970; Sigelman and Simpson, 1977; Muller, 1985; Weede, 1987; Boyce 1996; and Wickham-Crowley, 1992). An examination of recent literature on the economic causes of civil war in developing countries, suggests that inequality posited as an important cause of conflict (Schock, 1996; Boyce, 1996; Nafziger and Auvinen, 1997; Stewart, 1998; Elbadawi, 1992; Collier, 2000b; Collier and Hoeffler, 2001a). Schock (1996) tests the hypothesis that economic inequality is positively related to violent conflict, using quantitative cross-national lagged panel data to examine political violence between 1973 and 1977. He reaches a result that supports the hypothesis. Boyce (1996) stresses that the main causes of violence in El Salvador have been inequality of income. He also finds unequal distribution of land a more potent reason for inequality of income in El Salvador. An empirical study by Nafziger and Auvinen (1997) indicates that income inequality (based on the Gini index) is associated with political conflict and complex humanitarian emergencies. Stewart (1998) demonstrates a positive relation between horizontal inequalities and civil conflict, by examining case studies of developing countries such as Afghanistan, Burundi, Cambodia, El Salvador, Guatemala, Haiti, Liberia, Nicaragua, Rwanda, Sierra Leone and Somalia. Elbadawi (1999) advances poverty and ethnic fractionalisation as main causes of civil war. Collier (2000b) and Collier and Hoeffler (2000) mention that greed and not grievance causes civil wars. Other studies by Collier and Hoeffler (1998; 2002a; 2002b) propose that inequality does not have a significant impact on the likelihood of internal conflict.

With these debates, we are going to examine the relation between inequality and conflict in the Middle East region. These countries have received little attention in the empirical literature on the relationship between inequality and conflicts. This research will help to fill the gap.

1.3.3.3   Natural resources and conflicts

Here, the struggle about access to and control over important resources (such as water, oil, gold, diamonds, productive land etc.) is the *differentia specifica* of the conflict. Inequities in the distribution, use, needs, desires, and consequences of resources management have been sources of tension and international and intra-state disputes. According to some resource conflict researchers (Ehrlich, Gleick and Conca, 2000) four important conditions influence the likelihood that resources will be the object of military or political action: (1) the degree of scarcity; (2) the extent to which the supply is shared by two or more groups/states; (3) the relative power of those groups; and (4) the ease of access to alternative sources. The most present approach in the resource conflict literature is 'resource scarcity' as a main conflict contributor. This approach links resources, considers resource scarcity (supply induced, demand induced or absolute scarcity), as well as environmental degradation, as key conflict issues (Homer-Dixon, 1999). Homer-Dixon and Percival (1997), stressing the causal pathways between conflicts and resources in some developing countries, argue that under certain conditions, the scarcity of renewable resources such as cropland, forests and water, generate social effects (such as poverty, migration, and weak institutions) and produce tensions and conflicts.

The literature on civil war in developing countries (note that conflicts in many Middle Eastern countries are interstate wars) emphasises poverty (as a result of growth failure) and horizontal inequalities (not vertical) on the grievances side; and natural resource abundance on the greed side (Murshed and Tadjoeddin, 2009). For some scholars, natural resources may provide reasons as to why internal conflicts are fought. There have been several studies regarding the relationship between natural resources and conflict. A study by Ross reaches the conclusion that natural resources have contributed to the onset, duration, and intensity of many conflicts (Ross, 2001). Research by Collier and Hoeffler (2000, 2002a, 2002b) suggests that countries whose wealth is dependent on the export of primary commodities are prone to civil violence. Collier and Hoeffler argue that conflict may be explained by either grievance or greed, but conclude that if we want to best understand the causes of contemporary civil wars we should concentrate more on the greed of rebel groups than on explanations based on grievance.[6]

There are at least eight complementary mechanisms that would explain the relationship between the variables, natural resources and conflict:

- Natural resources could be a way to finance rebellions.
- If natural resources are concentrated in a particular part of a country then this may encourage dissatisfied persons in that region to break away.

- Natural resources may be associated with grievance rather than greed. This may happen when natural resources are seen as unjustly distributed, as in Sierra Leone and Nigeria.
- Governments should not establish strong institutions if they depend on natural resources rather than taxation for their continuation (see Moore, 2001).
- The manufacturing sector of an economy dependent on natural resources could be weakened by fluctuations in the value of natural resources (Dutch disease).
- Countries dependent on natural resources may be more susceptible to terms-of-trade shocks.
- The availability of natural resources in certain areas could encourage other parties to engage in or foster conflict (see Dashwood, 2000; and Meldrum, 2000).
- In some cases there may be an observed correlation between primary resource dependence and conflict even if natural resources do not cause conflict.

Table 1.1 Conflicts linked to resource wealth during 1960–2015

	Duration	*Type*	*Resources*
Afghanistan	1978–	Lootable	Gems, opium
Syria	2011–	Unlootable	Oil, gas
Kuwait	1990–1991	Unlootable	Oil
Burma	1949–	Lootable	Timber, gems, opium
Cambodia	1978–1997	Lootable	Timber, gems
Iran	1980–1988	Unlootable	Oil, gas
Congo Republic	1997	Unlootable	Oil
Democratic Republic of Congo	1996–1998	Both	Copper, coltan, diamonds, gold, cobalt, coffee
Lebanon	1975–1990	Lootable	Forestry
Indonesia (West Papua)[a]	1969–	Unlootable	Copper, gold
Liberia	1989–1996	Lootable	Timber, diamonds, iron, palm oil, cocoa, coffee, marijuana, rubber, gold
Egypt	2011–	Unlootable	Copper, gold
Peru	1980–1995	Lootable	Coca
Sierra Leone	1991–2000	Lootable	Diamonds
Libya	2011–	Unlootable	Oil
Iraq	1991–	Unlootable	Oil
Israel	1963–	Both	Diamond, gas, gems

Source: Adapted from Paul Collier and Anke Hoeffler, 'Greed and Grievance in Civil War', Policy Research Working Paper no. 2355 (Washington, DC: World Bank, 2001).

a. Conflict did not generate 1,000 battle deaths in any twelve-month period.

1.3.3.4   *Social contracts and conflicts*

As we have mentioned in the previous literature review, there are several factors which contribute to the risk of violent conflict such as: inequality, poverty and natural resources appropriation. Some societies have such conditions but still do not descend into violent conflict. The main reason behind that is what Addison and Murshed (2001) call 'social contracts', meaning a framework of widely agreed rules, both formal and informal, that govern the allocation of resources, including resource rents and the peaceful settlement of grievances. If this contract is feasible and enforceable, it can be enough to hold down, if not eradicate, the probability of a violent conflict.

1.3.4   *Conflict management procedures (CMP)*

How can a conflict be reduced? The management of conflict has been an area of concern and interest to scientists for many years. Conflict management designates in the first instance the perception of the mediator (conflict adviser or conflict manager), who is called upon to help both parties. One can speak about conflict dealing also when during the conflict both parties look for a consensual solution, without asking for external assistance. The forms of approaching and dealing with conflicts could be of a very different nature. In compliance with Reimann (2005) there are consequently three forms of dealing with conflict that are to be outlined: conflict settlement, conflict resolution, and conflict transformation.

The conflict management procedure (CMP) is a step-by-step procedure to identify joint local satisfying positions for cooperation among belligerent groups (see Isard and Smith, 1983). Joint local satisfying actions are small cooperative arrangements that are comparatively stable, or less likely to re-escalate. This mutual improvement joint action was first developed by Isard (see Isard, 2002 and Isard and Moyersoen, 2003). Isard and Moyersoen (2003) explore how prospect theory can be relevant and effective in real conflict situations. The authors start with the proposal in Isard and Hara (2003a, 2003b), where building a new hotel would create 11,000 to 21,000 jobs and increase Israeli security 18.3% to 35%. Isard and Moyersoen (2003) acknowledge that it is more valuable to base experimental evidence on actual past conflict, and argue that a stable position can be reached by using elements of prospect theory. The authors take the French–Flemish conflict and propose to build a hotel in Brussels. Knowing that Brussels is the capital of the Flemish population, Flemish concerns with urban beautification and high French unemployment are factors that make such a proposal acceptable to both participants and guarantee a stable position. Using a MATLAB computer program and best estimates, the authors create a map of a possible utility function for the French and Flemish for different portions from a supposed total pie of $100 million. Their next step is to be aware of the veto power of French–Flemish participants and to take into consideration the positive effects of rational interactions. On the basis of utility mappings we find that there are

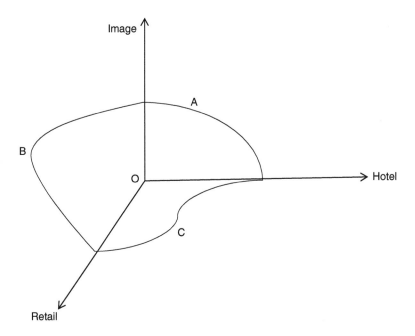

Figure 1.1 The utility possibility frontier from CMP

Note: A and B are the two local satisfaction points and the curve ABC is the utility possibility frontier.

two locations that are local joint satiation points for both participants (see Figure 1.1). Isard and Moyersoen (2003) conclude that in certain conflicts it may be possible to indicate local joint satiation points, but that there is a need for more advanced and deeper research.

CMP combines two theoretical tools: the prospect theory developed by the Tversky School and the related intertemporal choice theory developed by Ainslie and Herrnstein (1981); and the hierarchical process analysis and procedures developed by Saaty (1980). CMP is based on three main steps: i) the elicitation and analysis of conflict; ii) the detection of stable neighbourhood positions; and iii) deliberation. In elicitation and analysis we will first identify the crucial actors and policy objectives; second, elicit the relative importance of each policy objective for each actor; third, elicit the sensitivity factors; and finally combine AHP procedure with sensitivity analysis to estimate the preference step-function for all actors and objectives. The elicited information allows us to estimate a preference step-function for each objective and for all actors. We will follow a similar strategy to that used by Isard and Chung (2000) (see Table A.8.1 for more information). The second phase in CMP detects local stable positions, and the third phase includes a deliberation process with the involved parties about what sort of joint project would be coherent with the detected satisfying position.

This research is concerned with effective conflict analysis that leads to workable mediation or management in public policy decision-making. For such decision-making we abandon the optimisation approach from a normative standard economic perspective, in which agents have preferences suggested by neoclassical economics. Instead we would like to propose a conflict management procedure by drawing up a topical mental accounting framework: that is to say, by using a descriptive set of cognitive operations that guide agents to evaluate their options. In general, decision theory and conflict analysis is normative or prescriptive: it is concerned with identifying decisions to take, and assuming an ideal decision taker who is fully informed, able to compute with perfect accuracy, and fully rational. However, multiple researches in the last decades indicate that we realistically cannot assume that people are rational beings. Kahneman and Tversky (1979) have developed an alternative 'descriptive' mental accounting framework, which they call 'prospect theory', which aims to be consistent on how people take in real-world decisions. The central principle in prospect theory and topical mental accounting is that people adapt to hedonic sensations, and therefore utilities are determined by gains and losses from a particular reference point rather than by overall wealth.[7] In this section we will analyse how prospect theory is relevant in conflict analysis and how it can be mobilised as a tool for conflict mitigation.

1.4   The main research paradigm in the manuscript

Conflicts are an intractable and analytical problem for traditional neoclassical economics. The problem arises from the emphasis of neoclassical economics on win-win aspects of economic exchanges and the resulting gains from trade. In recent years neoclassical economics has highlighted imperfectly specified and enforced property rights as a major source of conflicts. The methodology of our research will embrace the neoclassical agenda:

- Agents are driven by self-interest.
- Agents have pre-determined and exogenous goals.
- Agents can use markets to 'get rich'.
- Agents and groups can get rich by 'appropriating, grabbing and confiscating', as property rights are neither fully specified nor fully enforced, which leads to a trade-off between production and appropriation activities and potential conflicts.

In the following subsections we will explain the most important elements of our major research methodologies.

1.5   Plan of the research monograph

Chapter 1 is a brief introduction to our research. The rest of the chapter sequence of our manuscript is as follows:

1.5.1 Chapter 2

This chapter will focus on this relatively new and rapidly expanding branch of knowledge, which will be of great value for understanding issues of conflict management and prevention, especially from the perspective of the developing world. This chapter will help us understand the sources of conflict and how to mitigate and manage conflict in developing societies. The aim is to understand conflicts from a multidisciplinary vantage point. Chapter 2 examines the source of conflicts in a context in which democratic principles and market ethos are introduced into a prototypical developing economy or society. For historical reasons, the society is envisaged as comprising two sectors: agricultural and industrial. Governments wield significant control over the allocation of capital across these sectors, and typically influence the terms of trade between them. The forces of democratisation instil an electoral motive for an incumbent government that determines optimal (inter-sectoral) terms of trade and optimal capital allocation for the government.

This chapter will highlight entitlement failures to explain conflicts in such societies. We will focus upon the issues of violent conflicts being driven by entitlement failures. The approach of entitlements failure can be an important step forward – especially from the perspective of the developing world – for appraising the sources of conflict and mitigating and managing conflict in less developed societies. In this chapter we extend the entitlement failure approach to the specific context of human security and not just food security: the entitlement set of a household constitutes the goods and services that the household can command, or acquire, by converting its endowments like assets, incomes and labour, into goods and services through market exchanges (see Sen, 1976 and 1981). In the context of famines and food insecurity, Sen (1976; 1981) and others have employed the entitlement approach to explain why the distribution problems can cause famines and food insecurity in a society, despite the successful operation of various markets including asset markets and food markets (see Edkins, 1996; p. 550). In other words, despite the efficiency of an exchange mechanism like modern markets, market prices can change in such a fashion that the food entitlements (or purchasing capacity) of many households can fall below the minimum quantities of foods. As a result, these households either choose to starve (Ravallion, 1986), or are forced to starve (Sen, 1981, p. 176), facing the increased risk of annihilation. What we argue in Chapter 2 is that certain forms of human insecurities, like famines, can arise from deadly conflicts as a result of an exchange entitlement failure, or exchange entitlement decline. As a direct consequence many households are exposed to such stark insecurities caused only by changes in relative prices in otherwise efficient markets. Such changes in relative prices can be brought about by various exogenous shocks. For us, the main intuition is that serious human insecurity from collective violence and group conflicts can only take place due to entitlement failures.

In order to model the intuition, we posit the following: given the endowments of a household, or an identifiable segment of a population, the household can acquire security from four sources, first and foremost, a typical household can purchase security from private sources like purchasing small arms and personal security networks; second, and most importantly, a typical household receives security from sub-national governments in the form of public security networks like police forces; third, security is also provided to private households by the national governments in the form of defence networks; and finally, households also receive some forms of security from the international community and civil society when the previous three sources fail to guarantee the minimum security to human lives and human dignity in a country. Households pay direct and indirect taxes and other prices for ensuring security from conflicts. When households face violent conflicts in a society, the possibility arises that the purchasing power of a household is not sufficient to purchase the minimal level of security due to changes in prices in other markets. Similar to deaths from famines, ordinary households can now face deaths and destruction from exchange entitlement failures in physical securities. In other words, if security problems arise because of exchange entitlement failures, one should be able to detect both theoretical and empirical links between vulnerability of the households and market prices – especially prices of primary goods and oil prices – in a conflict-ridden society like the Middle East. The main thrust of the chapter is to build, develop and hone theories and empirics to explain how and why and whether exchange entitlements have triggered the catastrophic conflicts in the Middle East and North Africa.

1.5.2   Chapter 3

In Chapter 3 we assume that defence spending, like arms imports, is like a public good that influences the regional economy. To be more specific, our model posits that defence spending in a regional economy offers public infrastructure that in turn influences the costs of production of local firms, which thereby influence the competitive positioning of the regional economy in the national context. The theoretical models will establish three important insights in the context of defence spending: first, it is essential to disaggregate an economy into competing components to analyse how defence spending impacts on different sectors and regions of an economy. As an example, each region can have different preferences for defence spending, like arms imports. How does the political system aggregate the diverging preferences of citizens? We will undertake the disaggregation by breaking up each of the seven economies into two distinct groups, namely, rural and urban, which will help us understand the determination of defence spending in a society with multiple stakeholders with divergent interests. We will use a theoretical model of interest group rivalry to explain the equilibrium defence spending. From the data set, by applying the cointegration analysis, we will analyse whether and how different sectors/regions have divergent impacts on defence spending. Second, we will also examine various other factors that will have impacts on the equilibrium in the allocation of government budgets. The main intuition of our theoretical model is as follows: political power, or government, plays a crucial role in determining military spending and its allocation. If the political power is rational, it is going to use its defence spending to influence its reputation instrumentally for achieving certain political ends. Since the government has power to determine military spending with diverse impacts on the economy, interest groups will easily form and use 'pressure tactics' to wrench benefits from defence spending. We assume that there are multiple interest groups in an economy, which compete against each other to influence defence spending. For our analysis, we posit that there are two regional groups who form the rival interest groups: first, we have the rural interest group (RIG) and second, we have the urban interest group (UIG). As our empirical section will confirm, a bipartite division of interests groups is a reasonable abstraction for the Middle East and North Africa. We posit that the political power, or government, faces these two interest groups in two separate arenas: let us call Arena I as being where the RIG seeks to influence the political power to achieve its ideal mix and level of defence spending. In a similar note, Arena II is the contest ground for the UIG and the political power. The political power has two options: (i) either it chooses to accommodate the political pressure from the interest group, which we call 'Relent', or (ii) the political power chooses an aggressive response, which we call 'Resist'. There are two types of political power and the political power only knows its true type: political power is either 'Weak' or 'Strong'. So, the incumbent government, after elections have taken place, can either be a 'Strong Government' or a 'Weak Government'. The uncertainty about the true nature of the government creates grounds for the political power to choose defence spending strategically: if the games are repeated without a known finite end date, then the government has an incentive to influence the subjective estimates about its type so that the government can have a free rein in the determination of defence spending or its allocation. More importantly, if the true type of the government is not known a priori, then the government will have to teach the 'foolish challenger' that the government is strong – but this is costly for all. In summary it is shown that the 'bad or fuzzy' information about the type of government, and its relationships with potential interest groups, can pay the political power to pursue the optimal defence policy from its own point of view. However, this is feasible only for a short time, given the updating of subjective beliefs of interest groups. In the medium run, we also establish that the political power will succumb to pressure group politics in its pursuits of defence policy. We then apply the econometric models to lend support to the theory.

In this chapter we will also examine the empirical foundation to our models by applying the time series analysis to seven countries from the region: five from the Middle East and two from North Africa as in Chapter 2. We introduce several new variables to empirically determine the nature of the equilibrium outcome. Finally and most importantly, since we don't have reliable data on the regional allocation of defence spending, we examine the impacts of various factors on the dynamics of arms imports in the seven countries from the region during 1960–2013. By so doing we will explain (long-term) new determinants of militarisation, like arms imports, of a region hitherto not considered in the literature.

As examples, we will raise and answer relatively simple questions: how does the long-term vulnerability of a nation impact on its and regional arms imports? Do arms imports of a country destabilise the long-term vulnerability of another nation in the region? Do arms imports in the Middle East and North Africa have anything to do with the global oil market? Does urbanisation promote militarisation of the region? Many other factors will be shown to bear a long-term cointegrating relationship with arms imports. We are thus able to detect important determinants of militarisation of the region and confirm the direction of causality in the context of militarisation of the Middle East and North Africa.

1.5.3   Chapter 4

Chapter 4 explores causes and consequences of terrorism in the Middle East and North Africa. The term 'terrorism' is mostly used to convey the meaning of a violent action that is perpetrated and politically motivated, targeting non-combatant citizens of a country by sub-national groups or clandestine agents, with a clear intention to influence an audience. International terrorism involves international targets, international audience and foreign, or multinational, perpetrators. The literature on terrorism and counterterrorism has well-recognised contributions from economists for more than three decades. Since the terrorist attack on US soil on the 11 September 2001, there has been a virtual explosion of research with important studies on the economic causes of terrorism and its economic consequences. Many excellent research publications appeared on investigating the structural determinants of terrorism. Interesting behavioural questions were posed about who becomes a terrorist. Obviously, as an indispensable aid to policymaking, economists offer models to examine the optimal counterterrorism policy to deter terrorism, break terrorist networks and arrest radical mobilisation. One of our major contributions to the literature is to apply the vulnerability index to the terrorism research for understanding whether and how terrorism impacts on the vulnerability of the chosen nations during 1968–2009. We will also seek to establish the reverse causality: how vulnerability of a nation, among other economic factors, impacts on terrorism. Once again the period of study is dictated by the availability of data on terrorism in the region from February 1968 to December 2009. The following important lessons were learnt: first and foremost, there is a long-term equilibrium relationship, both economically meaningful and statistically significant, between the regional terrorism index and the vulnerability of all seven nations in the region. However, the vulnerability of nations has a heterogeneous impact on regional terrorism. As opposed to the strand of research led by Eckstein and Tsiddon (2004), we find that terrorism does not have an unequivocal impact on the vulnerability of a nation. In their work, terrorism raises death rates and thereby raises the discount rate to cause misallocation of investment. We argue and establish that terrorism lowers vulnerability for some nations but enhances resilience in others. The heterogeneous effect materialises through some interesting channels, which will have significant policy implications. Second, we also find that global warming increases terrorism in the region – the effect is also statistically significant. Third, the global oil market has its strong influence on terrorism: the larger the global demand for oil, the lower will be the incidence of terrorism in the region. However, the oil price has a counter-balancing impact on terrorism in the region. We also note interesting pictures from the Granger causality results.

1.5.4 Chapter 5

The Israeli–Arab conflict is a protracted social conflict with the following characteristics: duration (protractedness) of a 'high-conflict NRR' (normal relations range), fluctuations in the intensity and frequency of interaction, conflict spillover into all domains, strong equilibrating forces, and the absence of distinct termination (Azar et al. 1978). The conflict has become so complicated that facile solutions are non-solutions. Despite the enduring conflict, relations do not remain at war level but fluctuate both bilaterally and regionally. In Chapter 5 we will propose a participatory conflict management procedure (CMP) that aspires to discover stable points for collaboration between confrontational parties. Stable points are mutual joint cooperative arrangements that diminish the probability of conflict re-escalation. The data for the CMP will be gathered through two experiments. The first will be a questionnaire whose main purpose is to identify the crucial objectives for each party. The second experiment is intended to elicit the sensitivity of each policy objective for each actor. Once the data is gathered, we will seek to determine all possible joint actions that might lead to a stable position between the two parties.

The CMP consists of three main phases:

- Phase 1: Elicitation and conflict analysis
    - Identifying the crucial actors and policy objectives:
        - Identifying the crucial actors in the conflict;
        - Determining the most important objectives for the actors in the conflict;
        - Identifying which objectives for which actor are costly or beneficial; and
        - Sorting the objectives in coherent categories.

- • Eliciting the relative importance of each policy objective for each actor:
  - ○ Comparing pair-wise the different categories for each actor in the conflict;
  - ○ Comparing pair-wise the different subsets of objectives within each category for each conflict; and
  - ○ Calculating the overall relative importance of each objective for each actor in the conflict.
- • Eliciting the sensitivity factors:
  - ○ Eliciting the interval sensitive factor of each objective for each actor;
  - ○ Eliciting the utility sensitive factor of each objective for each actor;
- • Combining the AHP-procedure with the sensitivity analysis to estimate the preference step-function for all actors and objectives.

- ■ Phase II: Detecting Stable Neighbourhood positions
  - • Operationalisation of reference dependent preference structure:
    - ○ Determining the one-parameter hyperbolic discount function;
    - ○ Operationalising the reference dependent preference structure.
  - • Detecting a common stable neighbourhood position:
    - ○ Determining stability levels for each possible allocation bundle;
    - ○ Selecting the most common robust or stable neighbourhood position,
- ■ Phase III: The deliberation phase

We will work with a very small group (between four and six persons) to elicit in-depth data on the Arab–Israeli conflict. We believe working larger groups will slow down the process without guaranteeing better results. A better strategy might be to repeat the methodology with different small focus groups and evaluate the coherence between the different results. We will have two groups, one representing the Arabs and the other representing the Israelis. Agents for each group will be selected from the university and will be well informed about the conflict, and each one will be considered as representing well the current interests of his/her government. Two field experiments will give us the background data. The first experiment will help us determine the objectives for each actor. The second experiment will specify which objectives are more crucial, and the sensitivity of each objective for each party, by using Saaty's scale (see Table A.8.1 for more details). Here, we wish to elicit the sensitivity of each policy objective for each actor. We can expect that some objectives are more crucial than others, and that the sensitivity of most objectives differs between the parties. The procedure consists of two questions for each objective for each actor. The first question assesses how large a concession for a given policy objective may differ from its most preferred position before the actor perceives the decrease as a significant loss in utility. The second question measures what the drop in utility actually is for each objective, if a significant concession (answer question a) occurs. When data is gathered from both experiments, the MATLAB program (version 7, release 14) will be used to run the data in order to verify the stability of all possible collaborative actions among the conflicting parties. After running the model we can determine what sorts of actions in the real world endorse the detected positions, and evaluate their feasibility.

1.5.5 Chapter 6

The purpose of this Chapter is to explore the global arms race, herd mentality among decision-makers and their impact on the regional economies of the Middle East and North Africa. The arms race is an immense issue confronting our globe and so is herd mentality in the arms race. Ours is a first small step towards understanding the possibility of informational cascades and herding among decision-makers in the context of the arms race and to search for some empirical validation of our model. It begs a question of why we need herding to justify arms races. In the context of incomplete information, the latest models of arms races explain the possibility of the detente equilibrium and the information acquisition/learning phase such that there is nothing sacrosanct, or automatic or instantaneous, about the onset and continuation of the arms race. These new developments in the arms race literature tend to contradict and discount the findings of the earlier Richardsonian framework traditionally applied to explain arms races by the action–reaction type of interactions between nations. Our major contribution is to bring informational cascades into the incomplete information setting to highlight how human irrationalities, fears and phobias can still play immense roles in triggering, fuelling and propelling catastrophic arms races in our contemporary world.

We model the arms race as anarchy in that it is a system in which rival nations engage in military build-ups to defend economic resources without an effective regulation, or protection, from above. Military build-ups are costly since they require inputs that will diminish the resources for producing the economic good (e.g. GDP). Military spending is important for advancing national interests in order to protect, or expand, economic resources. We also assume that the economic output (GDP) has a positive feedback to the production of military output. In this mixed model the military build-up of a nation is shown to depend, *inter alia*, on what the rival expects one's rivals to do. From this interdependency, we derive a game of military build-ups and the relevant Nash characterisation as a combination of mutually best responses in the context of incomplete information. In the context of arms race models with incomplete information, a number of recent works highlighted the relevance of communication and social learning in preventing the arms race. The incompleteness of information motivates nations to learn from social interactions, which is the primary intuition of our chapter that allows a necessary extension of the literature by developing a comprehensive model of informational cascades in the arms race and tests its validity from the dynamics of military spending by major players in the global arms market. We find, due to herd sentiments, there is a non-zero probability that the military spending and arms race will never be predicated on an objective consideration of the costs and benefits and dangers associated with arming. In the post-Cold War era, the annual spending of $1 trillion on global military build-ups is not only a steep price to pay for the arms race but is also socially inefficient since – despite myriads of private signals that reveal the right choice as de-escalation – nations seem to herd on the incorrect choice of arming with positive probability. The decision to get armed and subsequently embroiled in a war and ensuing violent conflicts can be driven by herd sentiments: every nation is individually rational to arm being ready to fight a last *'bloody war'*, even if all nations have overwhelming (private) information that there is absolutely no necessity to do so. In other words, everybody will willingly embrace the 'wrong behaviour' even when there is enough evidence in favour of espousing the 'right behaviour', which can give a gentle nudge to our civilisation along the precipice of meaningless self-destruction. As our research confirms, there is clear evidence of the arms race being driven by herd sentiments in the Middle East and North Africa, which is the most militarised region of the globe.

1.5.6   *Chapter 7*

Conflicts have deep social and economic effects on the economies of developing countries. Chapter 7 offers a fresh discussion on inequality and its relation to conflicts. Marxist theories and theories of ethnic conflicts have stressed the relationship between economic inequality and political violence. Conflicts are one of the main concerns of any country, whatever political, social or economic situation it may be in. Conflicts are generally categorised as 'major' and 'minor' based on the level of intensity and the number of casualties. Middle Eastern countries experienced a dramatic increase in the number of conflicts in the 1990s. In this chapter we will investigate the causes of this unprecedented change in incidence using a panel of conflict estimates for ten Middle Eastern countries for the period 1963–1999. The fixed effects model is used to control for unobservable country-specific effects that result in a missing-variable bias in cross-sectional studies. More importantly, the fixed effects model is chosen since the main goal of this study is to investigate what factors have caused substantial changes in the number of conflicts over time within countries, rather than to explain variations in conflicts across all ten countries.

To understand the relevance of *justice* in the Middle East and North Africa, we develop an index of the status of women in a country to measure, or capture, justice in the seven countries from the region during 1968–2009. These seven countries are the countries chosen for other chapters (Chapters 2–6). We then choose the average value of the country-level indexes for the seven nations to arrive at the average justice index (*AJI*) for the region of the Middle East and North Africa. We use the Johansen test results to determine the long-term cointegrating relationships between justice and other variables in the region. Appropriate causality tests are undertaken to confirm the direction of causality. Some of the important findings are as follows once we introduce *AJI* in the econometric modelling: first, an improvement in justice (*AJI*) in the region increases terrorism for the entire region. Some explanations will be offered. Second, as we have noted already, as the average per capita income of the region increases (decreases), regional terrorism declines (increases). The inverse relationship between income and terrorism is a time-honoured, though often challenged, adage in economics. Third, there is a positive and statistically significant relationship between militarisation and terrorism in the region. Thus, one can argue that terrorists strategically react to counterterror strategies like arms imports. Fourth, terrorism bears a direct relationship with the average long-term vulnerability of the entire region. The effect is also statistically significant. Finally, the global warming factor contributes positively to terrorism in the region. The regional justice is Granger caused by all the chosen variables in our analysis. The terrorism variable is marginally significant, but all others are statistically significant: economic progress (Granger) causes justice while the increase in vulnerability also (Granger) causes justice. Regional terrorism is also (Granger) caused by pursuits of justice in the region. We also note that economic performance is (Granger) caused by the justice variable for the region. Militarisation is a product of justice as the militarisation of the region is also (Granger) caused by the justice variable in the region. The rest of the Granger causality results are known and confirmed from Chapter 4 and Chapter 7. All other statistical tests are also satisfactory for the rank and lag determination.

1.5.7 Chapter 8

Chapter 8 is a summary of findings and the conclusion.

Notes

1 The Middle East is a geographical area without any precisely defined borders, but usually including Bahrain, Egypt, Iraq, Iran, Israel, Jordan, Kuwait, Lebanon, Oman, Palestinian Territories, Qatar, Saudi Arabia, Syria, Turkey, United Arab Emirates and Yemen.
2 There have been several conflicts in the Middle East since 1948: Arab–Israeli conflict, Jordan–Syria tensions, Jordan government–Palestinian Liberation Organisation war, Lebanese civil war, Libya–Egypt tensions, Kuwait invasion, Iraq–Iran war, and the invasion of Iraq.
3 Crises in the Arab–Israeli conflict: Palestine partition (1947), Sinai Incursion (1948), Hula drainage (1951), Qibya (1953), Gaza raid (1955), Suez war (1956), Qalqilya (1956), Rottem (1960), Jordan waters (1963), El-Samu (1966), Six Day war (1967), Karameh (1968), Beirut Airport (1968), War of Attrition (1969), Libyan plane

(1973), Israel mobilisation (1973), Yom Kippur War (1973), Entebbe raid (1976), Syria mobilisation (1976), Litani operation (1978), Iraq Nuclear Reactor (1981), Al-Biqaa Missiles-1 (1981), Lebanon Invasion (1982), Al-Biqaa Missiles-2 (1985), Operation Accountability (1993), and Operation Grapes of Wrath (Ben-Yehuda and Mishali-Ram, 2006).

4 This study looked at data from 1870 until 1914.

5 The Gini coefficient is an index between 0 and 1, where 0 corresponds to perfect equality (everyone gets exactly the same income) and 1 corresponds to perfect inequality (one person gets all the income and others get nothing).

6 Collier and Hoeffler (2002b) state: 'We test a "greed" theory focusing on ethnic and religious divisions, political repression and inequality. We find that greed considerably outperforms grievance.'

7 The three main results from prospect theory are:

1. Evaluation of decisions occur on the basis of a certain reference point: In simple situations involving outcomes under uncertainty (lotteries), prospect theory finds, first, that people think of consequences as increments (or decrements) to current wealth, where current wealth (and other positions of status) serve only as reference points from which changes are made.

2. People are risk averse: People tend to be more sensitive to decreases in their wealth than to increases. Kahneman and Tversky (1979) observe a ratio of just over 2:1 in several gambling experiments. For example, the experiment wherein a bet was made that would yield a 2.5:1 ratio – a 50-50 bet to win $25 or lose $10 – was rarely accepted. Those results are reflected in the value function – presented by Kahneman and Tversky – since it has a kink at the origin. The function is concave when positive and convex when negative.

3. The value function displays diminishing sensitivity: When people associate their utility values with improvements, these values fall off with the size of the improvements. The difference in subjective value between a gain of $100 and a gain of $200 is greater than the difference between a gain of $1,100 and a gain of $1,200.

2   Insecurity from entitlement failures in the Middle East and North Africa

2.1   Introduction

Why do people get into conflict? This is a question that is neither well understood nor fully addressed by social scientists. This chapter will focus on this question, at the base of a relatively new and rapidly expanding branch of knowledge, which will be of great value for understanding issues of conflict management, especially from the perspective of the developing world, and help us understand both the sources of conflict and how to mitigate and manage conflict in less developed societies. In this chapter we apply the entitlement failure approach to the specific context of human security: the entitlement set of a household constitutes the goods and services that the household can command, or acquire, by converting its endowments like assets, incomes and labour into through market exchanges (see Sen, 1976 and 1981). In the context of famines, Sen (1976; 1981) and others have employed the entitlement approach to explain why the distribution problems can cause famines and food insecurity in a society, despite the successful operation of various markets including asset markets and food markets (see Edkins, 1996; p. 550). In other words, despite the efficiency of an exchange mechanism like markets, market prices can change in such a fashion that the food entitlements (or, purchasing capacity) of many households can fall below the minimum quantities of foods. As a result, these households either choose to starve (Ravallion, 1986), or are forced to starve (Sen, 1981, p. 176), facing the increased risk of annihilation: certain human securities like famines arise because of an exchange entitlement failure, or exchange entitlement decline, such that many households are exposed to such stark insecurities due mainly to changes in relative prices in otherwise efficient markets. Such changes in relative prices can be brought about by various exogenous shocks. For us, human insecurity from violent collective, or group, conflicts can take place due to entitlement failures: given the endowments of a household, or an identifiable segment of a population, the household can acquire security from four sources: first and foremost, a typical household can purchase security from private sources like purchasing small arms and personal security networks; second, and most importantly, a typical household receives security from sub-national governments in the form of public security networks like police forces; third, security is also provided to private households by the national governments in the form of defence networks; and finally, households also receive some forms of security from the international community when the previous three sources fail to guarantee minimum security to human lives and human dignity in a country. Households pay direct and indirect taxes and other prices for ensuring their security. When households face violent conflicts in a society, the possibility arises that the purchasing power of a household is not sufficient to purchase the minimal level of security, due to changes in market prices. Similar to death from famine, ordinary households can now face death and destruction from exchange entitlement failures in physical securities. In other words, if security problems arise because of exchange entitlement failures, one should be able to detect both theoretical and empirical links between vulnerability of the households and market prices – especially prices of primary goods – in a conflict-ridden society like the Middle East. The rest of the chapter is built to develop the theories and the empirics to explain how and why and whether exchange entitlements have triggered the catastrophic conflicts in the Middle East.

The aim of this research is to understand conflicts from exchange entitlement failures. First, modern markets cannot be fully understood without a brief analysis of globalisation since most economies and their markets have been seriously impacted by globalisation. In other words, market ethos plays a significant role in most countries, including the Middle East. Second, modern societies are also significantly influenced by the political ethos of democratisation. Thus, we will choose a multidisciplinary approach in this chapter. In order to do that we will ask simple questions: what are the (economic) incentives for and constraints on conflicts? Why in some societies do conflicts recur, while other societies retain their peaceful character? The analysis will be undertaken in the context of globalisation, which has spurred the twin forces of democratisation and privatisation in developing nations.

In recent years economics has turned its attention to the explanation of conflicts. Some interesting microeconomic models have been developed, yet there are still gaps that motivate current research. Hirshleifer (1988, 1989, 1995a, and 2000) put forward models to explain conflicts in terms of three economic variables: 1) preferences, 2) opportunities within constraints, and 3) prevailing perceptions. Hirshleifer in his work highlights a contest to explain conflict as a means to make economic gains. One of his main contributions to the field is to introduce a Tullock-type contest success function that came to be called 'conflict technology' in the relevant literature. In light of the conflict technology, with an economic prize from conflicts akin to that of a contest, Hirshleifer offers an equilibrium conflict as a Nash equilibrium of the proposed contest so that conflicts are chosen as mutual best responses of micro agents.

The pioneering work of Grossman (1991, 1999) also shares the notion of conflict, but in a richer setting: Grossman reduces society to three groups: first, there is a group of peasants who decide to choose between two activities – to fight, or to produce an agricultural product. The second group represents a government agency that taxes the peasants and thereby collects booty and raises an army to protect the booty. The third group is a rebel group, which recruits and raises a rebel army from the peasants to fight the government for the booty. The rebel group funds its activities by looting peasants. Grossman posits rebellion as business, and sees this as one of the most distinguishing features of conflicts: insurgents are similar to bandits or pirates who engage in rebellion and conflicts to make profit. Thus, the new model of Grossman is more intricate than the models of Hirshman although the fundamental notion of both is that conflicts are akin to a contest for acquiring resources, as opposed to a peaceful participation in a market exchange that involves mutually beneficial trade. Conflicts are a zero-sum game – there is only one winner, who takes the whole stake.

In this way conflicts come to be seen as a product of rebellion akin to an industry that creates profit-making opportunities from an act of piracy. The rebel group has an increasing marginal cost of recruiting fighters from the peasantry and a declining marginal benefit in terms of the increased probability of winning the contest and the prize with the increasing size of its armed force. Economic equilibrium is struck where the marginal cost of employing one more soldier is balanced by the marginal benefit of so doing.

Against the backdrop of this strand of economic theory, political scientists traditionally argue that conflicts and rebellions are actuated by political protests that are driven by deep-rooted *grievances*. These grievances are precipitated by a host of social factors like inequality, racial, ethnic or religious intolerances, and oppression of one group by another. The exploitation of one group by another has received serious attention from Hirshleifer (2000) who calls this proclivity of human beings to gang up on others as Machiavelli's theorem, which can shape preferences and stir up grievances, and exaggerate the opportunities that may arise from conflict. Political science literature highlights two elements that exacerbate conflicts: first, the *type* of political regime has been isolated as a determinant of conflicts (see Hegre et al., 2001). There is some evidence to suggest that more democratic countries have a lower risk of war (see Collier and Hoeffler, 1998, 2002a, 2002b). Second, economic inequality is believed to be an important determinant of conflicts, though recent economic studies have not found any systematic relationship between inequality and conflict (see Collier and Hoeffler, 2002a, 2002b). In their studies, however, Collier and Hoeffler note low per capita income and low growth rates as contributing factors.

2.2   Twin forces of globalisation: conflicts with democratisation and the spread of market ethos

Globalisation is a multidimensional issue whose various facets of economic, financial, technological and social and political processes continually transform global economy, society and polity. It is generally recognised that the process of globalisation has been significantly aided by the fall in the cost of communication and transportation and led to an inevitable shrinkage of our globe into a quasi-'global village', characterised by an integration typically observed in traditional village communes. One therefore views globalisation as a complex process that gradually unleashes a series of transitions: the process begins with an increased integration of the world economy through trade and investment networks. It is well understood that this stage of increased integration turns on the pivot of decreasing transaction costs associated with trans-border trade and investment. Declining transaction costs are typically explained in terms of technical progress that reduces the price of communication and transport. Declining transaction costs have direct and positive impacts on cross-border trade, and on portfolio and direct investment. Another kind of transaction cost is the agency cost which generally increases with international trade. The economic consequence of increased integration is twofold: first, nations become more interdependent in economic terms; and second, there arises a perception that trans-border trade and investment offer tremendous and often unprecedented economic opportunities for a nation. The first transition thus results in an increased integration of the world economy – through a mesh of multinational investment, trade flows and flows of financial capital – with an equally important transition in the perception of the importance of trans-border trade and investment as a vehicle of economic progress and prosperity for a nation. The second transition impacts on the realm of national management, as national governments actively respond to the benefits accruing to those nations that entertain openness to foreign trade and investment. As nations compete against each other to take home the spoils of the world economy, policymakers agree that the main barrier to the acquisition of spoils lies in the domestic economic structure, characterised by the labyrinth of controls that has been a by-product of the Keynesian era of de-globalisation.

The sequence of a nation's integration into the world economy and its development of trans-border trade and investment triggers a third transition, which paves the way for homogenisation of economic ideologies, the convergence of macroeconomic and trade policies and the consequent adoption of measures of democratisation, privatisation and liberalisation. This transition typically takes place in social and economic spheres. Whether the transition in terms of the spread of market ethos and democratisation creates special economic and social scenarios in developing nations that drive conflicts in these nations is the question that motivates this research.

To understand the seriousness of this question let us try to understand how conflicts seem to be banished from a democratic, market-based nation. The Smithian perspective on market competition highlights a congruence of interests of market participants: say a buyer wants some milk and is ready to give some money to the milkmaid for it, and the milkmaid wants money and is, therefore, ready to give a carton of milk in exchange. This exchange allows each to achieve a goal and thereby help each other. In a complex market mechanism, however, economic problems are often embedded in conflicting interests. The market mechanism can easily handle congruent interests, but may fail to resolve conflicts in a harmonious or fair fashion (see Sen, 1984b). To redress such conflicts the visible hand of government is usually invoked (Ostrom, 1987).

In this work we highlight two types of conflicts, market conflicts and political conflicts, and weave them together to illuminate an important intersection between economy and polity. We consider conflict at the market level in the usual fashion, as a dual economy with two distinct markets, agricultural and industrial. By applying the simple reasoning of general equilibrium, we obtain the balance between these two markets. The major departure from usual general equilibrium models is twofold: first, we argue that governments in developing nations still exercise significant control over agricultural products to avoid food shortage crises and to influence the incomes of farmers; and second, that in developing nations governments mediate the allocation of capital between agricultural and industrial sectors. As a result, the market mechanism in developing nations is influenced by relevant public policies. Thus, the first type of conflict in our model is sectoral conflict, that is, between industrial and agricultural sectors, in the allocation of capital as well as in the determination of inter-sectoral terms of trade (relative price). This is the first facet of our model.

The introduction of public policies in the context of rural and industrial markets in our model allows us to link the second type of conflict, the political conflict, with the first type, sectorial. Since, the availability of public resources is fixed, it is modelled that there is no congruence of interest of the agents coming from these two sectors. As Hirsch (1977) notes, 'what winners win, losers lose'. Any allocation of capital will entail political costs and benefits that a self-seeking government – driven by electoral motive – will try to exploit. An incumbent government will naturally choose an allocation that will maximise the probability of its re-election. Our model on probabilistic voting has antecedents in the literature: Lindbeck and Weibull (1987) and Dixit and Londregan (1994) adapt the probabilistic model to examine public policies that redistribute income to narrow groups of voters. They assume that the various groups differ in their preferences for political parties and, thereby, identify the political characteristics of a group that make it an ideal candidate for receiving political largesse. These authors study the major determinants of the political success of a special interest group. In contrast, we begin with the political characteristics of voters and then apply the probabilistic voting theorem to determine the electoral equilibrium that is driven by political largesse in the form of public policies and inter-sectoral terms of trade. This is how our model resolves political conflicts.

The resolution of political conflict can have serious ramifications for the product markets due to its impact on the allocation of capital and the determination of relative prices. This is indeed a serious point to consider: traditional political theory highlights the failure of majority-rule voting caused by the absence of a stable electoral equilibrium. As a result, political instability can create significant instability in product markets. This is where we apply the probabilistic voting theorem to highlight the existence of a stable voting equilibrium, to establish that democratic political markets are well organised to promote the vote-maximising allocation of infrastructure that will, in turn, lend stability to the product markets: the model predicts that the vote-maximising government adopts an optimal allocation of capital and optimal terms of trade, which induce an electoral equilibrium that, in turn, maximises the government's chances of re-election. From this perspective, the economic outcome driven by agricultural and industrial markets depends on electoral equilibrium and, hence, on voters' preferences and characteristics. In light of the equilibrium we offer sources of conflicts and crises in such nations.

2.3   The role of privatisation in globalisation: as a vehicle of change of capital ownership and structure

Privatisation of public enterprises involves an increased trust in the efficiency of the market principle in comparison with the efficacy of the government. This ideological backdrop engendered a series of debates in the 1980s and 1990s. Despite serious questions and concerns, privatisation has been promoted with great zest in developed and developing countries alike since the 1980s. In a series of papers published in the early 2000s, the economic consequences of privatisation are considered welfare-enhancing (see Kikeri and Nellis, 2001; Shirley and Walsh, 2001 among many). However, the consequences of privatisation are mainly considered in advanced economies, and specifically in high-tech sectors like telecommunications. There is reason to believe that the economic consequences of privatisation are, at best, controversial in developing nations. From the work of Rodrik et al. (2002) and Jalilian et al. (2003) we know that the economic effects of privatisation are predicated on the quality of the regulatory regimes and governance institutions.

During the 1980s and 1990s, privatisation of public enterprises was a common economic event that rocked Africa, Asia, Australia, South America and Eastern and Western Europe (Kikeri, Nellis and Shirley, 1992). Western European nations provide a nice cameo of privatisation: Great Britain and France led the major forces of privatisation in Western Europe. In Great Britain, large and important industries such as telecommunications, gas and electricity were privatised. In France, large industrial and financial conglomerates cropped up from public enterprises. On the other hand, West Germany, Italy and the Netherlands had a somewhat cavalier approach, selling public shares in industrial companies and banks (see Knauss, 1988); and no measures were taken to privatise major public utilities such as telecommunications and postal services. It was widely recognised that these utilities were inefficient, yet privatisation was pushed to the background. The governments attempted to reduce inefficiency by initiating changes in the internal organisation of these public utilities. In Austria, Belgium and Scandinavian nations, the forces of privatisation have been in low gear.

In many Eastern European countries, privatisation bids are a step towards a capitalistic economic system. Privatisation measures have also been taken in many Asian, African and South American nations, mainly to embrace a capitalistic economic system. These nations of Asia, Africa and Eastern Europe are typically characterised by absence of stock markets and experienced managerial teams, and beset with inadequate industrial organisation, lack of comprehensive legal frameworks and a lack of appropriate market institutions. Thus, the bids of privatisation in these nations are significantly different from the bids in industrial nations with well-developed capitalistic economic systems. In non-industrial nations, privatisation aims to lay down the structures of market economies, while in Western economies the aims of privatisation are mainly to improve the efficacy of the capitalistic economic system.

The conventional wisdom in this context is that public enterprises are heavily inefficient. There are three types of inefficiency noted in the literature. First, the cost of production in public enterprises is argued to be significantly higher than the cost of similar services provided by private enterprise. Public provision of municipal services is shown to be very costly in comparison with their private provision in the United States (see Donahue, 1998). Second, public enterprises have lower profitability relative to private firms in similar businesses (see Lopez de Silanes, 1993). Third, public firms are more inefficient in the utilisation of resources than private firms (see Mueller, 1989; and Vining and Boardman, 1993). These conclusions are supported by recent findings of the World Bank that 'efficiency improves after privatisation' (see Boycko et al., 1996). This leads to questions about the reason for the inefficiency of public enterprises. The explanation is that public enterprises, instead of maximising efficiency, address the needs of vote-maximising politicians (Boycko et al., 1996).

The secret behind improvement in efficiency is the change in management behaviour, caused by three factors (Bös, 1994): first, privatisation entails less government intervention, which allows flexibility in management. Second, the management of a privatised firm is more responsive to market forces due to bankruptcy threats and capital market discipline (see Kay and Thompson, 1986). Third, the management of a privatised firm has less power in influencing government policy and political favours since the ties between firm and government are snapped by privatisation. Thus, privatisation not only provides more decision-making and strategising power to the management, but also makes the firm more reliant on the market mechanism. As a result, the management – in order to survive and prosper – must enhance the market value of the firm given the available resources. The corollary is that management will enhance efficiency in the bid to increase the market value of the firm.

However, privatisation is controversial in all societies – partly because of its political and ideological leanings and partly because of its adversarial relation with labour unions. It is true that privatisation alters the distribution of power within a society: economic decisions are transferred from the hands of policymakers and bureaucrats to private managers, while the management becomes responsible to shareholders rather than society or government. Socialistic models of ownership are replaced by capitalistic ones. Privatisation also impinges on the institutional aspects of labour markets. Privatisation is normally accompanied by a reduction in a trade union's power and political influence. As an example, privatisation of the electricity industry in Great Britain was a means to weaken the stranglehold of the miners' union (see Bös, 1994, p. 3). Similar motives behind privatisation have been reported from West Germany, where the wheels of privatisation have been clogged by trade unions that exert a strong influence on political parties.

Does privatisation necessarily augment efficiency? The intended effect of privatisation on efficiency critically depends on the entry of private firms to enhance competition and reduce the monopolistic power of the privatised firm. Foreign firms, in particular, play an important role in promoting competition and encouraging technology that will lower production costs. However, foreign entry also creates problems of expatriation of profits. Foreign investors compound the problem, since an excess of foreign investment will influence strategies of privatised firms, and these may be antithetical to national goals. In Great Britain and France, governments obviated this problem by retaining a 'golden share' of the privatised firm, giving them a veto power against takeovers and undesirable changes in policies. It is important to note that privatisation directly affects the budget deficits of the government. Governments lose future dividends from a privatised firm, although they can raise revenues from selling their assets. It is generally recognised that the former outweighs the latter (see Yarrow, 1986).

Privatisation may thus have an adverse effect on the government budget and, thereby, on government expenditure on infrastructure. The decline in government expenditure on infrastructure has dual effects: first, it has a recessionary impact as it lowers effective demand in the Keynesian sense. Second, a decline in the availability of infrastructure will increase the cost of production and, thereby, acts on the competitiveness of the entire economy. Hence privatisation is a mixed bag, and the immediate effects may be counterproductive. At the least, privatisation has political implications that may overshadow economic rationales.

In what follows we posit that privatisation is an instrument in the armoury of a government in a developing nation. By choosing the precise bid of privatisation, such governments alter the allocation of capital. Hence, we need to subdivide developing nations into two categories: the first is the group of nations with the least developed status, where governments still tweak the allocation of capital by direct control. The second group includes those where allocation of capital takes place through the market mechanism, although governments may still have significant power in dictating the allocation of capital, acting as a gatekeeper of capital through their choice of privatisation bids. What follows in the next section is important for both types of nations.

We now turn to the question of the political determinants of capital allocation.

2.4   The politics of capital allocation: a new model of conflict from exchange entitlement failures

The primary idea here is to break an economy into different sectors characterised by regional features and allow them to produce locally and exchange with each other. The process of exchange will give rise to flows of goods and services mediated by inter-sectoral terms of trade. On the basis of this disaggregation we will search for sectoral inequality and imbalance as sources of conflict in a traditional society. In what follows we develop a model in terms of two sectors, although it can easily be extended to a multi-sector economy.

2.4.1   The basic setting of exchange entitlements

Assume we have a dual economy that has two sectors: industry and agriculture. Thus there is a single term of trade which we label TOT. The output Y_i in sector i is given as the following production function, in which L_i is employment and K_i is capital in sector i:

$$Y_i = f(L_i, K_i) \tag{1a}$$

The output in each sector is shared by bargaining among claimants. In the industrial sector the bargaining takes place between owners and workers, while in the agrarian sector the bargaining takes place between a rural oligarchy and workers. The individual share of output of workers in sector i is ϑ_i. Each sector thus has economic agents who also participate in politics by casting their votes. There are N_i voters in sector i and S_i; a fraction of them vote for the incumbent political party. Thus S_i is the sensitivity of voters from sector i, which is the exposit probability that a randomly selected voter from sector i will vote for the incumbent government. Thus, the votes in favour of an incumbent government are labelled as V and given in equation (1b):

$$V = S_1 N_1 + S_2 N_2 \tag{1b}$$

Voters' sensitivities in two sectors are given as:

$$S_1 = H(\vartheta_1),\ S_2 = h(\vartheta) \tag{1c}$$

Table 2.1 Description of the dual economy

Industry (1)	Agriculture (2)
Industrial Output: $Y_1 = F(K_1, N_1)$	Agricultural Output $Y_2 = G(K_2, N_2)$
$S_1 = H(\vartheta_1), \dfrac{\partial H}{\partial \vartheta_1} > 0$	$S_2 = h(\vartheta)$
$\dfrac{\partial^2 H}{\partial \vartheta^2} < 0$	$\dfrac{\partial h}{\partial \vartheta_2} > 0, \dfrac{\partial^2 h}{\partial \vartheta_2^2} < 0$
Share of Owner = T_1	Share of Oligarchy = T_2
$\vartheta_1 = p(Y_1 - T_1)/N_1$	$\vartheta_2 = (Y_2 - T_2)/N_2$

Note S_i, the sensitivity of voters from sector i, increases with the sectoral share of workers ϑ_i. We don't assume specific functional form besides the functional form of S_i in equation (1c) at this stage. We label the TOT as p. We offer the necessary details of these two sectors in Table 2.1.

Nash bargaining outcome

The bargaining takes place in each sector to maximise the so-called Nash product n_i:

$$n_1 = \text{Nash Product} = (Y_1 - T_1)^\alpha * T_1^{1-\alpha} \qquad \text{Industry}$$
$$n_2 = \text{Nash Product} = (Y_2 - T_2)^\beta * T_2^{1-\beta} \qquad \text{Agriculture}$$

where α, β are the bargaining powers of the industrial owner and the rural oligarchy respectively. Thus we can define T_i as the following:

$$T_1 = f(\alpha, Y_1) \tag{1d}$$

$$T_2 = f(\beta, Y_2) \tag{1e}$$

The first order condition to maximise the Nash product is given as:

$$\frac{dn_1}{dT_1} = T_1^{1-\alpha} * \alpha (Y_1 - T_1)^{\alpha-1} * (-1) + (Y_1 - T_1)^\alpha * (1-\alpha)T_1^{-\alpha} = 0 \tag{1f}$$

which gives us

$$T_1^{-\alpha} * \left(Y_1 - T_1\right)^{\alpha-1} \left[-T_1\alpha + \left(Y_1 - T_1\right)\left(1-\alpha\right)\right] = 0 \tag{1g}$$

$$Y_1\left(1-\alpha\right) - T_1\left(1-\alpha\right) - T_1\alpha = 0 \tag{1h}$$

$$Y_1\left(1-\alpha\right) = T_1\left(1-\alpha+\alpha\right) \tag{1i}$$

The optimal share of the owner and the oligarchy are given in (1j) and (1k)

$$T_1^* = \left(1-\alpha\right)Y_1 \tag{1j}$$

$$T_2^* = \left(1-\beta\right)Y_2 \tag{1k}$$

The per capita tax in sector i is given as

$$t_1^* = T_1^*/N_1 = \left(1-\alpha\right) \cdot \frac{pY_1}{N_1} = \left(1-\alpha\right)py_2 \tag{1l}$$

$$t_2^* = \left(1-\beta\right)\frac{Y_2}{N_2} = \left(1-\beta\right)y_2 \tag{1m}$$

Define y_1 as the per capita income in industry and y_2 as the per capita income in agriculture.

The per capita share of workers in sector i is given as

$$\vartheta_1 = p\left(Y_1 - T_1^*\right)/N_1 \tag{1n}$$

or,

$$\vartheta_1 = p\left(Y_1 - Y_1 + \alpha Y_1\right)/N_1 \tag{1o}$$

$$\vartheta_1 = \alpha\left(pY_1\right)/N_1 \tag{1p}$$

$$\vartheta_2 = \beta.Y_2/N_2 \tag{1q}$$

We know the per capita income in each sector is given as

$$Y_1/N_1 = y_1 \tag{1r}$$

$$Y_2/N_2 = y_2 \tag{1s}$$

So the individual labour share in each sector is reduced to

$$\vartheta_1 = p.\alpha.y_1 \tag{1t}$$

$$\vartheta_2 = \beta.y_2 \tag{1u}$$

The voter sensitivity in each sector is given as

$$S_1 = H(\vartheta_1) = H(p\alpha y_1) \tag{1v}$$

$$S_2 = h(\vartheta_2) = h(\beta y_2) \tag{1w}$$

The political characteristics are given as the overall voter sensitivity v:

$$v = \frac{V}{N_1 + N_2} = H(p\alpha y_1)\frac{N_1}{N_1 + N_2} + h(\beta y_2)\frac{N_2}{N_1 + N_2} \tag{1x}$$

$$n_1 = \frac{N_1}{N_1 + N_2} \tag{1y}$$

$$n_2 = \frac{N_2}{N_1 + N_2} = 1 - n_1 \tag{1z}$$

2.4.2   Vote-maximisation and electoral motives of the incumbent government

The basic theoretical insight is that exchange entitlement failures can be more fundamental than political forces. Thus, we assume the existence of a democratic set-up in our model and establish that exchange entitlements can create insecurity problems despite the existence of democratic forces in a society. The lack of democratic forces can further exacerbate the problems driven by exchange entitlement failures. Thus, we consider our analysis in a set political set-up in which the national governments pay attention to the welfare of their citizens. As a simplification, we posit that the basic motive of an incumbent government is to maximise votes, or political support, which is not necessarily the same as maximisation of the probability of re-election. This is the fundamental assumption about the electoral motive of an incumbent government in our model. Thus, the function that is of relevance to an incumbent is equation (2a) which is the vote function:

$$V = H(p\alpha y_1)n_1 + h(\beta y_2)n_2 \tag{2a}$$

In our model the incumbent government maximises votes V by choosing the TOT, p, and the allocation of available capital between sectors K_1 and K_2, while p, K_1 and K_2 determine Y_1 and Y_2 wherefrom the shares of worker-voters are determined. The goal of the government is to maximise votes subject to the constraints laid down in the previous section.

Optimisation problem of the incumbent government

The incumbent government seeks to maximise the following:

$$\text{Maximise.}\{V = H(p\alpha y_1)N_1 + h(\beta y_2)N_2 \Sigma p, K_1, K_2\} \tag{2b}$$

$\{K_1, K_2\}$

subject to

$$Y_1 = F(L_1, K_1) \tag{2c}$$

$$Y_2 = G(L_2, K_2) \tag{2d}$$

$$K_1 + K_2 = \overline{K} \tag{2e}$$

Hence, we can reduce the capital allocation to the following simple rule:

$$\frac{K_1}{\overline{K}} + \frac{K_2}{\overline{K}} = 1 \tag{2f}$$

$$k_1 + k_2 = 1 \tag{2g}$$

$$k_1 = 1 - k_2 = k \tag{2h}$$

Thus the choice of capital allocation for the incumbent government is reduced to the choice of k.

2.4.3 Optimal choice of capital allocation and entitlement failure

The foundation of our model is built on the idea that the choice of capital allocation is dependent on the political calculations of the incumbent government, which is driven mainly by instincts for political survival. The allocation of capital leads to the creation of sectoral supplies and incomes and corresponding sectoral demands, wherefrom the equilibrium terms of trade arise. Our central question is whether the choice of an optimal allocation of capital, on the basis of political calculations, can cause a *distribution failure* for the poor that drives them to starvation and consequent violent conflict. The first order condition for maximisation is given as (3a):

$$\frac{\partial v}{\partial k} = \frac{\partial H}{\partial y_1} * \frac{\partial Y_1}{\partial k} * \frac{1}{N} + \frac{\partial h}{\partial y_2} * \frac{\partial Y_2}{\partial k} * \frac{1}{N_2} = 0 \tag{3a}$$

From equation (3a) we know

$$p\frac{\partial H}{\partial y_1} * \frac{\partial Y_1}{\partial k} * \frac{1}{N_1} = \frac{\partial h}{\partial y_2} * \frac{\partial Y_2}{\partial k_2} * \frac{1}{N_2} \tag{3b}$$

Wherefrom we can derive the shares of workers in each sector as implicit functions of p, y and k:

$$\vartheta_1^* = p \cdot \alpha \cdot y_1^* \left(k^* \right) \tag{3c}$$

$$\vartheta_2^* = \beta \cdot y_2^* \left(k^* \right) \tag{3d}$$

A distribution-failure arises if the vote-maximising choices lead to individual income shares of workers in either sector that are smaller than a critical minimum that is necessary for survival. That is:

$$\vartheta_i^* < \overline{\vartheta} \tag{3f}$$

Note that $\overline{\vartheta}$ is the critical value of ϑ below which workers will starve due to a distribution failure; consequent social problems will arise that will gradually push the sector towards violence. As an example, if $\vartheta_1^* < \overline{\vartheta}$ then the industrial sector may encounter conflict as workers' incomes are less than the critical minimal income necessary for survival. What is important is that the survival problem can be expressed in terms of an allocation of capital problem: there is a maximum, or upper-bound, of k, Max k^*, beyond which the agricultural sector will suffer violent conflict as the allocated capital is too little to give workers a minimum income. In a similar vein, there is a minimum k, Min k^*, such that the allocation of capital below Min k^* will drive the industrial sector into strife as workers' shares fall below the critical minimum. It is possible for conflicts in one sector to move to the other sector.

What is interesting in this two-sectoral model is that whether the capital allocation k^* is safe or otherwise will be reflected in the inter-sectoral price

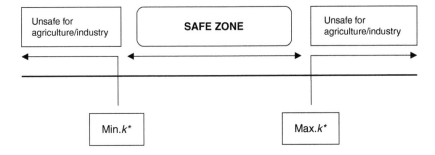

The condition for the nonexistence of a safe zone is given by Min.k^* > Max.k^*

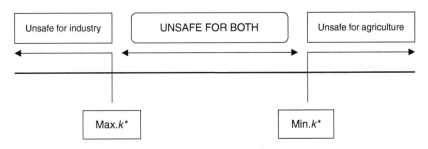

Figure 2.1 Allocation of capital and conflicts

ratio, TOT p. Thus, there will be a crisis if the TOT exceeds a critical value as given in the following (see Figure 2.1):

$$p > \frac{\beta \vartheta_1^*}{\alpha \vartheta_2^*} * \frac{Y_2^{*-1}}{Y_1^{*-1}} \tag{3g}$$

The important question now is what determines the inter-sectoral terms of trade p? We turn to this in the following subsection.

2.4.4 Determination of the intersectoral term of trade (TOT)

The finding of the model calls forth a seemingly easy question of the determinants of the TOT, p. In other words: what determines p? The answers are not simple since the agricultural TOT is influenced by a host of market and extra-market factors like demand and supply, price controls, price subsidies, procurement prices, input subsidies and so on. It is in fact a Pandora's box that we seek to take a quick look in. Some possibilities are outlined below as starting points for analysis:

- One possible means of determining p is in terms of a bargaining game between industrialists and the agro-oligarchy. Relative bargaining power will determine p and explain whether the critical value of p is crossed, unleashing a series of sectoral conflicts.

- p can be determined for the equality of demand and supply in the industrial sector given the balance between demand and supply in the agricultural sector. Thus, one may like to hold the price of agricultural commodity as a datum (administered price) and determine p by equating the demand and supply in the industrial sector. In this case it is important to understand how we can endogenously derive the excess demand function to determine p.

In what follows we examine the demand and supply mechanism to determine the TOT p.

2.4.4.1   Demand for industrial goods

Assuming a fixed proposition of income α_i of Y_i is spent on industrial goods, we can write the demand for industrial goods as:

$$D_I = \alpha_1 * Y_1 + \alpha_2 * Y_2 \tag{4a}$$

One can make α_i sensitive to the price ratio p:

$$\alpha_1 = \left(\alpha_o - \alpha_1 p\right) \tag{4b}$$

$$\alpha_2 = \overline{\alpha}_o - \alpha_2 p \tag{4c}$$

Hence the demand for the industrial goods is reduced to

$$D_I = \left(\alpha_o - \alpha_1 p\right)Y_1 p + \left(\overline{\alpha}_o - \alpha_2 p\right)Y_2 \tag{4d}$$

$$\text{or, } D_I = p\left(\alpha_o - \alpha_1 p\right)F\left(K_1, N_1\right) + \left(\overline{\alpha}_o - \alpha_2 p\right)G\left(K_2, N_2\right) \tag{4e}$$

$$\text{or, } D_I = p\left(\alpha_o - \alpha_1 p\right)N_1 F\left(\frac{K_1}{N_1}, 1\right) + \left(\overline{\alpha}_o - \alpha_2 p\right)N_2 G\left(\frac{K_2}{N_2}, 1\right) \tag{4f}$$

In order to make calculations in terms of k, we make a simplification:

$$\overline{K} = K_1 + K_2 = N_1 \tag{4f$'$}$$

As a result, we can write:

$$\frac{K_1}{N_1} = k^*, \frac{K_2}{N_2} = 1 - k^* \tag{4g}$$

After substituting (4f') and (4g) into equation (4f) we arrive at the demand for the industrial good as:

$$D_I = p(\alpha_o - \alpha_o p) N_1 F(k^*) + N_2 (\overline{\alpha}_o - \alpha_2 p) G(1 - k^*) \tag{4g'}$$

2.4.4.2 Supply of industrial goods

From the postulated production function we know

$$S_I = Y_1 = F(K_1, N_1) = N_1 * F\left(\frac{K_1}{N_1}, 1\right) = N_1 * F(k^*, 1) \tag{4h}$$

We express the excess demand function as

$$X_D = D_I - S_I \tag{4i}$$

Hence,

$$X_D = p(\alpha_o - \alpha_1 p) N_1 F(k^*) + N_2 (\overline{\alpha}_o - \alpha_2 p) G(1 - k^*) - N_1 F(k^*, 1) \tag{4j}$$

or,

$$X_D = F(k^*) N_1 [p(\alpha_o - \alpha_1 p) - 1] + (N_2 \overline{\alpha}_o - N_2 \alpha_2 p) G(1 - k^*) \tag{4k}$$

Further simplifications yield the following:

$$X_D = F(k^*) N_1 [p\alpha_o - p^2 \alpha_1 - 1] + N_2 \overline{\alpha}_o G(1 - k^*) - N_2 \alpha_2 pG(1 - k^*) \tag{4l}$$

or,

$$X_D = F(k^*) N_1 \alpha_o p - \alpha_1 F(k^*) N_1 p^2 - F(k^*) N_1 \\ + N_2 \overline{\alpha}_o G(1 - k^*) N_2 \alpha_2 pG(1 - k^*) \tag{4m}$$

Hence,

$$X_D = \left[F\left(k^*\right) N_1 \alpha_o - G\left(1 - k^*\right) N_2 \alpha_2 \right] p - \alpha_1 F_1 \left(k^*\right) N_1 p^2$$
$$+ N_2 \alpha_o G\left(1 - k^*\right) - F\left(k^*\right) N_1 \tag{4n}$$

Equation (4n) can be reduced to a simple quadratic equation:

$$X_D = A_1 p - A_2 p^2 + A_3 \tag{4o}$$

The excess demand function is a quadratic function of the TOT p and the slope of the excess demand function is equal to

$$\frac{dX_D}{dp} = A_1 - 2 A_2 p \tag{4p}$$

The excess demand function and its slope will play an important role in the determination of an equilibrium TOT p and its stability properties as highlighted in the following subsection.

2.4.5   The existence and stability of equilibrium terms of trade in a bi-sectoral model

The existence and stability of an equilibrium TOT requires that the excess demand function is a continuous and inverse function of p which is true if $p < A_1 / 2 A_2$ and that will give $\frac{dX_D}{dp} < 0$. Since there are two goods in the system, from Walras' law we know that if one market is in equilibrium the other market will also be in equilibrium. Hence for the existence of an equilibrium TOT we need the following single condition to be met:

$$X_D = A_1 p - A_2 p^2 + A_3 = 0 \tag{4o$'$}$$

The above equilibrium condition as a quadratic equation gives us two roots p^*:

$$p^* = \frac{-A_1 \pm \sqrt{A_1^2 + 4 A_2 A_3}}{-2 A_2} \tag{5a}$$

$$\text{Or, } p^* = \frac{A_1}{2 A_2} \pm \frac{\sqrt{A_1^2 + 4 A_2 A_3}}{2 A_2} \tag{5b}$$

Note that from the stability condition we know that only the smaller root is stable; hence, the stable equilibrium TOT is given by p^*:

$$p^* = \frac{A_1}{2A_2} - \frac{\sqrt{A_1^2 + 4A_2 A_3}}{2A_2} = \mu(k^*) \qquad (5c)$$

Now we try to predict how the equilibrium p^* will respond to changes in p^* as an exercise in comparative static. It is a huge problem, since the functional forms are too complex to yield a ready-made answer. So we adopt the following steps to provide an answer to this question:

• *Step 1:*

We first look at the first term of the equilibrium price p^*:

$$\frac{A_1}{2A_2} = \frac{F(k^*)N_1\alpha_o - G(1-k^*)N_2\alpha_2}{\alpha_1 F_1(k^*)(N_1)} \qquad (5d)$$

This can be reduced to:

$$\frac{A_1}{2A_2} = \frac{\alpha_o}{\alpha_1} - \left[\frac{G(1-k^*)N_2\alpha_2}{F_1(k^*)N_1\alpha_1}\right] \qquad (5e)$$

Differentiating (5e) with respect to k gives (where h_{ij} are parameters)

$$\frac{d(A_1/2A_2)}{d.k^*} = -\frac{h_{11} * -G'N_2\alpha_2 - [.h_{12}]F_1'N_1\alpha_1 G[h_{13}]}{[F_1(k^*)N_1\alpha_1]^2} < 0 \qquad (5f)$$

• *Step 2:*

Let us call $T = \dfrac{A_1^2 + 4A_2 A_3}{4A_2^2} = \left(\dfrac{A_1}{2A_2}\right)^2 + \dfrac{A_3}{A_2^2}$ \qquad (5g)

Differentiating (5g) with respect to k yields:

$$\frac{d(T)}{d.k^*} = 2 * \frac{A_1}{2A_2}\left[\frac{d(A_1/2A_2)}{d.k^*}\right] + A_3 * \frac{d}{d.k^*}\left(\frac{1}{A_2^2}\right) \qquad (5h)$$

Note the following:

$$\frac{d}{d.k^*}\left(\frac{1}{A_2^{2}}\right) = \frac{-2A_2\left(\frac{d.A_2}{d.k^*}\right)}{A_2^{4}} \tag{5i}$$

$$\frac{d}{d.k^*}\left(\frac{1}{A_2^{2}}\right) = -\frac{d.A_2/d.k^*}{A_2^{3}} \tag{5j}$$

Note that: $\dfrac{d.A_2}{d.k^*} = \alpha_1 N_1 F_1^{'}\left(k^*\right) > 0$ ⠀⠀⠀⠀⠀⠀⠀⠀(5k)

The most likely case is that as k^* increases, the p^* will decline as the impact on supply will be stronger than the demand.

That is, it is expected that $\dfrac{dp^*}{dk^*} < 0$. However, there is no guarantee that this will be the case, for which we will offer restrictions in the next subsection to yield this result. However, if $\dfrac{dp^*}{dk^*} < 0$, the vote-maximisation by an incumbent government will require:

$$V = H\left(p^*, \alpha, Y_1\right)N_1 + h\left(\beta Y_2\right)N_2 \tag{5l}$$
$$p^* = \mu\left(k^*\right),\ Y_1 = F\left(k^*\right),\ Y_2 = G\left(1-k^*\right)$$
$$V = H\left[\mu\left(k^*\right), F\left(k^*\right)\right]N_1 + h\left[\beta.G\left(1-k^*\right)\right]N_2 \tag{5m}$$

$$\frac{\partial V}{\partial k^*} = N_1\left(\frac{\partial H}{\partial k^*}*\frac{\partial\mu}{\partial k^*} + \frac{\partial H}{\partial k^*}*\frac{\partial F}{\partial k^*}\right) - N_2\beta.h'.G' = 0 \tag{5n}$$

$$N_1\left(H'.\mu' + H'.F'\right) - N_2\beta.h'.G' = 0 \tag{5o}$$

Since our result is based on an assumption that it is very likely that $\dfrac{dp^*}{dk^*} < 0$, in what follows in the next subsection we offer a set of conditions that can ensure this inverse relationship between p^* and k^*.

2.4.6 An alternative formulation of the terms of trade

We can also make an alternative model. The demand for industrial goods is

$$D_I = p.\alpha_1.Y_1 + \overline{\alpha}_2 Y_2 \tag{6a}$$

Let us assume that α_1 = Constant, but that

$$\bar{\alpha_2} = \alpha_o - \alpha_2 p \qquad (6a')$$

Thus, the income effect and price effect cancel each other out in the industrial sector while the demand function for the industrial goods is assumed to be inversely associated with the TOT in the agricultural sector. This is the most likely demand function, given as:

$$D_I = p.Y_1.\alpha_1 + (\alpha_o - p\alpha_2)Y_2 \qquad (6b)$$

$$\text{Or, } D_I = p.\alpha_1.F(K_1, N_1) + (\alpha_o - p\alpha_2)G(K_2, N_2) \qquad (6c)$$

$$\text{Or, } D_I = p.\alpha_1.N_1.F(k^*) + (\alpha_o - p\alpha_2)N_2.G(1-k^*) \qquad (6d)$$

The supply function for the industrial goods is given as:

$$S_I = Y_1 = N_1.F(k^*) \qquad (6e)$$

The excess demand function is given as:

$$X_D = D_I - S_I \qquad (6f)$$

$$\text{Or, } X_D = p.\alpha_1.N_1.F(k^*) - N_1.F(k^*) + (\alpha_o - \alpha_2 p)N_2.G(1-k^*) \qquad (6g)$$

$$\text{Or, } X_D = N_1.F(k^*)(p.\alpha_1 - 1) + (\alpha_o - \alpha_2 p)N_2.G(1-k^*) \qquad (6h)$$

Once again, by appealing to Walras' law, the equilibrium in the system is given by the market clearing for one market only. That is:

$$X_D = 0 \qquad (6h')$$

which gives rise to:

$$N_1.F(k^*)\alpha_1 p - N_1.F(k^*) + \alpha_o.N_2.G(1-k^*) - \alpha_2.N_2.G(1-k^*)p = 0 \qquad (6i)$$

$$\text{Or, } \left[N_1.F(k^*)\alpha_1 - \alpha_2.N_2.G(1-k^*)\right]p = \alpha_o.N_2.G(1-k^*) - N_1.F(k^*) \qquad (6j)$$

The equilibrium condition (6j) gives us the equilibrium TOT p^e as:

$$p^e = \frac{\alpha_o.N_2.G(1-k^*) - N_1.F(k^*)}{N_1.F(k^*)\alpha_1 - \alpha_2.N_2.G(1-k^*)} \qquad (6k)$$

Is there something that automatically makes the equilibrium TOT meaningful? Unfortunately, there is nothing sacrosanct about $p^e > 0$. If $p^e < 0$, the model breaks down. In order to prevent the collapse of the model, we require some parametric restrictions. In what follows we take a special case to drive our point home.

Let us assume $\alpha_2 = 0$ so that we can see how parametric restrictions can ensure a meaningful equilibrium price. For $\alpha_2 = 0$, we will have a special value of p^e as p^{ee}:

$$p^{ee} = \frac{\alpha_o.N_2.G(1-k^*)}{\alpha_1.N_1.F(k^*)} - \frac{1}{\alpha_1} \tag{6l}$$

For $p^{ee} > 0$ the following must hold:

$$\frac{\alpha_o.N_2.G(1-k^*)}{\alpha_1.N_1.F(k^*)} > \frac{1}{\alpha_1} \tag{6m}$$

$$\frac{\alpha_o.N_2.G(1-k^*)}{N_1.F(k^*)} > 1 \tag{6n}$$

$$G(1-k^*) > \frac{N_1}{N_2}.\frac{F(k^*)}{\alpha_o} \tag{6o}$$

The above conditions are necessary for making the equilibrium price p^{ee} economically meaningful.

2.4.7   *The new model of terms of trade and electoral motive*

Note that vote-maximisation calls forth:

$$\frac{\partial V}{\partial k} = \frac{\partial H}{\partial Y_1}.\frac{\partial Y_1}{\partial k}.\frac{1}{n_1} + \frac{\partial H}{\partial p}.\frac{\partial p}{\partial k}.\frac{1}{n_1} + \frac{\partial h}{\partial Y_2}.\frac{\partial Y_2}{\partial k}.\frac{1}{n_2} = 0 \tag{6p}$$

Note $\dfrac{\partial H}{\partial p} > 0, \dfrac{\partial H}{\partial Y_1} > 0$ $\tag{6p'}$

Since $\dfrac{\partial p^e}{\partial k} = \dfrac{-\alpha_1.N_1.F(k^*)G - \alpha_o.N_2.G(1-k^*)}{[.Z]^2} < 0$, there exists an interior

value of k that maximises votes and Z is a parameter.

Let us use a specific example here to take stock of our findings.

2.4.7.1 An example of exchange entitlement failures and collective violence

Let us assume

$$y_1^* = F(k_1^*) = \mu.k_1^*, \; y_2^* = G(k_2^*) = \lambda.k_2^* \tag{6p'}$$

We know $k_1^* = k^*$, $k_2^* = 1-k^*$ and from these functions we can derive the critical value of TOT as p^c such that for $p > p^c$ there will be a potential conflict and an ensuing crisis for the system.

Thus there is a potential conflict and a crisis if

$$p > p \frac{\beta.\vartheta_1^*}{\alpha.\vartheta_2^*} * \frac{y_2^*/\lambda}{y_1^*/\mu} = p^c \tag{6r}$$

or, if

$$p > \frac{\beta.\vartheta_1^*.\mu}{\alpha.\lambda.\vartheta_2^*} * \frac{\mu_2^*}{y_1^*} \tag{6s}$$

That is

$$p > \frac{\beta.\vartheta_1^*}{\alpha.\vartheta_2^*} * \frac{k_2^*}{k_1^*} \tag{6t}$$

that can be further reduced to

$$p > \frac{\beta.\vartheta_1^*}{\beta.\vartheta_2^*} * \left(\frac{1-k^*}{k^*}\right) \tag{6u}$$

For us the critical price ratio is p^c that is given as

$$p^c = \frac{1-k^*}{k^*} * \frac{\beta.\vartheta_1^*}{\alpha.\vartheta_2^*} \tag{6v}$$

Note that if $p > p^c$ at least one sector of our postulated economy will experience problems that can lead to violent conflict, as there is a distribution failure for workers in at least one sector. On the other hand, if $p < p^c$, everything is fine – the market mechanism works well and there is no distribution failure in either sector.

2.5   Determination of equilibrium TOT

We know that the excess demand for the industrial good is given as:

$$X_D = \left[\mu k^* N_1 \alpha_o - \lambda (1 - k^*) N_2 \alpha_2 \right] p - \alpha_1 \mu k^* N_1 p^2$$
$$+ N_2 \alpha_o \lambda (1 - h^*) - \mu h^* N_1 \qquad (6w)$$

that can be expressed as:

$$X_D = A_1 . p - A_2 . p^2 + A_3 \qquad (6x)$$

where the coefficients are given as:

$$A_1 = N_1 . \alpha_o . \mu . k^* - \lambda . N_2 . \alpha_2 + \lambda . N_2 . \alpha_2 \qquad (6y)$$

$$A_1 = A_{11} . k^* - A_{12} \qquad (6z)$$

$$A_2 = N_1 . \alpha_1 . \mu . k^* = A_{21} . k^* \qquad (6aa)$$

$$A_3 = N_2 . \overline{\alpha}_o . \lambda - N_2 . \overline{\alpha}_o . k^* - \mu . N_1 . k^* \qquad (6ab)$$

$$A_3 = N_2 . \overline{\alpha}_o . \lambda - k^* \left(N_2 . \overline{\alpha}_o + \mu . N_1 \right) \qquad (6ac)$$

$$A_3 = A_{31} - A_{32} . k^* \qquad (6ad)$$

It is possible to express the excess demand function $X_D = A_1 . p - A_2 . p^2 + A_3$ in terms of k^* and p as:

$$X_D = \left(A_{11} . k^* - A_{12} \right) p - A_{21} . k^* . p^2 + A_{31} - A_{32} . k^* \qquad (6af)$$

$$\text{or,} \quad X_D = A_{11} . k^* . p - A_{12} . p - A_{21} . k^* . p^2 + A_{31} - A_{32} . k^* \qquad (6ag)$$

$$\text{Hence,} \ X_D = k^* \left[A_{11} . p - A_{21} . p^2 - A_{32} \right] + A_{31} - A_{12} . p \qquad (6ah)$$

In order to determine the derivative of the excess demand function with respect to p we differentiate it to yield:

$$\frac{\partial X_D}{\partial p} = k^* \left[A_{11} - 2 A_{21} . p \right] - A_{12} \qquad (6ai)$$

The existence of an equilibrium and its stability are guaranteed if

$$\frac{\partial X_D}{\partial p} < 0 \text{ if } k^*\left[A_{11} - 2A_{21}.p\right] - A_{12} < 0 \tag{6aj}$$

that is, $\quad A_{11} - 2A_{21}.p < \dfrac{A_{12}}{k^*}$ $\tag{6ak}$

or, $\quad A_{11} - \dfrac{A_{12}}{k^*} < 2A_{21}.p$ $\tag{6al}$

$$p > \frac{A_{11}}{2A_{21}} - \frac{A_{12}}{2A_{21}} * \frac{1}{k^*} \tag{6am}$$

The existence of the equilibrium TOT and its stability are explained in Figure 2.2.

Note that X_D is downward-sloping near the equilibrium p^e and there is a unique intersection between the X_D and p axis and hence a single equilibrium p which is stable since the forces of excess demand and supply send it back to p^e if there is any displacement of p from p^e.

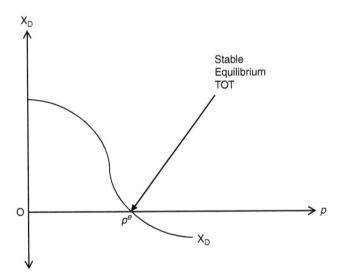

Figure 2.2 Existence and stability of equilibrium TOT
Note: p^e is the unique and stable equilibrium.

2.5.1   *Associated dynamics of the equilibrium path: electoral motive, optimal allocation of capital and the time-path of terms of trade*

We know the vote-maximising k^* is given by:

$$p \frac{\partial H}{\partial Y_1} * \frac{\partial Y_1}{\partial k} * \frac{1}{N_1} + \frac{\partial h}{\partial Y_2} * \frac{\partial Y_2}{\partial k} * \frac{1}{N_2} \tag{7a}$$

And we also know:

$$\frac{\partial Y_1}{\partial k} = \mu \quad \frac{\partial Y_2}{\partial k} = -\lambda \tag{7b}$$

Similarly, as we postulate:

$$S_1 = \frac{1}{2} Y_1^2 \quad S_2 = \frac{1}{2} Y_2^2 \tag{7c}$$

The sensitivity of voters in each sector is given by:

$$\frac{\partial S_1}{\partial Y_1} = y_1 \quad \frac{\partial S_2}{\partial Y_2} = y_2 \tag{7d}$$

The first order condition gives us:

$$p.y_1.\mu.\frac{1}{N_1} = y_2.\lambda.\frac{1}{N_2} \tag{7e}$$

or,

$$\frac{y_1}{y_2} = \frac{N_1}{N_2} * \frac{\lambda}{\mu} \tag{7f}$$

that can be further reduced to

$$\frac{p.\mu.k^*}{\lambda(1-k^*)} = \frac{N_1}{N_2} * \frac{\lambda}{\mu} \tag{7g}$$

or, $p.\mu^2.N_2.k^* = N_1.\lambda^2 - N_1.\lambda^2.k^* \tag{7h}$

From (7h) we derive the vote-maximising allocation of capital as

$$k^* = \frac{N_1.\lambda^2}{p.\mu^2.N_2 + N_1.\lambda^2} \tag{7i}$$

Note the following comparative static properties of k^* :

$$\frac{\partial k^*}{\partial p} < 0 \quad \frac{\partial k^*}{\partial N_2.\mu} < 0 \quad \frac{\partial k^*}{\partial N_1.\lambda} > 0 \tag{7j}$$

2.5.2 Excess demand function

We have derived the excess demand function as:

$$X_D = \frac{N_1.\lambda^2}{N_1.\lambda^2 + p.N_2.\mu^2}[...] + A_{31} - A_{12}.p \tag{7k}$$

that is,

$$X_D = \frac{N_1\lambda^2[...] + A_{31}[N_1\lambda^2 + N_2\mu^2 p] - A_{12}[N_1\lambda^2 p + N_2\mu^2 p^2]}{N_1\lambda^2 + pN_2\mu^2} \tag{7l}$$

2.5.3 Simple definition of equilibrium and disequilibrium adjustment

Our simple definition of instantaneous equilibrium requires $X_D = 0$, which gives rise to the following equilibrium condition:

$$N_1\lambda^2[A_{11}p - A_{21}p^2 - A_{32}] + A_{31}N_1\lambda^2 + A_{31}N_2\mu^2 p - A_{12}N_1\lambda^2 p \\ - A_{12}N_2\mu^2 p^2 = 0 \tag{7m}$$

that is,

$$a_1.p - a_2.p^2 + a_3 = 0 \tag{7n}$$

The disequilibrium adjustment is a chimerical tatonnement process for which we need to express the non-zero excess demand as the following:

$$X_D = \frac{a_1.p - a_2.p^2 + a_3}{m + n.p} \tag{7o}$$

2.5.4 The Walrasian tatonnement and the time path of terms of trade

Note that the time path of p is given by an adjustment in price in real time that is linked to the excess demand τ as the rate of adjustment:

$$p_{t+1} = \tau.X_D{}^t \tag{7p}$$

$$p_{t+1} = \frac{a_1 . p_t - a_2 . p_t^2 + a_3}{m + n . p_t} \quad \tau \tag{7q}$$

For the sake of simplification we set $\tau = 1$, which gives us:

$$m.p_{t+1} + n.p_t.p_{t+1} = a_1.p_t - a_2.p_t^2 + a_3 \tag{7r}$$

2.5.5   The relevant fixed point of the proposed time path:

The fixed point of the time path is defined as:

$$p_{t+1} = p_t = p^* \tag{7s}$$

that is,

$$m.p^* + n.p^{*2} = a_1.p^* - a_2.p^{*2} + a_3 \tag{7t}$$

$$(a_1 - m) p^* - (a_2 + n) p^{*2} + a_3 = 0 \tag{7u}$$

$$p_{1,2}^* = \frac{(a_1 - m) \pm \sqrt{(a_1 - m)^2 + 4a_3 (a_2 + n)}}{2 (a_2 + n)} \tag{7v}$$

The time path therefore is:

$$p_{t+1} (m + n.p_t) = a_1.p_t - a_2.p_t^2 + a_3 \tag{7w}$$

Roughly:

$$p_{t+1} (m + n.p_t) = B_1.p_t (L - p_t) \tag{7x}$$

$$p_{t+1} = \left(\frac{B_1}{m + n.p_t} \right) * p_t (L - p_t) \tag{7y}$$

2.6   The chaotic regime: simple model with complex dynamics

The time path is beset with chaotic dynamics if the following condition holds:

$$M^* = \frac{B_1}{m + n.p_t} > 3.73 \tag{8a}$$

$$B_1 > 3.73\left(m + n.p_t\right) \tag{8b}$$

$$p_t < \frac{1}{n}\left(\frac{B_1}{3.73} - m\right) \tag{8c}$$

Both these equilibria p_1^* and p_2^* are the steady state of the above price dynamics. It is instructive to see that the larger equilibrium relative price p_2^* is stable. The lower equilibrium price p_1^* is always unstable. Also note that p_1^* is stable if

$$p_t < \frac{1}{n}\left(\frac{B_1}{3.73} - m\right) \tag{8d}$$

It is now possible to characterise the dynamics: for $1 < M^* < 3$ the dynamics of relative price converge to the stable equilibrium p_1^*. This is the region of stability that plays an important role in equilibrium analysis as discussed in Gangopadhyay (2005, 2007). If due to parametric shifts M^* is increased above 3, p_1^* becomes unstable and the relative price converges to a stable 2-period cycle. As M^* is increased further the stable period cycles of n bifurcate into cycles of period $2n$. From Feigenbaum (1978) we know that the range of M^* values for which the nth cycle is stable shrinks at a geometric rate. For $M^* > 3.57$ the relative price evolves through a cycle of infinite period. The relative price is within the relevant bounds but never repeats. For a higher order the relative price may look like a random process, but it is fully deterministic (see May, 1976).

2.7 Exchange entitlement failures and violent conflicts in the Middle East: in search of evidence

The theoretical models establish that the evolving paths of prices in well-behaved markets can engender allocations of capital across sectors, which can in turn trigger entitlement failures. Such entitlement failures can stir a society and lead to a tipping point such that a large number of households can suffer from severe declines in exchange entitlements for security. Such declines can trigger collective violence and further accentuate the vulnerability of people in nations. The increasing vulnerability can further influence insecurity as the system is gradually pushed to an extremely fragile state in terms of security. As a casual observation, one may see such trends evolving in some nations in the Middle East and North Africa over a long period of time. In this section we will apply standard econometrics to assess if there is any evidence that decline in exchange entitlements in the form of swings in relative prices – possibly driven by factors like climate changes – can explain the long-term vulnerability in the region.

2.7.1   *Vulnerability of the Middle East and North Africa: the background*

It is customary to argue that the entire globe needs a better and effective planning for a drier future. It is also being realised that the Middle East can especially suffer from global warming. Thus, global warming can have significant implications in terms of conflicts in the Middle East. Climate scientists have long raised a serious concern about the impact of climate changes on conflicts in the Middle East: from the meteorological data, researchers showed that natural variability alone could not explain the trends in wind, rain and heat that led to massive droughts in the Middle East (Kelley et al., 2015; Hsiang et al., 2015; Welzer, 2012). Such droughts intermingled with poor governance and high rates of employment tend to cascade into severely violent conflicts in the Middle East. In other words, many of these authors argue that the Middle East seems to suffer from long-term vulnerability due mainly to sustainability problems created and propelled by weather patterns. These natural disasters and man-made disasters feed on each other to push the Middle East towards a cycle of collective violence and destruction. In this section of the book, our goal is to look for evidence for the aforementioned thesis: climatic changes cause vulnerability to the Middle East and vulnerability triggers violent conflicts in the region. In what follows, we try to create an indicator, or index, of long-term vulnerability for the Middle East. We then try to assess if the index can be linked to various types of conflicts and violence in the region.

2.7.2   *Developing an index of vulnerability for the Middle East and North Africa*

We develop an index of vulnerability for seven countries in the region of the Middle East and North Africa: 1) Libya, 2) Syria, 3) Iraq, 4) Iran, 5) Egypt, 6) Lebanon and 7) Israel. We choose four different types of factors for each country during 1960–2013 to develop the vulnerability index (VI): the first factor to measure long-term vulnerability of a country is the overseas development assistance and aid (*ODA*). This is an economic variable that shows the reliance of a country on overseas donors and foreign governments for economic and social development. In other words, the *ODA* measures the vulnerability of a country in the eyes of the donor countries: the higher the *ODA* is, the greater is the perception of the donor countries about the long-term vulnerability of the receiving country. The second factor derives from the environmental sustainability of a country which indicates the carbon footprint of the region and is being measured by the per capita carbon emission (*CO2*) in a country. The larger the *CO2*, we posit that the larger is the vulnerability due to potential environmental hazards. The third factor is the source of vulnerability due to collective violence in the regions. We measure the impacts of collective violence on the vulnerability of people in terms of three indicators, *INFANTD*, *MMORT* and *DEATHR*. *INFANTD* is the infant death rate, $MMORT$ is the male mortality and $DEATHR$ is the death rate in a country. Collective violence not only impacts on the mortality of people and hence increases these three variables but also makes a society extremely fragile by raising these three variables. Since we also use female mortality as an explanatory variable in our subsequent analysis, we have not used the female mortality in creating the index of vulnerability. Finally, we take into consideration the impact of the agricultural sector on the sustainability of a society: we have taken three indicators for this purpose, $ARLAND$, $FOODPROD$ and $CEREALPROD$: $ARLAND$ is the per capita arable land in a country while $FOODPROD$ and $CEREALPROD$ are indices of food productivity and cereal productivity in a country. Despite the predominance of the oil sector in the economy the agrarian economy still plays an important part in the Middle East for providing employment and ensuring food security in the region. The decline in $ARLAND$ is a major source of migration and conflicts along with fluctuations in water resources. Since the data on water resources is unavailable, we have chosen $ARLAND$ as an indicator of the pressure of resources in the country. Food insecurity is an important source of vulnerability in the region and the slowing down of $FOODPROD$ is a serious concern in the region. We have hence chosen $FOODPROD$ as an indicator variable for vulnerability. In a similar vein, $CEREALPROD$ is an indicator of the long-term viability of maintaining livestock and a stalling of its productivity will pose serious problems in the food chain of the region.

2.7.3   The index of vulnerability from the principal component analysis

We apply the principal component analysis (PCA) to the above eight variables, namely ODA, $CO2$, $INFANTD$, $MMORT$, $DEATHR$, $ARLAND$, $FOODPROD$ and $CEREALPROD$ for seven nations in the Middle East and North Africa – Libya, Syria, Iran, Iraq, Israel, Egypt and Lebanon. For each variable we have observations during 1960–2013. The PCA enables us to derive an index of vulnerability for each of these nations during 1960–2013. By analysing the dynamics of vulnerability of each nation over time, we will find important long-term determinants of vulnerability in the Middle East and North Africa. It is important to emphasise that the PCA is a statistical procedure that applies an orthogonal transformation of the variables to create a new set of observations of correlated variables into a set of values of uncorrelated variables. These new and linearly correlated variables are the principal components such that the number of principal components is less than or equal to the number of original variables. What is important for us is to note that the PCA undertakes transformation in such a way that the first principal component has the largest possible variance, which thereby accounts for the maximum variability in the data. Each succeeding component in turn has the highest variance with the additional constraint that it is orthogonal to the preceding components. The resulting vectors are an uncorrelated orthogonal basis set. The principal components are orthogonal since they are the eigenvectors of the symmetric covariance matrix. We use the first PCA as the basis for deriving the vulnerability index of each country so that the weights from the PCA accord us the case that explains the greatest variability in the eight variables chosen to reflect vulnerability in the region. We label the vulnerability of Libya as *VIL* and define *VIL* as the following:

$$VIL = w_1*ODA + w_2*CO2 + w_3*INFANTD + w_4*MMORT$$
$$+ w_5*DEATHR - w_6*ARLAND - w_7*FOODPROD$$
$$- w8*CEREALPROD \quad\quad\quad\quad (9a)$$

Note that the coefficient w_6, w_7 and w_8 are negative, reflecting the fact that the vulnerability of a nation declines with improving productivity and availability of arable land in the country. All other variables increase vulnerability of a nation as their values go up. It is also important to stress that the PCA is sensitive to the relative scaling of the original variables, so we have used various scaling techniques including normalisation so that our findings are not sensitive to the chosen scales. All the reported findings are not sensitive to scales. In Table 2.2, we offer the values of the weights from the first PCA for each country.

In Figure 2.3 we present the vulnerability index of the seven nations during 1960–2013. The dynamic paths of vulnerability for each nation show wide fluctuations along with significant variations. From the figure it seems that the paths of stochastic trends call for the application of the cointegration

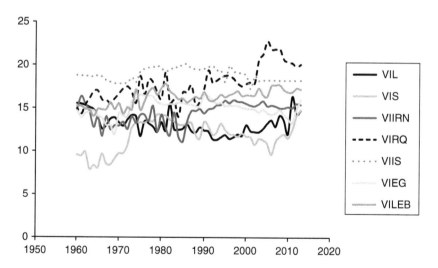

Figure 2.3 The dynamic paths of the vulnerability index
Note: Other variables of interest are presented in Table 2.3.

Table 2.2 The weights in the vulnerability index

Country	Variable	ODA	CO2	INFANTD	MMORT	DEATHR	AL*	FP*	CP*
Libya	VIL	0.02	0.48	0.15	0.17	0.16	0.17	0.15	0.13
Syria	VIS	0.005	0.14	0.15	0.16	0.15	0.15	0.15	0.13
Iran	VIIRN	0.05	0.12	0.15	0.10	0.13	0.12	0.15	0.14
Iraq	VIIRQ	0.03	0.16	0.057	0.09	0.21	0.21	0.19	0.3
Israel	VIIS	0.15	0.15	0.16	0.17	0.07	0.17	0.07	0.10
Egypt	VIEG	0.002	0.15	0.16	0.16	0.13	0.16	0.05	0.14
Lebanon	VILEB	0.05	0.13	0.14	0.14	0.13	0.14	0.12	0.13

Note: Constructed from the PCA data obtained from the development indicators of the World Bank.
* AL: ARLAND; FP: FOODPROD; CP: CREALPROD

Table 2.3 Important variables

Variable	Labelling	Function
Average global temperature	LNT	Natural Log
Global oil production	LNO	Natural Log
Food price in a country	FP	Natural Log
Food price inflation in a country	FPI	
Global oil price	OP	Natural Log
Oil price inflation	OPI	
GDP per capita of a nation	GDP*	Natural Log
Arms imports by a nation	ARIM*	Natural Log
Change of relative price of food over inflation	RPOFO=FPI-OPI	

Note: *ARIM* data obtained from SIPRI. We will use ARMIM and GDP in Chapters 3–4.
* These variables will be used in other chapters

analysis to explore the long-term relationships of vulnerability across nations and exchange entitlements failures.

2.7.4 Long-term dynamics in the Middle East and North Africa: cointegration analysis

In what follows we apply the cointegration analysis to investigate any relationship between relevant variables from their long-term (dynamic) patterns. Here at the outset we emphasise that our study calls forth the cointegration analysis since most of economic and social variables have stochastic trends. In other words, the data has unit roots, which begs a question of the relevance of using cointegration methods. In clearer terms one can simply question the tenability of the usual regression methods to the relevant time-series variables with unit roots. The answer is that standard regression models are estimated with the standard assumption of stationarity, implying that the variables are not trending, or if they are, that the trend is a deterministic time trend and not stochastic. In other words, the economic variables are $I(1)$ and not $I(0)$, then regressing $I(1)$ variables on each other creates enormous problems that the usual chi square statistic, F tests and t distributions are no longer valid. Thus, there are statistical problems with applying standard statistical tools to $I(1)$ variables (see Johansen et al., 2000; Juselius, 2006 among others). As the subsequent analysis shows, it is possible to examine the long-run co-movements between trending variables, as well as short-run dynamic adjustment and feedback effects within the same model. Furthermore, the model allows us to focus on the shocks that had a long-run permanent effect on the variables of the system. In this sense, the analysis may potentially provide results on causal mechanisms in the long run. Annual data from 1960–2013 are obtained from the development indicators of the World Bank and food prices are obtained from various local sources and supplemented by the consumer price index data obtained from the World Bank. Except for Lebanon, we are able to create a consistent data set for the average food prices during 1960–2013. The oil price data and global output and global temperature data came from the Earth Policy Institute and were downloaded from the website www.earth-policy.org. The data is expressed in natural logarithmic forms except for inflationary figures and relative prices being the difference between food price and oil price inflation rates. We employ the Johansen (1991) approach of detecting cointegration for examining the long-term relationship between relevant variables. As a prerequisite of cointegration analysis we undertake the unit root tests – Augmented-Dickey-Fuller (ADF) tests and Zandrew tests – for both constant and constant trend terms and noted all variables to $I(1)$ as some results reported in Table 2.4. We also used the minimisation of MAIC to determine the optimal lag for each variable.

After ensuring the variables are $I(1)$ and their first differences $I(0)$, we apply the Johansen approach to assess the long-term relationship (see Johansen, 1991) in the following section.

2.8　Interdependency and vulnerability in the region

In this section we start off with the cointegration analysis to examine if there is any evidence of inter-country vulnerability in the Middle East during 1960–2013. The analytical question is simple for us: is there any evidence that vulnerability of one country impacts on another? In order to answer the question we test the following empirical equation:

$$VI_i = F(VI_j) \tag{10a}$$

where i is the country whose vulnerability is the dependent variable. VI_j is the set of vulnerability indices for all other countries except country i. $F(.)$ is a function for which VI_i is the dependent variable and VIj are independent variables.

This section reports our empirical results of the long-run relationship between the vulnerability index of a country and the indices of vulnerability of other countries as the key explanatory variables. The long-run elasticities of the independent variables and their t-ratios are reported in Table 2.6. Table 2.5 summarises the Johansen's Cointegration test statistics. The Johansen test results indicate that there is at least one cointegrating vector based on the maximum trace statistics/tests. Thus, from Table 2.5 we can conclude that our model (equation 10a) with two or more variables is a fair representation for the chosen countries in the Middle East and North Africa.

Table 2.6 presents the long-run estimated relationship between the vulner-ability of a country and the explanatory variables, which are normalised on

Table 2.4 Basic tests for unit roots and optimal lags

VARIABLES	TESTS			Integration	First Difference	
	Lags		ADF			
Criterion	MIN. MAIC		Statistic	ADF TEST	ADF and Zandrews tests	
Vulnerability Index						
VIL	3		-0.98	I(1)	-4.43, I(0)	
VIS	2		-1.04	I(1)	-4.71, I(0)	
VIIQ	1		-2.82	I(1)	-5.74, I(0)	
VIIN	2		-3.41	I(1)	-4.75, I(0)	
VIE	1		-2.47	I(1)	-4.46, I(0)	
VILEB	3		-1.31	I(1)	-4.23, I(0)	
VIIS	1		-1.35	I(1)	-6.46, I(0)	
Price Variable	ADF Statistic, Integration			Lags, ADF for First Difference		Integration: Δ RPIF
RPIF (Libya)	-2.47, I(1)			4, -5.57		I(0)
RPIF (Syria)	-1.48, I(1)			2, -4.48		I(0)
RPIF (Iraq)	-2.05, I(1)			2, -5.31		I(0)
RPIF (Iran)	-1.84, I(1)			4, -535		I(0)
RPIF (Israel)	-2.38, I(1)			2, -5.11		I(0)
RPIF (Lebanon)						
RPIF (Egypt)	-1.98, I(1)			4, -4.48		I(0)

Other Variables

Variable	Value	Order
ARMIM (Libya)	−2.76, I(1)	2, −9.81	I(0)
ARMIM (Syria)	−2.51, I(1)	1, −5.77	I(0)
ARMIM (Iraq)	−2.22, I(1)	1, −4.68	I(0)
ARMIM (Iran)	−2.20, I(1)	1, −480	I(0)
ARMIM (Israel)	−1.34, I(1)	1, −6.48	I(0)
ARMIM (Lebanon)	−2.19, I	2, −4.46	I(0)
ARMIM (Egypt)	−3.97, I(0)*		
GLOBOLO	−2.31, I(1)	1, −4.56	I(0)
LNT	−3.18, I(1)	7, −17.56	I(0)
PCGDP (Libya)	−1.13, I(1)	1, −3.75	I(0)
PCGDP (Syria)	−2.57, I(1)	2, −5.57	I(0)
PCGDP (Iraq)	−1.37, I(1)	1, −4.97	I(0)
PCGDP (Iran)	−2.12, I(1)	2, −4.46	I(0)
PCGDP (Israel)	−2.59, I(1)	1, −5.11	I(0)
PCGDP (Lebanon)	−2.49, I(1)	3, −3.63	I(0)
PCGDP (Egypt)	−3.39, I(0)	1, −5.46	I(0)

Table 2.5 Optimal lag choices and ranks of cointegrating variables

Country	HQIC, SBIC	Lag	Vec Rank	Trace Stat	CV*
Libya	1.53, 2.1	4	2	14.81	15.41
Syria		1	1	13.25	29.68
Iran	14.27, 14.75	2	1	21.08	29.68
Iraq	21.94, 22	2	1	22.23	29.68
Israel	1.96, 2.02	2	1	7.94	29.68
Egypt	−6.27, 2.3e⁻⁸	2	1	27.34	29.68
Lebanon	11.74, 11.61	1	1	22.66	29.68

* 5% Critical Value

the dependent variable. The coefficients of the explanatory variables have the expected signs in most of the equations. We have removed the explanatory variables that are statistically significant. The following cases emerge from the Johansen test:

• The vulnerability of Libya has a long-term association with two countries in the Middle East, namely, Iraq and Israel. For both these countries the long-term relationship is negative and statistically significant, which implies that an increased vulnerability in Iraq and Israel has lowered vulnerability in Libya. However, VIL is positively influenced by the vulnerability of Egypt, which is statistically and economically significant. It is also important to note that VIL does not have any impact (positive or negative) on any other country's vulnerability, as can be seen from the first column of Table 2.6.

• There are two countries in the region that exert influences on the maximum number of countries chosen in the analysis. Both Iraq and Israel determine the vulnerability of all other nations. In turn, the vulnerability of Iraq is influenced only by Israel and Egypt. Similarly, the vulnerability of Israel is propelled only by Iraq and Egypt. What is interesting is that Iraq and Israel increase each other's vulnerability in the long run. On the other hand, the vulnerability of Egypt lowers the vulnerability of Iraq and Israel.

• The vulnerability of Israel bears a positive (negative) relationship with Iraq (Egypt) only. Both the coefficients are extremely small. Thus Israel has insulated its long-term vulnerability quite successfully from the group of nations chosen from the Middle East and North Africa.

• The vulnerability of Lebanon seems to impact only on Egypt. Yet the vulnerability of Lebanon is favourably impacted on by Syria, Iran, Iraq and Israel while Egypt exerts an unfavourable influence.

• The vulnerability of Egypt is favourably influenced by vulnerability in Syria, Iran, Iraq and Israel. The exception is Lebanon whose vulnerability seems to bear a positive long-run relationship.

Table 2.6 Vulnerability and its long-term relationships

	VIL	VIS	VIIRN	VIIRQ	VIIS	VIEG	VILEB
VIL	–			–4.44*	–33.99*	18.73*	
VIS		–					
VIIRN			–	2.08*	15.92*	–8.77*	
VIIRQ				–	**7.64***	–4.21*	
VIIS				0.13*	–	–0.55*	
VIEG	–0.57*	–0.17*	–0.35*	–0.84*	–		**1.20***
VILEB	–0.47*	–14.7**	–0.29*	–0.69*	0.82*	–	

* Significant
** Marginally significant

- The vulnerability of Iran bears an unfavourable relationship with the vulnerability of Iraq and Israel. Egypt has a favourable influence on the vulnerability of Iran. Iran exerts a favourable influence on Egypt and Lebanon and no other impacts on the vulnerability of five other nations from the region.
- The vulnerability of Iraq, Iran and Libya are strongly influenced by other nations as we can see from the sizes of coefficients. There is no other nation in the region that has such strong impacts (positive or negative).

In the next subsection, we investigate the factors that can create such vulnerability for each country.

2.9 Consequences of weather, oil and food prices for regional vulnerability: cointegration analysis

In order to undertake the cointegration analysis, we have first derived the optimal lag and ranks from the trace statistics. We have not reported the results as the results are very similar to Table 2.5, which implies the presence of at least one long-term relationship for each dependent variable. Our econometric model is given by the following equation:

$$VI_i = F(LNT, LNO, RPFO_i) \tag{10b}$$

where VI_i is the vulnerability index of country i, which is assumed as a function (F) of LNT, LNO and $RPFO_i$. We did not use the other variables for equation (10b). However, they will be used in the next cointegration analysis. We could not gather reliable data on food prices for Lebanon, so we have not employed the cointegration analysis for Lebanon. The findings are interesting:

- The rising global temperature seems to have adversely impacted on Syria, Israel and Egypt by raising their vulnerability indices as the first column of Table 2.7 shows. However, the coefficient of global temperature for Egypt is not statistically significant. For all other nations, the rising global temperature is rather beneficial and all coefficients are statistically significant.

- There are four countries for which the rising global output of oil increased their (long-term) vulnerability, as we can see from column 3 of Table 2.7, and they are Libya, Iraq and Israel though the coefficient is not statistically significant for Egypt. It is also important to note that the magnitude of the oil output effect is very small for Israel. The increasing global output of oil lowered the long-term vulnerability of Syria and Iran.
- The impact of *RPFO* (*TOT* movement of food price relative to oil price), which is taken as a proxy of the exchange entitlement, from the sixth column of Table 2.7, shows that there is evidence of exchange entitlements failure in four countries except Syria and Iran. The elasticity coefficient of Syria is very small. So, the only exception is Iran where the *TOT* did not increase vulnerability. In other words, as the theory shows, improvements in *TOT* in favour of agriculture can create long-term vulnerability for many nations in the Middle East and North Africa.

In what follows we have used another model to test the robustness of our results on the impact of the rising temperature and the rising oil production in the region. We have taken the food price variable in the natural logarithmic form. Our postulated model is as follows:

$$VI_i = F(LNT, LNO, FO_i) \tag{10c}$$

The only difference between (10b) and (10c) is FO_i.

We present the results in Table 2.8. We find that the rising global temperature has increased the vulnerability of all countries in our study except Libya.

Table 2.7 Cointegration coefficients of the vulnerability index

	LNT	LNP	LNO	FP	RPFO	Constant**
VIL	−185.84*		21.31*		0.37*	3.93
VIS	99.27*		−5.6*		−0.0013*	−256.04
VIIRN	−3.022*		−228*		−3.002*	280
VIIRQ	−145.7*		3.01*		0.004*	355.78
VIIS	37.72*		0.63*		0.003*	
VIEG	19		1.78		0.083*	
VILEB^						

^ Data on food price inflation not available
* Statistically significant
** Normalised by Johansen's approach

Table 2.8 Cointegration: an alternative model

	LNT	LNO	FP
VIL	−166.27*	6.07*	−0.45*
VIS	90.24*	−5.47*	−0.036
VIIRN	−6.11	4.14	−0.71*
VIIRQ	116.66*	−2.7	0.20*
VIIS	46.4*	0.66	0.003***
VIEG	60.94*	−1.9***	0.03
VILEB	^	^	^

* Statistically significant

^ Missing data for the country

The coefficient is not statistically significant for Iran. Except for Libya, the evidence shows that the long-term effect of the rising global temperature (column 2 of Table 2.8) is quite devastating for the region. The effect of the global oil output (demand) is mixed. For Libya the LNO increased its vulnerability while for Syria the rising LNO reduced its vulnerability (see column 3 of Table 2.8). For all other nations there is no meaningful long-run relationship between vulnerability and the global oil output. Finally, if we only look at the dynamics of food prices (ignoring the sectoral terms of trade) the picture changes: for all nations except Iraq, changing (increasing) food prices lowered their vulnerability, though elasticities are small in magnitude. The rising food prices increased the vulnerability of Iraq and Israel but the effect on Israel is very small. For Egypt and Syria the coefficients are not statistically significant.

2.10 The long-run dynamics of price variables

We employed the cointegration test to discover long-term relationships between price variables and other global factors. The model we test is the following:

$$PRICE\text{-}VARIABLE_i = F\,(PRICE\text{-}VARIABLE_j, LNT, LNO, FP_i) \quad (10d)$$

where the dependent variable is either the food price inflation (*FP*) or the oil price inflation (*OILPINF*), which is

$$PRICE\text{-}VARIABLE_i = (FP_j, OILPINF) \quad (11a)$$

In Table 2.9, we only present the food price inflation result for Libya (*FPL*) and various specifications. Table 2.9 offers the results from the Johansen approach to detect cointegration. The following picture emerges:

Table 2.9 Cointegration: the Johansen approach

	FPS	FPIRQ	FPIRN	FPE	FPIS	OILPINF	LNT	LNO
FPL	0.27**	0.05*	0.77*	−0.52*	−0.09*	−0.36*	−88.7*	−3.55
OILPINF	0.25**	2.76*	−2.41*	0.94	0.23*		−0.16*	−1.2*
LNO						−0.16*	−12.2*	
OILPINF							7.4**	−60*
OILPINF	−2.29*	3.66*	−3.53*	0.76*	0.27*		24.73*	

* Statistically significant

** Marginally significant

- First, the food price inflation in Libya (*FPL*) bears a long-term relationship with food price inflation rates in many other countries of the region. This is the case with countries as well, though we have not reported the results for other countries. The second row of Table 2.9 gives the results for Libya. The second row of Table 2.9 also shows the statistically and economically significant (long-run) relationship between food price inflation at the country level (*FPL*) and oil price inflation at the global markets (*OILPINF*) and long-term rising global temperature (*LNT*). Similar observations are made for other nations, but not reported for conserving space.
- It is also interesting to note that oil price inflation (*OILPINF*) shows a long-term dependence on both food price inflation (*FPL*) and global warming (*LNT*).
- We have three different specifications for the long-term relationship between global warming (LNT) and oil price inflation (*OILPINF*). Except for the third row of Table 2.9, the rising global temperature (*LNT*) has raised the global oil price with highly significant elasticities and statistical significance for the other two specifications.

In a nutshell, we find evidence that various country-specific, regional and global factors have combined to propel the long-term vulnerability of the chosen countries from the Middle East and North Africa. The region will need to plan for managing a cascading regional vulnerability, food price inflation, oil price inflation and rising global temperature. Our results establish that there are regional and global implications of the vulnerability of the individual nations in the Middle East and North Africa.

2.11　Summary

We find that the introduction of market ethos and democratisation in developing nations can create a fragile economic and social system in the Middle East. We show the existence of a political equilibrium that maximises the probability of the re-election of an incumbent government. In the equilibrium, we derive the optimal allocation of capital as well as the optimal value of inter-sectoral terms of trade between agriculture and industry. The central issue is whether the political equilibrium is economically meaningful. We articulated two sets of conditions for it: first and foremost, the political equilibrium must ensure a minimal distribution for both industrial and agricultural agents. Otherwise, there will ensue a distribution failure and survival problems for economic agents that will, in turn, drive conflicts in such societies. Secondly, the political equilibrium and the consequent economic outcome must be stable so that small changes do not threaten a distribution failure. The findings are of great importance: we have demonstrated the existence of a region of capital allocation such that if the optimal allocation of capital lies within this specific region there does not arise any distribution failure. Allocation of capital within this safe region renders the system crisis-free and there is no economic source of conflict. If the capital allocation is not contained within this safe region, economic crises, distribution failures and conflicts characterise the outcome either in agriculture or in industry. In addition, we have established that under a specific and reasonable condition, the postulated economic and political system will fail to engender the safe region. As a result, there will be crises, distribution failures and conflicts in agriculture or industry or both, depending on the allocation of capital between these sectors. We also found that the dynamics of the political equilibrium can create enormous instability and fragility, such that chaotic regimes are characteristic of the expected economic and social outcome. At the empirical level, we find evidence that various country-specific, regional and global factors have combined to propel the long-term vulnerability of the chosen countries from the Middle East and North Africa. The region should search for a mechanism to manage and curb a cascading regional vulnerability, food price inflation and oil price inflation with the rising global temperature. Our results establish that there are regional and global implications of the vulnerability of the individual nations in the Middle East and North Africa. In Chapter 4 we will present coordinated policy interventions for reducing the long-term vulnerability of the region.

3   Interest group politics and defence spending

3.1   Politics of allocation of defence spending in a bi-sectoral model

In this section we assume that defence spending is like a public good that influences the regional economy. To be more specific, our model posits that defence spending in a regional economy offers public infrastructure that in turn influences the costs of production of local firms, which thereby influence the competitive positioning of the regional economy in the national market. Defence spending also withdraws public funds from other investment projects. So regional impacts of defence spending can vary significantly and trigger diverse types of interest group politics: some regions may clamour for more defence spending while others can oppose if the net effect is not favourable. It is hence important to disaggregate an economy to analyse the determination of defence spending for understanding how political and economic factors impact on the level of defence spending.

3.1.1   Introduction to the main ideas

In terms of bare essentials, our theoretical model will be similar to the strategic trade and investment models. These have attracted serious criticisms on two grounds: that their conclusions are extremely sensitive to assumptions about the mode/nature of competition and that the optimal rent-seeking policy loses much of its gloss once we consider the political costs associated with the policy (Dixit and Grossman, 1986, p. 234). An important step towards a better understanding of this issue requires us to endogenise the mode of competition and also to explicitly introduce government policymaking in this context. Our proposed work makes both the nature of competition and government policymaking endogenous, and thereby provides a framework in which defence spending, the conduct of firms and political decisions are endogenously determined. Our theoretical model is therefore an enhancement of the existing models of strategic investment and trade.

Our central concern is to address two critical issues of government involvement in the context of strategic investment models. One of these is that the nature of competition plays an important role in determining whether government policy has the intended, desired effects. It is important to model the nature of competition endogenously in this context, since government policy can significantly influence the nature of competition through its effect on defence spending (Dixon, 1986). Second, the promotion of one set of firms represents a 'taxation' of others. Government policy thus entails a political cost, an important ingredient for formulating government policy. Existing literature does not make both government policy and the nature of competition endogenous. This creates a major difficulty with the rent extraction argument since political costs constrain a government's behaviour while the benefits from strategic government policy largely depend on the endogenous degree of competition. An optimal government policy will thus be misconstrued unless we determine these elements endogenously.

We combine two distinct ideas – the probabilistic voting model and the conjectural variations model – to endogenise the nature of competition and the government policy on defence spending. First of all, the probabilistic voting model is a recent development in political theory to counter the time-honoured predictions of traditional political theory (Wittman, 1989): social thinkers have argued that democratic governments are plagued by the absence of a stable electoral equilibrium and the risk of expropriation of minorities by majorities. The probabilistic voting model, by assuming a universally concave votes-to-offers curve, establishes the existence of a stable voting equilibrium and suggests that the expropriation argument is 'an optical illusion'. The probabilistic voting model will allow us to endogenise relevant government policy. Second, the conduct of regional firms has been made endogenous in the very important contribution of Bresnahan (1982), popularly known as the conjectural variations model. Laitner (1980), Bresnahan (1982), Kamien and Schwartz (1983) and Perry (1982) question the robustness of the Cournot model as an equilibrium concept by using the model of consistent conjectured reactions. A conjectural variation is a conjecture by one firm about how another firm will adjust its decision variable in response to adjustments by the first firm. The consistent conjectural equilibrium is believed to be a rational expectations equilibrium that collectively confirms individual expectations about changes in the decision variables. It is argued that the Cournot equilibrium is not generally a consistent conjectural equilibrium. However, there are problems with this approach: the consistent conjectural equilibrium is not equilibrium, since each firm can unilaterally change its output to make more profits (Bresnahan, 1982, p. 937). Experimental evidence indicates that agents do not converge on the consistent conjectural equilibrium (Holt, 1982). It is also recognised that the conjectural variations parameter is not observable in principle. It has been noted that these models lack a game theoretic foundation (Shapiro, 1989). Yet it is widely held that conjectural variation models are still very important in examining scenarios underpinned by complex dynamic processes.

The simplified story of our model subsumes the following: we examine government policy that is concerned with an allocation of defence spending between two different regions, or locations. We postulate that defence spending brings a host of local goods to the regional economy, like roads, electricity, water supply and security. It is argued that the location of defence spending will determine the short-run cost functions of firms in these locations. These costs of production will, in turn, determine the nature of competition in the product market.[1] As a result, government policy will endogenously determine the degree or nature of competition in the market. On the other hand, this allocation of defence spending enables us to analyse the political cost: the promotion of an industrial location is an implicit taxation of firms in other locations. As the government increases defence spending in a location, voters from this constituency increase their political support for the incumbent government while this government loses votes from the other location. An allocation of defence spending thus influences voters' evaluation of the government, and this evaluation constrains government policy on defence spending that, in turn, impinges on voters' evaluation. In the proposed equilibrium of the game, the government chooses the optimal allocation that influences the voters' evaluation that, in turn, maximises the probability of re-election of the incumbent government. The optimal allocation will determine the nature of competition in the product market.

The game unfolds over two stages: in stage I, the government allocates defence spending in order to maximise its probability of re-election given the voters' preferences and characteristics. Thus, at stage I an electoral platform is created. In stage II, two firms with different production bases compete for a unified market. At the perfect Nash equilibrium of this sequential game, the government achieves an electoral equilibrium that maximises votes cast in it favour. This optimum allocation of defence spending provides a winning electoral platform to the incumbent government from which the costs of production for firms and the nature of competition in the product market emerge.

3.1.2   *Allocation of defence spending in the bi-sectoral model*

The basic setting of the model is taken from Gangopadhyay and Elkanj (2009) and Gangopadhyay and Chatterji (2009) and we then introduce the need for reputation building to explain the equilibrium level of defence spending. The basic setting (Sections 3.1.2.1–3.1.2.3) is from Gangopadhyay and Elkanj (2009).

We consider a national market that has duopolists with distinct production locations. Our model is consistent with a finite number of locations, or regions in an economy. We assume that these location choices have already been made and, hence, the location of a firm is part of the history. It is also assumed that the national economy consists of these locations. The government has a given amount of tax revenue that is to be distributed between these locations for defence spending. The impact of the defence spending will reduce costs of production. Thus the larger is

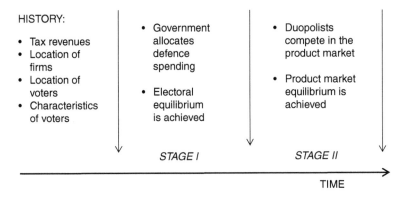

Figure 3.1 Time structure of decisions

defence spending in location i, vis-a-vis j, the lower is the cost of production of the firm at location i. We further assume that buyers are located in such a fashion that the cost of transport is zero so there is a single price that prevails in the market. The market is thus characterised by the following sequential game (see Figure 3.1): at stage I the electoral equilibrium is achieved and that, in turn, determines the distribution of defence spending. The distribution of defence spending determines the costs of production of the duopolists/oligopolists in stage II of the game; they engage in competition in the product market to capture the largest possible market shares.

The solution to the game is proposed in a recursive fashion. We first determine the market outcome at stage II and then trace back to stage I, a technique popularly known as the logic of backward induction. Rationality and complete information dictate that both these firms and the government will form their expectations by looking ahead and foreseeing the product market equilibrium of stage II. If agents behave in this fashion, they are said to have rational expectations. In stage I all these agents adopt their optimal actions based on rational expectations. The outcome is the perfect Nash equilibrium of the proposed game.

3.1.2.1 Stage II: Nature of competition in the product market

We introduce the following assumptions to characterise the product market.

Assumption 1: Industry demand function (inverse) is linear:

$$p = a - bX \tag{1}$$

where p and X are price and output respectively and a, $b>0$.

Assumption 2: There are two regions, or locations, for defence spending. We assume that firm i is based at location i, for $i = 1, 2$.

Assumption 3: The cost of production of firm i is as follows:

$$c_i = c_i(X_i, G_i) = mX_i^2 / G_i \tag{2a}$$

where
  X_i : output of firm i, $i = 1, 2$
  G_i : allocation of defence spending to location i where firm i is located.

The marginal cost is hence given as MC_i :

$$MC_i = 2mX_i / G_i \tag{2b}$$

Thus MC_i is increasing in X_i given G_i and decreasing in G_i given X_i :

$$\partial MC_i / \partial X_i = 2m / G_i > 0 \tag{2c}$$
$$\partial MC_i / \partial G_i = -2mX_i / G_i^2 < 0 \tag{2d}$$

The profit function of firm i is as follows:

$$\Pi_i = X_i(a - bX) - mX_i^2 / G_i \tag{3a}$$

It is assumed that the firms have non-zero conjectural variation and, hence, we get the following for firm 1:

$$d\Pi_1 / dX_1 = a - 2bX_1 - bX_2 - bX_1(dX_2 / dX_1) - 2mX_1 / G_1 \tag{3b}$$

We define the conjectural variations as the following:

$$\varphi_1 = (dX_2 / dX_1), \varphi_2 = (dX_1 / dX_2) \tag{3c}$$

Hence the reaction functions in quantity decision of the duopolists are the following:

$$X_1 = (a - bX_2) / (2b + \varphi_1 b + 2m / G_1) \tag{3d}$$
$$X_2 = (a - bX_1) / (2b + \varphi_2 b + 2m / G_2) \tag{3e}$$

The consistency condition is that the change of X_1 with respect to X_2 along (3d) must be self-confirming. That is, the slopes of the reaction functions must be equal to the appropriate conjectural variations. Hence:

$$\varphi_2 = [-b / (2b + b\varphi_1 + 2m / G_1)] \tag{4a}$$

$$\varphi_1 = [-b / (2b + b\varphi_2 + 2m / G_2)] \tag{4b}$$

The consistency conditions (4a) and (4b) give the following:

$$2b\varphi_2 + \varphi_1\varphi_2 b + 2m\varphi_2 / G_1 + b = 0 \tag{5a}$$

$$2b\varphi_1 + \varphi_1\varphi_2 b + 2m\varphi_1 / G_2 + b = 0 \tag{5b}$$

Subtracting (5b) from (5a) will yield:

$$(\varphi_2 / \varphi_1) = [b + (m / G_2)] / [b + (m / G_1)] \tag{5c}$$

The more negative φ_1 firm 1 believes that firm 2 is more accommodating. Thus, at the consistent conjectural equilibrium all expectations are ex post confirmed and, hence, (φ_2 / φ_1) is a measure of the relative competitiveness of firm 1.

Definition 1: We define (φ_2 / φ_1) as the degree of competitiveness of firm 1 vis-à-vis firm 2.

The larger (φ_2 / φ_1) is, the more accommodating firm 1 is; and vice-versa. It is instructive to note that the degree of competition depends on the allocation of defence spending G_1 and G_2. We now turn to the explanation of G_1 and G_2 that will in turn determine the degree of competition.

3.1.2.2 Stage I: Electoral equilibrium

Citizen voters have two entitlements: as an economic agent, each voter has entitlement to returns from the firm at his location. We assume that the higher the profit of a firm, the larger the economic return to the citizen residing in the location in which the firm operates. As a voter he has an entitlement to influence the rules of the game: that is, the allocation of defence spending. This allocation, in turn, affects his economic returns. It is assumed that each citizen exercises the voting rights in his own interest. The rational government chooses the allocation of defence spending (rules of the game) that will give rise to nominal returns to voters and will, in turn, maximise its votes. The electoral equilibrium is the optimal allocation of defence spending that maximises the votes cast in favour of the incumbent government.

In order to determine the allocation of defence spending G_1 and G_2 we now look at the electoral equilibrium of stage I. We apply the probabilistic voting theorem to explain the electoral equilibrium (see Wittman, 1989). It is assumed that voters are located in two locations of defence spending. Within a location, voters have an identical preference for defence spending. Thus, there are two groups of voters and their preferences are represented by their utility functions $U_1(G_1 - G^a)$ and $U_2(G_2 - G^b)$ and S_1 and S_1 are the sensitivity parameters of these groups of voters. G^a and G^b are respectively the 'ideal points' of voter groups 1 and 2 given their tax burdens. For instance, S_1 represents the extent to which voters from group 1 based at location 1 decrease their support/vote for the political party in response to a divergence between G_1 and these voters' preferred allocation of defence spending G^a. We specify the votes-to-defence spending function as:

$$V_1 = 50 + n_1 S_1 (U_1(G_1 - G^a)) \tag{6a}$$

$$V_2 = 50 + n_2 S_2 (U_2(G_2 - G^b)) \tag{6b}$$

Suppose G^* is the total tax revenue to be distributed and group i of voters is located at location i. Each group splits votes equally between two parties when both the parties offer the same defence spending.[2] Otherwise, a party loses votes as its defence spending offer deviates from the 'ideal point' of a group. From Wittman (1989) we know that vote-maximising electoral equilibrium is ensured when the following first order condition is satisfied:[3]

$$n_1 S_1 (\partial U_1 / \partial G_1) = n_2 S_2 (\partial U_2 / \partial G_2) \tag{6c}$$

Assumption 4: We specify the utility functions of the two groups of voters as the following:

$$U_1(G_1 - G^a) = -(G_1 - G^a)^2 \tag{6d}$$

$$U_2(G_2 - G^b) = -(G_2 - G^b)^2 \tag{6e}$$

The above formulation of the utility function suggests that voters dislike both shortfalls and over-allocation of defence spending to their respective localities. The latter needs an explanation: voters may dislike an over-allocation if it leads to congestion and pollution.[4]

Proposition 1: If equations (14d) and (14e) capture voters' preferences and equations (6a) and (6b) are the votes-to-(defence spending)offer functions, then the optimal allocation G_1 and G_2 of the defence spending that maximise the votes of the incumbent government are given by:

$$G_1 = w_1(G^* - G^b) + G^a(1 - w_2) \tag{7a}$$

$$\text{where } w_1 = (n_2 S_2) / (n_1 S_1 + n_2 S_2) \tag{7b}$$

$$\text{Similarly, } G_2 = w_2(G^* - G^a) + G^b(1 - w_2) \tag{7c}$$

$$\text{where } w_2 = (n_1 S_1) / (n_1 S_1 + n_2 S_2) \tag{7d}$$

Proof: Simple substitutions yield the result.

Equations (7a)–(7d) establish that political elements such as n_i, S_1 and S_2 are critical ingredients in determining G_1 and G_2 given G^*. If the incumbent government wants office and voters want defence spending, then the vote-maximising government allocates defence spending to create an electoral equilibrium platform that is sensitive to voters' characteristics. The vote-maximising allocation of defence spending influences the nature of competition due to its effect on the costs of production of duopolists. The higher the allocation that a particular location gets, the lower is the cost of production of the firm based there. This firm, with its lower costs, will be able to extract larger profits from the output market.

3.1.2.3 Electoral equilibrium and the nature of competition

From equations (7c) and (7d) it is evident that the allocation of government investment in defence spending depends on w_1 and w_2 given the exogenously determined budget and the 'ideal points' G^a and G^b. It is instructive to note that w_1 and w_2 depend on the sizes of these voter groups – n_1 and n_2 – and their political sensitivities, S_1 and S_2, to the non-fulfilment of their demand for defence spending. From equation (5c) we know that the nature of competition in the product market depends on the ratio of G_1 and G_2 given the values of a and b. Hence, combining (5c) and (7a) through to (15d), we argue that political elements such as the size of the groups (n_i) and the political sensitivities of these voters, S_1 and S_2, are the main determinants of the degree of competition, (φ_2 / φ_1) in the product market. In order to highlight this finding let us consider two special cases.

Assumption 5: Suppose each group of voters wants all available funds G^* to be ploughed back into their respective localities. Hence,

$$G^* = G^a = G^b \tag{8a}$$

Proposition 2: In the perfect Nash equilibrium of the proposed sequential game, the degree of competition $(\varphi_2^*/\varphi_1^*)$ lies between the Cournot and Bertrand values and is sensitive to the political landscape of the simplified society.

Proof: In the perfect Nash equilibrium all agents hold rational expectations about the market outcome at stage II which are given by equations (3d) and (3e). The rational expectations outcome in turn depends on the allocation of defence spending G_1 and G_2 at Stage I. Given the rational expectations outcome, the incumbent government chooses G_1 and G_2 at stage I to maximise votes. Suppose voters' ideal points are given by Assumption 6, then we know:

$$G_1 = [(n_1 S_1)/(n_1 S_1 + n_2 S_2)]G^* \tag{8b}$$

$$G_2 = [(n_2 S_2)/(n_1 S_1 + n_2 S_2)]G^* \tag{8c}$$

Substituting (8b) and (8c) we get:

$$(\varphi_2 * / \varphi_1 *) = [bG * + m(n_1 S_1 + n_2 S_2) / (n_2 S_2)] / \qquad \text{(9a) QED.}$$
$$[bG * + m(n_1 S_1 + n_2 S_2) / (n_1 S_1)]$$

Equation (9a) establishes that the equilibrium degree of competition $(\varphi_2 * / \varphi_1 *)$ is determined by the political factors $(n_i S_i)$ of the society – given the cost and demand conditions. It is also evident that the equilibrium values lie between the Cournot and Bertrand values.

3.2.1.4   *Defence spending: a new model of reputational equilibrium in interest group politics*

The political power, or government, plays a crucial role in determining military spending and its allocation, as we have seen in the basic model. If the political power is rational, it is going to use its defence spending to influence its reputation as an instrument for achieving certain political ends.

Since the government has power to determine military spending with diverse impacts on the economy, interest groups will easily form and use 'pressure tactics' to wrench benefits from defence spending. If an interest group tries to influence the government for specific targets in defence spending, we label the behaviour as 'Wrench'. If an interest group decides not to influence the defence policy, we label the decision as 'Waver'. We assume that there are multiple interest groups in an economy who compete against each other to influence defence spending. For our analysis, we posit that there are two regional groups who form the rival interest groups: first, we have the rural interest group (RIG) and second, we have the urban interest group (UIG). As our empirical section will confirm, a bipartite division of interests groups is a reasonable abstraction for the Middle East and North Africa.

We posit that the political power, or government, faces these two interest groups in two separate arenas: let us call Arena I where the RIG seeks to influence the political power to achieve its ideal mix and level of defence spending. In a similar note, Arena II is the contest ground for the UIG and the political power. The political power has two options: i) either it chooses to accommodate the political pressure from the interest group, which we call 'Relent', ii) or the political power chooses an aggressive response, which we call 'Resist'. There are two types of political power and the political power only knows its true type: political power is either 'Weak' or 'Strong'. So, the incumbent government, after elections have taken place, can either be a 'Strong Government' or a 'Weak Government'. The payoffs will determine the nature of government in our analysis. The payoffs to the players are shown in Table 3.1.1.

Table 3.1.1 Payoffs to agents in Arena I

RIG's & Government's Choices	Payoff to RIG	Payoff to Strong Government	Payoff to Weak Government
Waver	0	A	a
Wrench and Resist	−1	0	−1
Wrench and Relent	B	−1	0
Reputation (R_1)		R_1	$1-R_1$

The government is modelled as either 'Strong' or 'Weak'. It is Strong if it can resist pressure tactics from the RIG. It is Weak if the government is expected to succumb to the pressure from the RIG in Arena I. The payoff structure is explained by the nature of the contest:

- If RIG wavers it gets nothing and the government is free to pursue its defence policy and the payoff to either type of government is a.
- If RIG decides to wrench and the government resists, then the RIG makes a loss (−1). The payoff to a strong government (0) is greater than the payoff to a weak government (−1).
- If RIG decides to wrench and the government chooses to relent, the interest group gets b, its maximum return. The strong government loses face more than a weak government by capitulating, so the payoff to a strong government (−1) is less than the payoff to a weak government (0).
- R_1 is the probability assessment by the RIG about the type of the government being 'Weak'. So $(1-R_1)$ is the subjective probability assessment that the government is 'Strong'.

The contest game gets played in the second arena (Arena II) between the government and the urban interest group (UIG). We present the details of the contest game in Table 3.1.2.

Table 3.1.2 Payoffs to agents in Arena II

UIG's & Government's Choices	Payoff to UIG	Payoff to Strong Government	Payoff to Weak Government
Waver	0	H	h
Wrench and Resist	−1	0	−1
Wrench and Relent	j	−1	0
Reputation (r_1)		r_1	$1 - r_1$

The structure of the payoff in Table 3.1.2 is similar except for the values h, j and the probability assessment r_1. One can linearly read Table 3.1.2 from the explanation of Table 3.1.1.

Observation 1: When $R_1=0$ and $r_1=1$, the government is known to be immune from the pressure tactic in Arena II. However, its reputation is low in Arena I and the government is expected to capitulate to the pressure from the RIG. Consequently, the defence policy (spending) will be influenced by the preferences of the RIG.

Observation 2: When $R_1=1$ and $r_1=0$, the government is known to be immune from the pressure tactic in Arena I. However, its reputation is too low in Arena II and the government is expected to capitulate to the pressure from the UIG. Consequently, the defence policy (spending) will be influenced by the preferences of the UIG.

Observation 3:

Consider the case where $\qquad R_1 < \dfrac{b}{1+b}$ $\qquad$ (9b)

A minor manipulation will yield:

$$-R_1 + (1 - R_1)\, b > 0 \qquad (9c)$$

The left hand gives the expected payoff to the RIG from wrenching. Since by construction the payoff to the RIG from wavering is zero (0), then (9c) gives us the condition that the expected payoff from 'Wrench' is greater than that from 'Waver'. Therefore in Arena I the RIG will seek to influence the defence policy and spending.

Observation 4:

Consider the case where $\qquad r_1 > \dfrac{j}{1+j}$ $\qquad$ (9d)

In this case the gain from wrenching in Arena II by the UIG is greater than the gains from wavering. Hence the UIG will put pressure to shape the defence policy close to its own preferences.

Observation 5: Assuming $R_1=r_1$, such that both groups share their probability assessment about the government, consider the possibility where

$$r_1 = R_1 < \frac{j}{1+j} < \frac{b}{1+b} \qquad (9e)$$

Both these interest groups have incentives to challenge the government in order to influence the defence policy, or spending. Such attempts can lead to political crises, or at least the government will choose a compromised policy as a combination of the ideal preferences of the two interest groups.

Observation 6: If the reputation is such that

$$\frac{j}{1+j} < r_l = R_l > \frac{b}{1+b} \tag{9f}$$

then neither interest group has incentives to challenge the defence spending. The government will be free to pursue an independent defence policy – independent of the interest groups. The value of its reputation is such that neither interest group wants to test out the government in the contest. This is an interesting, some may call it stunning, result from ambiguity: neither interest group believes that the political power is truly strong, yet the political power stays immune from challenges. In other words, the government is not strong, yet it enjoys some room to manoeuvre in deciding the defence spending and its allocation. The government has the limited autonomy to undertake its defence policy without challenges from powerful interest groups.

All these observations are true for single-shot games. The main frame of interactions is ideally captured by a finitely repeated game (say, at the end of the term of a government). If the game is finitely repeated, the logic of backward induction will not make any material change from the outcomes considered in the one-shot versions as above.

If the games are repeated without a known finite end date, then the government has an incentive to influence the subjective estimates about its type so that the government can have a free rein in the determination of defence spending or its allocation. More importantly, if the true type of the government is not known a priori, then the government will have to teach the 'foolish challenger' that the government is strong – but this is costly for all. So, for the conditions given by (9b)–(9e), the government will disclose its true type and be influenced by either or both interest groups. But if condition (9f) holds, and if there is not a clear end date for the game, the government will engage in reputation building over time to stall any interest group pressures. This is what we summarise in the first result:

Result 1: By exploiting the logic of mixed strategy equilibrium, the reputational dynamics, or path, of the political power is given by equation (9g) such that there is no incentive for RIG to influence the defence policy where t represents time:

$$\frac{dR1}{dt} = (1+bt)^t \tag{9g}$$

Result 2: By exploiting the logic of mixed strategy equilibrium, the reputational dynamics, or path, of the political power in Arena II is given by equation (9h) such that there is no incentive for UIG to influence the defence policy where t is the time:

$$\frac{dr1}{dt} = (1 + jt)^t \qquad\qquad (9h)$$

In summary it is shown that the 'bad or fuzzy' information about the type of the government and its relationships with potential interest groups can pay the political power to pursue the optimal defence policy from its point of view. However, this is feasible only for a short-time and also along the above paths that give the updating of subjective beliefs of interest groups. Otherwise, the political power will succumb to pressure group politics in its pursuit of defence policy. If the interest groups want to seek the strength of the political power, it prefers a challenge in the arena where the government is strong.

Result 3: If the UIG and RIG are unsure about the true type of the government and expect the arrival of information concerning the true nature of the government from its actual defence spending, then, due to an option value from waiting, the interest groups will have an optimal waiting time before challenging the government (see Gangopadhyay and Gangopadhyay, 2008). During this waiting time, the government is free to choose the defence policy but will be subject to heavy pressure from interest groups once the waiting period is over.

So, there may be a temporary lull when defence spending is not subject to interest group pressures, but more often than not there will be pressure from interest groups on the political power to choose the defence policy to the benefit of the interest groups. However, which group wins to influence the political power is an empirical question that we will address in the next section.

3.2   Political economy of the determination of defence spending in the Middle East and North Africa: a case study of arms imports

In this section we examine the empirical foundation to our models by applying the time series analysis to seven countries from the region: five from the Middle East and two from North Africa as Chapter 2 has done. So, we refer our readers to the empirical section of Chapter 2 for relevant details. The theoretical models establish three important insights in the context of defence spending:

- First, it is essential to disaggregate an economy into competing components. Each component has different preferences for defence spending, or arms imports. We undertake the disaggregation by breaking up each of the seven economies into two distinct groups, namely, rural and urban.
- Second, various other factors like degrees of competition and political behaviour of interest groups will determine the equilibrium in the allocation of government budgets.
- Finally, since we don't have data on the regional allocation of defence spending, we examine the impact of various factors on the dynamics of arms imports in the seven countries from the region during 1960–2013.

Our simple theoretical model for estimation, ignoring the time script, is postulated as the following:

$$ARIM_i = F(P^A, (P^{POWER})_i, THREAT_i) \qquad (10a)$$

As explained in Chapter 2, $ARIM_i$ is the natural log of the value of arms imports of country i; in the constant US dollar of 2012, P^A is the price of arms in the international market and $(P^{POWER})_i$ is the purchasing power of the country i. The variable $THREAT_i$ is the perception of internal and external threats which motivate the national government to bolster the national defence by importing arms. From our models in Chapter 2 and Chapter 3, one can explain these variables as:

$$P^A = EXCH_i^* P \qquad (10b)$$

P is the international price of a basket of arms and $EXCH_i$ is the exchange rate that converts the international currency (US\$) to the local currency.

We define the purchasing power of the national government as the following:

$$(P^{POWER})_i = f(GDP_i, FPINF_i, OILP) \qquad (10c)$$

where GDP_i is the per capita nominal GDP and $FPINF_i$ is the food price inflation in country i and $OILP$ is the price of oil in the international market. Since we will take into consideration the population, we have chosen the per capita GDP to reflect the purchasing power of an average citizen of a country to invest in modern arms and ammunitions. Food price inflation and oil prices will determine the real per capita GDP of a country, so we have introduced them to reflect the price variables.

The $THREAT$ equation is postulated as:

$$THREAT_i = Q(VI_i, URPG_i, LRPL_i, RG_i) \qquad (10d)$$

Note VI_i is the vulnerability index of country i introduced in Chapter 2. We have used several specifications of the index to check for robustness. $URPG_i$ is the rate of growth of the urban population, RG_i is the growth of rural population and $LRPL_i$ is the natural log of rural population in country i. The basic intuition is that rural and urban people have different preferences for defence spending and they belong to different interest groups with different bargaining power to influence government budgetary decisions. Combining (10a)–(10d) yields the empirical model as the following:

$$ARIM_i = \Omega(EXCH_i, GDP_i, FPINF_i, OILP\ VI_i, URPG_i, LRPL_i, RG_i) \quad (11a)$$

Note that Ω is a compound function in (11a). In the following subsection we apply the econometric tools to equation (11a) to mainly determine the long-run relationship between arms imports and other factors.

Table 3.2.1 Optimal lag choices and ranks of cointegrating variables

Country	FPE/HQIC, SBIC	Lag	Vec Rank	Trace Stat	CV*
Libya	$-2.2e^{-21}$, -18.2	2	1	142.81	156
Syria	No results	No results	No results	No results	No results
Iran	No results	No results	No results	No results	No results
Iraq	$-1.3e^{-16}$, -18	2 (4)	4	67.54	68.34
Israel	-9.47, 3.45	4	5	46.49	47.41
Egypt	26.2, 18	4	6	26.36	29.68
Lebanon	12.96, 20.84	4	5	41.13	47.21

* 5% Critical Value

3.2.1   Interdependency and vulnerability in the Middle East and North Africa

In this subsection we start off with the cointegration analysis to examine if there is any long-run foundation to equation (11a) in the seven countries from the Middle East and North Africa during 1960–2013. The analytical question is simple for us: is there any evidence that the dependent variable ($ARIM$) exhibits a long-run relationship with the postulated independent variables? In order to answer the question we test the following empirical equation:

$$ARIM_i = \Omega(EXCH_i, GDP_i, FPINF_i, OILP\ VI_i, URPG_i, LRPL_i, RG_i) \quad (11a)$$

This section reports our empirical results of the long-run relationship between the dependent variable ($ARIM_i$) and the array of independent variables chosen in equation (11a) as the key explanatory variables. The long-run elasticities of the independent variables and their t-ratios are reported in Table 3.3. Table 3.2.1 summarises the Johansen's cointegration test statistics. The Johansen test results indicate that there is at least one cointegrating vector based on the maximum trace statistics/tests. Thus, from Table 3.2.1 we can conclude that our model (equation 19a) with two or more variables is a fair representation for the chosen countries in the Middle East except Syria and Iran. As a consequence, we have presented results for the other five nations in Table 3.2.1 and Table 3.2.2.

Table 3.2.2 presents the long-run estimated relationship between $ARIM$ of a country and the explanatory variables, which are normalised on the dependent variable. The coefficients of the explanatory variables have the expected signs in most of the equations. We have removed the explanatory variables that are statistically insignificant. The following cases emerge from the Johansen test:

• The case of Libya is an interesting example: first of all, all coefficients except the exchange rate, are negative. Ceteris paribus, as the exchange

Table 3.2.2 Long-term determinants of arms imports

ARIM	NV_i	GDP_i	$EXCH_i$	$FPINF_i$	OILP	RPG_i	$UPGR_i$	$LRPL_i$
Libya	−13*	−0.55	25*	−0.9*	−0.24*	$-2e^{-11}$	−0.3	−47*
Syria	NA	NA	NA	NA	NA	NA	NA	NA
Iran	NA	NA	NA	NA	NA	NA	NA	NA
Iraq	4.52*	3.81*	−0.003*	0.02*	−0.25*	−4.13*	−.80	37.4*
Israel	−5.2*	14.4*	−4.5*	0.007**	−0.11*	−7.5*	−25*	−16*
Egypt	0.5	−10*	−1	−0.9*	−0.02*	222*	−0.2	6
Lebanon	27*	−21*	0.03*	0.12*	−.10	169*	−4**	55*

* Statistically significant

** Marginally significant

NA: No long-run results

rate depreciates (appreciates), the Libyan government spends more (less) money for importing arms. This suggests that the Libyan government has been targeting a particular basket of arms from importers. We see similar effects of exchange rates for Lebanon though the elasticity is very small. However, for Israel, Iran and Egypt we see the usual price effect: as the price of arms imports increases with rising exchange rates, or depreciation of local currencies, the demand for arms imports is elastic to reduce their spending on imported arms.

• For Libya, however, all other variables have negative impacts on its arms imports as the second row of Table 3.2.2 shows. It is also interesting to note that the per capita *GDP* (*GDPL*) does not have a statistically significant impact on the arms imports of Libya. This further confirms the possibility of a targeting behaviour for using imports to acquire specific arms. Interestingly, the rural sector plays an important role in deescalating arms imports: both the growth of rural population and its size seem to reduce arms imports and they are economically and statistically significant. However, there is no statistically significant relationship between the urban sector and arms imports in Libya. Finally, the Libyan government seems to have responded to the rising vulnerability of the nation by investing more public money into other public projects than arms imports as the negative coefficient of row 2 and column 2 of Table 3.2.2 shows. So, there is some evidence that the Libyan government might have been more progressive than what was shown in the generally accepted picture about it. The rising food price inflation, as row 2 and column 5 of Table 3.2.2 shows, also confirms that the Libyan government – ceteris paribus – did reduce arms imports to feed its own people. The rising oil bonanza from rising oil prices, as row 2 and column 6 of Table 3.2.2 confirms, reduced arms imports. One plausible explanation behind this observation is the response of the government to pump extra resources into the oil sector as the returns have been high from oil production. Alternatively, the oil prize bonanza could have augmented the bargaining power of the domestic producers of arms and other industrial goods, which resulted in a long-term negative coefficient between *ARIM* and *OILP*.

- As column 6 of Table 3.3 shows, the oil bonanza – contrary to the general opinion – has reduced arms imports in the long-run for all other countries. The oil bonanza, as a consequence, has promoted peace by reducing arms imports in the region.

- From column 5 of Table 3.2.2 we note that the food price inflation, in the long-run, lowers arms imports for Egypt and Libya though the impacts are not big. This shows that both Libya and Egypt were targeting a basket of arms. This is so since food price inflation raises the general inflation rate and results in *seigniorage* (inflation tax) and the national government has more money to spend. Yet both Libya and Egypt reduce their arms imports, ceteris paribus, as the seigniorage increases. In the long-run, the national governments of Israel, Iraq and Lebanon tend to increase their arms imports as the seigniorage rises.

- As the second column of Table 3.2.2 shows, Israel like Libya increases (decreases) arms imports as the long-term vulnerability falls (rises). Both national governments of Israel and Syria tend to consider arms imports and vulnerability as substitutes. We find the exact opposite scenario for Iraq, Lebanon and Egypt, though the elasticity for Egypt is not statistically significant. For these three nations, the arms imports rise (fall) in the long-run as the vulnerability rises (falls). One can argue that arms imports and vulnerability are complements for the decision-makers in Lebanon, Iraq and Egypt. There is some reason to believe that these three nations also use arms imports as a strategy to promote their long-term vulnerability.

- In the long-run, as column 8 of Table 3.2.2 shows, the growth of the urban population bears an inverse relationship with arms imports for all countries. Urbanisation could thus be a vehicle for de-escalating the arms race in the Middle East and promoting peace. We will examine the issue in greater detail in Chapter 6.

- Columns 7 and 9 of Table 3.2.2 confirm that both the size of the rural population and its growth are important determinants of arms imports: first and foremost, for Libya and Israel both the size and growth of rural populations have negative relationships with their arms imports and both are economically and statistically significant. For Egypt and Lebanon, the effects of the rural sector on their arms imports are exactly the opposite: the larger the dominance of the rural sector in terms of population, the larger is the growth of militarisation, or arms imports. In Iraq we see a mixed case: the size of the rural population exerts an upward pressure on its arms imports while the growth of the rural population lowers demand for imported arms. One plausible rationale is that the newer generations want to move away from arms imports to promote peace in Iraq. This is an important issue of demography that we will address in Chapter 6 and Chapter 7.

In what follows, in Section 3.2.2, we will seek to assess if global warming and the global oil market play any role in driving the arms imports in the region.

3.2.2   Implications of global weather and the oil market for arms imports in the Middle East and North Africa: a long-term analysis

In order to undertake the cointegration analysis, we have first derived the optimal lag and ranks from the trace statistics, which we report in Table 3.2. In this subsection we use the (natural log of) total arms imports in our chosen seven nations as the dependent variable. The trace statistics show the presence of at least one long-term relationship for the dependent variable. Our econometric model is given by the following equation:

$$\Sigma ARIM = F\,(LNT,\,LNO,\,LNP) \tag{11b}$$

Note that $\Sigma ARIM$ is the sum of (log of) $ARIM$ of each country, which is postulated as a function (F) of LNT, LNO and LNP. T, P and O are respectively the average global temperature, price of oil and global output of oil and LN is the logarithmic transformation of the variables. We present the long-term cointegration results in Table 3.3:

- If we take $\Sigma ARIM$ as a proxy for the militarisation of the region, then the rising global temperature has an economically meaningful and statistically significant impact on the militarisation of the Middle East, which can be seen from the first two rows of the second column of Table 3.3. From the data we find some concrete evidence that global warming has increased militarisation of the region during a haul of 1960–2013.
- There is no evidence that the global oil production did have any palpable impact on the militarisation of the region. Though the results show a negative effect, the coefficient does not have statistical significance.
- The impact of oil price, on the contrary, from the third column of Table 3.3, shows that there is strong evidence that the rising oil price can significantly reduce militarisation in the region.
- The issue of militarisation is given short shrift in this chapter, as we will devote considerable attention to militarisation in Chapter 6.

3.2.3   The long-run dynamics of arms imports in the region

Modern nations rarely engage in costly wars and bloody conflicts, yet they devote a sizeable proportion of their economic resources to defence spending,

Table 3.3 Cointegration coefficients of arms imports from the Johansen approach

	LNT	*LNP*	*LNO*	*Constant***
$\Sigma ARIM$	1366.98*	−14.78*	−10.28	−3677.55
Z Stat	9.20	−4.59	−0.94	
Optimal Lag	Min. FEP	Min AIC	Min HQIC	Min SBIC
1	1.0e⁻⁷	−4.75	−.4.46	−3.98
Vec Rank	Trace Stat	CV***	Parm	eigenvalue
0	54.90	47.21	20	
1	27.23*	29.68	27	0.41

* Statistically significant
** Normalised by Johansen's approach
*** 5% Coefficient of variation

which is commonly known as defence burden. It was widely held that defence burden had acted as deterrence against open wars. In other words, the capacity to hurt one's rival can be used as a motivating factor for rivals to avoid war and influence another state's *rational* behaviour. Despite the fact that defence burden is neither necessary nor sufficient to prevent wars, as the new research shows, the average defence burden of our globe has been stable roughly at 3% of the global GDP with a standard deviation of less than 1%. Thus, defence spending can have a large opportunity cost. Out of the top ten nations in terms of defence burden, six are from the Middle East. It has long been established that emulation within a regional group – popularly known as *security webs* – plays an important role in propelling defence spending by a nation. Despite being a major issue in the regional context, there is no existing theoretical model to explain the precise determinants of defence burden. Ours is a first attempt to offer an economic model for explaining the determination of defence burden. In this chapter we develop simple theory and direct evidence from the Middle East to highlight a common thread that runs through these nations to understand the precise determinants of defence burden. A detailed analysis will be offered in Chapter 6 of the book.

3.3   Discussion and conclusion

The Smithian perspective on competition highlights a congruence of interests of market participants: for example, if a buyer wishes to buy milk and is prepared to offer money in return, and the seller (milkmaid) wants money and is willing to give milk in exchange for the money. This exchange allows each to achieve one's goal and they thereby help each other. In a complex market mechanism, however, economic problems are often embedded in conflict. It is recognised that the market mechanism can easily handle congruent interests but may fail to resolve conflicts in a harmonious or fair fashion (see Sen, 1984b). To redress such conflicts, the visible hand of government has usually been invoked (Ostrom, 1987). In this work we highlight two types of conflicts – namely, market conflicts and political conflicts – and, thereby, attempt to weave them together to illuminate an important intersection between the economy and the polity. We introduce conflicts at the market level in the usual fashion as market rivalry – two prototype firms compete against each other for market shares. By applying the simple game theoretic reasoning, we obtained the equilibrium market outcome. However, the core of the problem remains that the emerging market outcomes, the conduct of firms, market shares and take-home profits of these rivals critically depend on the choice of their strategic variable and, hence, on the nature of competition.[5] Dixon (1986) introduces consistent conjectural variations to make the degree of competition endogenous in a strategic investment model and establishes that the degree of competition is driven by the investment decision of firms since capital stocks impinge on costs of production. We exploit this intuition of Dixon's by focusing on the impact of defence spending, as opposed to private capital, on costs of production. The introduction of defence spending in our model allows us to link the second type of conflict, namely the political conflict, with the first type. Since, the availability of defence spending is fixed, it is modelled that there is no congruence of interests of agents coming from two distinct locations: as Hirsch (1977) notes, 'what winners win, losers lose'. An allocation of defence spending will naturally entail political costs and benefits that a self-seeking government – driven by electoral motive – would try to exploit. An incumbent government will naturally choose an allocation to maximise the probability of its re-election. Our model on probabilistic voting has antecedents in the literature: Lindbeck and Weibull (1987) and Dixit and Londregan (1994) adapt the probabilistic model to examine public policies that redistribute income to narrow groups of voters. They assume that the various groups differ in their preferences for the political parties and thereby identify the political characteristics of a group that makes it an ideal candidate for receiving political largesse. The upshot is that these authors mainly study the major determinants of the political success of a special interest group. On the contrary, we start off with the political characteristics of voters and then apply the probabilistic voting theorem to determine the electoral equilibrium that is driven by political largesse in the form of defence spending. This is how our model resolves political conflicts.

The resolution of political conflict can have serious ramifications for the product market, due to its impact on the allocation of defence spending. This is a serious point to consider: traditional political theory highlights the failure of majority-rule voting caused by the absence of a stable electoral equilibrium. As a result, political instability can create significant instability in product markets. This is where we apply the probabilistic voting theorem to highlight the existence of a stable voting equilibrium to establish that democratic political markets are well organised to promote the vote-maximising allocation of defence spending that will, in turn, lend stability to the product markets: the model predicts that the vote-maximising government adopts an optimal allocation of defence spending that induces an electoral equilibrium that, in turn, maximises its chances of re-election. In this perspective, the nature of competition, structure industry and conduct of firms in an oligopolistic market critically depend on this electoral equilibrium and hence on voters' preferences and characteristics. The degree of competition is thus identified with the equilibrium allocation of defence spending and becomes a continuous variable, rather than a binary variable. It captures intermediate situations between the pure Bertrand and Cournot cases. We also find important comparative-static results that show that the structure and conduct of firms, and the nature of competition in oligopolistic markets, will be sensitive to political characteristics.

Future extensions of the work are desired on two fronts: voters' preferences should be made dependent on the final good's price and thus on the nature of competition. This extension will enhance our understanding of the nature of equilibrium by providing circular interdependence between government policy and market outcomes. Second, important extension is possible by allowing voters to 'vote with their feet'. This extension will once again provide circular interdependence between government policies and market outcomes.

At the country level, we find interesting and diverse long-run estimated relationships between militarisation ($ARIM$) of a country and the explanatory variables, which are normalized on the dependent variable. The coefficients of the explanatory variables have the expected signs in most of the equations. Some of the most interesting results are as follows: in the long-run the growth of the urban population bears an inverse relationship with arms imports for all seven countries in the region. The link between urbanisation and militarisation is hitherto unknown in the literature. Urbanisation could thus be a vehicle for de-escalating the arms race in the Middle East and promoting peace. We will examine the issues of militarisation in greater detail in Chapter 6. We also argue that both the size of rural population and its growth are important determinants of arms imports but their effects vary across nations: first and foremost, for Libya and Israel both the size and growth of rural populations have negative relationships with their arms imports and both are economically and statistically significant. For Egypt and Lebanon, the effects of the rural sector on their arms imports are exactly the opposite: the larger the dominance of the rural sector in terms of population, the larger the growth of militarisation, or arms imports. In Iraq we see a mixed case: the size of the rural population exerts an upward pressure on its arms imports while the growth of the rural population lowers demand for imported arms. At the empirical level, for the entire region, we find many interesting results: if we take $\Sigma ARIM$ as a proxy for the militarisation of the region, then the rising global temperature has an economically meaningful and statistically significant impact on the militarisation of the Middle East and North Africa. From the data we also find some concrete evidence that global warming has increased militarisation of the region during a long haul of 1960–2013. However, there is no evidence that the global oil production did have any palpable impact on the militarisation of the region. Though the results show a negative effect, the coefficient does not have statistical significance. The impact of the oil price, on the contrary, shows that there is strong evidence that the rising oil price can significantly reduce militarisation in the region.

Notes

1 Arrow and Kurz (1970) and Barro (1990) have stressed the importance of public infrastructure as a substitute for private capital in the production function. Thus, an increase in public infrastructure in an industrial location, ceteris paribus, reduces cost of production of all firms in that location. Alternatively, one may assume that public infrastructure reduces costs due to the 'iceberg' effect of Samuelson (1954): if public infrastructure is inadequate then a large portion of the goods produced will be wasted and will fail to reach consumers. An increase in public infrastructure therefore reduces cost by facilitating trade. Public infrastructure has assumed significance in Europe as EC-funded infrastructure projects aim to create strategic advantages for member nations (Martin and Rogers, 1995). As examples, the Channel Tunnel, high-speed rail network and new telecommunication networks have been undertaken in recent years to boost industrial development and convergence in Europe.
2 Why should voters care for infrastructure? One plausible explanation is that voters are the stakeholders of the firms, both as shareholders and employees.
3 It can be checked that the second order condition is automatically satisfied.
4 It is important to note that a simple concave utility function, where voters are happier the more infrastructure investment they get but decreasingly so, will provide similar results.
5 From an early work of Marshak and Nelson (1962) we know that if the production structure is inflexible, then the Cournot outcome is a natural conclusion. On the other hand, if production is completely inflexible, then the Bertrand outcome is the likely candidate. It is argued that if production is more flexible, then the MC functions are steeper. The nature of competition is introduced as an external assumption in Brander and Spencer (1983, 1985), Dixon (1985), Dixit (1984), Eaton and Grossman (1986), and Yarrow (1986).

4 Dynamics of terrorism in a fragmented world

The Middle East and North Africa conundrum

4.1 Introduction

The term 'terrorism' is mostly used to convey the meaning that a violent action is perpetrated and politically motivated, targeting non-combatant citizens of a country by sub-national groups or clandestine agents, with a clear intention to influence an audience. International terrorism involves international targets, international audience and foreign, or multinational, perpetrators. The literature on terrorism and counterterrorism has well-recognised contributions from economists for more than three decades. Since the terrorist attack on US soil on 11 September 2001, there has been a virtual explosion of research with important studies on the economic causes of terrorism and its economic consequences. Many excellent research publications appeared on investigating the structural determinants of terrorism. Interesting behavioural questions were posed about who becomes a terrorist. Obviously, as an indispensable aid to policymaking, economists offer models to examine the optimal counterterrorism policy to deter terrorism, break terrorist networks and arrest radical mobilisation.

In order to understand terrorism, terror incidents and their deterrence and also government–terrorist negotiations and the *strategic* use of violence, it is important to understand the inner workings of terrorist organisations. The initial work was undertaken by Chai (1993), who strained the new institutional economics to better understand how terrorists choose their strategies. It was in 2007 when the resource constraint of terrorist organisations came to the forefront of research with a pioneering paper by Shapiro and Siegel (2007). Their primary intuition is that terrorist organisations suffer from the agency problem: terrorist leaders, often political representatives, openly or clandestinely recruit a network of operators who undertake terrorist-related activities. The principal is the leader/s while the operators are the agents. The principal is responsible for financial and other resources and delegates the task of terrorism to the operators. The operators thus have delegated responsibility to act on behalf of the principal. Since the operators may engage in rent seeking, there arises a gap between the intended outcome and the actual outcome in terms of terrorist activities. In order to control the delegated agents, the leaders often choose to underfund the activities (see Shapiro and Siegel, 2007). The important insight is that financial return is an important determinant of terrorism since the operators suffer from inadequacy of funds. So, the operators are engaged in fund-seeking activities and looking for avenues to improve the financial returns from terrorism. In other words, when an organisation is filled up with resources, the agency problem is a non-sequitur. Resources don't have much impact on incidents of terrorism. However, if resources become sufficiently scarce, cooperation within the terrorist organisation becomes difficult, that can in turn impact on the frequency and deadliness of terrorist attacks. Thus choking terrorists' funds can be an effective deterrence in counterterrorism tactics only after a critical threshold is reached, at which point it becomes highly effective. The cooperation and agency issues can be overcome by a terrorist organisation by increasing cohesion within the terrorist organisation linking terrorism to religion (e.g. Berman 2003; Iannaccone and Berman 2006). This literature argues that religious organisations, with their effective screening mechanisms and strong barriers to entry for non-members, are suitable to reduce agency problems and cooperation problems, by choosing members who are likely to be highly committed and willing to contribute to the group's mission without having financial, or other, motives.

Another important element within a terrorist organisation, as highlighted by Siqueira (2005) and Bueno de Mesquita (2008), is rivalry, or factionalisation, within a group. Siqueira (2005) studies the interaction of militant and political wings of a terrorist organisation. He shows that the actions of one of these factions can have spillover effects on the other, whether or not the factions coordinate with one another. As a result, the existence of competing factions can increase or decrease the overall level of violence. The precise relationship between factionalisation and violence depends on how internal divisions affect public (and donor) support for the terrorist movement and the complementarities or substitutabilities between attacks by the various factions. The model, thus, adds to the argument in Bloom (2005) that factional rivalry is a key force behind escalation in terrorist conflicts.

Bueno de Mesquita (2008) investigates the formation of a splinter faction in a model with the following elements: first, the model endogenises both the affiliation and mobilisation of recruits. Second, the model also endogenises the choice of ideological positions by terrorist leaders. The model highlights that many factors that decrease terrorist mobilisation do so at the cost of increasing ideological extremism. For instance, a strong economy is found to decrease terrorist mobilisation but also increase the extremism of terrorist factions, and decrease the likelihood of a splinter faction forming. He argues that this suggests that economic shocks have competing micro-level effects on the expected level of violence that might not be observed in the type of macro-level data employed in many of the studies of the relationship between terrorism and the economy described above. Thus, understanding the internal politics of terrorist organisations is critical, not only for understanding government–terrorist negotiations, but also for assessing the root causes and consequences of terror.

In economics, an important inquiry concerns whether the root causes of terror derive from economic inequality and deprivation through the channel that deprivation acts as the grease in the wheels of radical mobilisation. Many studies address the causal connection between deprivation and inequality to terrorism by adapting and exploiting both cross-country and over-time variations in the state of the economy and in the level of terrorism. Unfortunately, there is no convergence in findings: the results are sensitive to the choices of model specification, covariates, and the measurement and operationalisation of an acceptable definition of the level of terrorism. In important contributions, Blomberg, Hess and Weerapana (2004) and Drakos and Gofas (2006b) find a statistically significant negative correlation between measures of economic performance and the levels of terrorist violence. However, many subsequent works contradicted the negative correlation. As an example, Krueger (2007) notes that there is evidence that the wealthier the country is, the more likely the probability of a terrorist attack on the country will increase. There is no role of economic performance for the home country of a terrorist attack. In a similar vein, in an important work by Li and Schaub (2004), it has been found that terrorism does not bear any statistical relationship with foreign direct investment (FDI) or portfolio investment. They find that economic development in a country and in its major trading partners will reduce terrorism in the network of these countries. However, all these findings suffer from the general weakness in the quality of data. More importantly, most studies fail the test of causality. One must bear in mind that these are the major weaknesses in the literature. In another important work, Abadie (2006) addresses both of these issues within a cross-country setting: on the data side, Abadie uses the Global Terrorism Index instead of using the standard count-data of terrorist attacks or fatalities. The dependent variable on terrorism of Abadie is the Global Terrorism Index of the World Market Research Centre. The index uses five factors for forecasting: motivation, presence, scale, efficacy and prevention of terrorism. The problem with the econometric model is the potential endogeneity between economic performance and the level of terrorism risk: poor economic performance causes terrorism and terrorism causes poor economic performance. He uses the instrument of being a country landlocked as a dummy as for national GDP. The identification assumption is that landlocked status directly affects GDP but does not affect the risk of terrorism through any mechanism other than its effect on GDP. Abadie finds that, controlling for other factors (including the level of political freedom), there is no statistically significant relationship between per capita GDP and terrorism risk in the instrumental variables estimates.

The other approach is to avoid the problem of endogeneity by not using cross-country models. Instead, such papers swivel on the individual details involving specific terrorist conflicts: for instance, Krueger and Maleckova (2003) and Berrebi (2003) study the individual characteristics of terrorist operatives from Hezbollah and Hamas, respectively. They underscore that terrorist members and operatives are, themselves, neither poor nor poorly educated. On the contrary, their economic and educational statuses tend to be on a par with, or even better than, the averages in their respective societies. As a corollary, Krueger and Maleckova (2003) argue that, since terrorists neither suffer from poverty nor deprivation in terms of education, the economy and education cannot credibly explain terrorism. In contradiction to the above, Bueno de Mesquita (2005b) develops a formal model to show that, although the evidence regarding the socio-economic status of individual terrorists is of considerable interest, it does not lead to the conclusion that poverty is not an important ingredient in terrorist mobilisation. The key element in Bueno de Mesquita's (2005b) model is that terrorist hierarchies use screening for potential recruits on what they call 'terrorist ability'. The ability of a terrorist and one's effectiveness as a terrorist is positively correlated with one's socio-economic status. In other words, better-educated people make better terrorists. Benmelech and Berrebi (2006) marshal empirical evidence that better-educated terrorist are indeed more effective in carrying out difficult tasks. The key question is as follows: what determines the 'ability' of a terrorist in one's skills in terrorism? Unfortunately, the ability is often positively correlated with income, or education. Both income and education are determined by the state of the economy. So, the state of the economy and economic performances can still trigger and propel terrorism. In other words, the state of the economy can and will determine the quality and the supply/ quantity of potential terrorists. The endogeneity issues between terrorism and economic factors naturally lead to more problems: what is the precise effect of terrorism on a country's economy? This literature is reviewed in considerable detail in Enders and Sandler (2006). One common observation that comes out of this literature is that it is very difficult, if not impossible, to measure the macroeconomic effects of large-scale terrorist attacks. In calculating the costs, the study must take into account a wide variety of direct effects like productive lives lost, infrastructure destroyed etc. Even if one can measure these direct effects, there are far too many and difficult-to-measure indirect effects like time and efficiency lost to increased airport security, deadweight loss from increased taxes for compensations to victims of the attacks, stock market consequences of terrorist attacks so the impact is unknown.

Alternative studies have taken two forms: isolating the effects of terrorism on specific types of economic activity (like tourism or FDI) or on the economy of a specific country. With regard to the former, Abadie and Gardeazabal (2005) argue that terrorism alters the allocation of investment capital by increasing risk and decreasing expected returns. Their estimates show that increased terrorism risk in a country decreases foreign direct investment in that country by a significant amount. In a similar vein, Sandler and Enders (2008) also find large negative effects of terrorism on foreign direct investment in Greece and Spain. Similarly, Enders, Sandler and Parise (1992) find that terrorism significantly reduced tourism in Greece, Italy and Austria.

Two important studies estimate the effect of terrorism on economic growth in particular conflict zones. Abadie and Gardeazabal (2004) examine how ETA terrorism has diminished economic growth in the Basque Country of Spain. They are able to do so because ETA terrorism has been overwhelmingly concentrated in this one region. Given this concentration, they statistically construct a 'synthetic' Basque Country based on other Spanish regions and compare its growth (free from terrorism) to the growth of the actual Basque Country. Their analysis suggests that ETA terrorism has decreased per capita GDP in the Basque Country by 10 percentage points since the onset of Basque terrorism in the 1960s. Eckstein and Tsiddon (2004) employ an intervention-style time series methodology to study the effects of terrorist attacks on the Israeli economy. They find that terrorism depresses growth, but that the effects of any given attack are relatively short lived. In this chapter we offer a new economic model of terrorism to seek answers to three critical questions for the Middle East and North Africa:

- First and foremost, what are the long-term determinants of terrorism in the Middle East and North Africa?
- Second, has terrorism changed the long-term economic dynamics of the region?
- Finally, is terrorism in the Middle East impacted by various global factors?

In their work Blomberg, Hess and Orphanides (2004) argue, having controlled for various country specific effects by including dummy variables in their cross-country growth regressions, that such studies to measure the impact of terrorism on an economy are 'crude' estimations at best. Enders and Sandler (2006) also posit that different 'institutional structures and levels of terrorism' make cross-country analysis of terrorism suspect (Enders and Sandler, 2006, p. 214; Sandler and Enders, 2008). In this chapter we plough new grounds to examine the effects of terrorism on the Middle East economy on a case-by-case basis however we also include the regional impacts. We also estimate the determinants of terrorism in the region by introducing new variables hitherto not applied to the terrorism research.

4.2   Economic modelling of terrorism

In the literature, two formal models by Eckstein and Tsiddon (2004) and Abadie and Gardeazabal (2008) were proposed, to study the impact of terrorism on the economy, each focusing on particular factors and channels through which terrorism affects the economy. Eckstein and Tsiddon (2004) chose a closed economy model to argue that terrorism raises the discount rate, which in turns translates into a reduction of income and other macroeconomic variables. On the other hand, Abadie and Gardeazabal (2008), by exploiting an open economy model, take capital outflows as a consequence of terrorism.

The adverse effect of terrorism on the economy materialises through the capital flight.

Eckstein and Tsiddon's (2004) is one of the few studies that formally model to examine the effect of terrorism on the economy. They extend the Blanchard-Yaari Model (Yaari, 1965; Blanchard, 1985) by introducing the idea that terrorism increases the death rate in a country. Thus, they postulate that terrorism results in an exogenous increase in death rates, which in turn changes important economic behaviours in a country. They argue that changes in (perceived) life expectancy caused by terrorism impacts adversely on an economy through a series of reactions of government and individual economic agents. Governments usually respond to terrorism by consuming more defence goods, whereas economic agents change their consumption and investment patterns. The theory posits that the increase in the probability of death – caused by terrorism – motivates economic agents to use a larger rate of discounting for future incomes. As a result, economic agents, in order to increase the current needs relative to future needs, reduce steady states' level of investment in the short run and consumption and production in the long run. By extending the Blanchard-Yaari Model, with the introduction of terrorism and defence spending in the model, they find an intertemporal substitution in consumption and investment with a strong long-run effect. They do this by making the death rate endogenous.

4.3 Global roots of regional conflicts

The main argument of this chapter is to posit conflicts as a product of continuing international chasms, splits and differences of political and social ideologies. We argue that conflicts are, to some extent, driven by international tension, or global, ideological and geopolitical factors. Notwithstanding the global influence, local factors – such as income inequality, income growth or lack of it, and the influence of political institutions – can and do exacerbate conflicts. We will start our discussion with a glimpse of the great global conflicts, as current conflicts have roots of global origin, and are products of what is known as international tension. Comprehensive models will capture the feedback between local factors and international tension, and will explain various subtle inter-temporal dynamics of conflicts, violence, and terrorist activities. In order to set the stage ready, we plot the terror attacks on the globe during 1968–2009 in Figure 4.1.

The time path of global attacks displays very complex dynamics, which we will address for the region in the next section. In what follows we provide a brief history of international tensions that could have driven global terrorism during 1968–2009.

The idea of ideological chasms and global tension is not new: Rattinger (1975) introduced it into the basic Richardson-type model. International tension was quantified in terms of verbal statements made by nations embroiled in conflict. In a work on Iraq–Iran conflict, Abolfathi (1978) introduced

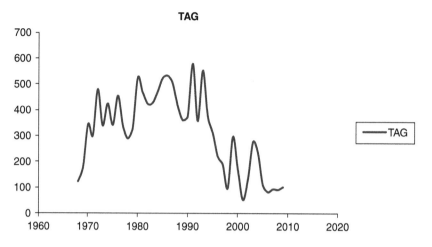

Figure 4.1 Time profile of global terror attacks during 1968–2009

US–Soviet Union rivalry as an explanatory variable. In a differential game, international tension, as measured by the sum of military expenditure, has been modelled by Zinnes et al. (1978) to explain the arms race. Our model differs significantly from these models as we focus on actual conflicts and derive an endogenous index of international tension-driven conflict, instead of an exogenous measure of international tension. As a result, our model, with its empirical questions and findings, is significantly different from the early attempts.

4.3.1 Emergence of the new era of globalisation

Globalisation is a multidimensional concept having various important facets that entail economic, financial, technological, and social and political processes, which continually transform the global economy, society and polity. This chapter will focus on seven key aspects of globalisation: trans-border trade, trans-border movement of capital, the emergence of a new international order, diffusion and homogenisation of economic cultures and institutions, labour market consequences, governance issues, and prospects and problems of our global economy and society. The choice of these themes is not fortuitous: they have been chosen to illuminate the complex path that globalisation has trod.

It is generally recognised that the process of globalisation has been significantly aided by the fall in the costs of communication and transportation, leading to a shrinkage of our globe into a quasi-'global village' characterised by an integration typically observed in traditional village communes. We therefore view globalisation as a complex process that gradually unleashes a series of transitions: the process starts off with an increased integration of the world economy through trade and investment networks. It is well understood that the start of this stage of increased integration turns on the pivot of decreasing transaction costs of trans-border trade and investment. Declining transaction costs are explained in terms of technical progress that reduces the cost of communication and transport. Declining transaction costs have a direct and positive impact on cross-border trade and portfolio and direct investment.

The economic consequence of this increased integration is twofold: first, nations become more interdependent in economic terms. Second, there arises a *perception* that trans-border trade and investment offers tremendous and often unprecedented economic opportunities for a nation. The first transition thus results in an increased integration of the world economy – through a mesh of multinational investment, trade flows and flows of financial capital – with an equally important transition in the *perception* of the importance of trans-border trade and investment as a vehicle of economic progress and prosperity. The second transition impacts on the realm of national management, as national governments actively respond to this new perception of great benefits to those nations that entertain relevant openness to foreign trade and investment. As a number of nations vie with each other to take home the spoils of the world economy, policymakers come to agree that the main barrier to the access of these spoils lies in the domestic economic structure characterised by the labyrinth of controls that has been a by-product of the Keynesian era of de-globalisation. This leads to the third transition that paves the way for homogenisation of economic ideologies, convergence of macroeconomic and trade policies, and the consequent adoption of measures of domestic liberalisation. For any national government, options are pretty limited – either it chugs along with the pre-existing regime of economic control with limited global trade as pursued by China and India, or it ditches the olden economy and replaces it with a functional market mechanism, openness to trans-border trade, liberalisation of domestic and external sectors and exchange rates, and privatisation of state-owned enterprises. That the majority of nations had taken the second option represents an unprecedented convergence of economic ideologies during the 1980s and 1990s. This common act of nations, as though to the dictate of a common script, has consolidated the process of integration of the global economy.

The final transition typically takes place in the social and economic spheres of our globe as a direct consequence of these previous transitions. The process of globalisation can thus be reduced to this simple and uncomplicated fable which highlights various, possibly virtuous, transitions that lie within a plethora of enormously complicated subplots, without which it is impossible to understand the process, consequences and ramifications of globalisation.

4.4   Partnerships in conflicts and terrorism: can there be endogenously-driven terror cycles?

Chaotic behaviour can characterise many important facets of economics (Saari, 1996). We now know that complex and unpredictable behaviour is not only a product of complex systems with many degrees of freedom but can also be caused by simple and deterministic dynamic systems. Since the early 1980s, a series of important papers has highlighted the relevance of non-linear dynamic models exhibiting chaotic dynamical behaviour in economics (see Benhabib and Day, 1982; Day, 1982; Jensen and Urban, 1984; Hommes, 1991 and 1993).

4.4.1   Basic Setting

From the previous sections, we formulate terror groups as specific assets which are financed and 'owned in some sense' by global/international decision-makers. Like any asset we now postulate a quasi-market for terror assets and explore how market equilibrium and equilibrium asset price dynamics will evolve. In this segment we draw attention to some very complex behaviour that occurs in simple models of equilibrium asset prices in quasi-markets that we have already postulated. In our quasi-market, for each asset there is a group of buyers and a group of sellers. We posit that both buyers and sellers of an asset face a gamble regarding the future value of an asset, related to the unknown element of law enforcement. At the point in time, one can only make honest guesses. In reality, the value of the asset may increase or decline. We derive the asset price dynamics associated with terror activities based on the expected value of this gamble. This example is, in its context, structurally stable although the underlying dynamics are not straightforward. We find that the dynamics of this model are represented by a quadratic map of the type that is well recognised in the literature on chaos. Although asset price dynamics are completely deterministic, we show that these dynamics can evolve in a chaotic fashion under a set of usual parametric restrictions.

4.4.2   Heuristics

The unusual dynamics of terrorism in the Middle East and North Africa can be confirmed from Figure 4.2 in which we plot terror attacks in the seven chosen countries (see the footnote to Figure 4.2) along the vertical axis and years of attack along the horizontal axis. The figure shows a serious spike in terror attacks, though the dynamic path for each country is complex. In Figure 4.3 we plot the time dynamics of aggregate terror attacks ($ATAR$) on the seven countries of the region. The same apparent picture of a sudden spike with a complex temporal path is observed from Figure 4.3.

We consider the basic model of terrorism in Figure 4.4. The foundation of our model is rooted in the work of Chai (1993) who applied the new

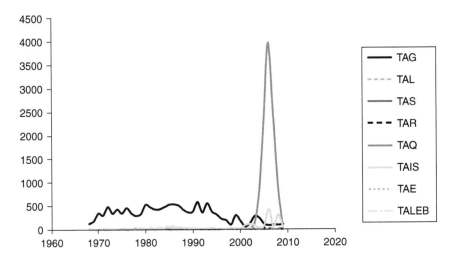

Figure 4.2 Time profile of terror attacks in the region

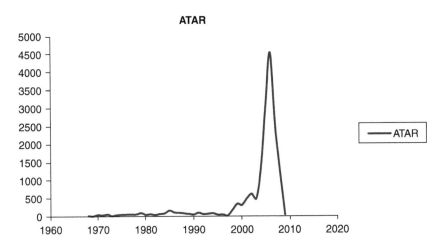

Figure 4.3 Time profile of aggregate terror attacks in the region

institutional economics to understand terrorist organisations. Following the work of Chai (1993) and Shapiro and Siegel (2007), we dichotomise a terrorist organisation into two interdependent cells: first, we have the terrorist leaders and political representatives who are depicted in the top right-hand box of Figure 4.4. Terrorist leaders recruit a network of operators who undertake terrorist-related activities. The network of operators is described in the

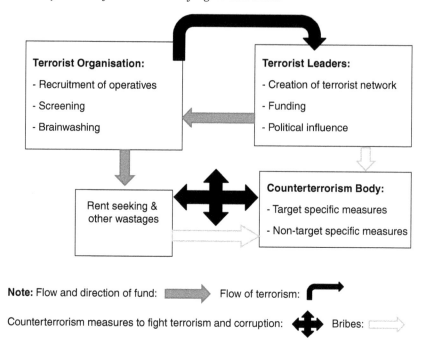

Figure 4.4 The complex web of terrorism

left-hand box. The leaders are responsible for financial and other resources and delegate the task of terrorism to the operators. Thus, funds flow from the left box to the right box. In return terror-related activities flow from the left to the right box. As we know from the literature, the terrorist operators may engage in rent seeking, which is depicted as a downward flow of funds and resources out of the operatives' cell. Resources can also flow from the operatives' cell to the counterterrorism authority as bribes. The terrorist leaders can also bribe the counterterrorism authority directly. From Bloom (2005), Siqueira (2005) and Bueno de Mesquita (2008) we know that the terrorism will critically depend on screening, brain-washing, rent seeking and factionalisation among terror operatives. These problems will also be predicated on the degree of cooperation among operatives due to imperfect group cohesion within the terrorist organisation as highlighted by Berman (2003) and Iannaccone and Berman (2006). Finally, both terrorist leaders and their operatives strategically respond to the counterterrorism strategies and counterterrorism in turn depends on terrorist activities. The complex web is described in Figure 4.4 as the basic model of terrorism that will be deployed to derive important insights.

The main intuition is that the web should be smoothly functioning in converting potential terrorist assets into real assets and actual terrorist activities to influence the public policy in favour of the terrorist leaders. The leaders face hindrances from the counterterrorism authority. The leaders also face hindrances due to agency problems within the network of operatives. If potential assets are converted into actual assets too quickly, then the system becomes fragile due to agency problems within the organisation. On the one hand, if the process is too slow, then the counterterrorism authority will predict and thwart the terror attacks. Thus, we posit, there is threshold in the speed of adjustment in the market for terrorism. If the actual speed is below the threshold, then the system converts to a Nash equilibrium and the terror leaders and their network will home in on the Nash equilibrium to create terror attacks. On the other hand, if the speed adjustment is above the threshold, the system will be chaotic for leaders and their operatives to rationally unleash terror attacks. Rational terrorists will then stay away from terror activities and wait for the more opportune moment. What we intend to show is that a host of national and regional factors can determine the speed of adjustment at which potential resources are converted into terrorist assets and will thereby influence terrorism in a country or a region.

Here we posit no fundamental difference between the price of a terror asset and the value of the terror asset. The price reflects the value to the terror operatives and their leaders. At date t the asset price can take two values – either a high or a low one. The high value materialises if the agency problems, recruitment and monitoring of operatives issues are overcome within a terrorist organisation. We define the high value as $(R^N + \Delta_t)$ while the probability of its occurrence is $(1-\lambda)$; and the low value is $(R^N - \Delta_t)$ and the corresponding probability is λ. The low value materialises when the terrorist organisation succumbs to the above organisational problems. One may presume that R^N is the long-run value/price of the asset and Δ represents a short-run deviation from the long-run value. It is further postulated that the probability of low price (λ) is positively related to the magnitude of deviation Δ (ignoring the time subscript):

$$\lambda = \eta\Delta \text{ where } \eta > 0 \text{ and } \Delta \neq 0 \tag{1a'}$$

(1a') indicates that the larger the magnitude of deviation from the long-run value/price, the larger is the probability that the asset price will assume the lower of the two possible values. We expect to stamp out any irrational exuberance by the assumption in (1a').

We call V_t the expected value of a gamble of holding the terror asset at date t, which is given as:

$$V_t = R^N + (1-\eta R^N)\Delta_t - n\Delta_t^2 \tag{1a}$$

We postulate that the demand for the asset at date $t+1$ (D_{t+1}) bears a positive relation with the expected value of the gamble at date t (V_t):

$$D_{t+1} = c + dV_t \tag{1b}$$

The assumption (1b) is free of controversies.

We postulate that supply of the asset at date $t+1$ (S_{t+1}) bears a negative relation with the value of the asset at date t (V_t):

$$S_{t+1} = a - bV_t \tag{1c}$$

The assumption (1c) is not too comfortable: as the value of the asset increases, the terror groups find it difficult to supply more units. One way of rationalising the assumption is that the terror groups have finite and fixed needs for financial resources and motivation of terrorists which they can raise with a lower floating of the terror asset given the increase in the price/value of each unit of asset. If equation (1c) is different to what has been postulated, we will need additional conditions to derive our central results.

The excess demand for a terrorist asset at date $t+1$ is X_{t+1}:

$$X_{t+1} = (c-a) + (d+b)V_t \tag{1d}$$

The price of the terror asset is assumed to display a finite pace of adjustment as described in

$$\Delta_{t+1} = KX_{t+1} \tag{2a}$$

$$\Delta_{t+1} = k(c-a) + k(d+b)V_t \tag{2b}$$

while k is the speed of price adjustment.

Thus, $\Delta_{t+1} > 0$ if $k(a-c)/(d+b) < V_t$ \hfill (2c)

And $\Delta_{t+1} < 0 \, \Delta_{t+1} < 0$ if $k(a-c)/(d+b) > V_t$ \hfill (2d)

Based on these we propose the following lemma.

Lemma 1: The dynamics of price of the terror asset is captured by the following difference equation:

$$\Delta_{t+1} = m - h\Delta_t + A\Delta_t^2 \tag{3a}$$

where $m = k(c-a) - k(d+b)R^N$ \hfill (3b)

$$h = k(1 - nR^N)(d+b) \tag{3c}$$

$$A = k(d+b)n \tag{3d}$$

Proof: Substitution of (2b) and (2c) into (3b) yields the result. QED.

Lemma 2: The above dynamics has two fixed points Δ^*, Δ^{**}:

$$\Delta^* = \left[(1+h) - \sqrt{\{(1+h)^2 - 4Am\}}\right]/(2A) \tag{4a}$$

$$\Delta^{**} = \left[(1+h) + \sqrt{\{(1+h)^2 - 4Am\}}\right]/(2A) \tag{4b}$$

Δ^{**} is always unstable. Δ^* is stable if

$$\left[\sqrt{\{(1+h)^2 - 4Am\}}\right] < 2 \tag{4c}$$

Proof: The derivation, being simple, is omitted. QED.

If the equilibrium, Δ^*, is stable, then the asset price dynamics (3a) in the asset market will drive prices to the equilibrium. This happens if the initial price is close enough as dictated by (4c). If the price at any date t should go beyond Δ^{**}, then this unstable fixed point will cause the asset price to diverge. As a consequence, the system will fail to reach the equilibrium and the possibility of a self-fulfilling prophecy in terrorism for terrorists will disappear. A corollary of it is the impossibility of predicting the long-run outcome of a terrorist attack and a rational terrorist organisation will not be able to choose an optimal strategy in the context of terror strikes. For the asset prices to be bounded it is imperative that the following is true:

$$\Delta_t < \Delta^{**} = \Delta^{\max} \text{ for } t = 0,1,2,3.... \text{ and} \tag{4d}$$
$$\Delta_t > h/A - \Delta^{**} = \Delta^{\min} \text{ for } t = 0,1,2,3.... \tag{4e}$$

Thus, asset prices will be bounded if the initial price lies on the interval $\left[\Delta^{\min}, \Delta^{\max}\right]$ and

$$\sqrt{\{(1+h)^2 - 4Am\}} < 3 \tag{4}$$

If the restrictions on the parameters and initial prices, equations (4d)–(4f) hold, the asset price dynamics remain bounded between $\Delta^{\min}$ and $\Delta^{\max}$. Following Feigenbaum (1978) we now apply the change of variable technique that will transform the non-linear price dynamics to the logistic equation of May (1976).

Lemma 3: The quadratic asset price dynamics (3a) are equivalent to the following logistic equation with an appropriate transformation of the variable Δ:

$$P_t = h(\Delta^{**} - \Delta_t)/M \tag{5a}$$

$$M = 1 + \sqrt{\left\{ (1+h)^2 - 4Am \right\}} \tag{5b}$$

$$P_t = BP_{t-1}(1 - P_{t-1}) \tag{5c}$$

Proof: The derivation is omitted. QED.

For $1 < M < 3$ the price converges to the stable equilibrium Δ^*. If $M > 3$ then Δ^* becomes unstable and the asset prices converge to a stable two-period cycle. As M is increased further the stable period cycles of period n bifurcate into cycles of $2n$. At $M = 3.57$ the asset prices evolve through a cycle of infinite period. The asset prices are within the relevant bounds but they never repeat. For a higher order, the asset prices may look like a random process but they are fully deterministic. For values of M greater than 3.57 we can have even more complex behaviour.

Result 1: The asset prices evolve through a cycle of infinite period and hence never repeat themselves if

$$Am > \left[6.60 - (1+h)^2 \right] \Big/ 4 \tag{6a}$$

As a result, it is not possible for terrorists to have self-fulfilling expectations. They will not be able to coordinate their multiple stakeholders and the probability of a successful terrorist strike will decrease.

Result 2: In order to place these results in a sharper focus we consider a special case where $R^N = 1/\lambda$; then we know $h = 0$, $A = k(d+b)\lambda$, $m = (c-a) - k(d+b)(1/\lambda)$. Then the chaotic dynamics emerge at

$$(1+h)^2 - 4Am > 6.60 \tag{6b}$$

The substitution of h, A and m will reduce (6b) to

$$1 + 4k(d+b)(d+b+\lambda a - \lambda c) > 6.60 \tag{6c}$$

Thus, the chaotic dynamics emerge if the speed of price adjustment is beyond a threshold:

$$k > k^* = 1.4 \Big/ \left[(d+b)(d+b+\lambda a - \lambda c) \right] \tag{6d}$$

The price dynamics converge to the stable equilibrium if the speed of price adjustment k is such that

$$k < k^{**} = 0.75 \Big/ \left[(d+b)(d+b+\lambda a - \lambda c) \right] \tag{6e}$$

4.4.3   Observation

It is now well recognised in economics science that chaos cannot be given short shrift as an outcome of highly artificial models. Seemingly innocuous models can exhibit chaotic dynamic behaviour, as confirmed in this chapter. The source of the chaotic behaviour in this chapter is in the series of complicated decisions that economic agents make to buy, or sell, an asset on the basis of the expected value of the proposed gamble involving unknown future (asset) prices. The resultant asset price dynamics do not have sufficient refined properties that may eventually lead to radical behaviour (Saari, 1996). It is therefore the basic nature of the economic problems that confront decision-makers in the asset market that triggers chaotic dynamic behaviour in asset prices. The upshot is that the speed of price adjustment can be a critical factor in determining whether asset price dynamics evolve through a cycle of infinite period. We are able to derive two critical values of the speed of price adjustment k^* and k^{**}: if the actual speed of price adjustment k is such that $k > k^*$ then the asset prices remain bounded but never repeat. Thus the price dynamics exhibit chaotic dynamical behaviour for $k > k^*$. Asset prices can show time behaviour that is seemingly random but is purely deterministic. In this case, terrorists fail to make long-run predictions even though they act in a deterministic world. Time profiles that start very close together will separate exponentially. On the other hand, for values of speed of price adjustment k such that $k < k^{**}$, the asset price dynamics converge on a stable equilibrium. As a result, the terror agents can predict and achieve the terror equilibrium and counterterrorism will fail to prevent terrorist attacks. On the other hand, for k such that $k > k^*$, the system will not converge on a unique equilibrium and terrorist organisations will fail to coordinate their activities effectively. As a result, the effectiveness and incidence of terrorism will decline. Thus, any factor that influences the speed of price adjustment can have a long-lasting effect on terrorism. It is now an empirical question to assess the factors that promote and the factors that inhibit terrorism. In the following section we will address the empirical foundation to the theory.

4.5   The calculus of terrorism: causes and consequences of terror strikes in the Middle East and North Africa

In the existing literature, there are two strands of thought to understanding the economic consequences of terrorism: the formal models by Eckstein and Tsiddon (2004) and many other works focus on a very particular factor and specific channels through which terrorism affects the economy. In their work Eckstein and Tsiddon (2004) choose a closed economy model and put forward the proposition that terrorism raises the discount rate, which in turns translates into a reduction of income and other macroeconomic variables. The pertinent question in this context is whether terrorism

Table 4.1 Data and variables of interest for terrorism

Variable	Definition	Data Source
Terrorism Index: $(TI_1)_i$	Natural Logarithm of Annual Terror Incidents in Country i	RAND Database of Worldwide Terrorism Incidents (1968–2009)*
Terrorism Index: $(TI_2)_i$	Ratio of terror incidents in the i_{th} (chosen) country and terror incidents in the rest of the world	Calculated from the data from the Rand Database of Worldwide Terrorism Incidents
Regional Terror Index: RTI_1	$RT1=LN(\Sigma i\,(TI)i)$, for $i=1,2...7$ – the chosen seven countries	As above
Regional Terror Index: RTI_2	$RT_2=[(\Sigma i\,(TI)i]/[(\Sigma n-7\,(TI)n-7)$, $(n-7)$ denotes the rest of the world excluding 7 countries.	As above
AVVI	Average/Arithmetic Mean of the vulnerability index (VI) of seven nations chosen.	Calculated from the VI of individual countries presented in Chapter 2.
AVM	Average of military imports in natural logarithmic value for the chosen nations.	Calculated from ARMIM of each nation presented in Chapter 3.
AVGDP	Average (log) of per capita GDP of the region in the 2012 US$	Calculated from the individual per capita GDP of nations as in Table 3.2 in Chapter 3
ALLARIM	Natural log of annual arms imports by the seven nations.	Calculated from data in Chapter 3.

Note: The terror data set is created by the authors after downloading incidents from www.rand.org/nsrd/projects/terrorism-incidents.html.

palpably impacts on the vulnerability of a segment of population in a country, or region such that agents change their behaviour, which will then adversely impact on the macroeconomic performances of the region, or country. The implicit assumption is that terrorism increases the vulnerability of the targeted group as their death rates and mortality rates rise and such rises then alter investment and consumption behaviours of private agents along with far-reaching changes in public investment. In Chapter 2 we have introduced, developed and calculated the vulnerability index (VI) for seven nations from the Middle East and North Africa for which we have data from 1960 to 2013. Table 4.1 defines the variables and data sources.

One of our major contributions to the literature is to apply the vulnerability index to the terrorism research for understanding whether and how terrorism impacts on the vulnerability of the chosen nations during 1968–2009. We will also seek to establish the reverse causality: how vulnerability of a nation impacts on terrorism among other economic factors. Once again the period of study is dictated by the availability of data on terrorism in the region from February 1968 to December 2009. Abadie and Gardeazabal (2008) were proposed to study the impact of terrorism on the economy. On the other hand, Abadie and Gardeazabal (2008) by exploiting an open economy model take capital outflows as a consequence of terrorism. The adverse effect of terrorism on the economy materialises through capital flight.

The following important lessons we arrive at from Table 4.2.1 and Table 4.2.2: first and foremost, there is a long-term equilibrium relationship, both economically meaningful and statistically significant, between the regional terrorism index (RTI_2) and the vulnerability of all seven nations in the region. However, the vulnerability of nations has heterogeneous impacts on regional terrorism: we note that increases (decreases) in vulnerability in Libya, Syria and Iran, Israel will increase (decrease) terrorism in the region. In other words, there is a direct relationship between RTI_2 and the vulnerability of these nations. However, the relationship reverses for Iraq, Egypt and Lebanon with an inverse relationship between RTI_2 and the vulnerability of these three nations. As opposed to the strand of research led by Eckstein and Tsiddon (2004), we find that terrorism does not have an unequivocal impact on the vulnerability of a nation, in their work death rates. Terrorism lowers vulnerability for some nations but enhances resilience in others. The heterogeneous effect materialises through some interesting channels, which we will explore in the subsequent sections.

Second, we also find that global warming (LNT) increases terrorism in the region – the effect is also statistically significant. Third, the global oil market has its influence on RTI_2: the larger the global demand for oil, the lower will be the RTI_2. However, the oil price has a counter-balancing impact on terrorism in the region.

In Table 4.2.2 we present the Granger causality results that can offer further insights into the relationship between terrorism and other variables of interest. We present the results for the first index of terrorism only as the results are not sensitive to the choice of index of terrorism. First, we note that there is no evidence of Granger causality running from country-specific vulnerability and regional terrorism. This does not preclude the possibility of Granger causality from lagged values of the vulnerability to terrorism since it takes time for vulnerability to create terrorism. Second, there is evidence that regional terrorism (RTI_1) has the Granger causality for vulnerability in Syria, Iraq, Iran, Egypt and Lebanon. There is no such evidence for Israel and Libya. Third, global warming (LNT) has Granger causality for vulnerability in Libya, Syria, Iraq, Israel, Egypt and Lebanon. We don't find any causality running from global warming to vulnerability in Iran. Finally, we also find the evidence of Granger causality from the global oil market to national vulnerability for Libya (LNO and LNP), Syria (LNO), Iraq (LNO, LNP), Israel (LNP), Egypt (LNP) and Lebanon (LNO and LNP).

Table 4.2.1 Cointegration between terrorism and vulnerability from Johansen approach

	VIL	VIS	VIIR	VIIQ	VIIS	VIEG	VILEB	LNT	LNO	LNP
RTI_1	50.0*	47.3*	71.4*	−7.1*	14.75*	−7.22*	−59*	20.4*	−5.2*	6.5*
Z	11.09	10.74	18.31	8.43	2.30	−5.86	−11.13	4.9	−9*	8.8*

Note: The variables in the first row are defined in Chapter 2 as the vulnerability of the chosen nations.

Table 4.2.2 Important sources of Granger causality for terrorism

Dependent Variable	Causal/Excluded Variable	Chi²	Prob>Chi²
RTI₁	No Regional Causes		
VILIBYA	*VIRAN*	16.9	0.0000*
VILIBYA	*VIIRAQ*	11.41	0.003*
VILIBYA	*VIEGYPT*	7.94	0.019**
VILYBIA	*LNT*	10.4	0.006*
VILIBYA	*LNO*	14.8	0.001*
VILIBYA	*LNP*	6.02	0.049**
VILIBYA	*ALL*	76.8	0.0000*
VISYRIA	*RTI₁*	5.63	0.06**
VISYRIA	*VIIRAN*	15.64	0.0000*
VISYRIA	*VIIRAQ*	6.7	0.034**
VISYRIA	*VIEGYPT*	9.4	0.009*
VISYRIA	*LNT*	16.53	0.0000*
VISYRIA	*LNO*	18.21	0.0000*
VISYRIA	*ALL*	75.49	0.0000*
VIIRAN	*VILIBYA*	5.55	0.06**
VIRAN	*LNT*	6.03	0.049**
VIIRAQ	*ALL VARIABLES*	Min=8.75	Max=0.013
VIISRAEL	*RTI₁*	5.11	0.075**
VIISRAEL	*VIEGYPT*	13.607	0.001*
VIISRAEL	*LNP*	12.31	0.002*
VIISRAEL	*ALL*	66.49	0.0000*
VIEGYPT	*RTI₁*	9.45	0.001*
VIEGYPT	*VILYBIA*	18.85	0.0000*
VIEGYPT	*VISYRIA*	11.9	0.003*
VIEGYPT	*VIIRAN*	5.44	0.06**
VIEGYPT	*VILEBANON*	12.21	0.002*
VIEGYPT	*LNP*	5.38	0.06**
VILEBANON	*ALL*	Min=7.04	Max=0.03

Note: We have expanded the abbreviations, for instance *VIL* is now *VILibya*, as the variable name.

4.6 Arms imports as a counterterrorism strategy: militarisation and terrorism in the Middle East and North Africa

An important insight into the problem of optimal counterterrorism through military interventions is due to Enders and Sandler's (1993) postulation that terrorism is intrinsically linked to government policies to rout terrorism. In their work they argue that terrorists respond strategically to counterterrorism measures, which will engender the 'substitution effect.' That is, rational terrorists, on watching an increase in a particular government counterterrorism program, will switch tactics. Terrorists will pursue attacks less affected by the government's efforts. In a large body of literature, a variety of empirical studies confirm that counterterrorism generates such effects (Enders and Sandler 1993, 2002; Enders, Sandler and Cauley, 1990; Im, Cauley and Sandler 1987).

As an example, Enders and Sandler (1993) argue that when the United States installed metal detectors in airports in the 1970s, hijackings went down but other forms of terrorism increased. Both Bueno de Mesquita (2007) and Powell (2007a, 2007c) build on this insight in order to home in on the optimal division of counterterrorism resources in game theoretic models. Bueno de Mesquita's (2007) analysis (which is primarily focused on why we observe suboptimal counterterrorism) is restricted to a zero-sum game between the terrorists and the government where the government allocates resources prior to the terrorists attacking. Powell (2007a, 2007c) offer a greater range, developing games that are simultaneous or sequential moves (respectively) and that need not be zero sum. The relevant message from Bueno de Mesquita (2007) and Powell (2007c) is the following: first, both show the possibility that the government can invest in counterterrorism that is not target-specific (as examples, border security or intelligence). The advantage of such measures is that it is more difficult for terrorists to substitute away from them. Thus, as the number of targets that need to be defended increases, counterterrorism that is not target specific becomes more effective.

From Table 4.3 we detect the strengths of the insights of Bueno de Mesquita (2007) and Powell (2007a, 2007c): first and foremost, we find that arms imports by a nation, as a proxy for counterterrorism measures, have heterogeneous effects as predicted by Bueno de Mesquita (2007) and Powell (2007a, 2007c) in the context of the Middle East and North Africa. As the signs of their coefficients show in Table 4.3, arms imports as a counterterrorism measure in Israel, Iraq and Lebanon are target-specific as such imports are met with increased incidents of terrorism. On the contrary, arms imports for Libya, Syria, Iran and Egypt help their counterterrorism strategies to move away from target-specific projects, which will see a decline in terrorism in the region. There are various other channels through which the heterogeneous effects materialise. We will turn to the other channels in the next section.

Once we take stock of the Granger causality, as in Table 4.4, we see that arms imports of Libya, Syria, Iran, Iraq and Lebanon have causal effects on regional terrorism. It is also important to stress from Table 4.3 that imports of Libya, Syria and Iran reduce regional terrorism, while such imports for Iraq and Lebanon intensify regional terrorism. Arms imports thus are a mixed bag for the region.

Table 4.3 Cointegration between terrorism and arms imports

	ARIML	*ARIMS*	*ARIMIR*	*ARIMIQ*	*ARIMIS*	*ARIMEG*	*ARIMLEB*
RTI_1	−1.66*	−2.17*	−0.115	7.28*	7.06*	−7.22*	2.719*
Z	−17.23	−4.7	−0.12	8.43	12.58	−5.86	4.42

* Statistically significant as shown by the values of Z

Table 4.4 Granger causality Wald tests for terrorism

Dependent Variable	Excluded Variable	Chi²	Prob>Chi²
RTI_1	ARIML	68.9*	0.0000
RTI_1	ARIMS	14.80*	0.001
RTI_1	ARIMIR	6.601**	0.037
RTI_1	ARIMIQ	10.84*	0.004
RTI_1	ARIMLEB	11.7*	0.003
RTI_1	ALL	100.09	0.0000

* Statistically significant
** Marginally significant

Table 4.5 Optimal lags and ranks: statistical results

Lag Order	Min. AIC	Min. HQIC	Min. SBIC	
4	$7.4e^{-50}$*	−97.76*	−86.38*	
VECRANK	Parm	Eigenvalue	Trace Stat	5% Confidence Value
0	132		525.9	277.71
1	153	0.95	399.91	233.13
2	172	0.91	300.68	192.89
3	189	0.88	213.14	156
4	204	0.78	152.57	124.24
5	217	0.75	95.24	94.15
6	228	0.65	53.58*	68.52

Note: Constructed by the authors from various statistical tests conducted in STATA.

In Table 4.5 we presented some background statistical results to confirm that the Johansen's method to derive the cointegration relationship in the context of arms imports is robust. As examples, both the lag order and the trace statistics support the choice of vecrank and the optimal lag so that the cointegrating long-term relationship between terrorism and arms imports is statistically justified.

4.7 Terrorism, global warming and the global oil market: is there a missing link?

In Table 4.7 we present the long-term cointegration relationship between terrorism in the Middle East and North Africa (RTI_1) and annual global temperature (*LNT*), annual global oil output (*LNO*) and average annual oil price (*LNP*) during 1968–2009. The results shown are the Johansen test results for these variables. Both the optimal lag and vector rank confirm the existence of at least one cointegrating relationship among the variables. The Johansen tests confirm that increases in *LNT*, *LNO* and militarisation

Table 4.6.1 Cointegration equation for terrorism in the region

Dependent Variable	Variable 1	Variable 2	Variable 3	Variable 4
RTI_l	LNT	LNP	LNO	ALLARIM
	108.5*	−2.3378*	6.52*	0.20*
Z Value	4.36	−6.46	3.10	8.91
Optimal Lag	Min. FEP	Min AIC	Min HQIC	Min SBIC
1	$1.0e^{-7}$	−2.3	−1.90	−1.07
Vec Rank	Trace Stat	CV***	Parm	eigenvalue
0	102.02	68.52	30	.
1	60.21	29.68	39	0.64
2	28.69	15.41	46	0.54

* Significant
** Marginally significant
*** 5% Confidence value

Table 4.6.2 The Granger causality test for terrorism

Dependent Variable	Excluded Variable	Chi^2
RTI_l	LNP	9.29*
RTI_l	LNO	3.6**
RTI_l	ALLARIM	26.3*
ALLARIM	RTI1	5.3*
ALLARIM	LNT	7.5*

* Granger causality (strong)
** Granger causality (weak)

of the region (increase in *ALLARIM*) increase terrorism in the region. However, the oil price hike (*LNP*) reduces terrorism in the region. In a nutshell, we find evidence that global warming and militarisation are important causes of terrorism in the Middle East and North Africa for the chosen nations. The global oil market is a mixed bag: oil production increases terrorism while oil price inflation lowers terrorism. More detailed studies are necessary to explore the link between the global oil market and terrorism in the region.

In Tables 4.6.1 and 4.6.2 we present the Granger causality test results for variables that are found to cause the dependent variables. First and foremost, we find evidence that the global oil market Granger causes terrorism in the region. However, we find no evidence of causality for global warming. An extended analysis will be undertaken to understand the role of global warming in

Table 4.7.1 Definitions of variables

Acronym	Definition of the Variable
GDPL	Per capita GDP of Libya in 2012 US$
GDPS	Per capita GDP of Syria in 2012 US$
GDPI	Per capita GDP of Iran in 2012 US$
GDPQ	Per capita GDP of Iraq in 2012 US$
GDPIS	Per capita GDP of Israel in 2012 US$
GDPE	Per capita GDP of Egypt in 2012 US$
GDPLB	Per capita GDP of Lebanon in 2012 US$

Note: Constructed from the data source given in Chapter 2.

the next subsection. It is important to note that militarisation (*ALLARIM*) Granger causes terrorism in the region. In turn, both global warming and terrorism in the region Granger cause militarisation of the region. As a result, one can safely conclude that the region has been seriously impacted by global warming, global oil markets and militarisation.

4.8 The impact of per capita GDP on terrorism in the Middle East and North Africa

In this subsection we will explore the long-term relationships between the per capita GDP and terrorism in the region. The per capita GDPs of the seven chosen nations are chosen as the explanatory variables and the dependent variable is the regional index of terrorism (RTI_l). In Table 4.7.1 we present the acronyms for the variables. In Table 4.7.2 we present the long-term relationship between terrorism in the region and country-specific per capita GDP. The observations are as follows: first and foremost, the per capita GDP has heterogeneous effects on terrorism in the region: as the per capita GDP rises (falls) in Libya, Syria and Lebanon, regional terrorism declines (rises). For Iran, Iraq, Israel and Egypt the impacts are the reverse: as their per capita GDP rises (falls) terrorism rises (declines). We will offer explanations for the heterogeneity in the next subsection. Second, we also note that the impacts of oil price and quantity have reversed once we introduce the per capita GDP variables, though the global oil market has a strong and statistically significant impact on regional terrorism. Third, in Table 4.9, equation 1 shows that the per capita GDP of each country – except Israel – Granger causes terrorism in the region. So, not only do we find evidence of heterogeneous long-term effects of per capita income of a country on regional terrorism, but we are also able to establish the causality of per capita GDP in determining regional terrorism. Finally, equation 1 also shows that the global oil market (*LNO* and *LNP*) and global warming (*LNT*) Granger cause regional terrorism (see Table 4.8).

Table 4.7.2 Per capita GDP as the determinant of terror strikes in the region

	GDPL	GDPS	GDPI	GDPQ	GDPIS	GDPE	GDPLB	AVM	AVVI	LNT	LNO	LNP
I^	-65*	-7*	30*	2*	88*	36*	-92*	8*	32*	74*	-3*	2*

^ Dependent variable I is RTI_1

Table 4.8 Granger causality Wald test results

Dependent Variable	*Causal Variable*	*Chi²*	*Prob>Chi²*	
Equation 1				
RTI₁	*GDP Libya*	12.4	0.0000*	
RTI₁	*GDP Syria*	3.8	0.03**	
RTI₁	*GDP Iran*	4	0.03**	
RTI₁	*GDP Iraq*	8	0.038*	
RTI₁	*GDP Israel*	6	0.05**	
RTI₁	*GDP Egypt*	6.72	0.042**	
RTI₁	*GDP Lebanon*	6.8	0.04*	
RTI₁	*AVM*	50	0.0000*	
RTI₁	*AVVI*	23	0.0000*	
RTI₁	*LNT*	10.87*	0.034**	
RTI₁	*LNO*	6.16	0.05**	
RTI₁	*LNP*	15.53	0.0000*	
RTI₁	*ALL*	148	0.0000*	
Equation 2				
GDP	**RTI1**	**LNT**	**AVM**	**AVVI**
GDP LIBYA	4.5**	5.06*	**0.23**	7.8*
GDP SYRIA	1.64	0.20	0.18	1.2
GDP IRAN	9.10*	12.43*	1.39	3.2***
GDP IRAQ	11.47*	1.91	3.5***	7.9*
GDP ISRAEL	4.47**	1.91	2.08	5.4*
GDP EGYPT	4.47*	2.01	2.08	5.5*
GDP LEBANON	27*	7.1*	14.35*	0.92

Equation 3			**Equation 4**	
Dependent Variable	Causal Variable	Chi²	Dependent Variable	Causal Variable (Chi²)
AVM	GDP LIBYA	5.34*	AVVI	*RTI₁ (26*)*
AVM	GDP IRAQ	10.25*	AVVI	*GDP Libya (49*)*
AVM	GDP ISRAEL	8.37*	AVVI	*GDP Syria (36*)*
AVM	GDP EGYPT	17*	AVVI	*GDP Iran (40*)*
AVM	GDP LEB	17.98*	AVVI	*GDP Iraq (56.2)* *
AVM	LNP	13.75*	AVVI	*GDP Israel (21.37*)*
			AVVI	*GDP Egypt (9.01*)*
			AVVI	*GDP LEB (4.5**)*
			AVVI	*AVM (12.34*)*
			AVVI	*LNT (24.61*)*
			AVVI	*GDP Egypt (9.01*)*
			AVVI	*GDP LEB (4.5**)*
			AVVI	*LNP (6.34*)*
			AVVI	*LNO (16.24*)*

* Statistically significant
** Marginally significant

4.9   Regional snapshot of terrorism: dynamics of average vulnerability and average militarisation and their impacts on regional terrorism

In order to provide the regional snapshot of terrorism, we consider a model involving the regional variables including RTI_1, $AVGDP$, $AVARIM$, $AVVI$. All variables are in natural logarithms and they are integrated of order 1, $I(1)$. $AVGDP$ gives the annual average per capita income/GDP in the region, $AVARIM$ is the annual average of arms imports in the region and $AVVI$ is the annual average of the vulnerability index of the region. In addition to the regional variables, we also choose global variables LNT, LNO and LNP. It is instructive to note that the average value is calculated from the data of the seven chosen countries from the Middle East and North Africa. Table 4.9 presents the results for Johansen cointegration tests. The optimal lag and the rank tests establish at least one cointegrating (long-term) relationship among variables with an optimal lag of at least 2.

The long-term relationships offer some interesting insights: first, as the average per capita income/GDP of the region increases (decreases), regional terrorism declines (increases). The inverse relationship between income and terrorism is a time-honoured, though often challenged, adage in economics. There are many channels, as we discussed in the introduction to this chapter, through which per capita income exerts an influence on terrorism. It suffices to say that the opportunity costs of terrorism for terrorist operatives increase with rising per capita GDP and, hence, one should expect an inverse relationship between terrorism and per capita income of the region. Second, there is a small and positive and marginally significant statistical relationship between militarisation ($AVARIM$) and terrorism in the region. Thus, one can argue that arms imports are an integral component of counterterrorism strategy in the region and it is effective in deterring terrorism. Third, terrorism bears an inverse relationship with the average vulnerability of the region as the extensive literature has highlighted. The effect is statistically significant. The global factors all contribute positively to terrorism in the region though the impact of oil price on terrorism is marginally (statistically) significant. From Table 4.10 we find that $AVGDP$, $AVARIM$ and $AVVI$ Granger cause regional terrorism. From Table 4.9 we also note that the cointegrating relationship shows that the $AVGDP$ is negatively impacted by all variables except $AVVI$. Thus, economic growth in the region took place at the cost of its long-term sustainability. Global warming has a strong negative effect on the per capita income of the region. The global oil market exerted a negative influence on the per capita income as well. All coefficients are at least marginally significant. Regional terrorism, regional militarisation and regional vulnerability have Granger caused $AVGDP$. From the global oil market, LNP has Granger causality for the regional per capita income, $AVGDP$.

Regional vulnerability is (Granger) caused by all the variables chosen as Table 4.10 shows. Except $AVGDP$, all other explanatory variables lower

Table 4.9 Cointegration with the Johansen normalisation

Dependent Variable	Explanatory Variable	Coefficients (Z statistic)
RTI_1	AVGDP	−28*
	AVARIM	0.7**
	AVVI	−9.45*
	LNO	39.1*
	LNP	1.8**
	LNT	38*
AVGDP	RTI1	−0.33*
	AVARIM	−0.02**
	AVVI	0.33*
	LNO	−1.39*
	LNP	−0.06*
	LNT	−13.62
AVVI	RTI_1	−0.15**
	AVGDP	2.9*
	AVARIM	−0.07**
	LNO	−4.1*
	LNP	−0.19
	LNT	−40*
AVARIM	RTI_1	1.42**
	AVGDP	−4*
	AVVI	−13*
	LNO	5.5*
	LNP	2.59*
	LNT	54.7*

* Statistically significant
** Marginally significant

Table 4.10 The Granger causality: revisited

Dependent Variable	Excluded Variable	Chi²
RTI_1	AVGDP	3.75**
RTI_1	AVARIM	28.35*
RTI_1	LNO	5.1*
RTI_1	ALL	35*
AVGDP	RTI_1	4.13*
AVGDP	AVARIM	6.5*
AVGDP	AVVI	10*
AVGDP	LNP	3.7**
AVARIM	RTI_1	5.85*
AVVI	RTI_1	8.83*
AVVI	AVGDP	7.6*
AVVI	AVARIM	3.8**
AVVI	LNT	5.38*
AVVI	LNO	5.2*

* Statistically significant
** Marginally significant

regional vulnerability. This counter-intuitive result can be due to the aggregate picture of the region as factors have heterogeneous, often contradictory, effects on nations so that the aggregate picture masks individual country-specific effect. A detailed analysis will be offered in the next subsection.

The militarisation bears a long-run and positive relationship with regional terrorism (to counter terrorism), global warming and global oil markets. The impacts of *AVGDP* and *AVVI* on the regional militarisation are negative. Only terrorism (Granger) causes the militarisation of the region. A more detailed analysis will be offered in Chapter 6.

4.10   A complex chain of virtuous dynamics

Let us consider a positive shock to the average per capita GDP (*AVGDP*) to the group of seven nations. The effects of the shock are explained in Figure 4.5: the shock arises at the extreme left of the figure. The shock unleashes Granger causality on various variables as described by one of the arrows. The cointegration equations will determine the signs of change (+) or (–) for individual variables, which will further unleash Granger causality and the chain of reactions will continue. Given the empirical foundations of the cointegration equations and the Granger causality, the initial shock creates a series of changes such that the variables gradually change to recreate the same shock at every future point. One can visualise the recreation of the shocks by looking at the end states of the figure at which we can see *AVGDP* (+). This means that the shock starts again and creates similar changes to take the region to a higher and higher per capita GDP and lower and lower states of terrorism. We call this a virtuous dynamics. If the national governments of the region can coordinate their policies to create a massive income shock (positive), or lower terrorism – the regional system will create a virtuous dynamics as confirmed by the cointegration equations and the Granger causality. In Chapter 5 we focus

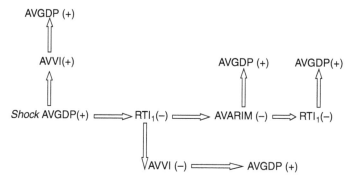

Figure 4.5 The virtuous dynamics from income shocks in the region

our attention on how to coordinate public policies to create the gale force to overcome terrorism and economic backwardness simultaneously.

All nodes hide complex long-term adjustment processes and Granger causality, but the effects mutually change each other in such a way that the above figure shows a virtuous dynamics. If we have an adverse shock, it will create exactly the opposite chain and the system will gravitate to bigger and bigger disasters. The upshot is that the system is extremely fragile for creating, maintaining and propelling peace and prosperity. Once we appreciate the fragility, then appropriate coordination can be undertaken to promote peace.

4.11   Conclusion

Terrorism is not only a clandestine operation but also extremely fragile – as our models establish on the basis of recent developments. We further find that terrorism has tenuous relationships with the national and regional economy, national and regional vulnerability and international factors like the global oil market. We further find that terrorism is often propelled by climatic factors like global warming. Not only does terrorism have the complex feedback mechanisms with the economy, polity and vulnerability of people, terrorism also makes an economic and social system fragile. In a system characterised by extremely fragile and equally dangerous dynamics of terrorism, environmental threats, and other forms of vulnerability, we are able to explore important determinants of terrorism in the Middle East and North Africa. We are able to explain how terrorism impacts on the regional economy, its security and long-term viability. We also find important impacts of terrorism on the economic, political and social systems of the Middle East. We are also able to shed invaluable light on the pathway to peace in such a fragile system. In Chapter 5 we will explain how micro-management can reduce fragility and build a stable society in the Middle East.

5 Conflict management procedure and its application to the Middle East

5.1 Introduction

The many peace plans (described in the Appendix) found little success, but did point out the areas of particular concern for Israelis and Palestinians: the status of Jerusalem, the treatment of refugees, border demarcation, and Israeli settlements in contested territory.

On 11 March 2004, India's cricketers made a 40-day tour of Pakistan for the first time in 14 years, in a step considered by many as a significant move towards strengthening the fragile peace between the two countries. About 8,000 Indian fans travelled to Pakistan to watch the event. On 7 April 2005, two buses crossed the border between the nations: a small but significant event, because it betokened a mutual improvement joint action. The main purpose of such a joint action is to break the ice between two parties and make the ensuing peace process irreversible.

Joint actions work to achieve global stability. Global stability is a position reached when all issues between two countries are regulated peacefully and the probability of war re-escalation between the two countries is so minor that it no longer enters into the calculations of the two parties (see Figure 5.1, which shows that the ball remains at the bottom always at the end). Local Stability is a state of affairs where a small perturbation of the system does not change the joint status quo position between belligerent groups (Axelrod, 1990; Newman, 1961) (see Figure 5.1, which indicates that small perturbations can't move the ball to a different hole) as articulated by Moyersoen (2007).

CMP combines two theoretical tools: First, it uses the prospect theory developed by Kahneman and Tversky (1979), and the related inter-temporal choice theory developed by Ainslie and Herrnstein (1981). Second, it uses the analytical hierarchy process and procedures (AHP) developed by Saaty (1980) and Isard and Azis (1999). CMP is based on three main steps: the first is elicitation and conflict analysis, the second phase in CMP detects local stable positions, and the third phase includes a deliberation process with the concerned groups regarding what kind of joint project would accord with the discovered satisfying position (Moyersoen, 2007).

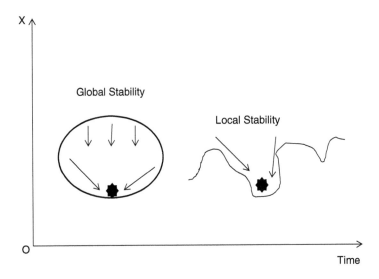

Figure 5.1 Global and local stability

In this chapter we are searching for an effective intervention in public policy decision-making through conflict analysis, using the prospect theory developed by Kahneman and Tversky (1979). Kahneman and Tversky (1979) explored how people take decisions in state of affairs involving uncertainty about outcomes. They have found that there is little empirical support for using rational analysis and prescription when taking a decision under uncertainty. For example, in simple situations (like the lottery where there is uncertainty about the result) they have found that people think of consequences as increments (or decrements) to current wealth (current wealth serves as reference points from which changes are made). In addition, when people relate their subjective values with improvements these values drop with the size of improvements. For example, the difference between a gain of $100 and a gain of $200 is greater than the subjective difference between a gain of $1,100 and $1,200 (the same concept works on loss, where the difference between a loss of $100 and a loss of $200 is greater than the subjective difference between a loss of $1,100 and $1,200).

5.1.1 A descriptive foundation for irrevocable decisions in conflict escalation

An irrevocable decision is a decision that is impossible to revoke, retract or change, which alters the stable status quo in a way that is difficult to forecast, and where the decision-maker is faced with a credible risk in time to face

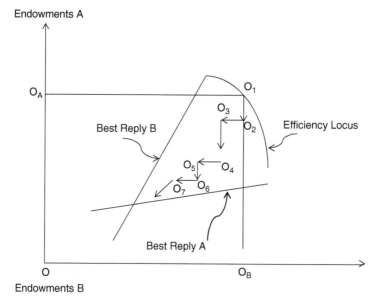

Figure 5.2 A simple model of conflict escalation

important negative consequences of the decision (Luterbacher, 2004). To understand this we will take the Israd-Smith model of conflict escalation to understanding an irrevocable decision between two parties A and B (Figure 5.2). Figure 5.2 describes an argument between A and B on how to divide the burden of a public good project.

The figure carries two best reply lines, one for actor A and the other for actor B. Each point on best reply line A gives the best investment for a given particular outlay of group B for the project (any point on best reply line A would optimise benefits for actor A). Any point on the arc, the efficiency frontier, denotes joint actions that are neither strongly nor weakly dominated by some other joint action. The initial equilibrium position between actor A and B is point O_1. If we assume that actor A is an adventurous person who wants to maximise his benefits, he will try to decrease his contributions from O_1 to O_2 in the project to move closer to his best reply line A. At O_2 actor B becomes poorer compared to O_1, so he learns from A and decreases his contributions to move from point O_2 to O_3, closer to his best reply line B. This scenario continues until both actors A and B have moved away from an efficient solution (efficient frontier) and become worse off. The irrevocable decision is the decision taken by actor A to deviate from point O_1 to O_2, which is difficult to revoke, retract or change.

5.1.2 *Inter-temporal choice theory to identify local stable positions*

In view of the fact that actors are myopic in their decision taking, we have to introduce time discounting as a key instrument for conflict deliberation. If one actor intends to bargain for another agreement as an alternative to the planned agreement, he or she is aware that this will hold up the bargaining course. Altering an agreement needs cautious bargaining, which is a time-squandering process that heightens the risk of re-escalation. Utility discounting is intended to include all explanations that reduce one's expected utility for alternative outcomes, such as bargaining time, changing tastes, uncertainty etc. We presume that alternative agreements engaging insignificant changes from the suggested proposed agreement have to be discounted at a rate not more than that for agreements involving significant changes.

As a result of prospect theory assumptions, in CMP we will apply discounting models in which the shorter term has higher discount rates than the longer term. Looking at the literature we find three common discounting formulas:

1. $F(d) = \dfrac{1}{d}$ (see Ainslie, 1975)

2. $F(d) = \dfrac{1}{(1+\alpha d)}$ (see Mazur and Hernstein, 1988)

3. $F(d) = (1+\alpha d)^{-\beta/\alpha}$ where $\alpha, \beta > 0$ (see Loewenstein and Prelec, 1991)

For this chapter we will choose the second model by Herrnstein and Mazur because it is simple, clear, and easy to deploy. To measure the distance between a possible and an alternative position, we will take the absolute difference between the positions for all accounted objectives divided by two (see the formula below).

$$d(A(x,y,z) \rightarrow B(x',y',z'))$$

$$d(A \rightarrow B) = \frac{|x-x'| + |y-y'| + |z-z'|}{2}$$

Each objective for each party will have a different level of conflict sensitivity factor. The sensitivity factor reflects the degree of sensitivity of each party to a change from their most preferred policy action for a given objective. Sometimes a small change from their most preferred action for an objective may lead to a severe decrease of utility: this kind of objective is a conflict sensitive objective. In a non-conflict sensitive objective, a 10% or 15% change from the most preferred position will not cause a great difference for the actor. As a result, in non-conflict objectives we require low discount rates to trigger preference reversals, and for conflict objectives we need higher discount rates to trigger preference reversals. The lowest discount rate for the non-conflict

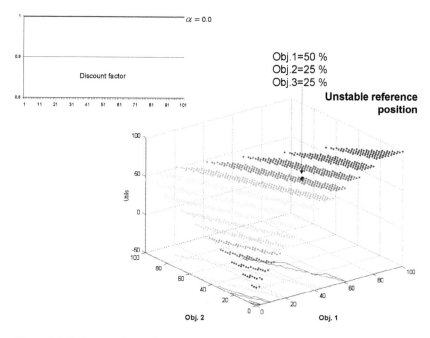

Figure 5.3 Reference dependent preference structure alpha = 0

objectives may trigger preference reversal in such a way that the proposed reference action becomes of greater importance compared to all other policy actions as a credible and stable position for mutual cooperation.

Using the discounting formula and the distance measurement, we will be able to determine if the reference position is stable or not. For example, we may have three objectives with reference position for Objective 1 = 50%, Objective 2 = 25%, and Objective 3 = 25%. Objectives 1, 2 and 3 are measured on the x-, y-, and z-axes respectively. We can find the reference position for Objective 3 by subtracting Objective 1 and Objective 2 from 100%. The z-axis shows the level of utile.

As an example we will take three different cases for alpha. First, when alpha is equal to zero. This mean there will be no discounting. The reference position is not stable because the actors have alternative beneficiary positions (see Figure 5.3).

Second, when alpha is equal to 0.03. As alpha get higher the positions close to the reference position are discounted less than positions further away. The reference position is still unstable (see Figure 5.4).

Third, when alpha is equal to 0.07. The reference position is stable. This means the reference position is stable at level alpha equal to 0.07 (see Figure 5.5).

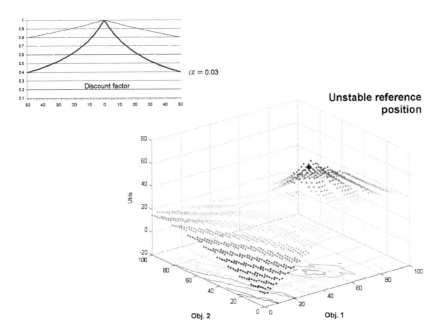

Figure 5.4 Reference dependent preference structure alpha = 0.03

This method will discover further possible solutions if we take into consideration more objectives that divide the parties.

5.1.2.1 *Identifying local satisficing positions of conflict in the Middle East*

The conflict between Arabs and Israelis is a brutal conflict that has been going for more than 60 years. The conflict between the two involves several key elements such as: struggle over land, Palestinian right of return, the status of Jerusalem, border demarcation, and Israeli settlements in contested territory.

Conflict management procedures are based on four main phases: first, the eliciting phase, second the estimation of the stepwise preference structures, third the detection of stable neighbourhood positions and fourth the deliberation phase (Moyersoen, 2007) (see Figure 5.6 for all stages of CMP).

5.2 Phase 1: elicitation and conflict analysis

In this phase we will try to determine three main points: first, identifying the crucial actors and major policy objectives in the conflict; second, identifying the relative importance of the objectives and categories for different groups;

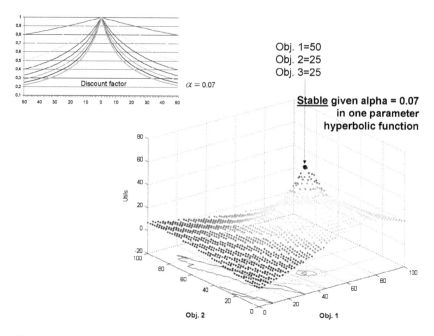

Figure 5.5 Reference dependent preference structure alpha = 0.07

and finally identifying the sensitivity factor (how crucial each objective is for each party) for each objective for each group.

5.2.1   *Identifying the crucial actors and policy objectives*

Before formally meeting any of the participants, we listed 25 main objectives for both parties. In the meeting with the two parties, they identified 18 objectives important in the current conflict between the Arabs and Israelis. In another meeting we sorted these objectives into four different categories: political issues, social issues, economic issues, and social and tourism issues (see Table 5.1).

5.2.1.1   *Political issues*

The first objective is establishing diplomatic relations between the two groups. Since its establishment, the State of Israel has suffered from diplomatic isolation and boycotts by Arab countries.[1] Many Arab countries still have no formal diplomatic relations with Israel, but some have established diplomatic relations, including Egypt,[2] Jordan,[3] and Mauritania; Israel also has trade relations with Qatar, Morocco, Tunisia and the Sultanate of Oman.[4]

Phase 1: Elicitation and conflict analysis

1. Identifying the crucial actors and policy objectives
   i. Identifying the crucial actors in the conflict
   ii. Determining the most important objectives for the actors in the conflict
   iii. Identifying which objectives for which actor are costly or beneficial
   iv. Sorting the objectives in coherent categories

2. Eliciting the relative importance of each policy for each actor
   i. Comparing pair-wise the different categories for each actor in the conflict
   ii. Comparing pair-wise the different subsets of objectives within each category for each conflict
   iii. Calculating overall relative importance of each objective for each actor in the conflict

3. Eliciting the sensitivity factors
   i. Eliciting the interval sensitive factor of each objective for each actor
   ii. Eliciting the utility sensitive factor of each objective for each actor

Phase 2: Detecting stable neighbourhood positions

1. Operationalising the Reference dependent preference structure
   i. Determining the one-parameter hyperbolic discount function
   ii. Operationalising the Reference dependent preference structure

2. Detecting the common stable neighbourhood position
   i. Determining stability levels for each possible allocation bundle
   ii. Selecting the most common robust or stable neighbourhood position

Phase 3: The deliberation phase

Figure 5.6 Overview of conflict management procedures (CMP)

The second objective is to solve the Palestinian refugee problem. As a result of the 1947 partition plan and the 1948 war, the refugee problem has been created (Laqueur, 1968). The third and fourth objective is Israel's withdrawal from Arab-occupied territories and recognising and respecting each other's sovereignty, and territorial and political independence (the term 'occupied territories' refers to land lost by Arab countries after the 1967 war).

The fifth objective is to freeze all settlements including expansion of existing settlements in the West Bank and Golan Heights. These settlements cause disagreement and disputes between the Palestinians and Israelis.

Table 5.1 List of objectives

List of Objectives	
A. Political Issues	1. Establishing diplomatic relations between the two parties
	2. Solving the Palestinian refugee problem
	3. Israeli withdrawal from Arab occupied lands (West Bank, Gaza Strip, Golan Heights and Chiba'a Farms)
	4. Recognise and respect each other's sovereignty, territorial and political independence
	5. Freeze all settlement building including expansion of existing settlements in the West Bank and Golan Heights
	6. Establish an independent Palestinian State (West Bank and Gaza Strip)
	7. Jerusalem becomes an international zone
B. Security Issues	8. Make strong and visible efforts to stop individuals and groups from attacking Israel
	9. Cut off public funding, private funding, and all other forms of support for individuals and groups engaged in violence against Israel
	10. Ensure that Israel stops attacking and using destructive powers against Palestinians and Lebanese
	11. Ensure that Israel respects all UN Resolutions
C. Economic Issues	12. Terminate Arab economic boycotts of Israel
	13. Secure rightful water shares
	14. Develop economic mutual cooperation
D. Social and Tourism Issues	15. Provide free access to places of religious and historical significance
	16. Reopen and maintain roads and railways
	17. Allow free movement of goods and people
	18. Stop propaganda against each other

The sixth objective is to establish an independent Palestinian State. The State of Palestine on the Gaza Strip and West Bank is a proposed country currently controlled by the Palestinian National Authority. This State was declared in Algeria on 15 November 1988 but has never in fact been an independent state, because it has never had sovereignty over any territory. The seventh objective is to make Jerusalem an international zone.

5.2.1.2   Security issues

For many years, the Middle East region has suffered from instability and insecurity because of continuous Israeli/Arab conflict. This region is the most militarised region in the world, with one-third of arms imports going to Middle East countries (Bureau of Verification and Compliance, 2000). Given the importance of security issues to Israel, Israel chose to create nuclear weapons. This placed huge pressure on neighbouring states to follow Israel down the nuclear pathway.[5]

This section has four main objectives: first, make strong and visible efforts to stop Lebanese[6] and Palestinian[7] individuals and groups from attacking Israel. Second, cut off public funding, private funding, and all other forms of support for individuals and groups engaged in violence against Israel. Third, ensure that Israel stops using destructive powers against Lebanese and Palestinians. Finally, ensure Israel respects all United Nations Resolutions.

5.2.1.3 *Economic issues*

The first objective is the termination of Arab economic boycotts of Israel. After the Israeli declaration of independence in 1948, the members of the Arab League[8] decided upon a formal boycott: 'Jewish products and manufactured goods shall be considered undesirable to the Arab countries.' All Arab 'institutions, organisations, merchants, commission agents and individuals' were called upon 'to refuse to deal in, distribute, or consume Zionist products or manufactured goods' (Bard, 2007). The boycott has three levels. The primary boycott forbids all Arab citizens from buying, selling, or entering into a business agreement with Israelis (government or citizens). The secondary boycott forbids all Arab companies to do business with Israel. The tertiary boycott forbids doing business with a company that deals with companies that have an operational base in Israel.

Some states have formally ended the boycott, such as Egypt (1979) and Jordan (1994). Others have established trade offices with Israel, such as Morocco, Tunisia and the Sultanate of Oman. The Gulf Cooperation Council (GCC) has declared the end of the boycott with Israel, as a step towards peace and regional cooperation in the Middle East (Foreign Trade Barriers: The Arab League, Office of the United States Trade Representative, 2007). One remarkable feature of the Arab–Israeli conflict is that although there is a total lack of interaction between the two parties, there is no effective 'secondary boycott' between them (Gleditsch, 1967).

The second objective is to secure rightful water shares between Israel and neighbouring Arab countries. Water resources occupy an important role in the bilateral negotiations of the Middle East. As a result of water scarcity in Israel, Israel has water issues with each of the following neighbouring countries: Syria, Lebanon, Jordan, and the Palestinians (see Table 5.2). The only extant water agreement is between Israel and Jordan, signed on 26 October 1994. Syria and Lebanon have no agreements with Israel, and there has been armed conflict over water, in particular the Litani River, between Lebanon and Israel.

The third objective is economic mutual cooperation between the two parties. The plan is to exploit the comparative resources of each country by regional cooperation, in order to produce competitive products which are beneficial for Israeli and Arab countries.

Table 5.2 Total water consumption

Country	Annual Renewable Water Resources (Km³/year)	Total Freshwater Withdrawal (Year 2000)	Per Capita Withdrawal (Year 2000)
Israel	1.7*	2.05	280
Jordan	0.9**	1.01	177
Syria	46.1**	19.95	1048
Lebanon	4.8**	1.38	385

Note: Constructed from data collected from the Pacific Institute: http://www.worldwater.org/data.html.

* 2001 estimation

** 1997 estimation

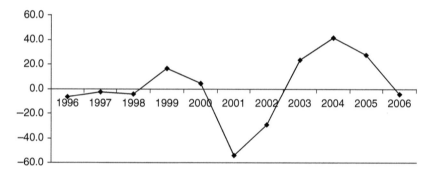

Figure 5.7 Percentage change on tourist arrivals to Israel

Note: Constructed from data from the Israel Bureau of Statistics.

5.2.1.4   *Social and tourism issues*

Because of continuous instability in the Middle East, there is great volatility in the number of tourists visiting the region. Although the region is rich in highly attractive historical and religious places, instability remains an important factor in determining the number of tourists each year. For example, when there was a kind of stability in Israel at the onset of the peace talks in 1991, Israel experienced an increase in international tourist arrivals (Mansfeld, 1999). After the 2000 Palestinian Intifada, there was a significant fluctuation in the number of tourists arriving in Israel (see Figure 5.7).

The first objective is to provide free access to places of religious and historical significance. The second objective is to reopen and maintain roads and railways between Israel and neighbouring countries. The third objective is to establish free movement of goods and people. The final objective is to stop propaganda against each other.

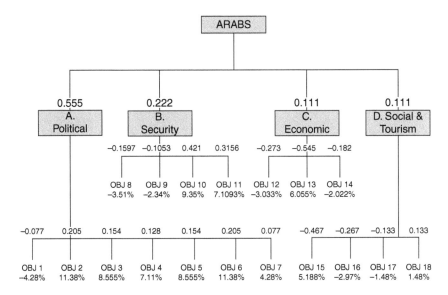

Figure 5.8 The relative weight of each objective for the Arabs

5.2.2 *Obtaining the relative importance of each objective for both actors*

In this stage we will try to determine the relative importance of each objective for Israelis and Arabs. In order to do this we will use a special scale developed by Saaty (1980). At the first level we started by identifying the relatively more important issues for each objective. We found that political issues were the most important for the Arabs, while security issues were most important for Israelis. At the second level we identified the relative importance of each issue for each actor, using the Saaty scale. This process discovered that for the Arabs the political issues had an importance of 55.55%, the security issues 22.22%, the economic issues 11.11% and the social and tourism issues 11.11%. For the Israelis, the political issues had an importance of 23.08%, the security issues 46.15%, the economic issues 15.38%, and the social and tourism issues 15.38% (see Figures 5.8 and 5.9).

After identifying the relative importance of each issue, we will identify the relative importance for each objective. This procedure will allow us to calculate the relative weight of each objective for each group. The relative weight provides an idea of which objective is important for only one of the parties, and will allow us to estimate preference structures for the two groups in the conflict. The preference structures provide vital information for detecting stable joint positions for cooperation. For example, for the Israelis the objective of recognising and respecting mutual sovereignty, territorial, and political independence (Objective 4) obtained a weight of 0.259. Multiplying this weight by the relative importance of the political issue, we get an overall

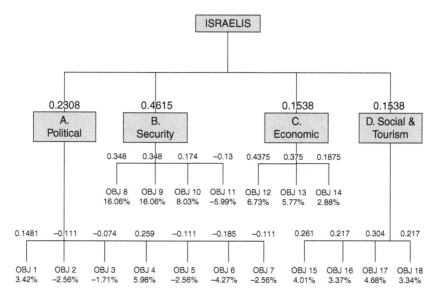

Figure 5.9 The relative weight of each objective for the Israelis

relative weight in percentage terms: 0.259 multiplied by the relative importance of political objective, 23.08%, to give 5.98%. The total relative weights
for the 18 objectives for each actor are equal to 100%.

Comparing the relative importance for each objective, we find that for the
Arabs the most important three policy objectives are the Palestinian refugee problem (Objective 2), establishing a Palestinian state (Objective 6), and
Israeli attacks on Lebanon and the Palestinians (Objective 10). The three
most important policy objectives for the Israelis are stopping individuals
and groups from attacking Israel (Objective 8), cutting off public and private
funding for those groups (Objective 9), and Israel stopping attacks against
Lebanon and the Palestinians (Objective 10). When comparing the relative
importance for both actors, we find that there are 5 objectives that are beneficial to both parties (Objectives 4, 10, 13, 15, and 18). The total relative weights
for these objectives are 29.183% for the Arabs and 27.13% for the Israelis.

5.2.3   *Eliciting the sensitivity factors*

After identifying the relative importance for each issue and the relative weight
for each objective, the next step is to identify the interval sensitivity factor
and the utility sensitivity factor. Those two factors will be used to estimate the
preference structure for each actor and for each objective. In this part we will
elicit the sensitivity of each policy objective for each actor. We can expect that
some objectives are more crucial than others, and that the sensitivity of most

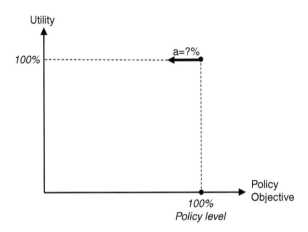

Figure 5.10 Identifying how large a concession in percentage

objectives differs between parties. The procedure consists of two questions for each objective for each actor.

When making a decision, individuals are faced with two cases: costly or beneficiary. Each actor is asked two questions:

a. How large should the concession be in percentage, from its most preferred position of the given policy objective before you perceive the decrease as a significant loss in utility? [See Figure 5.10.]

Table 5.3 shows the revealed interval sensitive factors for the two groups for the 18 objectives. As long as the policy is delivering 80% or 90% as an alternative of 100, it does not really matter for the actor, the policy delivery is perceived as adequate.

After calculating the elicited sensitivity factors for each policy objective, we need to estimate the subsequent interval sensitivity ratio. Multiplying the initial interval level with the interval sensitivity factor will give us the interval sensitivity ratio for the policy objective. For example, take Objective 10 for Arabs and Israelis. In Table 5.3 we can see that the Arabs have a 5% interval sensitivity factor for Objective 10, while the Israelis have a 40% interval sensitivity factor for same objective. Looking at Table 5.4, we see that the initial discrete level is 100% investment. If we take 5% of 100 we find the interval sensitivity ratio for the first interval, equal to 5. Consequently the dimension of the interval is from 100% to 95% and the initial interval level of the second discrete interval is 95.

Table 5.3 The elicited sensitivity factors for the Arabs and the Israelis for each policy objective

Policy Objectives	ARABS		ISRAELIS	
	Interval Sensitivity Factor	Utility Sensitivity Factor*	Interval Sensitivity Factor	Utility Sensitivity Factor*
Objective 1	60%	10	30%	10
Objective 2	10%	90	80%	20
Objective 3	5%	100	30%	20
Objective 4	20%	50	10%	50
Objective 5	20%	80	30%	10
Objective 6	5%	100	20%	60
Objective 7	20%	40	20%	30
Objective 8	10%	5	5%	100
Objective 9	30%	10	10%	80
Objective 10	5%	80	40%	10
Objective 11	10%	50	80%	5
Objective 12	20%	10	10%	50
Objective 13	20%	40	20%	40
Objective 14	30%	5	10%	30
Objective 15	30%	20	5%	30
Objective 16	20%	10	20%	10
Objective 17	30%	10	10%	10
Objective 18	20%	20	5%	10

* Most preferred position is equal to 100 utils

Table 5.4 Estimating the subsequent interval sensitivity ratio for Arabs (Objective 10)

Discrete Endowment Intervals	Initial Interval Level	Interval Sensitivity Factor	Interval Sensitivity Ratio	Dimensions of the Intervals
1	100	5%	5	100–95
2	95	Relative to initial	4.75	95–90.25
3	90.25	interval level	4.5125	90.25–85.74
4	85.7375		4.28688	85.74–81.45
5	81.4506		4.07253	81.45–77.38
6	77.3781		3.8689	77.38–73.51
7	73.5092		3.67546	73.51–69.83
8	69.8337		3.49169	69.83–66.34
9	66.342		3.3171	66.34–63.02
...	...		...	...

Table 5.5 Estimating the subsequent interval sensitivity ratio for Israelis (Objective 10)

Discrete Endowment Intervals	Initial Interval Level	Interval Sensitivity Factor	Interval Sensitivity Ratio	Dimensions of the Intervals
1	100	40%	40	100–60
2	60	*Relative to initial*	24	60–36
3	36	*interval level*	14.4	36–21.6
4	21.6		8.64	21.6–12.96
5	12.96		5.184	12.96–7.78
6	7.776		3.1104	7.78–4.67
7	4.6656		1.86624	4.67–2.8
8	2.79936		1.11974	2.8–1.68
9	1.67962		0.67185	1.68–1.01
....	....		....	....

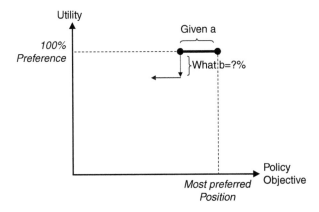

Figure 5.11 Identifying loss in utility

b. What is the percentage loss in utility if a significant concession (answer to question a.) occurs, from its most preferred position for a given policy objective? [See Table 5.5 and Figure 5.11.]

The answer to this question measures the drop in utility for each objective in percentages (where the most preferred position is 100 utils). If the policy objective is of great importance, then the drop in utility will be comparatively

Table 5.6 Estimating utility levels for Arabs (Objective 10)

Discrete Endowment Intervals	Dimensions of the Interval	Utility Sensitivity Factor	Utility Level
1	100–95	*−80*	100
2	95–90.25	*Constant utility*	20
3	90.25–85.74	*sensitivity factor*	−60
4	85.74–81.45		−140
5	81.45–77.38		−220
6	77.38–73.51		−300
7	73.51–69.83		−380
8	69.83–66.34		−460
9	66.34–63.02		−540
....	....		....

Table 5.7 Estimating utility levels for Israelis (Objective 10)

Discrete Endowment Intervals	Dimensions of the Interval	Utility Sensitivity Factor	Utility Level
1	100–60	*−10*	100
2	60–36	*Constant utility*	90
3	36–21.6	*sensitivity factor*	80
4	21.6–12.96		70
5	12.96–7.78		60
6	7.78–4.67		50
7	4.67–2.8		40
8	2.8–1.68		30
9	1.68–1.01		20
....	....		....

large. On the other hand, if the policy objective has low importance then the drop in utility will be relatively small (see Tables 5.6 and 5.7).

5.2.4   *Estimating the preference step-function*

After finding the utility levels and the relative weight, we can estimate the preference step-function for all objectives for both actors. Since objectives vary in importance for each actor, we should normalise the utility levels for

Table 5.8 Estimating preference step-function for the Arabs (Objective 10)

Discrete Endowment Intervals	Dimensions of the Interval	Utility Level	Relative Weight	Normalise Utility Level
1	100–95	100	9.35%	9.35
2	95–90.25	20		1.87
3	90.25–85.74	−60		−5.61
4	85.74–81.45	−140		−13.09
5	81.45–77.38	−220		−20.57
6	77.38–73.51	−300		−28.05
7	73.51–69.83	−380		−35.53
8	69.83–66.34	−460		−43.01
9	66.34–63.02	−540		−50.49
....	....	....		....

Table 5.9 Estimating preference step-function for the Israelis (Objective 10)

Discrete Endowment Intervals	Dimensions of the Interval	Utility Level	Relative Weight	Normalise Utility Level
1	100–60	100	8.03%	8.03
2	60–36	90		7.227
3	36–21.6	80		6.424
4	21.6–12.96	70		5.621
5	12.96–7.78	60		4.818
6	7.78–4.67	50		4.015
7	4.67–2.8	40		3.212
8	2.8–1.68	30		2.409
9	1.68–1.01	20		1.606
....	....	....		....

each objective based on its importance. For example, the relative weight of Objective 10 for the Arabs is 9.35% and the utility levels are found in Table 5.6. To find the preference step function we need to adjust each utility level according to the objective weight (see Tables 5.8 and 5.9).

5.2.5 *Sensitivity analysis*

At this stage we will plot the objectives where the x-axis indicates the interval sensitivity factor and the y-axis indicates the utility sensitivity factor (see Figures 5.12 and 5.13). For the Arabs, Objectives 3 and 6 are the most sensitive

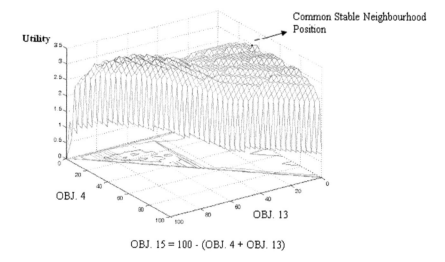

OBJ. 15 = 100 - (OBJ. 4 + OBJ. 13)

Figure 5.12 Common stable neighbourhood position for Arabs

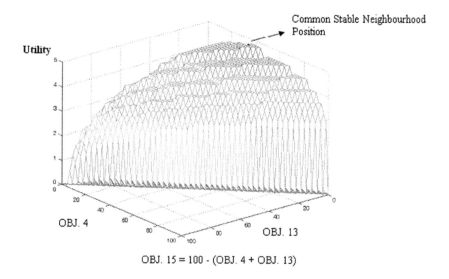

OBJ. 15 = 100 - (OBJ. 4 + OBJ. 13)

Figure 5.13 Common stable neighbourhood position for Israelis

issues, followed by Objectives 2 and 10. The Israelis are highly sensitive towards Objective 8, followed by Objectives 9 and 6. This means that the Arabs are highly sensitive towards the Israeli withdrawal from Arab occupied lands and declaring a Palestinian state; they will not be willing to make many concessions. For the Israelis, stopping individuals and groups from attacking Israel are perceived as the most sensitive, least negotiable, issues.

5.3   Phase 2: detecting stable neighbourhood positions

In this stage, CMP estimates reference dependent preference structures using the Mazur and Hernstein 1988 discounting model for each possible reference position for agreement. This reference dependent preference structure will direct the CMP to discover common stable neighbourhood positions. There are two steps in this phase: determining the stability level and detecting common stable positions.

5.3.1   *Determining the stability level*

CMP assumes that actors will move away from a proposed cooperative arrangement to another option, based on either the new position giving a higher utility than the old position, or the risk assessment of expensive delay while switching the reference position for an alternative. Positions involving larger alteration will be discounted by a lower average discount rate when compared with positions involving smaller alterations (see Mazur and Herrnstein, 1988). The discount parameter will indicate the stability level where the reference position becomes the most beneficial position. We will test all possible joint actions to reach the stable neighbourhood position with the highest level of stability.

To test all possible joint actions for Arabs and Israelis, we will use MATLAB software. There are 18 objectives for each actor, which means that there are 816 possible combinations involving three distinct policy objectives. We will also test robustness for every possible combination (2550 allocation for each possible combination). This means we will test 4,161,600 different positions using MATLAB software. The result of the MATLAB run illustrates the best ten feasible allocation bundles where allocation positions are stable for both Arabs and Israelis. Table 5.10 demonstrates the result of the MATLAB run; the second, third and fourth columns illustrate the combination bundle of policy objectives. Columns five, six and seven indicate the relative weights for each objective. Columns eight and nine show the utile levels for each group under the given allocation positions. The subsequent three columns indicate the stability for each allocation bundle (lower alpha means more stable, which means lower incentives to shift to an alternative position). The best bundle consists of an investment of 4% recognition and respect of mutual sovereignty, territorial, and political independence, 28% for securing equitable

Table 5.10 Common stable positions in the Arab–Israeli conflict

	Combination Policy Objectives			Weight of Each Policy Objective			Utility		Stability		
	Obj. A	Obj. B	Obj. C	Obj. A%	Obj. B%	Obj. C%	Arabs	Israelis	Arabs	Israelis	Common
1	4	13	15	4%	28%	68%	42.325	45.234	0.001	0.001	0.001
2	13	15	18	12%	34%	54%	38.154	18.958	0.001	0.001	0.001
3	4	15	17	18%	25%	57%	15.684	25.325	0.001	0.001	0.001
4	4	13	14	42%	15%	43%	17.254	15.287	0.001	0.001	0.001
5	10	15	18	15%	28%	57%	21.512	34.514	0.001	0.002	0.002
6	9	16	18	5%	42%	53%	19.628	24.581	0.002	0.001	0.002
7	7	10	15	16%	32%	52%	24.128	16.875	0.002	0.002	0.002
8	4	12	14	50%	15%	35%	45.218	35.286	0.003	0.002	0.002
9	11	15	16	50%	22%	28%	34.856	38.167	0.002	0.003	0.003
10	7	10	11	6%	65%	29%	41.365	40.286	0.003	0.003	0.003

water shares, and 68% for promoting free access to places of religious and historical significance. This bundle is the best when compared to others as it has the lowest alpha. All three objectives were previously identified by both Arabs and Israelis as beneficiary objectives.

5.4 Phase 3: the deliberation stage

Selecting the most common robust or stable neighbourhood position brought us to the following peace proposal:

1. Agreement between Arabs and Israelis about promoting free access to places of religious and historical significance: for example, declaring Jerusalem as a place to be accessed freely by Israelis and Arabs.
2. Establishment of a water reallocation agreement to include Israel, Palestine, Jordan, Lebanon and Syria.
3. Declaration of a celebratory day in recognition and respect of each other's sovereignty and territorial and political independence.

5.5 Conclusion

This chapter proposes a possible participatory conflict management procedure (CMP) that aspires to discover stable points for collaboration between confrontational parties. Stable points are mutual joint cooperative arrangements that diminish the probability of conflict re-escalation. We apply prospect theory developed by the Tversky School, and inter-temporal choice theory developed by Ainslie and Herrnstein, to assert the assumptions in the model.

The CMP process consists of four phases: indicating the crucial actors, objectives of each actor and the relative importance of each objective for the different actors; detecting local stable positions; embracing a certain process with the different actors about what sort of joint project would be coherent with the detected satisfying position; and finally reaching several crucial objectives for both parties. MATLAB (version 7, release 14) is used to verify the stability of all possible joint actions among the conflicting parties. The stable position detected by CMP consists of an investment of 4% for recognition and respect of mutual sovereignty, territorial and political independence, 28% for securing rightful water shares, and 68% for promoting free access to places of religious and historical significance.

Notes

1 There are 34 Arab and non-Arab countries that do not have formal diplomatic relations with Israel today: Afghanistan, Algeria, Bahrain, Bangladesh, Bhutan, Brunei, Chad, China, Comoros, Cuba, Djibouti, Guinea, Indonesia, Iran, Iraq, Kuwait, Lebanon, Libya, Malaysia, Maldives, Mali, Morocco, Niger, North Korea, Oman, Pakistan, Qatar, Saudi Arabia, Somalia, Sudan, Syria, Tunisia, United Arab Emirates and Yemen.

2 Egypt has had full diplomatic relations with Israel since signing the Israel–Egypt peace treaty in 1979.
3 Jordan has had full diplomatic relations with Israel since signing the Israel–Jordan peace treaty in 1994.
4 In October 2000, Israeli offices in Morocco, Tunisia and the Sultanate of Oman were closed after these three Arab countries suspended their relations with Israel.
5 Several Arab countries tried through the year to own nuclear weapons, including Iraq and Libya. On 6 September 2007 Israel attacked Syria targeting a partially built nuclear reactor in Northern Syria, near the Turkish border.
6 The main Lebanese group that had a direct armed conflict with Israel is Hezbollah. Hezbollah is a Shi'a Islamic organisation founded in the early 1980s in Lebanon during the Lebanese War. Hezbollah had several direct conflict incidents with Israel. The last conflict was the 2006 Lebanon war.
7 A number of Palestinian Liberation movements began to establish in the beginning of the 1950s with the major objective being to create a Palestinian state and destroy Israel. The first organisation to be established was Fatah at the end of 1957, which was founded by a group of Palestinians outside Israel/Palestine – among them was Arafat. Fatah supported and conducted violent attacks against Israel and Israeli citizens in order to achieve its ultimate goal of creating a Palestinian state. Although Fatah was established in the 1950s it was only in 1965 that Fatah started carrying out violent attacks inside Israel/Palestine through its military arm, 'Al-Asifa' (The Storm) (Cobban, 1984; Alexander and Sinai, 1989). The Palestinian Liberation Organisation (PLO) was founded on 2 June 1964 by the Arab League to represent the Palestinian people. In 1969, the Fatah managed to control the decision-making of the PLO and thus Arafat was appointed as the PLO chairman on 3 February 1969. Following the 1967 Arab–Israeli war the Popular Front for the Liberation of Palestine movement (PFLP) was established on 11 December 1967. The Popular Democratic Front for the Liberation of Palestine (PDFLP) was founded on 22 February 1969 followed by the establishment of the Palestinian Islamic Jihad (PIJ) in the 70s. The Islamic Resistance movement (HAMAS) was founded in 1988 after the first Palestinian Intifada (Palestinian uprising) with a main goal of establishing an Islamic Palestinian state in place of Israel.
8 The Arab League is a regional organisation of Arab States formed in Cairo on 22 March 1945. The current members of the Arab League are: Algeria, Bahrain, Djibouti, Comoros, Egypt, Iraq, Jordan, Kuwait, Lebanon, Libya, Mauritania, Morocco, Oman, Palestine, Qatar, Saudi Arabia, Somalia, Sudan, Syria, Tunisia, United Arab Emirates and Yemen.

6 Military spending

Decision-making in anarchy and herd instincts

6.1 Introduction

The annual military spending of the world today is about US$1 trillion, which has reached close to Cold War levels. The major producers and suppliers of conventional weapons are the five permanent members of the UN Security Council. These five members – the US, the UK, France, Russia and China – together contribute roughly 90% of reported conventional (global) arms exports. The major buyers of conventional arms are a handful of developing nations struggling with their developmental aspirations, deep poverty, internal violence and potentials for cross-border conflicts – ten developing nations absorb 61% of the arms exported to the developing world.[1] Since the five permanent members of the UN Security Council dominate the global arms trade, they have little incentives to introduce and enforce regulations and controls in the global arms market and, as a result, the global arms trade and the arms race continue unabated in a legal and moral vacuum. In the absence of meaningful regulation the global arms market, akin to anarchy, suffers from widespread corruption, bribery and kickbacks in the midst of which the top three armament firms usually share immense market spoils, for example, a whopping profit of $50 billion in 2012, from producing machines for aggravating human miseries. By the end of the Cold War, from Smith (1994), we now know how armament firms have regularly spread false rumours about military and naval programmes of various nations, engaged in scaremongering, played off one nation against another, influenced public opinion on armament through the control of media, and formed powerful arms cartels to promote the global arms race. It is often argued that the arms race has deepened the cycle of violence, oiled terrorism and increased human rights violation mostly in developing nations. Despite a great relevance of the arms race for the contemporary world, the traditional literature on the arms race – based on the Richardsonian action–reaction processes – made limited progress in explaining the factors responsible for triggering, fuelling and propelling the arms race (see Rider, 2009). It is only recently, as explored in Section 2.2 in full detail, that the latest game theoretic models of the arms race in Baliga (2011), Baliga and Sjöström (2004, 2008, 2011, 2013a, 2013b), and Baliga, Lucca and Sjöström (2013) provide a formalisation of the critical role of information revelation, transmission and pre-play communications to offer new insights into the dynamics of the arms race. In a similar vein, the latest vintage of international relations models, as reviewed in Section 2.1, highlights the role of social learning, information problems and information acquisition to explain the onset of the arms race (see Klein, Goertz and Diehl, 2006; Rider, 2009; Rider, Findley and Diehl, 2011). From these models we now know that there is nothing automatic, instantaneous or sacrosanct about the arms race as there is positive probability that the *détente* equilibrium will prevail to prevent the arms race from occurring.

In this work we develop a necessary expansion of the recent literature on the informational problems of the arms race by exploring rational inference of nations in social learning settings, which is popularly christened as information cascades.[2] Communications and learning are important when the underlying problem is about incomplete information about rival nations' preferences for arms build-up. Nations combine their own private information with that revealed by rival states' actions on military build-ups and we will establish that the herd instincts can motivate nations to arm themselves so that information cascades will fail to aggregate information.[3] In fully rational models of the arms race, information cascades occur once the information contained in a group's observed military build-ups becomes so great that an individual nation's private information can never ever affect its optimal military build-up. One can define herding as mutual imitation leading to a convergence of action as highlighted by Hirshleifer and Teoh (2003). Herds fail to eventually aggregate information if and only if an information cascade begins before the truth is revealed. This can occur in the long-run only if the environment is significantly 'coarse'. The obvious implication is that the military build-up is socially inefficient since, despite a plethora of private signals that reveal the right choice/action, nations chase each other on the incorrect and costly choice on arming with positive probability.[4]

In our model nations are like contenders, or rival claimants, that make sequential decisions on their individual efforts to produce economic goods and efforts to fight, or arm, in anarchy. Anarchy refers to a social arrangement in which contestants arm themselves to conquer and protect economic resources without effective regulation by higher authorities as in a hierarchy. To make the model tractable, we simplify by considering the sequential decision-making on arming, or military build-ups, by a representative agent from each cohort given the history of allocation of resources for military build-ups chosen by others.[5,6] We assume that there is a social norm on military build-ups, or allocation, that pre-exists the decision-making process and decision-makers do not have a prior knowledge of the public opinion/norm on the allocation (q^A) of resources to military build-ups. We assume that it is common knowledge that q^A can take either of two values and one can, hence, call q^A as the state of nature. Each cohort receives a signal about this state of nature.[7,8] We establish that there is no herding under a special condition.

On the other hand, herd mentality plays a decisive role if this condition is violated. In this case, agent, or cohort, *t* chooses the arms race regardless of the private signal that s/he receives.[9] We establish, to the best of our understanding, for the first time that the formation of war efforts (the arms race) and actual conflicts can be driven by *herd* instincts, which can have serious economic and social consequences. The upshot thus is that a decision to get armed and subsequently embroiled in a war and ensuing violent conflicts can be driven by herd mentality: everyone is individually rational to arm and fight a catastrophic war, even if all participants have overwhelming (private) information that there is absolutely no necessity to do so. In other words, everybody will willingly choose the 'wrong behaviour' even when there is enough evidence in favour of choosing the 'right behaviour'. Moreover, the decision to invest resources into fighting and ensuing conflicts will be plagued with an extreme fragility, due to the herd instincts. A little shift in the public opinion on conflicts can induce the herd to choose the opposite action that can trigger an avalanche of conflicts and crises. Thus the peace driven by pure herding can display razor's edge instability. So will conflicts.

The plan of the chapter is as follows: Section 6.2 offers the background to intuit the role of information cascades in the context of arms. Section 6.3 offers a modification of the Hirshleifer model. Section 6.4 examines anarchy in a sequential decision-making model to establish the precise conditions that can trigger herding among contestants in the context of the arms race. In Section 6.5 we provide an empirical foundation to the model of herding in terms of defence spending of the 50 most militarised nations during 1991–2009. Section 6.6 offers a new measure of herding to explore the empirical evidence of herding in the context of the arms race. Section 6.7 offers insights on the arms race in the Middle East. Section 6.8 concludes.

6.2   Related literature

Our current research introduces *herd* instincts in the context of anarchy for the very first time in the literature. In many economic decision-making processes, individuals are influenced by the decisions of others. As an example, the fashion industry thrives on the impact/influence of the group behaviour upon individual decisions. We now know that similar influences impinge on technology adoption, purchase and sales of assets and individual investment dynamics.[10] Herd behaviour in sequential decisions is a well-received doctrine. Scharfstein and Stein (1990) modelled sequential investment by agents/investors who care for their reputation as good forecasters. If these agents have correlated signals conditionally on the state of the world, investors will imitate, or copy, the behaviour of the first investor. This kind of modelling has come to be known as *reputational herding*.[11] In models of *statistical herding*, introduced by Banerjee (1992), and Bikhchandani and Hirshleifer (1992), agents maximise expected returns/profits in a common value environment and observe conditionally independent private signals of bounded precision, while still having access to watch the behaviour of others. Gradually, the accumulated evidence from observing earlier decisions is sufficiently strong to undermine the private information of a single decision-maker. The question about the source of herding begs an answer: herding arises because the observed behaviour of other investors affects the probability belief attached to different states of the world and also the payoff conditional on each state for an individual investor. Banerjee (1992), Bikhchandani and Hirshleifer (1992) and Welch (1992) and a large number of publications show the significance of informational cascades in modern investment markets. An informational cascade connotes a situation in which subsequent agents, based on the observations of others, make the same choice independent of their private signals. Informational cascades are argued to engender erroneous mass behaviour and cause fragility in a system.

6.2.1   Relevance of herding for international relations models of the arms race

Social scientists have always been tantalised by their unenviable task of explaining the arms race and consequent interstate (violent) conflicts, or wars. Until recently, both the international relations models of the arms race and the arms race games made very little breakthrough in understanding the *onset* of the arms race. In other words, the core of research on the arms race begs a fundamental question of why nations engage in the arms race. As will be discussed below in greater detail, the latest models of arms race games provide a formalisation of the critical role of information transmission and pre-play communications in triggering the arms race. It is noteworthy that the latest models of international relations models have also come to highlight the role of social learning in triggering the arms race.

The theory of the arms race has traditionally been examined in the Richardsonian action–reaction processes,[12] which fail to explain what triggers and then fuels the *costly* arms race (see Rider, Findley and Diehl, 2011). An exception is Rider (2009).[13] The primary justification of the arms race in international relations models is rooted in the deterrence theory (see Weede, 1980 and Glaser, 2000). Yet there are serious flaws in the justification as recognised and highlighted by leading scholars of the arms race: first, the arms race is an effective deterrence if it affects the capability distributions in favour of the actor. Yet most arms races will not improve the *relative* capabilities of the status quo states and, more importantly, military capabilities are only one component of successful deterrence (see Fearon, 1995; Rider, Findley and Diehl, 2011). Second, there is little empirical evidence that arms races can promote deterrence: Vasquez (1993) suggests that arms races are a reaction to *threat perception* and that this type of reaction, referred to as a power politics strategy, is most likely to cause conflicts. Moreover, the role of the arms race is linked to dispute escalation and a prior military dispute implies that the arms race is less likely to improve deterrence of future conflicts (see Valeriano, 2013).[14] Third, there is mounting evidence that the arms race produces long-term negative effects on domestic economies through rising budget deficits, decrease in capital formation and increased inflationary and taxation pressures (Cohen et al. 1996; Heo and DeRouen, 1998; Mintz and Huang, 1991; Ward and Davis, 1992).

Thus, an arms race inherently involves both immediate and potentially long-term costs while the precise benefits from military build-ups to nations are not clear to many researchers.[15] One plausible benefit from competitive military build-up is that a nation can deter potential aggression as highlighted by Morgenthau (1985), which is often labelled as the mutual-assured-destruction (MAD) doctrine. The strategy is effectively a form of Nash equilibrium in which neither side, once armed, has any *rational* incentive either to initiate a conflict or to disarm. The empirical finding contradicts the MAD doctrine (Gibler, Rider, and Hutchison 2005; Sample 1997, 1998). Due to the escalatory tendency of arms races, as discussed before, the question arises as to why states should take such a risky course of action.[16] It thus remains a mystery what *motivates* nations to engage in a costly arms race. In other words, the motivation for arming, or the decision-theoretic foundation of an arms race, has always challenged social scientists. The upshot of the recent research is that arms races and consequent wars take place in *enduring rivalries* (Kennedy, 1983; Diehl and Crescenzi, 1998; Diehl and Goertz, 2000). Dark shadows of interstate rivalries, or what is often called *rivalry competitions*, are believed to trigger and propel an arms race that can, in turn, culminate into violent wars.

The key issue concerning arms races in the dominant models of international relations centres around the dynamics of rivalry between potential competitors, as Thompson (2001b) defines rivalry when two states view 'each other as competitors, the source of actual or latent threats that pose some probability of becoming militarized, and enemies' (p. 560). In these models, information plays a central role in shaping the expectations of decision-makers of an arms race. Key elements of rivalries are that they are neither anonymous nor history-free and rivalries depend on both the 'push of the past' and the 'pull of the future' (Klein, Goertz and Diehl, 2006). That is, previous interactions and expectations of future interactions influence the dynamics of rivalries, which in turn reveals information on the potential threats and thereby impinges on the motivation for arming. The information dynamics assumes paramount importance as rivals *gradually* develop expectations that they will face security threats into the extended future from their rivals (see Diehl and Goertz, 2000).[17] The punctuated equilibrium model of rivalries, as propounded by Diehl and Goertz (2000), argues that the information dynamics can create historical 'lock-ins' as states are led to choose rivalry policies that are difficult to change over the course of the rivalry.[18] At the empirical level, Rider, Findley and Diehl (2011) consider arms races and wars from 1816–2000 by dichotomising states into rivalry population and non-rivalry population and conclude that arms races take place in the middle and later stages of *enduring* rivalry, which attests to the importance of information dynamics.

In this work we provide a necessary extension of the recent literature on the informational problems of the arms race by exploring rational inference of states in social-learning settings, which is often christened as information cascades. In the simplest model, a sequence of states, or leaders of these states, each choose in turn one of two options, A (to arm) or B (not to arm), each state observing all of one's predecessors' choices. They have common preferences over the two choices but do not know which is better. In our model, states know their own costs and benefits from military build-up, but they are unsure of the costs and benefits of their rivals from the arms race. In other words, the costs and benefits of arming often depend on the social, moral, political and psychological considerations of the leaders of states, which are often idiosyncratic and country-specific, or leader-specific. Communications and learning become important when the underlying problem is about incomplete information about rival states' preferences for arms build-up. States, or nations, combine their own private information with that revealed by rival nations' actions on military build-ups and we will establish that the herd instincts can drive states so that information cascades will fail to aggregate information.[19,20] In fully rational models of the arms race, information cascades occur once the information contained in a group's observed military build-ups becomes so great that an individual nation's private information can never ever affect its optimal military build-up. Herds fail to eventually aggregate information.

6.2.2   *Implications of herding for game theoretic models of the arms race*

In economics and, especially in game theory, arms races are explored as a coordination game in which the interactions between states carry the germs of coordination that will create multiple equilibria (see Baliga and Sjöström 2004, 2008, 2011). Politicians, or decision-makers, fully comprehend the negative consequences of the arms race and seek to avoid an arms race if their rival nations don't engage in arms build-up. However, they prefer to build-up military power if they believe their rivals will have arms build-up. The *strategic* interactions of nation states thus will thus create two possible pure strategy Nash equilibria as is well-recognised since Schelling (1966) and Jervis (1976): first, the arms race equilibrium in which both states engage in the arms race as the mutual best responses and second, the *detente equilibrium* in which both states optimally eschew the arms race. Traditionally, economists introduce uncertainty to select one of these equilibria (see Morris and Shin, 1998).[21] In a series of recent articles Baliga (2011), Baliga and Sjöström (2004, 2008, 2011, 2013a, 2013b) and Baliga, Lucca and Sjöström (2013) introduced information problems in arms race models and offered new insights into the rationale for arms races by considering explicit information transfers between actors like *cheap talk*.[22] In these models, a nation's type is modelled in terms of its preference for arming, while the true preference of a nation is treated as one's private information that is not immediately available to its rivals. For all types, the worst possible outcome is to have no military build-up while all other rivals have military build-ups. The type plays an important role in the determination of preference of a nation for arming if there is uncertainty about the intentions of its rivals about arming. At one end of the spectrum, there are 'hawks' for whom arming is a 'dominant strategy' and they engage in military build-up regardless of what their rivals do. At the other end of the spectrum are the 'doves' who prefer to arm if they are virtually sure that their rivals will arm.

In the traditional parlance of conflict models, driven by coordination games, even though each nation anticipates the rival nations to be a 'hawk' with a negligible probability, the unique Bayesian-Nash equilibrium is shown to be an arms race with probability one. In the latest developments of conflict models, on the contrary, the possibility of communication and information transmission about one's type has expanded the possible set of equilibria. The consequence of communication and information transmission has a dramatic effect as it reduces the probability of an arms race from one to almost zero.[23] If we view rivalry as a competition between two states over the disposition of some stake, then states will not immediately risk an arms race as they are aware that information transmission can establish the détente equilibrium. In other words, states and their decision-makers will devote real resources to understand their rivals' preferences for and constraints on arms build-up in which informational cascades can play an important role, which is the subject matter of this current work.

6.2.3 Herding in anarchy

Jack Hirshleifer (1995a) defined a system *anarchic* in which rivals seize and defend economic resources, without an effective regulation from above. In this classic work, Hirshleifer demonstrated that anarchy arises as an economic equilibrium of spontaneous order and is not *chaos* by any means. It is further argued that anarchy is a *fragile* equilibrium that can easily descend into formless 'amorphy', or chaos. Anarchy has also the tendency to become a more organised system, such as with hierarchy. To visualise an anarchic situation, one may like to ponder the state of Afghanistan before the US-led attack. It is generally recognised that anarchy as an equilibrium can only sustain when there are diminishing returns to fighting effort/conflicts and individual incomes exceed the viability minimum. This type of model attempts to explain many features of animal and human conflict. Anarchy is thus a social arrangement in which contestants arm themselves to conquer and protect economic resources, without effective regulation by higher authorities, or guiding social norms. The external relations of many modern nation-states are believed to remain mostly anarchic, which is often a source of global conflicts.

In an anarchic system, decision-makers have to divide current resources into two competing uses: (1) exploiting the currently-held assets in a productive manner and (2) seizing and defending a resource base. Thus, there are two technologies for each contender, or rival claimant: one is a technology of production and the other is a technology of appropriation, conflict and struggle (see Hirshleifer, 1991). The economic theory of anarchy explains conflict by modelling optimal behaviours of participants and offering an equilibrium conflict. The equilibrium conflict is a product of optimal group decisions to produce economic output and to arm such that no individual group has an incentive to unilaterally move away from this equilibrium. Thus one can view, following Hirshleifer (1991, 1995b), that the anarchy and conflict are a spontaneous order, which derives from the optimal behaviours of contesting agents. The anarchic equilibrium thus explains what fractions of a nation's resources will be devoted to fighting, or defence or military output. The collapse of an anarchic equilibrium can explain why and when a system dissolves into a tyranny, alternatively into an absolute chaos. This line of research is based on two limited assumptions: first, full information is assumed and second, a symmetrical Cournot-Nash solution is applied in which rational agents clinically use their full information to choose their optimal actions.

6.3   A simple model of herd behaviour in anarchy

We start with the basic Hirshleifer type model in order to appreciate the limitation and the precise contribution of our model.

6.3.1   The basic Hirshleifer type model

There are two rival political groups, or nations, in our prototype model, whose interests are mutually opposed. This kind of antagonism is akin to the one popularised by Plato as: 'the number of citizens should be sufficient to defend themselves against the injustice of their neighbours' (Laws, Book IV, translated by Jawett, 2012) In the context of federalism, Riker (1964) observed that the external military threats and potential conflicts led to the formation and consolidation of federal states, which initially started as independent regions. In the model there are two rival groups/claimants who aim to maximise their own incomes. The analysis can easily be extended to multiple claimants. At any point in time, each contender divides one's current resources between productive, or economic, efforts and fighting efforts. The fighting efforts may be directed at acquiring new resources at the expense of the rival or repelling the rival as rivals try to grab resources. Given the conflict technology and the production technology, the trade-off between war efforts and economic efforts is determined. Let us call e_i as the economic effort and E_i as the fighting effort of rival i (i $\forall 1, 2...n$) and the production technology of rival i for the economic goods is given as:

$$K_i = Me_i^{\alpha} \tag{1a}$$

We similarly assume that the military output Q_i is produced by a Cobb-Douglas production technology by rival i by using the war efforts E_i and a fraction of the economic output K_i also enters the production and we express the production function of the military output as the following:

$$Q_i = \Gamma_1 (\Gamma_2 K_i)^{1-\beta} E_i^\beta = \Gamma_1 \Gamma_2^{(1-\beta)} K_i^{1-\beta} E_i^\beta = \Gamma K_i^{1-\beta} E_i^\beta \tag{1b}$$

Γ, Γ_1 and Γ_2 are parameters and related by

$$\Gamma = \Gamma_1 \Gamma_2^{(1-\beta)} \tag{1c}$$

Expressing (1a) and (1b) in logarithms will give us:

$$k_i = m + \alpha \log e_i = m + \alpha h_i \tag{2a}$$
$$q_i = [\log \Gamma + (1-\beta)m + (1-\beta)(1-\alpha) + \beta H^*] + h_i [\alpha(1-\beta)-\beta] \tag{2b}$$

where $k_i = \log K_i$, $m = \log M$, $H_i = \log E_i$, $q_i = \log Q_i$, $h_i = \log e_i$, and from the resource constraint is given as

$$H_i + h_i = H^* \tag{2c}$$

Equation (2c) implies that efforts/resources have sectoral specificity such that there is a non-linear 'trade-off between guns and butter'. In the Hirshleifer model, a linear trade-off between e_i and E_i is assumed so that $e_i + E_i =$ constant, while we posit $e_i*E_i =$ constant. Our formulation assumes that resources, or efforts, can be transferred from one sector to the other only after some sort of transformation to make them suitable for the specific sector. We presume that peasants (militia) can't be simply transformed into an army (farmers). The formulation is not only more realistic but also simplifies our calculations.

We retain the basic structure of the Hirshleifer model. The main departure of our model is about the production and conflict technologies. We retain the assumption that the economic decision for a rival is to split the available resources between productive efforts and fighting efforts. These efforts determine economic output and military output. Military output depends on military efforts as well as on the economic output (or, national income) – this is the main departure of our model from the Hirshleifer model. We introduce further changes as described in the following postulates.

Postulate 1: We assume every rival confronts two dates T and $T + 1$. At date T rival i competes with other rivals in a contest for resources that has a financial return, or prize, X_i at date t. In other words, at date t there is a contest among rivals for Prize X_i while rivals instrumentally utilise their military output Q_i as a means to win the prize X_i. At date $t + 1$ rival i will have financial return Y_i that solely depends on the economic output K_i of rival i that is produced by the means of e_i. We assume the size of prize X_i to be endogenous and as a function of Q_i, which is given by equation (2d) in which B is a parameter and $B>0$,

$$X_i = Q_i^B \tag{2d}$$

Equation (2d) captures the 'glory' that the winner in any conflict takes away, which is an increasing function of the military output.

Postulate 2: We assume a time-separable utility function R_i for rival i while U_i^T, U_i^{T+1} represent the utility of rival i at date T and date $T+1$ respectively and taking r as the common discount rate we write R_i as:

$$R_i = U_i^T + [U_i^{T+1}/(1+r)] \tag{3a}$$

In the contest we define π_i as the contest success function, or probability of getting the prize X_i, for rival i. We express the payoff/utility of rival i at date T, U_i^T, as a logarithmic function of X_i and given by:

$$U_i^T = \pi_i \, \text{Utility} \,(X_i) = \pi_i \, \text{Utility} \,(Q_i^B) = \pi_i \log (Q_i^B) = B \, \pi_i \log Q_i \tag{3b}$$

We use the Tullock-type contest success function in which Π_i is the probability of success for rival i to win the prize X_i in a contest with n rivals, and π_i is the logarithmic of Π_i and given by:

$$\pi_i = \log \Pi_i \tag{3b'}$$

The contest success function Π_i is postulated to be the traditional one and given by:

$$\Pi_i = [Q_i/(Q_1+Q_2+\cdots+Q_n)] = (Q_i/Q^A)/n \tag{3c}$$

where

$$Q^A = (Q_1+Q_2+\cdots+Q_n)/n \tag{3c'}$$

After expressing (3c) in the logarithmic form and defining q^A as the logarithm of the average military output Q^A ($= \Sigma Q_i/n$),

$$\pi_i = (q_i-q^A-\log n) \tag{3c''}$$

The payoff/utility function of rival i at date T is as follows:

$$U_i^t = B \, \pi_i \log Q_i = B(q_i-q^A-\log n)q_i \tag{3d}$$

Postulate 3: The return at date $T+1$, Y_i, depends solely on K_i and given in equation (4a) where Θ is a constant:

$$Y_i = \Theta K_i = \Theta M e_i^\alpha \tag{4a}$$

The separable utility at date $T+1$, U_i^{T+1}, is as follows:

$$U_i^{T+1} = \text{Log } Y_i = y_i = \text{Log } \ominus M + \alpha \text{ Log } e_i \tag{4b'}$$
$$\text{Or, } U_i^{T+1} = c_i + (1-\alpha) + \alpha h_i \tag{4b}$$

where $c_i = \text{Log } \ominus M$, $y_i = \text{Log } Y_i$, $h_i = \text{Log } e_i$.

The overall payoff/utility of rival i, R_i, is given as:

$$R_i = B(q_i - q^A - \log n)q_i + [c_i + \alpha h_i]/(1+r) \tag{4c}$$

Rival i maximises the utility, or payoff, R_i given the production functions and the time constraints.

6.3.2   Interdependency in military build-ups and the Cournot-Nash characterisation

The rival i spends effort H_i to obtain the military output q_i. What is interesting is that the optimal use of H_i depends on the average military output q^A. Thus there is interdependency in the allocation of efforts between contestants/rival claimants: if rival claimant j increases their H_j, then q^A goes up, that will, in turn, increase the optimal effort of claimant i, in H_i. Hence, as in the rat race, each claimant i is driven by the knowledge that for lower q_i one must share a lower probability of protecting resources with less able rivals. Similarly, one is aware that for higher q_i one will enjoy a higher probability of protecting resources that one will share with rivals of higher ability. Why does not the rival raise the q_i to the maximum feasible level? In our model, the formation of a military output is costly because such formation reduces the effort to produce the economic output. Different rivals have different costs and the optimal military outputs arise from these costs. If all contestants behave in this fashion then the equilibrium efforts depend on the expectations of each contestant about the efforts of other rivals. We summarise these expectations as q^A that, which may be argued, is kind of an average opinion. Note that the model does not have any interaction if q^A is independent of q_is. An interactive model can only be utilised when q^A is predicated upon q_is.

In the Cournot-Nash characterisation we assume that as one changes one's effort, it will not affect the efforts of others, and hence q^A, will remain unchanged. This is a well-known assumption of Cournot models, known as the zero conjectural variations. On the other hand, each rival assumes that the rivals' efforts influence q^A. Note that the reaction function of rival i in allocating one's effort h_i, given the efforts of h_j by the other rival. Based on the reaction functions we shall derive the Cournot-Nash equilibrium in the allocation of efforts. The Cournot-Nash equilibrium effort is such that, once reached, no rival has any incentive to unilaterally deviate from the equilibrium allocation of efforts.

6.3.3   The Cournot-Nash equilibrium: strategic complements, fragility and herd-like behaviour

In order to derive the Cournot-Nash equilibrium allocation we follow two steps. In Step 1 we derive the reaction function of each rival. In Step 2 we derive the optimum allocation of efforts of these rivals from the equilibrium. To simplify further we express the beliefs of rivals about the average opinion in the following postulate.

Postulate 4: We define $E_i(q^A)$ as the subjective estimate/belief of rival i about the average opinion q^A. We express this as:

$$E_i(q^A) = 2\Psi_i q_j + \eta q_i \tag{6a}$$

We set $\eta = 0$ to simplify calculations. However, there is a twist here: the main intuition is that rival i expects/believes that rival j has a stronger influence on the average opinion. We establish the result with the assumption that rival i thinks s/he has no influence on the average opinion. Thus,

$$E_i(q^A) = 2\Psi_i q_j \tag{6b}$$

Step 1: Rival i's optimal choice involves the following:

$$\text{Maximise } R_i = B[q_i + q_i (q_i - q^A)] + R_i = B(q_i - q^A - \log n)q_i$$
$$+ [c_i + \alpha h_i /(1+r)] \{h_i\}$$

subject to the constraint function:

$$q_i = [\log \Gamma + (1-\beta)m + (1-\beta)(1-\alpha) + \beta H^*] + h_i [\alpha(1-\beta) - \beta] \tag{2b}$$
$$R_i = B(q_i - q^A - \log n)q_i + [c_i + (1-\alpha) + \alpha h_i]/(1+r) \tag{4c}$$
$$H_i + h_i = H^* \tag{2c}$$

The reaction function of rival i is:

$$q_i = \Psi_i q_j + V \tag{6c}$$

where

$$V = \alpha/[2(1+r)B(\beta - \alpha)(1-\beta)] \tag{6c'}$$

Step 2: The Cournot-Nash equilibrium is given by the consistency condition and, hence, the solution to the simultaneous equation system (6c). This will give us the equilibrium military output q_i^e:

$$q_1^e = V(1+\Psi_2)/[1-\Psi_1\Psi_2] \tag{6d}$$
$$q_2^e = V(1+\Psi_1)/[1-\Psi_1\Psi_2] \tag{6e}$$

The existence of equilibrium is guaranteed if $[1-\Psi_1\Psi_2]>0$. Substituting (6d) and (6e) into (2c) from (3a) we derive the optimal efforts corresponding to the Nash equilibrium as:[24]

$$\text{Log } H_1^e = [q_i^e - n - (1-\beta)k_1]/\beta \tag{7a}$$
$$\text{Log } h_1^e = [-q_i^e + n + (1-\beta)k_1]/\beta \tag{7b}$$

First, military build-ups are strategic complements, which create the multiplier effects that will in turn create the action–reaction models of the arms race. This induces the other group to respond by moving in the same direction. Second, decisions concerning fighting efforts are significantly influenced by herd instincts: subjective variations in beliefs of a group (changes in Ψ_1 or Ψ_2) can induce all to change their allocation of their efforts towards conflicts. One may say that these changes are not triggered by changes in the objective world as these changes take place in the subjective realm of decision-makers. Others, though have unchanged subjective beliefs, yet decide to go with the flow (herding) in their military build-ups (see Palley, 1995 for details).[25]

6.4 Sequential decisions and herd behaviour in defence spending

Herd behaviour in investment decisions is a well-received doctrine.[26] We consider a situation in which rival claimants make sequential decisions on their individual efforts to produce military output. One way of rationalising this sequential decision-making is to assume that every year a new cohort of decision-makers – representing these rivals – arrives, who can observe relevant actions of the past cohorts. Suppose there are N cohorts of decision-makers/rivals and N periods while the ith cohort makes a decision at date i, i ranging from 1 to N. Cohort 1 gets to choose their effort h_1 first and then Cohort 2 chooses h_2, and so on and so forth. Contestant i (representing cohort i) chooses the fighting effort h_i given the history of effort levels by the previous cohorts, to obtain the optimal military output q_i. Thus, the decision variable is h_i. Rival contestants do not have a *prior* knowledge of the average opinion q^A. It is common knowledge that q^A can take either of two values. One can call this q^A as the state of nature. Each cohort receives a signal about this state of nature. Each cohort has two possible optimal actions depending on the two possible states or two possible values of q^A. We state this story by assuming that q^A is chosen from a set of 2 possible values $Q=\{0, 1\}$. The state of nature, value of q^A, is set randomly at the beginning of the first period before any decision is made. The probability that $q^A=1$ is θ and the probability that $q^A=0$ is $(1-\theta)$. Rival t at date t has one private signal S_t such that Probability $(S_t=j|q^A=1)=W$. These private signals are independent and symmetric.

We reproduce equation (6c) and know from equation (6c), the optimal military output of rival i is:

$$q_i = V + q^A/2 \tag{6c}$$

Since q^A takes 2 values, the optimal q_i has two possible values q^* and q^{**}:

$$q^* = V \text{ for } q^A = 0 \tag{8a}$$
$$q^{**} = V+1/2 \text{ for } q^A = 1 \tag{8b}$$

The payoff to cohort i is R_i:

$$R_i(q^*) = B(V+V^2)+Y_i/(1+r) \tag{8c}$$
$$R_i(q^{**}) = B(1/4+V+V^2)+Y^i/(1+r) \tag{8d}$$

We now introduce fixed costs (F) of committing to conflict technology to drive our results home:

Assumption 1: $F_i = F_J$ for all i and j. It is assumed that

If $q^A = 0$ and $q_i = q^* = V$, $F_i = 0$.
If $q^A = 1$ and $q_i = q^{**} = V+1/2$, then $F_i = 0$.
If $q^A = 0$ and $q_i = q^{**} = V+1/2$, then $F_i = F_1$.
If $q^A = 1$ and $q_i = q^* = V$, then $F_i = F_2$.

The story is simple: the fixed cost is zero if rivals correctly read the signals and choose appropriate actions. The fixed cost is positive if and only if cohorts incorrectly interpret signals.

Assumption 2: At any date t, rival/cohort t receives a signal S_t such that

$$\text{Probability } \{S_t = j \text{ for } q^A = j\} = \mu \tag{9a}$$

Assumption 3: At any point in time t the prior probability that $q^A = 1$ is θ_t. Rival claimants can be of two types: first, rivals can be *overcautious*. Secondly, rivals can be *reckless*. We call a rival at date t overcautious if s/he receives a signal $S_t = 1$. What it means is that the rival at date t has received a signal that the average opinion is high and s/he hence chooses a larger (equilibrium) effort in building military power. On the other hand, a rival at date t is called reckless if s/he receives a signal $S_t = 0$. A reckless rival receives a signal that the average opinion is of low value and hence s/he chooses a lower (equilibrium) effort to build military might. Each rival can belong to one of these two types.

Note that a reckless type will update the probability that $q^A = 1$ by θ^-:

$$\theta^- = \theta(1-\mu)/[\theta(1-\mu)+\mu(1-\theta)] \tag{9b}$$

Similarly, an overcautious rival updates the prior as the following:

$$\theta^+ = \theta\mu/[\theta(1-\mu)+\mu(1-\theta)] \tag{9c}$$

Note that $\theta^- < \theta^+$ \hfill (9d)

A reckless rival's expected net return from $q*$ is

$$E(r_i(q*)) = B(V+V^2) + Y/(1+r) - F_2 + (1-\theta^-)F_2 \tag{9e}$$

Similarly, the expected net return from $q**$ is

$$E(r_i(q**)) = B(V+1/2)(V+3/2) + Y/(1+r) - (1-F_2) + \theta^-(1-F_2) \tag{9f}$$

A reckless type will choose $q*$ if

$$\theta^- > [F_2 + B(V+3/4)) - 1]/[2F_1 - 1] = L \tag{10a}$$

We define the value of θ as θ^C for which the following condition holds:

$$\theta^-(1-F_2) = \theta^C(1-F_2) = L \tag{10b}$$

That is

$$\theta^C = L\mu/[(1-\mu) + \mu L - L(1-\mu)] \tag{10c}$$

Observation 1: A reckless rival chooses $q*$ (the lower level of equilibrium effort) if

$$\theta > \theta^C \tag{10d}$$

S/he chooses $q**$ (the higher level of equilibrium effort in producing military output) if

$$\theta < \theta^C \tag{10e}$$

Observation 2: An overcautious rival chooses $q**$ if

$$\theta < \theta^{CC} \tag{10d'}$$

S/he chooses $q*$ if

$$\theta > \theta^{CC} \tag{10e'}$$

where

$$\theta^{CC} = L*(1-\mu)/[(1-\mu) - L*(1-\mu) + L*\mu] \tag{10c'}$$

Observation 3: Suppose the publicly held belief (θ) lies in the following interval,

$$\theta^C < \theta < \theta^{CC} \tag{11a}$$

If (11a) holds then rival t will choose $q*$ if the signal is $S_t = 0$ and rival t will choose $q**$ if the signal is $S_t = 1$. Thus, there will be no herding as one's action depends on one's private signals. There is no herding if (11a) holds. On the other hand, herd instincts play a decisive role if $\theta^C > \theta$ because rival/cohort, t chooses $q*$ regardless of the private signal that s/he receives. Similarly, herd instincts drive the formation of military might (military output) if $\theta^{CC} < \theta$ because rival t choose $q**$ regardless of the private signal that s/he receives. We establish, to the best of our knowledge for the first time, that the formation of military might, conflicts and war technology can be driven by herd instincts of Banerjee (1992) and Bikhchandani and Hirshleifer (1992) type.

6.5   Empirical foundation to herding in arms spending

The theoretical prediction of our model is the rather uncomfortable proposition that the arms race can be predicated upon the herd instincts of decision-makers, or nations, to follow each other in building their defence capabilities and war technologies, which can often be completely unnecessary and patently dangerous. Though the issue of herding in arms spending is an immense issue, our chapter is one of the very first to unravel if there is any evidence that nation states might follow each other in their decisions to build up military capability. To assess herding in the arms race, or defence spending, we examine the time profile of defence spending by the top 50 spenders on arms of our globe. They are the most militarised nations of our planet. We apply the standard tools to measure herding in defence spending by analysing the time profile of defence spending of these 50 nations in the post-Cold War era during the period of 1991 through 2009, for which we have data in the constant US dollar. Using the data set, we seek to capture the extent to which nation states collectively increase or decrease defence spending in each year.[27] We want to issue a caveat here: it is well-recognised in the literature that evidence on herding in financial markets based on the standard LSV indicator, developed by Lakonishok et al. (1992), is pronounced only over daily time intervals, which suggests that the LSV indicator measures the short-term nature of herding. When empirical tests are based on annual data, herd instincts become much less pronounced in financial markets in terms of the LSV indicator. As a result, we will also offer an alternative indicator to detect herding, in order to overcome the short-term aspects of the LSV indicator, in Section 6. At the outset it is also important to recognise that our results will be influenced by the classification of 50 nations into ten competing groups on the basis of their defence spending without paying any attention to their regional rivalry. As a result of the new global order, after the collapse of the Cold War, there is very little evidence of cross-border rivalry, conflicts and open wars between nations, though there are some exceptions. With the demise of the Cold War type of interactions, our classification suggests that nations of similar sizes compete with each other in the global arena for establishing their relative military supremacy within their respective reference groups. Since the primary goal is to detect herding, and not to precisely measure herding, we note that the reference group formation will impact on the precise value of the measure and not on the general detection of herding.

6.5.1 Evidence of herding in arms spending: empirical strategy

For our case study we look at the defence spending of 50 nations in constant dollar terms from 1989 to 2009. These 50 nations are first ranked in terms of their defence spending and then divided into ten groups on the basis of their ranks in terms of defence spending (see Table 6A.2). The first group consists of the top 5 nations in terms of defence spending – they are the permanent members of the UN Security Council. The next group consists of the next five nations and so on and so forth. In the context of social learning and herding, we examine three critical ingredients to measure herding: first we consider the annual change in defence spending and label the proportion of countries P_{it} of countries in group i at date t that increased their defence spending from the previous year. We then compute $E[P_{it}]$ as the expected proportion of the chosen 50 countries that increased their defence spending at date t, which is measured as the mean of all observed P_{it} for $i = 1,2..10$. In the context of financial markets the LSV index is based on the idea that herding occurs when decision-makers, nation states in our case, deviate from an *'average'* behaviour. It is important to note that their methodology is purely statistical and does not depend on any structural model. Let $LSV_{i,t}$ be the herding level of country i at period t. $LSV_{i,t}$ is calculated as follows:

$$LSV_{i,t} = |P_{i,t} - E[P_{i,t}]| - E[|P_{i,t} - E[P_{i,t}]|] \tag{12a}$$

$$P_{it} = I_{it}/5 \tag{12a'}$$

$$P_t = \sum_{i=0}^{10} P_{it} \tag{12a''}$$

Where $|\,|$ is the absolute value norm, $P_{i,t}$ is the proportion of countries in group i who increased their defence spending in period t. Thus I_{it} is the number of countries in group i that increase their levels of defence spending at date t from their individual levels of spending at date $t - 1$. Similar to previous studies, the proportion of all nations that increase their defence spending at date t is used as a proxy for $E[P_{i,t}]$. It is calculated by dividing the total number of times that nations increase their defence spending at date t by the total number of changes in defence spending date t. Tables 6A.3 and 6A.4 at the end of this chapter provide the figures on P_{it} and I_{it}. The primary intuition of the measure is that when there is no herding, then increases and decreases in defence spending are randomly distributed. If there are excessive increases, or decreases, then it is interpreted as herding behaviour. In the index on herding $E[P_{i,t}]$ represents the benchmark against which herding is assessed. It is the average proportion of increases in defence spending by all 50 nations in date t. Note that $E[|P_{i,t} - E[P_{i,t}]|$ is an adjustment factor. It is meant to account for the random variation of $E[P_{i,t}]$ under the null hypothesis that there is no herding among nations. Due to the assumption that the number of nations increasing their defence spending in each date t follows binomial distribution, $E[|P_{i,t} - E[P_{i,t}]|$ is calculated given the value of $E[P_{i,t}]$ and the total number of changes (increases and decreases) in spending. The adjustment factor $A(.)$ is calculated as the following k takes a value from 0, 1…5:

$$A(P_{it}, E(P_{it})) = \sum_{k=0}^{5} \binom{5}{k} P_i^k (1-P_i)^{5-k} \mid (k/5) - P_t \mid$$

(12b)

If $LSV_{i,t}$ is statistically significant from a value of zero, then there is evidence of herding behaviour among nations. In other words, LSV_{it} has a zero expected value under the hypothesis of no herding. Herding is measured by averaging $LSV_{i,t}$ among all ten groups of nations for the desired time period t and the overall measure is the average all groups of nations across time and we denote this overall measure of herding LSV. A common weakness of the index is that the adjustment factor, $A(p_{it}, E(p_{it}))$, overcorrects the estimated parameter (see Frey et al., 2007) and the evidence of herding is thus under-reported by the LSV measure. It is also instructive to note that for a group i $LSV_{it} > 0$ implies nations in group i herd by copying each other in increasing their defence spending while $LSV_{it} < 0$ implies that these nations copy each other in decreasing their defence spending. If one takes an increase (decrease/ unchanged) in defence spending as a vice (virtue), then $LSV_{it} < 0$ indicates virtuous herding while $LSV_{it} > 0$ measures what we call vicious herding. The overall LSV index for a year t is expressed as LSV_t:

$$LSV_t = \sum_{i=0}^{10} (LSV_{it})/10$$

(12b′)

6.5.2   *Data and relevant variables*

We collected the data on defence spending of each nation from the SIPRI webpage at constant 1999 prices. A total of 1,000 data points are collected from 1989 to 2009. We rank each country in terms of their defence spending in a descending order and put these 50 countries into 10 deciles, or groups with five members. The descriptive statistics are provided in Table 6A.1 at the end of this chapter. From the time series data on the defence spending of 50 countries we then calculate the variables I_{it}, P_{it}, $E(P_{it})$ and $|P_{i,t} - E[P_{i,t}]|$, $E[|P_{i,t} - E[P_{i,t}]|]$ and $A(P_{it}, E(P_{it}))$ wherefrom we derive the herding measures LSV_{it}, for each year and also the overall measure of herding LSV. In our work, note that P_t is the expected proportion of all 50 nations that increased their defence spending in year t, which is calculated as a mean of all the observed P_{it} in the year t. This P_t can be considered as an indicator of the overall defence policy that reflects the global environment involving potential conflicts. If every nation *independently* increases (or decreases) its spending in year t with probability P_t (or $1-P_t$), which is based rationally on global factors of potential conflicts, the observed value of P_i becomes close to P_t and the first term of LSV_{it} will become zero. If, on the other hand, nations in a group *collectively* increase or decrease their spending in a year, the observed value of P_{it} departs from P_t. The first term of LSV_{it} thus quantifies the extent to which nations' defence spending strategies in a year deviate from the overall spending strategy of the entire group of 50 leading nations in terms of overall defence spending in that year. The overall value of P_t thus represents the null hypothesis of no herding. Non-independent corrective increase and decrease amount to a larger value of the first absolute value. The last term $E|P_{it} - P_t|$ of the LSV measure of equation (12a) is subtracted so as to normalise the measure and make its mean zero under the null hypothesis of no herding.

6.5.3   Evidence of herding in arms spending from standard measures of herding

In early work the measure of herding has been used by Lakonishok et al. (1992), Grinblatt et al. (1995), and Wermers (1999), among others, to appraise the presence of herding instincts among institutional investors mainly in mutual funds. Herding on financial markets, using the same measure, has been detected to be economically and statistically significant. Lakonishok et al. (1992) report a value of 2.7 while Wermers (1999) calculated a value of 3.40 for the overall herding in financial markets. In interesting studies Uchida and Nakagawa (2007) applied it to the Japanese loan market while Weiner (2006) examined the role of herding in the oil market. Recent studies highlight the presence of herding in developmental aid-giving as the LSV index indicates a significant level of herding aid allocation, similar to that which is found on financial markets (see Frot and Santiso, 2009). Herding behaviour is believed to be pronounced in emerging markets as highlighted by various studies on the spillover effects of financial crises (see Ornelas and Alemanni, 2008; Bekaert and Harvery, 2000).

Overall herding in defence spending, as calculated in our study as per the standard LSV index, is roughly three-quarters of what has been observed in financial markets.[28] Our result shows that the overall LSV measure of herding in defence spending is significantly larger than the observed values of herding in the oil market, and also in the loan market. Herding in aid allocation is roughly a half of what is observed in defence spending according to our LSV measure. Herding is thus significantly pronounced in the context of defence spending. The annual values of the LSV_t measures are calculated by applying equations (12a)–(12b″) and are provided in Table 6.1.

Table 6.1 The overall *LSV* measure of herding in defence spending

Year	P_t	$1-P_t$	$|P_t - E[P_t]|$	$E[|P_t - E[P_t]|]$	LSV_t
1990	0.6170	0.3830	0.2268	0.1600	0.0668
1991	0.4894	0.5106	0.1979	0.1863	0.0116
1992	0.5000	0.5000	0.2000	0.1875	0.0125
1993	0.4600	0.5400	0.2800	0.1839	0.0961
1994	0.4600	0.5400	0.1680	0.1839	−0.0159
1995	0.4706	0.5294	0.1850	0.1855	−0.0005
1996	0.5098	0.4902	0.2800	0.1873	0.0927
1997	0.5294	0.4706	0.2200	0.2498	−0.0298
1998	0.5294	0.4706	0.2080	0.1855	0.0225
1999	0.6667	0.3333	0.2000	0.1665	0.0335
2000	0.6078	0.3922	0.1415	0.1677	−0.0262
2001	0.6667	0.3333	0.2133	0.1665	0.0468
2002	0.7059	0.2941	0.1811	0.1788	0.0023
2003	0.6471	0.3529	0.2200	0.1749	0.0451
2004	0.6863	0.3137	0.1345	0.1743	−0.0398
2005	0.4510	0.5490	0.2701	0.1839	0.0862
2006	0.6471	0.3529	0.2505	0.1749	0.0756
2007	0.7059	0.2941	0.1600	0.1788	−0.0188
2008	0.5490	0.4510	0.2101	0.1855	0.0246
2009	0.7059	0.2941	0.2000	0.1788	0.0212

It is imperative to note the time profile of the overall herding measure LSV_t of 50 countries presented in Figure 6.1. First, the measure of herding (LSV_t) displays a significant volatility over time with three significant spikes in 1993, 1996 and 2005 when the index LSV_t shot up above .08, which is nearly 2.5 times the value of *LSV* index observed in financial markets. For 1995, 2000 and 2004, the value of LSV_t turns out to be negative, which indicates nations have herded in reducing their defence spending, instead of increasing, for those three years. Second, if we take the average (absolute) value of 2.7 for the *LSV* index in financial markets as the benchmark, we note that the absolute value of LSV_t in defence spending has exceeded the benchmark of 2.7 in 1990, 1993, 1996, 1997, 2000, 2003, 2004, 2005, 2006. Finally, since the year 2001, the LSV_t has deviated significantly from its expected value of zero under the assumption of no-herding. Only twice, during the period of 2001–2009, the LSV_t is close to zero. In most years since 2001 the LSV_t has also exceeded the benchmark of 2.7.

In order to explain the source of volatility in the index of herding as depicted in Figure 6.1, we consider the 3-year average of LSV_t for our ten groups of nations. The 3-year averages of the herding values of individual groups are presented in Figure 6.2.

Some interesting features are immediately obvious from Figure 6.2. First and foremost, the top decile of nations in terms of defence spending have

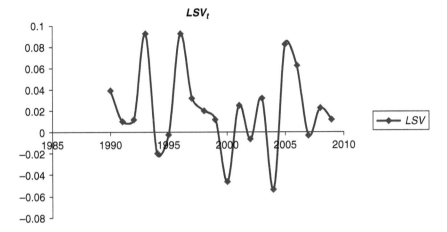

Figure 6.1 Time path of the overall index of herding (LSV_t) in defence spending

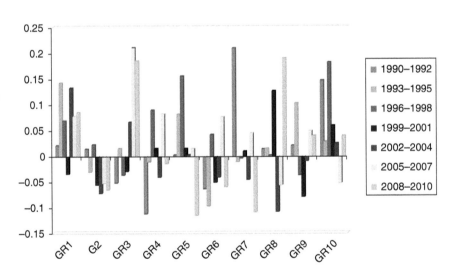

Figure 6.2 The 3-year average of herding index (LSV) for the top 10 decile nations

displayed a strong herding instinct to follow each other mainly to increase their defence spending (except in one phase). Thus, the top decile of nations seemed to have been motivated by what we call the vicious herding. We see the predominance of vicious herding at the other extreme since the lowest decile of nations also displayed an instinct to follow each other. We also note vicious herding in the third decile of nations. Secondly, we note a strong element of virtuous herding in the second and sixth deciles of nations that seemed to have followed each other in order to decrease, or keep unchanged, their defence spending. Other deciles have a mixed bag of virtuous and vicious herding. Finally, as a result of mutually opposing forces of vicious and virtuous herding, the LSV index of herding shows a great dose of volatility over time. Admittedly, the index cannot distinguish intentional herding, where nations wilfully imitate the spending behaviour of other nations from what is known as 'spurious herding' as defined by Bikhchandani and Sharma (2000), where groups facing similar information sets take a similar decision. However, this is the general difficulty with the available measures of herding.

The overall herding measure in Section 6.5.3 has been partly determined by the mutually opposing effects of virtuous and vicious herding. As a result, the observed value of herding is an understatement of actual herding that drives nations to copy each other in their decisions to choosing optimal defence spending. In what follows, we offer a simple index that does not dichotomise herding into virtuous and vicious herding instincts and instead offers an overall index in order to overcome the mutually opposing effects of virtuous and vicious herding.

6.5.4   *A modified measure of herding: vicious and virtuous herding*

In order not to separate the vicious herding from virtuous herding we offer a modified index of LSV,[29] called $MLSV_{it}$, such that we can capture the presence of herd mentality as

$$MLSV_{i,t} = |[|P_{i,t} - E[P_{i,t}]| - E[|P_{i,t} - E[P_{i,t}]|]|\qquad(12c)$$

By taking the absolute value of the difference between $|[P_{i,t} - E[P_{i,t}]|$ and the mean of $|[P_{i,t} - E[P_{i,t}]|$, we nullify the opposite effects of virtuous and vicious herding. The modified LSV now captures both the instincts of decision-makers to imitate, to increase and also decrease (or keep unchanged) their defence spending. Thus, $MLSV_{it}$ is often a better index of imitation than the standard LSV_{it} given by (12a). The overall $MLSV$ is an average measure of $MLSV_{it}$ over time $(1, 2 \ldots T)$ and thus:

$$MLSV = \sum_{i=0}^{10}\sum_{t=0}^{T}\frac{(MLSV_{it})}{T}\qquad(12d)$$

Note that (12d) is depicted as the higher horizontal line in Figure 6.3 and the modified measure of LSV_{it} is the uneven and light grey path, while the lower horizontal line is the average value of LSV in financial markets.

The modified measure of herding ($MLSV$) reveals an interesting picture as the average $MLSV$, as a measure of medium-term herd instincts, is more than 4 times the short-term LSV measure in financial markets. Though fluctuating, the medium-term $MLSV$ has always remained significantly above the average short-term LSV measures in financial markets. It is well-recognised that the LSV measure not only provides an understatement of herding, but is also more pronounced in the short-term responses. Once can thus safely conclude from the crude comparisons with the short-term measures of herding in financial markets that the evidence of herding in military build-ups is not less pronounced than the available evidence of herding in financial markets, oil markets, real estate markets or allocation of banking loans.

6.6   A new measure of herding in the arms race

In this section we will test for the presence of herding by investigating cross-sectional dispersions of changes in defence spending against the average change in defence spending within a group. The primary intuition is that such dispersions are meant to be low in the presence of herd behaviour.[30] In other words, a smaller cross-sectional dispersion indicates parallel movements with the cross-sectional mean defence spending, which in turn underscores a *consensus* among nations, or decision-makers, about the need for military build-up. The type of herding that these particular measures examine is system-based and is significantly different to the previous measures of herding, which refers to subgroups of nations behaving similarly in their efforts to military build-up. In the new measure individual behaviour follows the overall group behaviour. Although the cross-sectional standard deviation of returns is an intuitive measure for capturing herding, it can be considerably affected by the existence of outliers. That is why we will use the cross-sectional absolute deviation (CSAD) to measure the cross-sectional dispersion of changes in defence spending in this work. The $CSAD$ at date t is compared with the average change of defence spending for the major nations, or most militarised nations, of the world. The relationship between $CSAD_t$ and the average spending at date t is used to detect herd behaviour. In the presence of herding the relationship between $CSAD$ and average defence spending will be non-linear. In the absence of herding, the relationship will be linear. In the previous section we examined a measure of herding by using the distribution of changes of defence spending by 50 top spenders. In this section, the following equation explains the measure of herding and we use a cubic polynomial in the absolute value of the average change in defence spending (X) in our econometric models for detecting herd mentality in arms races. Our benchmark regression model for country i is as follows:

$$CSAD_t = \Sigma_N\{(X_{it} - X_t)/N\} \tag{13a}$$

where X_{it} is the observed change in defence spending in millions of dollars by nation i at time t and X_t is the cross-sectional average change in defence spending of N nations in the group at time t, while N is the number of nations

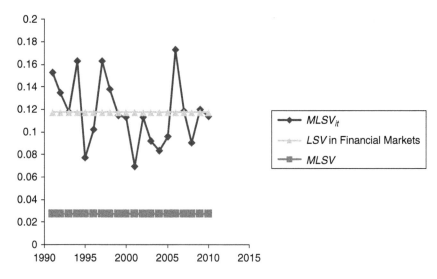

Figure 6.3 A modified *LSV* measure ($MLSV_{it}$) of herding in defence spending

in the group. We retain the same principle of grouping nations from the ranking of nations in terms of the size of defence spending as undertaken in Section 6.5.1.[31] We then model the relationship between *CSAD* and *X* as a non-linear equation:

$$CSAD_t = \alpha + \gamma_1 * X_t + \gamma_2 * X_t^2 + \gamma_3 * X_t^3 + error \tag{13b}$$

Table 6.2 provides the details of the regression result and we find all the coefficients are economically significant. All the coefficients, except γ_2, are statistically significant, which is consistent with the theory of herding, as will be explained subsequently. The empirical model provides us with the following (ignoring the time script):

$$CSAD = 1.29 - 0.39\ X - 0.11\ X^2 - 007\ X^3 \tag{13c}$$

$$\frac{d(CSAD)}{dX} = -0.39 + 0.22\ X - 0.021\ X^2 \tag{13d}$$

$$\frac{d^2(CSAD)}{dX^2} = 0.22 - .041\ X \tag{14a}$$

(13c) Implies:

$$\frac{d(CSAD)}{dX} = 0\ for\ X_{Min} = 5.34,\ X_{Max} = 5.37 \tag{14b}$$

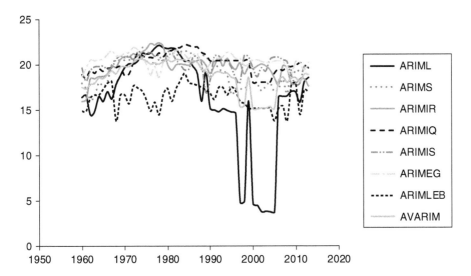

Figure 6.4 Evidence of herding in the arms race from the alternative measure

(14a) implies:

$$\frac{d^2(CSAD)}{dX^2} = 0 \ \ for \ X^{CR} = 5.37 \tag{14c}$$

Combining (13d), (14b) and (14c) one will get the wave function (reversed S-function) in the relationship between $CSAD$ and X, the positive association arising for the values of X within a narrow range of {5.34, 5.37}. Outside this range, there exists an inverse association between $CSAD$ and X, which is an indication of herd behaviour in defence build-up. It is instructive to note that the relationship between $CSAD$ and X will be U-shaped for values of X such that $0<X<5.34$. In other words, if $X<5.34$, the curve depicts that nations herd in their decisions to build up military might. On the other hand, if X lies in the region {5.34, 5.37}, our results show that the nations anti-herd. Nations herd once again if $X>5.37$.

Figure 6.4 illustrates the cross-sectional dispersion in defence spending with respect to the average cross-sectional change in defence spending.

In the absence of herding the relationship as described in (13b) will be linear and increasing. Except for a small interval of X, the relationship is neither linear nor increasing, which shows the presence of herd mentality in the arms race. Except for the narrow band of values for X in the region {5.34, 5.37}, the dispersion in defence spending in a group declines as the absolute value of the average change in defence spending in the group increases. We are thus

Table 6.2 A new measure of herding: regression results

Dependent Variable: CSAD

Method: Least Squares

Variable	Coefficient	Std. Error	t-Statistic	Prob.
Constant	$\alpha = 1.2968$	0.116263	11.15422	0.0000
X	$\gamma^{1}_{=}-0.3895$	0.094310	−4.130118	0.0008
X^2	$\gamma^{2}_{=}0.1169$	0.031711	3.688936	0.0020
X^3	$\gamma^{3}_{=}-0.0070$	0.002433	−2.902635	0.0104
R−squared	0.630061	Mean dependent var		1.295878
Adjusted R-squared	0.560698	S.D. dependent var		0.488648
S.E. of regression	0.323875	Akaike info criterion		0.759940
Sum squared resid	1.678323	Schwarz criterion		0.959086
Log likelihood	−3.599397	Hannan-Quinn criter.		0.798815
F-statistic	9.083461	Durbin-Watson stat		1.171171
Prob(F-statistic)	0.000959			

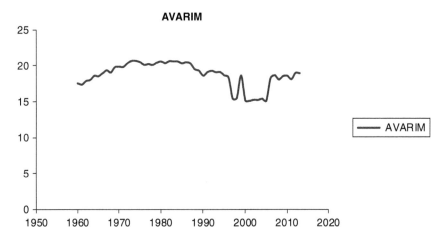

Figure 6.5 The dynamics of arms imports by individual countries to the region

able to show the existence, or possibility, of significant herd instincts in the arms race in the post Cold War era.

6.7 Arms race and herding in the Middle East and North Africa

In Figure 6.5 we present the logarithmic values of arms imports of the seven chosen countries from the Middle East and North Africa. The variables are defined in Chapter 4 and also at the beginning of Chapter 6. A quick look at

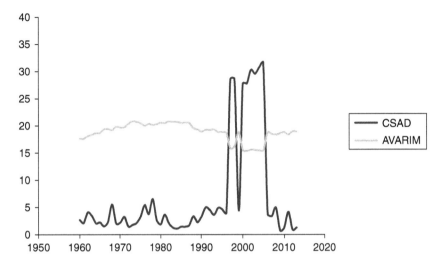

Figure 6.6 The dynamics of arms imports to the region

the figure confirms some serious fluctuations in the arms imports to the seven countries in the region during 1960–2013.

In Figure 6.6 we plot the average value (of logarithm) of arms imports to the region. $AVARIM_t$ is the average value of arms imports to the seven countries in the region in year t. For the tractability of notations, we have suppressed the time subscript in Figure 6.6. Until 1995, the variable $AVARIM$ shows a hill-shaped time path – it rises until 1984 and then starts declining until 1995. Since 1995, the variable shows wild fluctuations, though the trend has been rising since 1995.

In order to characterise the movement of the variable, $AVARIM$, we calculate the $CSAD$ of $AVARIM$ during 1961 to 2013 and plot the evolution of $CSAD$ during 1961–2013 in Figure 6.7. The plotting of $CSAD$ shows very strong fluctuations in $CSAD$ over time, which calls forth a formal statistical analysis of $CSAD$.

In order to fit a $\Delta CSAD$ as a function of ΔX, in what follows, we present the time series results for the $\Delta CSAD$ equation where Δ is the change operator:

$$\Delta CSAD_t = \alpha_0 + \alpha_1 \, \Delta X_t + \alpha_2 \, (\Delta X_t)^2 + \alpha_3 \, (\Delta X_t)^3 \qquad (15a)$$

We present the values of αs and their statistical significance in Table 6.3.

Since the cubic term is very small and statistically insignificant, we drop the cubic term to derive the $\Delta CSAD$ as a function of X_t. The herding equation:

$$\Delta CSAD_t = 0.091 - 43.70 \, \Delta X_t + 1.06 \, \Delta X^2 = F(\Delta X) \qquad (15b)$$

Table 6.3 Estimates of equation (15a)

Variables	Coefficients	Z
Constant (α_0)	0.91	2.55*
ΔX_t	−43.01	−7.04*
$(\Delta X_t)^2$	1.06	5.34*
$(\Delta X_t)^3$	0.005	1.2

*Statistically significant

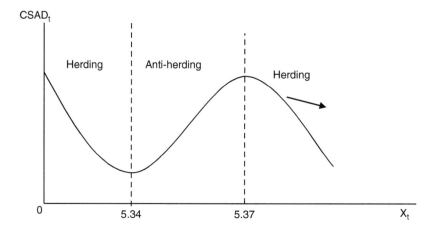

Figure 6.7 The dynamics of herding in arms imports to the region

The quadratic equation (15b) is integrated to arrive at the $CSAD_t$ equation which gives us two critical values of X, X^* and X^{**} (note not ΔX), such that the function $F(X)$ is an inverse function of X for $X^{**}<X<X^*$ since it has a negative slope for $X^{**}<X<X^*$ and $F(X)$ bears a positive relationship with X otherwise. By differentiating (15b) and equating it to zero, we derive $X^* = 0.01$ and $X^{**} = 43$. Since the maximum observed X for the Middle East and North Africa region is more than 0.01 and less than 20.61 for all years during 1960 to 2013, the relevant segment of the $F(X)$ function has always been in the zone $X^{**}<X<X^*$ for the Middle East and North Africa. For the region consisting of these seven nations $CSAD_t (= F(X))$ is steadily declining as X rises during 1960–2013. What we learn from the dynamics of $CSAD_t$ is that the nations in the region have herded on each other for importing arms from overseas. In simpler terms, these nations in the region spend significant resources to import arms – not because the decision-makers feel it is important to do so – but just by following each other. The impacts of herding on justice, equity and the economy will be examined in Chapter 7.

6.8 Concluding comments

The arms race is an immense issue confronting our globe and so is herd mentality in the arms race. Ours is a first small step to understand the possibility of informational cascades and herding in the context of the arms race and to search for some empirical validation of our model. It begs a question of why we need herding to justify arms races. In the context of incomplete information, the latest models of the arms race explain the possibility of the detente equilibrium and the information acquisition/ learning phase such that there is nothing sacrosanct, or automatic or instantaneous, about the onset and continuation of the arms race. These new developments in the arms race literature tend to contradict and discount the findings of the earlier Richardsonian framework traditionally applied to explain arms races by the action–reaction type of interactions between nations. Our major contribution is to bring informational cascades into the incomplete information setting to highlight how human irrationalities can still play immense roles in triggering, fuelling and propelling the arms race in our contemporary world.

We model the arms race as anarchy that is a system in which rival nations engage in military build-ups to defend economic resources without an effective regulation, or protection, from above. Military build-ups are costly since they require inputs that will diminish the resources for producing the economic good (e.g. GDP). Military spending is important for advancing national interests in order to protect, or expand, economic resources. We also assume that the economic output (GDP) has a positive feedback to the production of military output. In this mixed model the military build-up of a nation is shown to depend, inter alia, on what the rival expects one's rivals to do. From this interdependency, we derive a game of military build-ups and the relevant Nash characterisation as a combination of mutually best responses in the context of incomplete information. In the context of arms race models with incomplete information, a number of recent works highlighted the relevance of communication and social learning in preventing an arms race. The incompleteness of information motivates nations to learn from social interactions, which is the primary intuition of our chapter that allows a necessary extension of the literature by developing a comprehensive model of informational cascades in the arms race and tests its validity from the dynamics of military spending by major players in the global arms market. We find, due to herd sentiments, there is a non-zero probability that the military spending and the arms race will never be predicated on an objective consideration of the costs and benefits associated with arming. In the post Cold War era, the annual spending of $1 trillion on global military build-ups is not only a steep price to pay for the arms race but is also socially inefficient since – despite myriads of private signals that reveal the right choice on the arms race – nations seem to herd on the incorrect choice of arming with positive probability. The decision to get armed and subsequently embroiled in a war and ensuing violent conflicts can be driven by herd sentiments: every nation is individually rational to arm being ready to fight a 'bloody war', even if all nations have overwhelming (private) information that there is absolutely no necessity to do so. In other words, everybody will willingly embrace the 'wrong behaviour' even when there is enough evidence in favour of espousing the 'right behaviour', which can push our civilisation to the precipice of meaningless self-destruction. We also find evidence of herding in the arms imports in the region consisting of the seven nations from the Middle East and North Africa.

Appendix to Chapter 6

Table 6A.1 Descriptive statistics of annual defence spending of the top 50 countries

Year	Mean	Median	Maximum	Minimum	Kurtosis	Skewness
1989	31947.34	7882.5	528140	674	23.2	4.7
1990	30712.14	8254.5	504534	720	25	4.84
1991	23796.8	7004.5	442986	143	37	5.93
1992	23836.55	6683.5	468216	125	39	6
1993	22171	6450.5	443598	509	40	6
1994	21881.62	6071	416580	1614	39	6
1995	20275.77	5564	393996	941	41	6.21
1996	19845.42	5122	372569	705	40.32	6.14
1997	19788.33	5375	370627	1129	41	6.2
1998	19520.96	6022	362277	348	40.98	6.18
1999	19878.57	6101	363170	1784	40.82	6.16
2000	20643.1	6101	377228	1382	41.15	6.2
2001	21097.7	6141	380271	1243	40.94	6.1
2002	22396.71	6435	426982	1274	41.98	6.3
2003	23837.28	6538	485975	1682	43	6.4
2004	25141.16	6619	529673	1601	43.9	6.48
2005	26131.63	6619	554930	2268	44.2	6.5
2006	26950.26	7136	563549	2566	43.99	6.48
2007	27792.83	7412	578340	2337	43.78	6.46
2008	27798.81	7419	578350	2340	43.34	6.66
2009	27799.12	7425	5783380	2367	43.76	6.42

Note: Constructed from the SIPRI data.

Table 6A.2 Description of ten groups (deciles) of 50 nations

GR_1	GR_2	GR_3	GR_4	GR_5
USA	Germany	South Korea	Turkey	Poland
China	Japan	Brazil	Israel	Colombia
UK	S Arabia	Canada	Greece	Taiwan
France	Italy	Australia	UAE	Iran
Russia	India	Spain	Netherlands	Singapore

GR_6	GR_7	GR_8	GR_9	GR_{10}
Sweden	Mexico	Kuwait	Oman	Venezuela
Norway	Indonesia	Denmark	South Africa	Czech Republic
Chile	Thailand	Ukraine	Finland	Morocco
Algeria	Portugal	Switzerland	Egypt	Angola
Belgium	Pakistan	Malaysia	Austria	Iraq

Note: GR_i is the ith decile (group) of countries ranked in terms of their defence expenditure where $i=1..2..10$.

Table 6A.3 Observations on I_{it}

Year	1990	1991	1992	1993	1994	1995	1996	1997	1998	1999
I_{1t}	1	3	2	0	1	1	1	2	1	4
I_{2t}	3	1	1	4	2	2	3	4	4	4
IP_{3t}	2	2	3	4	3	3	1	3	3	4
I_{4t}	3	3	2	3	1	3	5	3	4	5
I_{5t}	5	2	3	5	3	3	5	5	3	3
I_{6t}	4	2	3	2	3	2	4	2	4	5
I_{7t}	5	5	4	2	3	4	3	2	1	3
I_{8t}	3	2	0	3	4	3	2	2	1	1
I_{9t}	2	3	4	1	3	0	2	4	3	3
I_{10t}	1	0	2	0	2	3	0	0	3	2
$[I_t/N_t]$	29/47	23/47	24/48	23/50	23/50	24/51	26/51	27/51	27/51	34/51

Year	2000	2001	2002	2003	2004	2005	2006	2007	2008	2009
I_{1t}	4	4	5	5	5	4	4	5	4	5
I_{2t}	4	3	3	4	3	2	2	3	2	4
I_{3t}	3	5	5	4	5	5	5	5	5	5
I_{4t}	3	2	3	2	3	3	5	2	3	5
I_{5t}	2	5	3	5	4	4	4	3	3	4
I_{6t}	3	3	3	2	3	2	0	4	2	3
I_{7t}	4	5	4	2	3	0	4	4	3	3
I_{8t}	2	2	3	3	3	2	2	4	4	1
I_{9t}	4	3	5	4	3	0	4	3	1	3
I_{10t}	2	2	2	2	3	1	3	3	1	3
$[I_t/N_t]$	31/51	34/51	36/51	33/51	35/51	23/51	33/51	36/51	28/51	36/51

I_{it}: Number of nations in Group i increasing defence spending at date t from the previous year.
I_t: At date t number of nations increasing defence spending from the previous year among all 50 nations. $N_t=50$

Table 6A.4 Observations on P_{it} and $E(P_{it})$ for each group of nations

Year	1990	1991	1992	1993	1994	1995	1996	1997	1998	1999
P_{1t}	1	3	2	0	1	1	1	2	1	4
P_{2t}	3	1	1	4	2	2	3	4	4	4
P_{3t}	2	2	3	4	3	3	1	3	3	4
P_{4t}	3	3	2	3	1	3	5	3	4	5
P_{5t}	5	2	3	5	3	3	5	5	3	3
P_{6t}	4	2	3	2	3	2	4	2	4	5
P_{7t}	5	5	4	2	3	4	3	2	1	3
P_{8t}	3	2	0	3	4	3	2	2	1	1
P_{9t}	2	3	4	1	3	0	2	4	3	3
P_{10t}	1	0	2	0	2	3	0	0	3	2
$E[P_{it}]$	29/47	23/47	24/48	23/50	23/50	24/50	26/50	27/50	27/50	34/50

*	2000	2001	2002	2003	2004	2005	2006	2007	2008	2009
$E[P_{it}]$	31/50	34/50	36/50	33/50	35/50	23/50	33/50	36/50	28/50	36/50

* We only show the overall figures for years

Notes

1 In 2011, as highlighted by the Grimmett Report of 2012, the three major markets of global conventional weapons in the developing world are Saudi Arabia (21%), India (13%) and the UAE (6%) while many other nations have continually upgraded their military capability.

2 In the simplest model, one may assume, a sequence of nations, or leaders of these states, each choose in turn one of two options, A (to arm) or B (not to arm), each state observing all of one's predecessors' choices. They have common preferences over the two choices but do not know which is better. States know their own costs and benefits from military build-up, but they are unsure of the costs and benefits of their rivals from the arms race. In other words, the costs and benefits of arming often depend on the social, moral, political and psychological considerations of the leaders of states, which are often idiosyncratic and country-specific, or leader-specific.

3 Social interactions influence individual (economic) decision-making in many situations. Herding fits in the broader spectrum of social interactions when agents lend primacy to learning from social interactions over and above their prior individual knowledge. Social interactions usually take place whenever an agent's return is a function not only of his own action but also depends on the actions of other agents in a given setting (Townsend, 1983).

4 There is an extensive literature on the relevance of social interactions and learning for economic behaviour in a wide range of contexts. As an example, Benabou (1993) considers social interactions in neighbourhoods with regards to education and crime. Diamond (1982) introduces social interactions in thick market externalities in trading. The literature has established social interactions can have a wide range of effects on the properties of the economic equilibrium: social interactions can lead either to conformity of behaviour, or to polarised actions (Bernheim, 1994). They can also cause multiplicity of equilibrium in cases in which equilibrium would otherwise be unique (Cooper and John, 1988). Cooper and Haltiwanger (1996) argue how social interactions can influence the dynamic equilibrium of a system.

5 We assume that in every period a new cohort of decision-makers, say politicians, arrives who can observe the relevant actions of the past cohorts and learn from the action of past decision-makers.

6 In all these models the authors displayed a tendency to 'herd' in their modelling techniques, maybe due to reputational concerns – or otherwise: a decision-making agent has a private signal about the state of the world, and the accuracy of this signal is predicated upon one's ability. There is publicly available information summarised as a public prior, which determines the likely state of the decision-making environment/world. The agent chooses an action on the basis of this public prior and one's own private information, or signals. There is a peer who observes the state of the world, the public prior, and the set of chosen actions by a multitude of agents. The peer can assess the quality of the agents' private information, which sheds light on an agent's ability. The decision-making agent's payoff depends on the assessment of the peer and s/he, hence, chooses to 'herd' in order to avoid being assessed as an agent of less ability, or 'dumb'.

7 Each cohort has two possible optimal actions depending on the two possible states, or two possible values of q^A. We state this story by assuming that q^A is chosen from a set of 2 possible values $Q = \{0, 1\}$. The state of nature, value of q^A, is set randomly at the beginning of the first period before any decision is made. The probability that $q^A = 1$ is θ and the probability that $q^A = 0$ is $(1-\theta)$.

8 Cohort t (at date t) has one private signal S_t such that Probability $(S_t = j | q^A = 1) = W$. If a condition holds then agent/cohort t will choose an action q^* if the signal is $S_t = 0$ and cohort t will choose q^{**} if the signal is $S_t = 1$.

9 Similarly, herd instincts drive the formation of war efforts and ensuing conflicts if there exists θ^{CC} such that $\theta^{CC} < \theta$ – agent, or cohort, t choose q^{**} regardless of the private signal that s/he receives.

10 Two phenomena are of particular interest to the profession, namely informational cascades and herd behaviour that can arise in several circumstances. Despite the fact that herd behaviour and informational cascades are interchangeably used in the existing literature, there is a significant difference in their precise imports. Informational cascades describe an infinite sequence of individual decisions in which individuals ignore their private information while making a decision. In herding, an infinite sequence of individuals makes an identical decision (see Smith and Sorensen, 2000). Herding thus implies that individuals choose the *same* action in a given circumstance, but they may have acted differently from one another if the realisation of their private signals had been different. In this paper we focus solely upon herd behaviour, or herding.

11 Note that reputational herding is feasible if better agents have more correlated signals on the state of the world. Without this correlation followers would have little incentive to copy predecessors' behaviour. However, Ottaviani and Sorensen (2002) have shown that this correlation is not necessary except in the degenerate case.

12 Measurement of the arms race is a contentious issue: the early index of the arms race by Wallace (1979; 1982) was called in question by Weede (1980) and Diehl (1983) as being non-comparable. A simple index of Diehl (1983) is often used to measure the arms race as 8% or more increases in military spending over at least 3 consecutive years by two rival states.

13 Primarily, arms races are viewed as an action–reaction process triggered, fuelled and shaped by real or perceived external threat (Buzan and Herring 1998, p. 83). One state, *fearing* a second state as a threat, embarks on a military build-up. The *rival* state, observing the action of the first state, reacts by augmenting its military power, which in turn motivates the first state to increase its military power and the arms race starts unravelling. Glaser (2000) notes that this action–reaction framework is consistent with several prominent international relations models such as the 'security dilemma, the spiral model, and structural neorealist theory' (2000, p. 225).

14 Jervis (1976) observes that military spending can pose a security dilemma, where a State retaliates against the build-up initiated by another State for fear of the rival's *intentions*. The reciprocated increases in arming potentially engender a spiral of hostilities, increasing the chances for the outbreak of armed conflict.

15 In an early and important work McGinnis and Williams (2001) examine the dynamics of arms acquisition in the US–USSR rivalry to find that the rivals did not react to one another in some sort of Richardsonian process. Rather, a *rivalry* was triggered and sustained by an underlying process by which the rivalry, or enmity, between the US and the former USSR came to be institutionalised. The belief systems of relevant decision- makers about each other became hardened. Arms acquisition then took place as the ongoing policy response to the perceived threat, not as the spiral model (Jervis, 1976) describes.

16 One way of rationalising military build-up is to treat arms races as costly signals to one's rival (Fearon 1995, pp. 395–396; Schelling 1966) to convey the (missing) information about the willingness of a state to bear the costs of wars. The signalling theory of the arms race has been challenged by many scholars as they argue that the resources spent on a military build-up constitute a sunk cost and, therefore, have no effect on deterring aggression if the relative position remains unchanged (see Fearon 1994, p. 579 and 1997, pp. 82–83).

17 The evolutionary model of rivalries (Hensel, 1999) posits that the early experience of competition determines whether the relationship develops into a *mature rivalry* with a potential for an arms race. Similarly, Maoz and Mor (2002) argue that states learn from their interactions early in a rivalry. Only when there are bad experiences do positions harden and seeds of mature rivalries are sown. Most rivalries 'die' in their nascent stages without the need for arming. Even among those rivalries that do mature, the rivals do not yet recognise themselves as being in a long-term competition and therefore have not yet adopted policies of enhancing their military capabilities. Thus, the evolutionary model highlights the information dynamics that plays an immensely important role in unravelling potential threats.

18 In the punctuated equilibrium framework, rivalries enter a 'lock-in' phase from interactions between rivals, which will establish the patterns that will in turn characterise the rivalry thereafter. In this phase, decision-makers take lessons from their interactions and begin to plan for the future, which is a type of learning paradigm for states.

19 States receive independent and equally strong private binary signals about the right choice on arming. In this setting, rational agents herd: once the pattern of signals leads to two more choices of one action than the other, all subsequent states ignore their signals and take that same choice of military build-up. This happens because two A choices (say) on the trail of equal numbers of A and B choices reveal (given the convenient simplification that people follow their own signal when indifferent) two signals favouring A; each subsequent mover, even with a B signal, thinks A is a better bet. Although everyone eventually chooses the same action, nobody confidently believes in its correctness because each understands that the herd, no matter how long, indicates only two signals favouring that action. Generalising this result, the rational social-learning literature finds that when action and signal spaces are both finite, and each signal is imperfect, rational people eventually 'herd' on an action because after a while every person imitates others' behaviour and ignores their own information, an 'information cascade'. Richer action spaces or richer signal spaces immensely reduce the probability that herds will form on the wrong action.

20 Our fundamental assumption is that action spaces are not rich enough to ensure that arming actions can reveal private information of states' true preferences for wars. We also assume away the possibility that signal spaces are not rich enough

to allow states to add new information to their predecessors' actions on military build-ups.

21 In the arms race model, a state might attach a small, but non-zero, probability that their rival is a 'warmonger'/aggressive type for whom arming is a dominant strategy. This probability creates the possibility that the benefit from arming is greater than the cost of arming at the margin, which will motivate each state to arm. Each state knows each rival thinks in an analogous fashion, which creates the multiplier effect and thereby escalates the arms race as a race to the bottom of the Pareto inferior equilibrium (see Schelling, 1966).

22 In these models, a state's type is modelled in terms of its preference for arming, while the true preference of a state is treated as a private information that is not immediately available to its rivals. There are some states that are hawks and some states that are doves. Hawks are the dominant strategy types and doves are the 'almost dominant strategy types'. Doves arm only in equilibrium.

23 In their work Baliga (2011, 2013), Baliga and Sjöström (2004, 2008, 2013a, 2013b) and Baliga, Lucca and Sjöström (2013) ignored the possibility of babbling equilibria in the cheap talk extension of the arms race game. In a babbling equilibrium states, just disregard the messages coming from their rivals. In the cheap talk extension of the arms race, states have private information about their true preferences for armament, then they send messages to their rivals and then take action on military build-up. In these models most states have the incentive to communicate that they are 'doves' while the 'almost hawks' – for whom arming is not a dominant strategy are incentivised to send the 'hawk' message. If all states send a 'hawk' message, then neither of them will arm if the probability of unilateral arming as a dominant strategy is small. Coordination then pays to avoid the arms race for all types of states except for the states who have arming as a dominant strategy.

24 One can detect herd-like behaviour in this context by looking at the comparative static properties of the Nash equilibrium: $\partial q_i^e / \partial \Psi_i > 0$, $\partial q_i^e / \partial \Psi_j > 0$; $\partial H_i^e / \partial \Psi_i > 0$; $\partial H_i^e / \partial \Psi_j > 0$; $\partial h_i^e / \partial \Psi_i = -V(1 + \Psi_j)/[\beta(1 - \Psi_i \Psi_j)^2] < 0$; $\partial h_i^e / \partial \Psi_j < 0$.

25 This dependence of the Cournot-Nash equilibrium on the subjective elements makes this equilibrium highly fragile. Simple fluctuations in subjective elements can have far-reaching impacts on the optimal efforts in producing military output. It is recognised that in games involving complementarities, consequences of idiosyncratic shocks get amplified through what is called a *multiplier effect* (see Vives, 2005).

26 The question about the source of herding begs an answer. Herding arises because the observed behaviour of other investors affects the probability belief attached to different states of the world and also the payoff conditional on each state. Banerjee (1992), Bikhchandani and Hirshleifer (1992), Welch (1992) and a large number of papers show the significance of informational cascades in modern investment markets. An informational cascade connotes a situation in which subsequent agents, based on the observations of others, make the same choice independent of their private signals. Informational cascades are argued to engender erroneous mass behaviour and cause fragility in capital formation.

27 Our methodology is taken from Lakonishok et al. (1992) who applied their measure known as LSV to detect herd behaviour among fund managers. This innovative index, LSV, measures the extent to which fund managers follow herd behaviour in investing in equity. The measure captures the extent to which fund managers deviate from average investment decisions, which depend on overall economic conditions to collectively buy or sell specific stocks. Due to its robustness, the measure gained substantial popularity and was applied to investigate herd behaviour in financial markets.

28 Frey, Herbst and Walter (2007) have shown by empirical simulations that LSV is biased downward. Thus the above measure points to an understatement of herding instinct among students. According to the LSV measure, one can therefore establish if subjects display *statistically* significant herding but not economically. So our finding has the same caveat, we are only able to establish the statistical significance of herding on the basis of the LSV index.

29 Both LSV and MLSV have the same interpretation: a measure of x implies that if the average fraction of changes that are increases was 0.5, then $50+k\%$ of the nations were changing their allocations of defence spending to an average recipient in one direction and $50-k\%$ in the opposite direction. As emphasised by Frey et al. (2007), LSV underestimates herding and is always much smaller than the true value. According to the MLSV measure, there is statistically significant herding as well as economically, as 12% of the changes in defence spending can be attributed to herding.

30 In the context of financial economics Christie and Huang (1995) and Chang, Cheng and Khorana (2000) applied the cross-sectional absolute deviation, (CSAD) as a measure of dispersion to detect herding in financial markets. According to Christie and Huang (1995), Chang et al., (2000); Caparrelli et al., (2004); Tan et al., (2008) and Chang, Cheng and Khorana (2000), herding can be detected comparing cross-sectional dispersion of asset returns with the overall mean of asset returns. This type of measure was initially applied to detect herding in special periods of extreme upward, or downward, movements in returns. However, it is later recognised that the measure can be used regardless of market turmoil or not.

31 We chose other possible groupings of nations and empirical results indicate the presence of herding.

7 Equity, justice and peace
Historical analysis

7.1 Introduction

Because of its geographical location, huge oil reserves, and strategic importance to the main players in international politics, the Middle East has been regarded as pivotal and unstable for the last 50 years. At the heart of the region's poignancy is the Israeli–Palestinian conflict, which has dominated domestic, regional, and world politics for more than five decades. The region has also hosted three wars not involving Israel (Iraq–Iran 1980–1988, Iraq–Kuwait 1991, and Iraq 2003). The region is, moreover, surrounded by other long-term conflict zones of our cotemporary world such as Sudan, Afghanistan and the Caucasus. In this chapter we will provide empirical analysis for the economic causes of conflicts for ten Middle Eastern countries and three regional countries: the Arab countries are Algeria, Egypt, Jordan, Kuwait, Morocco, Syria, and Tunisia. The three non-Arab countries are Iran, Israel and Turkey. The choice of countries is predicated upon the availability of relevant data.

The main strategy of our research is twofold: first, we seek to identify the factors that might cause dramatic changes in the number of violent conflicts in the Middle East between 1963 and 1999. The empirical analysis is performed using a unique panel of inequality estimates that cover ten countries over the selected period. This work estimates the effects of inequality and other variables on the intensity and level of conflicts, by applying two different measures. We look for specific economic and non-economic factors that can determine changes in violent conflicts in the region. Second, we explore the role of justice in promoting or preventing collective violence in the region by exploiting another data set for seven countries during 1968–2009. The main innovation is to create an index of justice and link it to collective violence and various factors behind such conflicts. The details are provided in Section 7.6.

A few quick observations are in order from Sections 7.2–7.5: first, our results indicate that inequality bears a negative relation with conflicts. The negative sign on the inequality variable indicates the special characteristics of a very imbalanced society where all opposition is crushed through heavy military presence and/or the very poor do not have the assets essential to initiate an armed rebellion. Second, a host of macroeconomic variables like inflation, military expenditure, and immigration have a positive relation with conflicts. Third, foreign direct investment (*FDI*) as a percentage of *GDP*, *GDP growth*, and workers' remittance are shown to bear a negative relation with the intensity and levels of conflicts.

The long-term relationships between terrorism and other variables offer some interesting insights in Section 7.6: first and foremost, as we find for the first time, improvement in *justice* (*AJI*), instead of lowering terrorism, increases terrorism for the entire region. Second, in the cointegration equation of per capita income of the region, we find that the coefficient of *justice* (*AJI*) for the region is negative and statistically significant, thus there is a price for justice in the region as justice lowers economic growth. What we find is that justice increases terrorism and also lowers economic opulence. In other words, justice is not a *free lunch*: the society will have to sacrifice something (growth and security) to have justice in the region. The critical question for us is whether *AJI* Granger causes *AVG*. Our results confirm that the per capita income in the region is (Granger) caused by regional terrorism justice and so is the long-term vulnerability.

The plan of this chapter is as follows: in Section 7.2.1 we discuss the role of inequality in conflicts. In Section 7.2.2 we examine the role of *GDP* in conflicts. In Section 7.4 we explore the relevant economic variables for the Middle East. In Section 7.5 we offer the model, data sources and empirical findings. In Section 7.6, we select the seven countries (as in previous chapters) from the Middle East and North Africa and examine if there are any long-term and causal relationships between violence and justice and economic factors. We also offer an aggregated analysis to home in on an average picture we choose the average values of various variables and examine their long-term dynamics during 1968–2009 to understand the determination of violence (conflicts), justice and relevant economic factors. We conclude in Section 7.7.

7.2   Conflicts, justice and inequality conflicts

7.2.1   *Conflicts and inequality*

Many studies have focused on discovering the relation between conflicts and inequality. As examples: studies done by Olson (1963), Sigelman and Simpson (1977), Hardy (1979), Weede (1981, 1987), Muller (1985), Park (1986), Muller and Seligson (1987), Midlarsky (1988), Londregan and Poole (1990), Boswell and Dixon (1990), Brockett (1992), Binswanger et al. (1993) and Schock (1996) have reached the conclusion that inequality in the allocation of resources and material goods such as land, wealth, income and other assets are linked with the occurrence of socio-political instability in several countries.

Although in general most theorists posit that there is a strong relation between inequality and violent conflicts, empirical work reveals three possible scenarios between these variables: (a) positive relation, (b) negative relation, and (c) no relation between the variables.

The first expectation is that economic inequality increases violent conflicts. There are two simple reasons for this positive relationship between inequality and incidence of conflicts. When economic inequality is high, poor people are envious of the richer people and, having nothing to lose, choose to force a redistribution of income. Conversely, rich people are greedy and have everything to lose; so they acquire the resources needed to prevent the redistribution of wealth. As economic inequality increases, conflict increases. There is interesting literature offering support for a positive relation between different forms of inequality and political and social conflicts (for example, Sigelman and Simpson, 1977; Muller, 1985; Weede, 1987). If we look at the recent literature on the economic causes of civil wars in developing countries, we will find inequality cited as an important factor (Schock, 1996; Boyce, 1996; Nafziger and Auvinen, 1997; Stewart, 1998; Elbadawi, 1992; Collier, 2000b; Collier and Hoeffler, 1998). In an important study Schock (1996) tests the hypothesis 'Hypothesis 1: Economic inequality is positively related to violent conflict'. The hypothesis is tested using quantitative cross-national lagged panel data which examines political violence between 1973 and 1977. He reaches a result that supports the proposed hypothesis. Boyce (1996) points out that the main reason behind the violent conflict in El Salvador is inequality (especially the unequal distribution of land). An empirical study by Nafziger and Auvinen (1997) 'indicated that high income inequality (based on the Gini Index) is associated with political conflict and complex humanitarian emergencies'. Stewart (1998) demonstrates proof for a positive relation between horizontal inequalities and civil conflict by examining case studies on developing countries such as: Afghanistan, Burundi, Cambodia, El Salvador, Guatemala, Haiti, Liberia, Nicaragua, Rwanda, Sierra Leone and Somalia. Elbadawi (1999) recognises poverty and the extent of ethnic fractionalisation as main causes of civil wars. Studies by Mitchell on the Philippines (Mitchell, 1969), Paranzino on South Vietnam (Paranzino, 1972), and Morgan and Clark on the United States (Morgan and Clark, 1973), gave further evidence on the positive relation between inequality and conflicts.

Another possible explanation is that economic inequality decreases violent conflicts. It may be that higher levels of inequality are associated with a powerful privileged minority, prepared and willing to use its power to suppress conflict. Another reason may lie in the social comparison processes of human beings. As Samuel Johnson said, 'it is better that some should be unhappy, than that none should be happy, which would be the case in a general state of equality'. That means some people will be unhappy under moderate economic inequality, while under pure economic equality, everyone is unhappy. This viewpoint is supported by Havrilesky (1980) as Havrilesky states,

> It is reasonable to assume that a discordance-minimizing distribution of income exists at some positive level of discordance and that a perceived change in the distribution away from this minimum toward either of the extremes of equality or inequality will generate increased discordance.
>
> (Havrilesky, 1980, p. 374)

Parvin (1973) proposes that

> It is therefore more reasonable to assume that an optimum level of income inequality exists for any level of per capita income. Subsequently, beyond this optimum level, the net effect of further redistribution of income toward more or less equality may imply increasing, not decreasing, political unrest.
>
> (Parvin, 1973, p. 272)

Other scholars have suggested that there is no direct relationship between inequality and violent conflict; and that there are more important factors involved such as absolute poverty, or mobilisation processes. It may be that economic inequality changes very gradually over time while conflict occurs erratically. There are a number of studies that support this result, including a study by Duff and McCamant on Latin America (1976), one by Powell on Western-style democracies (1982), Russo's study of South Vietnam (1972), and McAdam's (1982) and Spilerman's studies (1971) of the United States.

7.2.2   *GDP and conflicts*

Recent literature on the relation between violent conflict and GDP indicates that there is a negative relation between GDP and conflicts (Collier and Hoeffler, 2002a and 2002b; Fearon and Laitin, 2003). A study by Humphreys (2003) predicted the probability of war onset of 15% for a country with GDP per capita equal to $250. If this GDP per capita is doubled, then the probability of war will drop to 7.5%. Another study by Fearon and Laitin (2003) predicted a probability of 18% to countries with GDP per capita of $600. This probability decreased to 11% if the GDP per capita increased to $2,000 and to less than 1% for countries with GDP per capita of $10,000. How could be this explained? One of the explanations offered by Homer-Dixon (1994) and Fearon and Laitin (2003) is that wealthier countries are more capable of protecting their assets against rebels. Another explanation is given by Homer-Dixon (1994) where he states that poverty causes violence, and indicates to cases where scarcity leads to migrations that result in conflicts between identity groups over resources.

A study by Bates (2001) states if the value of assets increases in any economy, then people may increase their motivation to use violence. A study by Keen (2000) finds if there is a rise in the value of assets of a country this may lead to a rise in the value of controlling the state.

A study by Mack (2002) has raised an enquiry when he said that if increasing wealth would lead to a decrease in the amounts of conflicts, then why are we seeing the opposite? A possible explanation is presented by Humphreys (2003), who mentions that there might be other variables that outweigh the extenuating effects of increased wealth such as population sizes. Another reason is the uneven spread of global economic growth across different regions.

7.2.3   Trade and conflicts

Does international trade increase or decrease the likelihood of conflict? If country A increases its trade with country B, will this lead to a greater risk of conflict between these two countries? According to liberal theorists, if countries A and B have mutual trade then both are benefiting, so they would be reluctant to fight with a trading partner, as this might lead to 'commercial suicide'.[1] Others claim that if there is trade between two countries this will lead to a greater understanding of each other's culture. In Europe for instance, the formation of the European Union ended a century-old conflict and brought peace between Germany and France (Burn, 1961; Isard, 2002, 2004). Another view by the Baron de Montesquieu's, Spirits of the Laws (1979[1748]), states that commerce tends to promote peace between nations; mutual self-interest precludes war; trade also softens attitudes of peoples towards each other.

A number of studies have attempted to capture the impact of trade on peace. Polachek (1980) found that nations with the greatest amount of trade were the least hostile to each other. Another study by Oneal and Russett (1999) proved that peace and trade are highly correlated. A study by Murshed and Mamoon (2010) showed that more trade between India and Pakistan decreases conflict and any measures to improve bilateral trade would be a considerable confidence-building measure.

7.2.4   Conflicts and other economic variables

Economic growth may affect conflicts through several channels. Collier and Hoeffler (1998, 2000, 2002a, and 2002b) argue that civil conflicts are driven by economic opportunity rather than by political grievances: for example, young men would be more likely to take up arms when their expected income as fighters is higher than their income as agricultural workers. They found also that slow income growth, low per capita income, natural resource dependence, lower male secondary education enrolment, rebel military advantages and total population are all significantly and positively linked with the start of civil conflict. Democracy, they find, does not reduce the probability of civil conflict; this result supports their analysis of civil conflicts as being driven by economics rather than politics.

Elbadawi and Sambanis (2002) study the incidence of civil war and reach almost the same results as Collier and Hoeffler, except that they find democracy reduces the incidence of civil conflicts. A recent study by Boix (2003) develops a game theoretic model that describes different forms of conflict, ranging from civil war to guerrilla warfare, revolution, political assassination and riot, as the result of income inequality.

Low growth rates have both a direct and indirect relation with conflict. Barro (1991), Alesina and Perotti (1996), and Collier and Hoeffler (1998) find a significant negative relationship between investment, growth rates, and different measures of conflict. A paper by Benhabib and Rustichini (1996) presents a game theoretic structure to explain the conflict that occurs between two social groups over the allocation of resources (distribution of income). The conflict starts when each group tries to attain a larger share of output, either directly or by controlling the system of allocation. The strategic interaction between the two groups over the allocation of output affects the economy's power to enlarge or diminish the size of the pie, over time, and has an effect on growth at low or high levels of development, depending on the parameters of the production technology and the preferences.

Fearon and Laitin (2003) find that lower GDP per capita is significantly related to the onset of civil conflict, whereas democracy and ethnic diversity are not significantly related to violent conflicts.

7.3   Data and measurement

In what follows we describe the data and then undertake the empirical investigation about the impact of inequality on conflicts in the Middle East.

7.3.1   *Data on conflict and inequality*

Measuring conflict is a major problem in examining the relationship between conflicts and other variables. If we look at the existing literature on conflicts, we will find that most papers use the Correlates of War (COW) database. However, the lack of transparency of the COW database has been the focus of an exhaustive assessment by Sambanis (2002). Moreover, the database excludes conflicts which have fewer than 1,000 combat-related deaths per year. As a substitute for the COW database, we will use the new Armed Conflict Data database developed by the International Peace Research Institute of Oslo, Norway and the University of Uppsala, Sweden (PRIO/Uppsala). PRIO/Uppsala is more transparent and consistent than COW and records smaller conflicts, with a threshold of 25 battle deaths per year.[2] PRIO/Uppsala recognises three different intensity levels of conflict: Minor, Intermediate and War.

In this chapter we will use two different measures for conflicts. The first is a dummy variable that takes a value of one when a conflict has resulted in over 1,000 battle deaths in a given year and country. The second measure is a dummy variable that takes a value of one if the conflict is completely internal, and another which is equal to one when the conflict involves an external actor.

The inequality data are drawn from the 'Estimated Household Income Inequality Data Set' (EHII) – a global data set derived from the econometric relationship between UTIP-UNIDO, other conditioning variables, and the World Bank's Deininger and Squire data set (see http://utip.gov.utexas.edu/about.html). The University of Texas Inequality Project (UTIP) has produced an alternative global inequality data set, based on the Industrial Statistics database published annually by the United Nations Industrial Development Organization (UNIDO). This data set has approximately 3,200 observations over 36 years (1963–99). It is also based on source data that are much more likely to be accurate and consistent, both through time and across countries. However, the data do not measure household income inequality. UTIP-UNIDO is a set of measures of the dispersion of pay, using the between-groups component of a Theil index (Theil, 1972), measured across industrial categories in the manufacturing sector. While there is evidence that the UTIP-UNIDO measures provide a sensitive index of changes in distribution generally, the exact nature of the correlation between an establishment-based measure of manufacturing pay inequality and a survey-based measure of household income inequality is not clear, particularly in comparisons across countries.

Inequality is linked to a number of mathematical concepts such as skewness, variance and dispersion. Consequently, there are several methods to compute inequality, for example the McLoone Index, the coefficient of variation, range, range ratios, the Gini coefficient, and Theil's T statistic. The main justification for choosing Theil's T statistic is that it offers a more flexible structure that often makes it more suitable than other measures.[3] If we had permanent access to all necessary individual-level data for the population of interest, measures like the Gini coefficient or the coefficient of variation would be generally satisfactory for describing inequality. Yet, in the real world, individual data are hardly ever reachable, and researchers make do with aggregated data.

7.4 The empirical model

This chapter uses a model which addresses the findings of previous literature on conflicts. In this conceptual model, conflicts are considered a function of inequality, as well as of inflation, military expenditure, foreign direct investment, growth, workers' remittance, population, *GDP* per capita, military personnel, and immigration.

$$CON_{(it)} = \alpha_i + \beta_0 * INQ_{(it)} + \beta_1 * INF_{(it)} + \beta_2 * ME_{(it)} + \beta_3 * FDI_{(it)} + \beta_4 * GRO_{(it)}$$
$$+ \beta_5 * WRG_{(it)} + \beta_6 * POP + \beta_7 * PP_{(it)} + \beta_8 * MILPER_{(it)} + \beta_9 * IMN_{(it)}$$
$$+ \beta_{10} * DUM1_{(it)} + \beta_{11} * DUM2_{(it)} + \beta_{12} * DUM3_{(it)} + \varepsilon_{(it)} \qquad (7.1a)$$

Where:

- *i* stands for country index, *t* represents time period,
- *CON* is the conflict intensity, α_i is a country-specific intercept,
- *INQ* is the estimated income inequality,
- *INF* is annual inflation as measured by the year-to-year change in the consumer price index,
- *ME* is military expenditure as a percentage of GDP (constant 1995 $US),
- *FDI* is foreign direct investment as a percentage of GDP (constant 1995 $US),
- *GRO* is the real growth rate of the economy in the preceding period,
- *WRG* is the workers' remittance as a percentage of GDP,
- *PP* is GDP per capita (constant 1995 $US),
- *POP* is the total population
- *MILPER* is the number of military personnel
- *IMN* is the immigrant population to the US as a proportion of the population in the country of origin.
- *DUM1* is a dummy variable where 1 represents an Arab country and 0 a non-Arab country,
- *DUM2* is a dummy variable where 1 represents Shiite and 0 represents non-Shiite,
- *DUM3* is a dummy variable where 1 represents oil exporting countries and 0 non-oil exporting countries.

We will estimate equation (1a) by using a set of panel data including observations for ten Middle Eastern countries covering the period 1963–1999. Unfortunately, there are limited freely available data on Arab countries. As a consequence, we are unable to include more than seven Arab countries in this study: Algeria, Egypt, Jordan, Kuwait, Morocco, Syria and Tunisia. The three non-Arab countries are Iran, Israel, and Turkey.

In this study we will use the panel data that will allow us to control for unobservable time-invariant country-specific effects that result in a missing-variable bias. This problem is recognised in many studies such as Bruno et al. (1995), Ravallion (1995), Bourguignon and Morrison (1998), Deininger and Squire (1996 and 1998), and Forbes (2000). The fixed effect model setting will be used in this study for three main reasons. First, the fixed model will control unobservable country-specific characteristics and will reduce possible hetero-scedasticity problems rooting from probable differences across countries (Greene, 1997). Second, the fixed model is preferred for the reason that the most important objective of this study is to explore what factors have caused changes in intensity of conflicts over time within countries, rather than to explain variations in the intensity of those conflicts. Another reason for choosing the fixed effect model is because it is more appropriate when the focus is on a precise number of countries and the inference is limited to those countries (Baltagi, 1995).

7.5 The empirical results

In this section, we will inspect the theoretical considerations discussed above, using empirical evidence for ten Middle-East countries. We will construct two models based on the conceptual model and actual data. The first uses dummy variables to represent all conflicts with over 1,000 battle deaths in a given year and country. The second uses a simple dummy variable for civil and external conflicts with over 1,000 casualties in a given country and year. The two models estimated using a pooled model (ordinary least squares), fixed effects (accounting for heterogeneity across countries), and random effects (accounting for heterogeneity across countries and across time). We will analyse the impact of inequality on the intensity of conflict across ten major Middle Eastern countries for the period 1963–1999. Other independent variables collected are growth rate, *GDP* per capita, inflation, military expenditure, *FDI*, population, military personnel and immigration.

The results shown in Table 7.1 indicate that the signs of the parameters are almost all as hypothesised. Military expenditure, inflation, immigration and population increase the probability of war. Contrarily, *FDI*, growth, workers' remittance, and military personnel lower the probability of war. As for inequality, there is a negative relation between inequality and conflict intensity, indicating that increasing inequality by a unit would lower the intensity of conflict by 8.8%. An explanation for this might be that either higher levels of inequality are associated with a powerful privileged minority, prepared and willing to use its power to suppress conflict, or they may lie in the social comparison processes of human beings (as discussed in the literature review before).

Inflation and military expenditure both have a positive coefficient and are statistically significant with conflicts. A unit increase in inflation and military expenditure causes an increase in the level of intensity of conflicts by 0.23% and 1% respectively. Conversely, *FDI* as a percentage of *GDP*, growth, and immigration negatively affects conflicts. A unit decrease in *FDI* as a percentage of *GDP*, growth, and immigration causes increases in the intensity level of a conflict by 4.5%, 0.97%, and 213.25% respectively. This result is consistent with the theory that a lower growth rate increases the risk of conflict, as individuals in low-income situations have less to lose from conflict. Also the result of oil exports and *FDI* inflows leads to less conflict which supports the liberal peace idea where international trade reduces conflict (where inequality here is a proxy for a repression effect). As for the immigration variable, immigration is endogenous to the intensity of conflict. When a conflict occurs, the number of people emigrating increases. The size of immigration may proxy the intensity of conflict. The oil dummy variable (*Dummy3*) is statistically significant and has a negative coefficient, which decreases the incidence of conflicts by 11.07%.

Table 7.2 reveals a significant negative relation between conflict and inequality. We find that one unit increase in inequality results in a decrease in

Table 7.1 Regression results

Variable	(1) Pooled	(2) Fixed Effects	(3) Random Effects
Inequality	−0.033544 **	−0.08785***	−0.01197***
	(2.221113)	(−3.91938)	(−3.67083)
Inflation	0.002259 ***	0.002265***	0.002289***
	(4.635813)	(6.194494)	(4.831499)
Military Expenditure	0.007111***	0.010003***	0.008681***
as % of GDP	(3.619289)	(7.150603)	(4.506451)
FDI as % of GDP	−0.06452***	−0.04491***	−0.07949***
	(−4.29665)	(−4.60092)	−5.35128
% of yearly growth	−0.01207***	−0.00968***	−0.01268***
	(−5.93838)	(−7.08342)	(−6.43429)
Workers' remittance	−0.74007	−0.25281	0.26338
as % of GDP	(−1.61274)	(−0.80655)	(−0.58481)
GDP per capita	−5.50E−06**	−1.93E−06	−8.71E−07
	(−2.00716)	(−0.99617)	(−0.31498)
Yearly immigration to	2.914059***	2.132453***	2.693899***
the US as % of total	(3.617157)	(3.708477)	(3.450764)
population			
Military Personnel	−0.08351***	−0.11973***	−0.1558***
	(−4.36503)	(−6.80704)	(−6.80607)
Population	3.46E−06***	5.64E−07	5.60E−07
	(3.202762)	(0.62953)	(0.471964)
Dum1	0.02541	−0.04658	−0.04253
	(0.39732)	(−0.71234)	(−0.68167)
Dum2	−0.07197	−0.09292	−0.09531
	(−1.09901)	(−1.31957)	(−1.51985)
Dum3	−0.08389*	−0.11073***	−0.17558
	(−1.94246)	(−3.33142)	(−3.92191)
Constant		0.689813***	0.920071***
		(6.081123)	(5.228591)
Observations	348	348	348
Countries	10	10	10
Years	1963–1999	1963–1999	1963–1999
Adjusted R²	0.511366	0.535056	0.396787
R-squared	0.528264	0.544226	0.429816

Note: t-statistics in parenthesis.
***, **, and * indicate, respectively, statistical significance at the 1%, 5% and 10% level

the intensity level of conflict by 7.6%. Conflict decreases by 10.17%, 0.5%, and 145.06% for a one unit increase in *FDI* as a percentage of *GDP*, growth, and workers' remittance respectively. Here also the idea of liberal peace is supported by the positive relation between oil exports and *FDI* inflows with conflicts. On the other hand, a one unit decrease in inflation, military expenditure, and immigration causes a decrease in the intensity level of conflict by 0.07%, 0.7%, and 141.97% respectively. The results of dummy variable 2 and 3 indicate the importance of ethnicity and oil in increasing the intensity of a conflict. If we look at the *Dummy2* results we find that the greater the percentage of Shiite in the population, the lower is the intensity level of a conflict.

7.6 Justice, economics and terrorism in the Middle East and North Africa

The main goal so far is to identify the factors that caused dramatic changes in the intensity of conflicts in the Middle East between 1963 and 1999. The empirical analysis is performed using a unique panel of inequality estimates that cover ten countries over the selected period. We offer estimates of the effects of inequality and other variables on the intensity level of conflicts, using several measures. We looked for specific economic and non-economic factors that might determine changes in conflicts in the region. In what follows, we select the seven countries from the Middle East and North Africa and examine if there are any long-term and causal relationships between violence and justice and economic factors. We offer an aggregated analysis in Section 7.6; in order to home in on an average picture we choose the average values of various variables and examine their long-term dynamics during 1968–2009 to understand the determination of violence (conflicts), justice and relevant economic factors.

7.6.1 *Justice and terrorism: relevant variables to capture justice*

We have introduced most of the variables already in other chapters: i) the variables described in Table 4.1 in Chapter 4 are some of the relevant variables. In this subsection we choose the regional terrorism index (RTI_2) of Chapter 4 to capture violence in the region comprising of Libya, Syria, Iran, Iraq, Israel, Egypt and Lebanon. ii) We will also use $AVVI$ to capture the long-run vulnerability of the region. iii) The variable on the average arms imports of the region ($AVARIM$) will measure the militarisation of the region. iv) The variable $AVGDP$ measures the average per capita GDP of the region in log values and expressed in 2012 \$US. Table 4.1 presents the description and measurements of these variables and further details can be found in Table 3.2.2 of Chapter 3. We also include the global factors like LNT, LNP and LNO as discussed in Chapter 3 and Chapter 4. Note that LNT intends to capture the global warming variable while LNP and LNO capture the global oil market as discussed before.

There are two new variables that we have introduced for each country to capture social justice in the region: a) For each country we have chosen the log of female mortality rate ($LNFMORT$) as an indicator of gender equity. We have collected the relevant data for each country during 1968–2009 from the World Bank economic indicators as explained in Table 2.3. b) We have collected data from the World Bank economic indicators on the (log) of fertility rate ($LNFERT$) of women as an indicator of the social status of women in a country. Thus, we measure the social and economic status of women

Table 7.2 Alternative regression results

Variable	(1) Pooled	(2) Fixed Effects	(3) Random Effects
Inequality	−0.091573***	−0.076088***	−0.050859**
	(6.562322)	(−3.345247)	(−2.380208)
Inflation	0.000754**	0.000687***	0.001268*
	(2.037453)	(0.962346)	(1.929451)
Military Expenditure	0.000847	−0.007174***	−0.001500***
as % of GDP	(0.413624)	(−2.459804)	(−0.561813)
FDI as % of GDP	−0.001343	−0.101747***	−0.055210***
	(−0.102879)	(−4.580128)	−2.664835
% of yearly growth	−0.002592*	−0.004591***	−0.008972***
	(−1.675193)	(−1.585396)	(−3.320547)
Workers' remittance	−1.447443***	−1.450638**	−1.725907***
as % of GDP	(−4.213220)	(2.209611)	(−2.729125)
GDP per capita	4.04E-06**	7.43E-06*	7.59E-06*
	(1.995469)	(1.876433)	(1.947560)
Yearly immigration to	1.99490**	1.419658	2.295985**
the US as % of total	(2.075277)	(1.226688)	(2.108987)
population			
Military Personnel	0.064272***	−0.019566	−0.018299
	(3.977971)	(−0.582054)	(−0.572095)
Population	9.79E-06***	3.83E-06**	6.96E-06***
	(10.41271)	(2.139106)	(4.226150)
Dum1	0.118902	0.114587	0.145657*
	(1.587167)	(1.277340)	(1.656011)
Dum2	−0.566320***	−0.574763***	−0.570577***
	(−7.931723)	(−6.404488)	(−6.439276)
Dum3	−0.190909***	−0.395185***	−0.383280***
	(−4.190205)	(−6.127085)	(−6.092093)
Constant		1.556629***	1.137331***
		(5.937525)	(4.641377)
Observations	348	348	348
Countries	10	10	10
Years	1963–1999	1963–1999	1963–1999
Adjusted R²	0.680258	0.453933	0.424676
R-squared	0.691283	0.530822	0.446168

Note: t-statistics in parenthesis.
***, **, and * indicate, respectively, statistical significance at the 1%, 5% and 10% level

in a country by applying the principal component analysis to *LNFERT* and *LNFMORT* to calculate the weights w_1 and w_2 to derive the justice index of a nation i as $J.INDEX_i$:

$$J.INDEX_i = w_1 * \text{LNFERT} + w_2 * LNFMORT \qquad (7.1b)$$

We measure justice in a country i, $JUSTICE_i$, by the inverse of $J.INDEX_i$ in country i: the lower the female mortality, the higher is the gender justice. In a

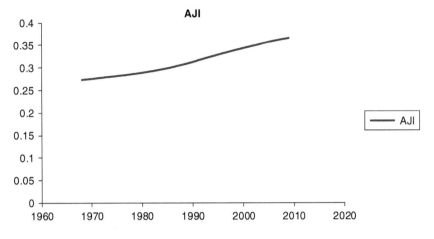

Figure 7.1 The time profile of justice (AJI) in the region

similar vein, we posit that the lower the fertility, the greater the gender justice is in a country. Our index of justice is expressed as the following:

$$JUSTICE_i = [1/JINDEX_i] \qquad (7.1c)$$

In other words, we choose a measure of the status of women in the country to measure justice in a country. We then choose the average value of $JUSTICE_i$ for the seven nations to arrive at the average justice index AJI in the Middle East and North Africa. We present the Johansen test results in the following table for testing the cointegration among relevant variables. We test two models – the difference between the two models is the absence and presence of the global warming variable (LNT) as an explanatory variable. We posit the long-term relationships as the following canonical model:

$$RTI_1 = F(AJI, AVARIM\ AVGDP, LNT, AVVI) \qquad (7.2)$$

In Figure 7.1 we present the time path that justice measured by AJI has taken in the region during 1968–2009. Though the AJI path is not steep, it shows continuous improvement in justice in the Middle East and North Africa. The econometric tests are presented in Table 7.3.

The important lessons from Table 7.3 are the following: first and foremost, there is a long-term equilibrium relationship, both economically meaningful and statistically significant, between the regional terrorism index (RTI_1) and the average per capita GDP ($AVGDP$), average vulnerability of all seven nations in the region ($AVVI$) and the average regional arms imports ($AVARIM$) and global warming (LNT), which we observed in some forms in

Table 7.3 Cointegration between terrorism and other regional variables

Dependent Variable	Explanatory Variable	Model 1: Coefficient	Z	Model 2: Coefficients	Z
RTI₁					
RTI₁	AJI	15.0	2.62	8.7	2.62
RTI₁	AVGDP	−9.59	−5.49	−10.8	−7.92
RTI₁	AVARIM	1.46	5.20	1.54	6.11
RTI₁	AVVI	2.58	4.07	2.67	4.52
RTI₁	LNT	–	–	162.07	3.70

Chapter 4. What is important is that we also detect a long-term relationship between terrorism (RTI_1) and the index of justice in the region (AJI).

The long-term relationships offer some interesting insights in Table 7.3: first and foremost, and as we find for the first time, improvement in justice (AJI), instead of lowering terrorism, increases terrorism for the entire region. In other words, empowerment of women does not seem to fight terrorism in the region. One can explain this phenomenon in two ways: i) As AJI improves, males face more competition and terrorism is a means to vent male anger. ii) As AJI improves, everyone in the society demands greater justice and terrorism arises as a violent demand for justice. This phenomenon is a very serious finding and we will invite more work to relate terrorism to the empowerment of women. Most importantly, more detailed study is called for to measure empowerment and then examine its impacts on terrorism. We will examine if there is Granger causality running from AJI and terrorism in Table 7.4. Second, as we have noted already, as the average per capita income ($AVGDP$) of the region increases (decreases), regional terrorism declines (increases). The inverse relationship between income and terrorism is a time-honoured, though often challenged, adage in economics. There are many channels, as we discussed in Chapter 4 and Chapter 6, through which per capita income exerts an influence on terrorism. It suffices to say that the opportunity costs of terrorism for terrorist operatives increase with rising per capita GDP and, hence, one should expect an inverse relationship between terrorism and per capita income at the regional level. Third, there is a positive and statistically significant relationship between militarisation ($AVARIM$) and terrorism in the region. Thus, one can argue that terrorists *strategically* react to counterterror strategies like arms imports. Fourth, terrorism bears a direct relationship with the average long-term vulnerability of the entire region ($AVVI$) as the extensive literature has highlighted. The effect is also statistically significant. Finally, the global warming factor contributes positively to terrorism in the region.

The regional justice is Granger caused by all the chosen variables as Table 7.4 shows. The terrorism variable is marginally significant, but all others are statistically significant: economic progress (Granger) causes justice while

Table 7.4 The Granger causality results

Dependent Variable	Excluded Variable	Chi²
AJI	RTI₁	2.8
AJI	AVGDP	17
AJI	AVARIM	4
AJI	AVVI	10.11
RTI₁	AVARIM	24.76
RTI₁	AJI	8.58
RTI₁	ALL	32
AVGDP	RTI₁	7.15
AVGDP	AJI	7.04
AVGDP	AVVI	8.8
AVARIM	AJI	8.4
AVARIM	RTI₁	5.85
AVVI	RTI₁	3.83
AVVI	AVGDP	5.7

the increase in vulnerability also (Granger) causes justice. Regional terrorism (RTI_1) is also Granger caused by justice (AJI). We also find that economic performance ($AVGDP$) is Granger caused by justice (AJI). Militarisation ($AVARIM$) of the region is also caused by justice (AJI) in the region. The rest of the Granger causality results are known from Chapter 4 and Chapter 7. All other statistical tests are also satisfactory for the rank and lag determination, which we don't report here.

7.6.2   Is there a price for justice?

It is amply clear from Section 7.6.1 that justice plays an important role in controlling violence in the Middle East and North Africa. In this subsection, we explore the price of justice. In simple words, our question is what is the trade-off to achieve justice in the region? In terms of analytical query, we seek to explore if justice lowers the average per capita income in the region. If not, justice is a regional public good: it promotes growth and reduces terrorism. So, the critical question for us is whether there is any long-term, cointegrating, relationship between economic growth and justice. Instead of economic growth, we will focus upon the per capita income of the region (AVG). Our baseline equation for cointegration is derived as follows:

$$AVG = -0.74*AJI - 0.092* RTI_1 - 0.148 *AVA - 0.24*AVV \qquad (7.3)$$

$$(-2.61) \quad\quad (-3.15) \quad\quad\quad (-6.64) \quad\quad\quad (-5.29)$$

In equation (7.3) the terms inside the parentheses give us the statistical significance of the relevant variables. We find that the coefficient of

Table 7.5 Does justice promote per capita GDP? The Granger causality test

Dependent Variable	Excluded Variable	Chi^2
AVG	RTI_1	7.15
AVG	AJI	6.91
AVG	AVV	8.82

cointegration for *AJI* is negative and statistically significant, thus there is a price for justice in the region as justice lowers economic growth. Justice increases terrorism and also lowers economic opulence. In other words, justice is not a free lunch, the society will have to sacrifice something to have justice. The critical question for us is whether *AJI* Granger causes *AVG*: we present the abridged results in Table 7.5.

Table 7.5 confirms that the per capita income in the region is (Granger) caused by regional terrorism justice and also the long-term vulnerability. So, in the collective struggle against violence and terrorism, justice is an important determinant of terrorism and economic well-being measured by the average per capita income of the Middle East and North Africa.

7.7   Conclusion

The main goal of this chapter is to identify the factors that caused dramatic changes in the intensity of conflicts in the Middle East between 1963 and 1999. The empirical analysis is performed using a unique panel of inequality estimates that cover ten countries over the selected period. This chapter estimates the effects of inequality and other variables on the intensity level of conflicts, using two different measures. We looked for specific economic and non-economic factors that might determine changes in conflicts in the region.

The data indicate that inequality has a negative relation with conflicts. More specifically, we find that a one point increase in inequality results in a decrease in conflict of 8.8% in the first model and 7.6% in the second model. As we have mentioned before the negative sign on the inequality variable indicates the special characteristics of a very imbalanced society where all opposition is crushed through heavy military presence and/or the very poor do not have the assets essential to initiate an armed rebellion (Baddely, 2005).

Inflation, military expenditure, and immigration have a positive relation with conflicts, while FDI as a percentage of GDP, growth, and workers' remittance has a negative relation with conflicts. In the first model, the most important factor that affects conflicts is the immigration variable, where a one point increase in immigration results in a 213% change in the intensity level of a conflict. In the second model, immigration and workers remittance highly affect the conflict variable. An increase in immigration results in an increase in conflict of 142%, while an increase in workers' remittance results in a decrease in conflicts of 145%. In both models the idea of liberal peace is supported where oil exports and FDI lead to less conflict.

The path of research commenced in this chapter shows good potentials for future research, because it exposes factors that have an effect on conflicts in Middle Eastern countries. However, it by no means exhausts all variables affecting the dynamics of conflicts in the Middle East region, and further research is indicated.

To understand the relevance of justice in the Middle East and North Africa, we choose an index of the status of women in the country to measure justice in the seven countries from the region. We then choose the average value of the indexes for the seven nations to arrive at the average justice index (*AJI*) in the Middle East and North Africa. We use the Johansen test results to determine the long-term cointegrating relationships between justice and other variables in the region. Appropriate causality tests are undertaken to confirm the direction of causality. Some of the important findings are as follows:

- First, an improvement in justice (*AJI*) in the region increases terrorism for the entire region. Some tentative explanations have been offered.
- Second, as we have noted already, as the average per capita income of the region increases (decreases), regional terrorism declines (increases). The inverse relationship between income and terrorism is a time-honoured, though often challenged, adage in economics.
- Third, there is a positive and statistically significant relationship between militarisation (*AVARIM*) and terrorism in the region. Thus, one can argue that terrorists strategically react to counterterror strategies like arms imports.
- Fourth, terrorism bears a direct relationship with the average long-term vulnerability of the entire region (*AVVI*). The effect is also statistically significant.
- Finally, the global warming factor contributes positively to terrorism in the region.
- The regional justice is Granger caused by all the chosen variables in our analysis. The terrorism variable is marginally significant, but all others are statistically significant: economic progress (Granger) causes justice while the increase in vulnerability also (Granger) causes justice.
- Regional terrorism is also Granger caused by justice. We also find that economic performance is (Granger) caused by justice in the region
- Militarisation (*AVARIM*) of the region is also (Granger) caused by justice in the region. The rest of the Granger causality results are known from Chapter 4 and Chapter 7. All other statistical tests are also satisfactory for the rank and lag determination, which we don't report here.

Notes

1 For more details see Angell (1933).
2 An armed conflict is defined in the PRIO/Uppsala database as follows:

> a contested incompatibility which concerns government and/or territory where the use of armed force between two parties, of which at least one is the government of a state, results in at least 25 battle-related deaths.

Refer to the PRIO website (www.prio.no/cwp/ArmedConflict) or the University of Uppsala website (www.pcr.uu.se).
3 Pedro Conceição and Pedro Ferreira (2000) provide a much more detailed analysis of these issues in their UTIP working paper 'The Young Person's Guide to the Theil Index: Suggesting Intuitive Interpretations and Exploring Analytical Applications'.

8 Summary and conclusion

8.1 Concluding comments

The Middle East remains unstable, with nearly 60 years of Israeli–Palestinian conflict, which has included 26 crises and six major wars. The region hosted two wars in Iraq (1991 and 2003) with the most international participants, as well as the bloodiest interstate war of that period (Iran–Iraq, 1980–1988). The region also witnesses rampaging civil wars in Iraq, Lebanon, Libya and Syria with an unending chain of bloodshed during the last five years. This monograph examines distinctive issues related to conflict in the Middle East and North Africa. The main aim of Chapter 2 is to understand conflicts from a multidisciplinary vantage point. In order to do that we ask the broad questions: what are the economic incentives for and constraints on conflicts? Why in some societies do conflicts recur, while other societies retain their peaceful character? The analysis argues that conflicts must be understood in the context of globalisation, which has spurred the twin forces of democratisation and privatisation in developing nations. Do these forces create a long-term vulnerability for the Middle East? In Chapter 2 we apply the principal component analysis (PCA) to the eight variables, namely *ODA, CO2, INFANTD, MMORT, DEATHR, ARLAND, FOODPROD* and *CEREALPROD* for seven nations in the Middle East and North Africa – Libya, Syria, Iran, Iraq, Israel, Egypt and Lebanon. For each variable we have observations during 1960–2013. The PCA enables us to derive an index of long-term vulnerability for each of these nations during 1960–2013. The existing literature has only highlighted the death rate (*DEATHR*) in exploring the sources of collective violence and its consequence. In this monograph we have extended the concept and measurement of vulnerability and its impacts on violence with the help of the PCA for the first time in the context of violence and wars. By analysing the dynamics of vulnerability of each nation over time, we are able to detect important long-term determinants of vulnerability in the Middle East and North Africa. This chapter then provides a comprehensive analysis of the long-term relationships between the index vulnerability of a nation and its neighbours' vulnerability. In other words, how the vulnerability of a nation impacts on regional vulnerability. We noted some interesting and hitherto unknown results. The chapter also introduces the basic concept of exchange entitlement failure and examines its role in the Middle East for exacerbating the vulnerability of the region. Interesting findings include the adverse impacts of global warming and the global oil market in exacerbating vulnerability of the region. We also find evidence that the divergence between food price inflation and oil price inflation has played a significant role in creating and driving vulnerability in the region. In a nutshell, in simple words, we have evidence to argue that various country-specific, regional and global factors have combined to create the long-term vulnerability of the chosen countries. The region will need to plan for managing a cascading regional vulnerability, food price inflation, oil price inflation and rising global temperature. Our results then establish that there are regional and global implications of the vulnerability of the individual nations in the Middle East and North Africa.

As we move to Chapter 3, it has two key ingredients. The first argues that the introduction of market ethos and democratisation in developing nations has created a fragile economic and social system. We demonstrate the existence of a political equilibrium that maximises the probability of re-election (or re-endorsement) of an incumbent government. This is an electoral equilibrium. In the equilibrium, we derive the optimal allocation of capital as well as the optimal value of inter-sectoral terms of trade between agriculture and industry. The central issue is whether the political equilibrium is economically meaningful. We derive two sets of conditions for it: first, the political equilibrium must ensure a minimal distribution for both industrial and agricultural agents, or a distribution failure will create survival problems for economic agents that will, in turn, drive conflict. Second, the political equilibrium and the consequent economic outcome must be stable so that small changes do not threaten a distribution failure. These findings are of great importance: first, we demonstrate the existence of a region of capital allocation such that if the optimal allocation of capital lies in this specific region there does not arise any distribution failure. Allocation of capital within this safe region renders the system crisis-free and there is no economic source of conflicts. If the capital allocation is not contained within this safe region, problems are expected to arise – economic crises, distribution failures and conflicts characterise the outcome either in agriculture or in industry. Second, we establish that under a specific and reasonable condition, the postulated economic and political system will fail to give rise to a safe region. As a result, there will be crises, distribution failures, and conflicts, either in agriculture or in industry or both, depending on the allocation of capital between the sectors. Third, we find that the dynamics of the political equilibrium can create enormous instability and fragility such that a chaotic regime will characterise the proposed economic and social outcomes.

In Chapter 3 we also highlight two types of conflicts, namely market conflicts and political conflicts involving interest groups, and attempt to weave them together to illuminate an important intersection between the economy and the polity. The introduction of the political determination of defence spending in our model allows us to link the second type of conflict, the political conflict, with the first. Since, the availability of defence spending is fixed, it is modelled that there is no congruence of interests between interest groups coming from two distinct regional locations, as Hirsch (1977) notes: 'what winners win, losers lose'. An allocation of defence spending will naturally entail political costs and benefits that a self-seeking government – driven by electoral motives – will try to exploit. An incumbent government will naturally choose an allocation to maximise the probability of its re-election. This is achieved by applying the probabilistic voting to the electoral competition as Lindbeck and Weibull (1987) and Dixit and Londregan (1994) adapt the probabilistic model to examine public policies that redistribute income to narrow groups of voters. They assume that the various groups differ in their preferences for political parties and, thereby, identify the political characteristics of a group that make it a suitable recipient of political largesse. These authors study the major determinants of political success of a special interest group. Instead, we apply the reputational model to explain the determination of defence spending to explain how interest groups can influence defence spending and how incumbent governments can thwart interest group politics, though only in the short term. In this chapter we then examine the empirical foundation to our models by applying the time series analysis to seven countries from the region: five from the Middle East and two from North Africa, as we did in Chapter 2.

The theoretical models establish three important insights in the context of defence spending: first, it is essential to disaggregate an economy into competing components. Each component has different preferences for defence spending, or arms imports. We undertake the disaggregation by breaking up each of the seven economies into two distinct groups, namely, rural and urban. Second, various other factors are expected to influence the political behaviour of interest groups, which will thereby determine the equilibrium level and allocation of defence spending. We introduce several new variables to empirically determine the nature of the equilibrium outcome. Finally and most importantly, since we don't have data on the regional allocation of defence spending, we examine the impacts of these factors on the dynamics of arms imports, or militarisation, in the seven countries from the region during 1960–2013. We explain the long-term determinants of arms imports hitherto not considered in the literature: as an example, the long-term vulnerability of a nation. Many other factors are shown to bear a long-term cointegrating relationship with arms imports. We are also able to determine important direction of causality in the context of militarisation of the Middle East and North Africa. In Chapter 3, at the country level, we find interesting and diverse long-run estimated relationships between arms imports ($ARIM$) of a country and the explanatory variables, which are normalised on the dependent variable. The coefficients of the explanatory variables have the expected signs in most of the equations.

Some of the most interesting results of Chapter 3 are as follows: in the long-run the growth of the urban population bears an inverse relationship with arms imports for all seven countries in the region. Urbanisation thus deters militarisation in all seven nations. The link between urbanisation and militarisation is hitherto unknown in the literature. As a corollary, urbanisation could thus be a vehicle for de-escalating the arms race in the Middle East and promoting peace. We will examine the issues of militarisation in greater detail in Chapter 6. In Chapter 3 we also find that both the size of the rural population and its growth are important determinants of arms imports but their effects vary across nations: first and foremost, for Libya and Israel both the size and growth of rural populations have negative relationships with their arms imports and both are economically and statistically significant. For Egypt and Lebanon, the effects of the rural sector on their arms imports are exactly the opposite: the larger the dominance of the rural sector in terms of population, the larger is the growth of militarisation, or arms imports. In Iraq we see a mixed case: the size of the rural population exerts an upward pressure on its arms imports while the growth of the rural population lowers demand for imported arms. In Chapter 3 at the empirical level, for the entire region, we find many interesting results: if we take the sum of military spending of the seven nations ($\Sigma ARIM$) as a proxy for the militarisation of the region, then the rising global temperature has an economically meaningful and statistically significant impact on the militarisation of the Middle East and North Africa. From the data we also find some concrete evidence that global warming has increased militarisation of the region during a long haul of 1960–2013. However, there is no evidence that the global oil production did have any palpable impacts on the militarisation of the region. Though the results show a negative effect, the coefficient does not have statistical significance. The impact of the oil price, on the contrary, shows that there is strong evidence that the rising oil price can significantly reduce militarisation in the region.

In Chapter 4 we explore the causes and consequences of terrorism. In the existing literature, there are two strands of thought to understand the economic consequences of terrorism: the formal models by Eckstein and Tsiddon (2004) and many other works focus on a very particular factor and specific channels through which terrorism affects the economy. In their work, Eckstein and Tsiddon (2004) choose a closed economy model and put forward the proposition that terrorism raises the discount rate, which in turns translates into a reduction of income and other macroeconomic variables. The pertinent question in this context is whether terrorism palpably impacts on the vulnerability of a segment of population in a country, or region so that agents change their behaviour, which will then adversely impact on the macroeconomic performances of the region, or country. The implicit assumption is that terrorism increases the vulnerability of the targeted group as their death rates and mortality rates rise, and such rises then alter investment and consumption behaviours of private agents along with far-reaching changes in public investment. In Chapter 2 we have introduced, developed and calculated the vulnerability index (*VI*) for seven nations from the region during 1960 to 2013. One of our major contributions to the literature is to apply the vulnerability index to the terrorism research for understanding whether and how terrorism impacts on the vulnerability of the chosen nations during 1968–2009. We also seek to establish the reverse causality: how vulnerability of a nation impacts on terrorism among other economic factors. Once again the period of study is dictated by the availability of data on terrorism in the region from February 1968 to December 2009.

Some important lessons from Chapter 4 are as follows: first and foremost, there is a long-term equilibrium relationship, both economically meaningful and statistically significant, between regional terror incidents and the average vulnerability of all seven nations in the region. However, the individual vulnerability of nations has heterogeneous impacts on regional terrorism: as examples, we note that increases (decreases) in vulnerability in Libya, Syria, Iran and Israel will increase (decrease) terrorism in the region. In other words, there is a direct relationship between terrorism and the vulnerability for these nations. However, the relationship reverses for Iraq, Egypt and Lebanon with an inverse relationship between terrorism and vulnerability of these three nations. Second, as opposed to the strand of research led by Eckstein and Tsiddon (2004), we find that terrorism does not have an unequivocal impact on the vulnerability of a nation, measured in their work by death rates. We note that terrorism lowers vulnerability for some nations but enhances resilience in others. The heterogeneous effect materialises through some interesting channels, which we explore in the subsequent sections. Third, we also evidence that global warming increases terrorism in the region – the effect is also statistically significant. Fourth, the global oil market has its influence upon terrorism: the larger the global demand for oil, the lower terrorism will be in the region. However, the oil price has a counter-balancing impact on terrorism in the region. The Granger causality results confirm the direction of causality as highlighted by the theoretical models.

An important area of research in terrorism is in the context of counterterrorism: an important insight into the problem of optimal counterterrorism through military interventions is due to Enders and Sandler's (1993) postulation that terrorism is intrinsically linked to government policies to rout terrorism. In their work they argue that terrorists respond strategically to counterterrorism measures, which will engender the 'substitution effect'. That is, rational terrorists, on watching an increase in a particular government counterterrorism program, will switch tactics. Terrorists will pursue attacks less affected by the government's efforts. In a large body of literature, a variety of empirical studies confirm that counterterrorism generates such effects (Enders and Sandler 1993, 2002; Enders, Sandler and Cauley, 1990; Im, Cauley and Sandler 1987). In our research we find that arms imports do not have unequivocal effects on each country of our study: counterterrorism measures do not work in Israel, Iraq and Lebanon as the imports are possibly target-specific. As a result, such imports are met with increased incidents of terrorism in these countries. On the contrary, arms imports for Libya, Syria, Iran and Egypt help their counterterrorism strategies, and arms imports possibly help them move away from target-specific projects, which will in turn see a decline in terrorism in the countries. There are various other channels through which the heterogeneous effects materialise. In this chapter we are also able to home in on the optimal policy to create a virtuous cycle to reduce terrorism, boost per capita income and reduce vulnerability.

In Chapter 5 we propose a participatory conflict management procedure (CMP) that aspires to discover stable points for collaboration between confrontational parties. Stable points are mutual joint cooperative arrangements that diminish the probability of conflict re-escalation. We work with a very small group (between four and ten persons) to elicit in-depth data on the Arab–Israeli conflict from two experiments. The first experiment lets us determine the main objectives for each actor. The second experiment determines which objectives are crucial, as well as the sensitivity of each objective for each party, using Saaty's scale (see Table A.8.1 in the Appendix for more details). This enables us to elicit the sensitivity of each policy objective for each actor. Some objectives are more crucial than others and the sensitivity of most objectives differs between the parties. The procedure consists of two questions for each objective for each actor. The first question senses how large a concession in percentage from its most preferred position, for a given policy objective, should be, before the actor perceives the decrease as a significant loss in utility. The second question measures, for each objective in percentages, what the drop in utility actually is, if a significant concession (answer question a) occurs from its most preferred position. MATLAB (version 7, release 14) is used to run the data in order to verify the stability of all possible collaborative actions among the conflicting parties. After running the model we select the most common robust or stable neighbourhood position, which allows us to determine specific sites of agreement where conflicts may be considered less valuable than the concessions granted to both sides: first, offering free access to places of religious and historical significance for both Arabs and Israelis; second, the agreement between all parties (Israel, Palestine, Jordan, Lebanon and Syria) on water allocation; and third, declaring a celebratory day which signifies the recognition and respect of each others' sovereignty, territorial and political independence.

The purpose of Chapter 6 is to understand the global arms race and its impact on the regional economies of the Middle East and North Africa. The arms race is an immense issue confronting our globe, and so is the herd mentality in the arms race. Ours is a first small step towards understanding the possibility of informational cascades and herding in the context of the arms race and the search for some empirical validation of our model. It begs a question of why we need herding to justify arms races. In the context of incomplete information, the latest models of arms races explains the possibility of the detente equilibrium and the information acquisition/learning phase such that there is nothing sacrosanct, or automatic or instantaneous, about the onset and continuation of the arms race. These new developments in the arms race literature tend to contradict and discount the findings of the earlier Richardsonian framework, traditionally applied to explain arms races by the action–reaction type of interactions between nations. Our major contribution is to bring informational cascades into the incomplete information setting to highlight how human irrationalities can still play immense roles in triggering, fuelling and propelling the arms race in our contemporary world.

In Chapter 6 we model the arms race as anarchy, that is, a system in which rival nations engage in military build-ups to defend economic resources without an effective regulation, or protection, from above. Military build-ups are costly since they require inputs, which will diminish the resources for producing the economic good (e.g. *GDP*). Military spending is important for advancing national interests in order to protect, or expand, economic resources. We also assume that the economic output (*GDP*) has a positive feedback to the production of military output. In this mixed model, the military build-up of a nation is shown to depend, *inter alia*, on what the rival expects one's rivals to do. From this interdependency, we derive a game of military build-ups and the relevant Nash characterisation as a combination of the mutually best responses in the context of incomplete information. In the context of arms race models with incomplete information, a number of recent works highlighted the relevance of communication and social learning in preventing arms races. The incompleteness of information motivates nations to learn from social interactions, which is the primary intuition of our chapter, that allows a necessary extension of the literature by developing a comprehensive model of informational cascades in arms races and tests its validity from the dynamics of military spending by major players in the global arms market. We find, due to herd sentiments, there is a non-zero probability that the military spending and arms races will never be predicated on an objective consideration of the costs and benefits associated with arming. In the post-Cold War era, the annual spending of $1 trillion on global military build-ups is not only a steep price to pay for an arms race but is also socially inefficient since – despite myriad private signals that reveal the right choice on arms races – nations seem to herd on the incorrect choice of arming with positive probability. The decision to get armed and subsequently embroiled in a war and ensuing violent conflicts can be driven by herd sentiments: every nation is individually rational to arm, being ready to fight a '*bloody war*', even if all nations have overwhelming (private) information that there is absolutely no necessity to do so. In other words, everybody will willingly embrace the 'wrong behaviour' even when there is enough evidence in favour of espousing the 'right behaviour', which can push our civilisation to the precipice of meaningless self-destruction. There is clear evidence of the arms race being driven by herd sentiments in the Middle East and North Africa.

In Chapter 7, the relationships between violent conflict and inequality are analysed. An econometric model is estimated using binary dependent variable techniques to capture the relation between violent conflict and inequality across Middle Eastern and Arab countries. We construct two models based on the theoretical model and actual data: the first is a dummy variable that takes a value of one when a conflict has resulted in over 1,000 battle deaths in a given year and country. The second is a dummy variable that takes a value of one if the conflict is completely internal, and another which is equal to one when the conflict involves an external actor.

For the purpose of this study we use the panel data that allows us to control for unobservable time invariant country-specific effects that result in a missing variable bias. The two models estimate using a pooled model (ordinary least squares), fixed effects (accounting for heterogeneity across countries), and random effects (accounting for heterogeneity across countries and across time). The other independent variables collected are the growth rate, *GDP* per capita, inflation, military expenditure, *FDI*, population, military personnel and immigration. The empirical analysis indicates a negative relation between inequality and conflict. Inflation, military expenditure, and immigration have a positive relation with conflicts, while *FDI* as a percentage of *GDP*, growth and workers' remittance have a negative relation with conflicts. In the first model, the most important factor that affects conflicts is the immigration variable; for the second model, immigration and workers' remittance strongly affect the conflict variable.

To understand the relevance of justice in the Middle East and North Africa, in Chapter 7 we also develop an index of the status of women in the country to measure justice in the seven countries from the region. We then choose the average value of the indexes for the seven nations to arrive at the average justice index (*AJI*) in the Middle East and North Africa. We use the Johansen test results to determine the long-term cointegrating relationships between justice and other variables in the region. Appropriate causality tests are undertaken to confirm the direction of causality. Some of the important findings are as follows:

First, an improvement in justice (*AJI*) in the region increases terrorism for the entire region. Some explanations are offered. Second, as we have noted already, as the average per capita income of the region increases (decreases), regional terrorism declines (increases). The inverse relationship between income and terrorism is a time-honoured, though often challenged, adage in economics. Third, there is a positive and statistically significant relationship between militarisation (*AVARIM*) and terrorism in the region. Thus, one can argue that terrorists strategically react to counterterror strategies like arms imports. Fourth, terrorism bears a direct relationship with the average long-term vulnerability of the entire region (*AVVI*). The effect is also statistically significant. Finally, the global warming factor contributes positively to terrorism in the region. The regional justice is Granger caused by all the chosen variables in our analysis. The terrorism variable is marginally significant, but all others are statistically significant: economic progress (Granger) causes justice while the increase in vulnerability also (Granger) causes justice.

Regional terrorism is also Granger caused by justice. We also find that economic performance is (Granger) caused by justice in the region. Militarisation (*AVARIM*) of the region is also (Granger) caused by justice in the region. The rest of the Granger causality results are known from Chapter 4 and Chapter 7. All other statistical tests are also satisfactory for the rank and lag determination, which we don't report here.

Appendix
A historical account of the conflicts in the Middle East

1.   Accounts of the conflicts in the Middle East before 1948

1.1   Introduction

This chapter traces the history of the modern conflict between Israel and Palestine from 4000 BCE to 1948 CE. It shows how Jews and Arabs diverged from a common source to become arch-enemies during the British Mandate over Palestine. It outlines the impact of World War II, the holocaust, treason, and terrorism on the Palestinian problem, and explains why Britain relinquished the Mandate in 1947, leaving the United Nations to resolve the land settlement problem. It demonstrates why this corrupted land settlement set the scene for almost 60 years of continuous war and terrorism in the Middle East.

1.2   Early history of the region

> No two historians ever agree on what happened, and the damn thing is they both think they're telling the truth.
>
> Harry S. Truman

In order to understand the Arab–Israeli conflict today, we need an overview of the history of Israel/Palestine land. The area that is now called Israel/Palestine is very small geographically (10,000 sq. miles at present) but huge in its historical importance. In addition to being home to the shrines of three religions, Israel/Palestine was conquered by many invaders throughout the years.

1.2.1   The Canaanites (ca. 2000 BC–1468 BC)

The first known inhabitants of Israel/Palestine were the Canaanites (the Levant) (Cattan, 1973). The Canaanites were a Semitic people with extraordinary industry and outstanding intelligence, who occupied Israel/ Palestine, Lebanon, and much of Syria and Jordan (Albright and Kunstel,

1990). H.G. Wells (1919) mentioned in his book *The Outline of History: Being a Plain History of Life and Mankind*, that

> What is called Palestine today was at that time the land of Canaan, inhabited by a Semitic people called the Canaanites, closely related to the Phoenicians who founded Tyre and Sidon, and to the Amorites who took, Babylon and, under Hammurabi, founded the first Babylonian Empire.
>
> Wells (1919, p. 73)

1.2.2 The Egyptians (ca. 1468–1200 BC)

During this period Israel/Palestine was part of Egyptian territory. The pharaoh left the Canaanites in control of their own territories with direct supervision from Egyptian and Canaanite commissioners. The Egyptians were astonished by the prosperous trade business of the Canaanite seaports of Gaza, Jaffa and Acca, which traded goods far and wide.

1.2.3 The Philistines (ca. 1200–975 BC)

The word Palestine is derived from the Philistines who lived in the southern coastal part of the country (Cattan, 1969; 1973). The Philistines, neither Arabs nor Semites, and also known as the Sea Peoples, originated from Crete. They attacked Israel/Palestine and devastated the cities. Once established in Israel/Palestine, they became the most powerful group there for more than two centuries.

1.2.4 The Israelites, the Kingdom of David (ca. 975–925 BC)

The Israelites were not the first inhabitants of Israel/Palestine but were invaders like others (Cattan, 1969). The conflict between the Philistines and the Israelites became unavoidable with the trade expansion of the Philistines into Arabia. In 975 BC the Israelites under the command of King David managed to defeat the Philistines, who were humiliated and never regained their supremacy. The successor to David was his son Solomon, most famous for the temple he built to offer sacrifices to God.

1.2.5 The Canaanite Phoenicians (ca. 925–700 BC)

The Israelites and the Philistines conquered approximately three-quarters of the Canaanite territories. As a result the Canaanites sailed to Tyre, where they established a vital city that became the centre of trade routes and gradually monopolised trade in the Mediterranean. Their strong trade powers led to a stronger army that invaded and conquered the Israel/Palestine region.

1.2.6   The Assyrians (ca. 700–612 BC)

The Assyrians came from Iraq; their capital city was Nineveh. When they fought they destroyed the towns and replaced the populace with people from different regions. They became infamous for the cruelty of their torture, which struck terror into everyone's heart. The Assyrians attacked Israel/Palestine and removed the residents to the Median Mountains, replacing them with colonists from Kutha in Iraq.

1.2.7   The Babylonians (ca. 586–539 BC)

The Babylonians lived in the area between the Tigris and Euphrates Rivers: Iraq in the present day. In 612 BC the Babylonians attacked the Assyrian Empire, which immediately collapsed. They then attacked Israel/ Palestine, destroying Jerusalem and burning Solomon's temple, and carried Jerusalem's leading Jewish citizens back to Babylon. These people were well treated and became very rich merchants.

1.2.8   The Persians (ca. 539–332 BC)

The Persians are Indo-Europeans, related to the Hittites, Romans, and Greeks. They created a huge empire that flourished for 200 years. In 539 BC the Persians destroyed the Babylonians and conquered the region from Asia Minor to India, including Turkey, Iran, Egypt, Afghanistan and Pakistan. In general, the Persians respected the customs and religious traditions of the diverse groups in their empire. They allowed the exiled Jews to return to the country in 538 BC (Cattan, 1969). The Jews living in Babylon returned to Jerusalem and built a second temple on the place where Solomon's temple had stood.

1.2.9   The Macedonian Greeks (ca. 332–70 BC)

The Macedonian Greeks crushed the Persians in Asia Minor and, upon reaching what is now called the Lebanon Coast, found that its kings were absent with the Persian fleet in the Aegean. The Macedonian Greeks conquered what is in the present day Egypt, Syria, Israel/Palestine and Lebanon.

1.2.10   The Romans (63 BC–637 AD)

In 63 BC the Roman general Pompey invaded Israel/Palestine, initiating seven centuries of Roman rule. In 70 AD the Romans destroyed the Great Temple in Jerusalem during the first Jewish Revolt against them (Minnis, 2001). Jericho and Bethlehem were destroyed when Jews revolted again between 132 and 135 AD; and the Jews were banned from Jerusalem. The Romans bestowed the name Palestina on the land known today as Israel/Palestine, and changed the name of Jerusalem to Aelia Capitolina. The Romans either killed the Jews or sold them as slaves. The Jews who survived left the country, dispersing throughout the Middle East.

1.2.11   The Arabs (AD 637–1260)

The Romans sensed the pointlessness of defending Palestina against the Arabs, so the Patriarch expressed his willingness to hand the keys of Jerusalem to Caliph Omar Ibn-AlKhattab[1] without using the sword. In 637 AD, the Caliph signed Jerusalem surrender terms[2] granting protection of the Christians, their property and churches. This was the first time that Jerusalem was conquered without slaughter. Many inhabitants converted to Islam, which became the major religion in the country (Cattan, 1969). The country remained under Arabian control for more than four centuries, with caliphs ruling first from Damascus, then from Baghdad and Egypt.

1.2.12   The Crusaders (AD 1099–1291)

In 1095, Pope Urban II made a plea to free Jerusalem from the Arabs. Thousands gathered to fight the Muslims. Many extended their target to include other infidels, particularly Jews. On 15 July 1009 the Crusaders captured Jerusalem and began to massacre the city's Muslims and Jews. Muslim, Christian and Jewish sources agree that exceptional quantities of blood were shed in the conquest of Jerusalem (Gil, 1997). The Crusaders forbade Muslims and Jews to live in Jerusalem.

1.2.13   The Ayubid Arabs (AD 1187–150)

The Ayubid were Muslims with Kurdish origins, who came from what is now Iraq. The Ayubid commander Saladin managed to become the Sultan of Syria and Egypt. In 1187 AD, Saladin defeated the Crusaders in Hittin, after which he besieged and captured Jerusalem. In contrast to the Crusaders' treatment of Muslims, Saladin offered forgiveness and a secure route home for the Crusaders and their families. The Jews returned to Jerusalem following Saladin's victory.

1.2.14   The Mamluks (AD 1260–1516)

The Ayibid were dependent on Turkish men who served in their army. These Turks were called Mamluks (which means 'owned' in Arabic) because they were captured in childhood and raised to become Muslim soldiers. The Mamluks became powerful, having the strongest organisation.

The Crusaders signed an agreement with the Mongols against the Muslims, and in 1258 the Mongols destroyed and burnt Baghdad's libraries on their way towards Jerusalem. In response, the Mamluks took control in Egypt and headed towards Jerusalem, where in 1260 AD they defeated the Mongols. The Mamluks destroyed the Crusaders' strongholds along Israel/Palestine's coastline as revenge for the Crusader alliance with the Mongols. Israel/Palestine became unimportant during the Mamluk period, and most of its ports were destroyed for fear of new Crusader attacks.

1.2.15   *The Ottoman Turks (AD 1516–1917)*

Israel/Palestine came under Ottoman rule after a bloody battle with the Mamluks in 1517 AD. The Ottoman Turks' rule in Israel/Palestine was to last four centuries, during which time Israel/Palestine never formed a political administration of its own (Bickerton and Pearson, 1986). The Turks paid little attention to Jerusalem because they considered it unimportant both politically and strategically. The land was divided into four districts connected administratively to the province of Damascus and ruled from Istanbul. In the Ottoman period between 1516–1831 AD, Israel/Palestine and the other Arab countries suffered from lack of knowledge, illiteracy, disease, few medical services and no developed ports. In November 1831, the long Dark Age reached an end when Ibrahim Pasha of Egypt invaded Israel/Palestine and opened Arabic schools, encouraging European missionaries to open schools to educate Christians.

The Ottoman Turks reoccupied the area in 1840 when Great Britain sided with them against Ibrahim Pasha. The Turks immediately closed the Arabic schools, but kept the missionary schools open. Europeans opened consulates and vice-consulates in Jerusalem and other seaports' interest in the region revived. As a result, the Jews' situation improved, and they revived the restricted Hebrew language. This eventually led to the founding of the Zionist movement. When World War I broke out, the Ottoman Empire sided with Germany against Great Britain.

1.2.16   *Zionism*[3]

A group of Jewish academics in Eastern Europe established a political lobby group called Zionism during the 1880s. Its objective was the creation of an independent Jewish nation state and the protection of Judaism and the Jewish tradition through the re-establishment of a Hebrew-based Jewish culture situated in the traditional Jewish homeland Eretz-Yisrael. Thomas Friedman says:

> The Zionists called for the ingathering of the Jews from around the world in Palestine and the creation there of a modern Jewish nation-state that would put the Jews on a par with all the other nations of the world. Most of the early Zionists either ignored the presence of the Arabs already living in Palestine or assumed they could either be bought off or would eventually submit to Jewish domination.
>
> (Friedman, 1995, p. 14)

Zionism was looked at as the solution to the Jewish dilemma, which was derived from two basic facts: the Jews were disseminated in various countries around the world; and in each country they formed a minority (Shlaim, 2001).

On 7 July 1882 a small group consisting of fourteen men and one woman landed in Jaffa, heralding the first modern wave of immigration to Israel/ Palestine that lasted from 1882–1903 (Bickerton and Pearson, 1986). The opposition of Arab leaders to the Jews' increasing immigration and purchase of land led them to exert pressure on the Ottomans to prohibit Jewish immigration and land buying. However, hearing of the bankruptcy of the Ottoman Empire, Zionist leader Theodor Herzl met the Sultan of the Ottoman Turks in May 1901 and offered to pay a substantial portion of the Ottoman debt in exchange for a charter allowing Zionists to colonise Israel/Palestine. The Sultan refused Herzl's offer, saying, 'I prefer being penetrated by iron to seeing Palestine lost' (Cattan, 1969). The Ottoman Regime suspended all land transfers to Jews when Zionists called for increased colonisation in Israel/Palestine in 1905. During the Ottoman period relations between the three religions in Israel/Palestine were peaceful and stable, but this changed after the arrival of British troops in 1917. For the Arabs inside Israel/Palestine, Zionism was a greater danger than the British Mandate: unlike the British, who had no desire to colonise, the Zionists perceived themselves as natives of the land.

1.2.17   The British (1917–1948)

After the outbreak of World War I, the Turks were forced to surrender Israel/Palestine to the British forces under General Allenby in September 1918. Within five weeks of occupying Israel/Palestine, the British Foreign Secretary Arthur Balfour made, on behalf of the British Government, a historic declaration in which he promised to support Zionist plans for a Jewish national home in Israel/Palestine (Laqueur, 1968). This declaration is considered by many to be the root of the Palestinian tragedy and of Arab–Israeli conflict (Cattan, 1973). The British also made an agreement (called the Sykes-Picot Agreement) with French and Russian governments, whereby Palestine should be placed under international administration (Laqueur, 1968; Reich, 1996). At the same time the British promised Husain, King of Hijaz and then Sharif of Mecca, that Israel/Palestine would be included in the zone of Arab independence if an Arab revolution was launched against the Ottoman Empire (Laqueur, 1968). In this way the British made three jointly opposing promises regarding the future of Israel/Palestine, the promises in the Sykes-Picot Agreement clashing with the promises made to both Zionists and Arabs (Peretz, 1996). These contradictory agreements, especially the one to Husain and the Balfour Declaration, set the stage for three decades of conflict during the British mandate on Israel/Palestine.

There are two main conclusions that can be derived from the brief history of Israel/Palestine land. First, the Muslims remained the inhabitants of Israel/ Palestine until the British Mandate. Second, the period of Jewish domination with complete independence was short compared with the history of Israel/ Palestine. Beatty, an archaeologist, states:

> all these [different peoples who had come to Canaan] were addi-
> tions, sprigs grafted onto the parent tree ... and that parent tree was
> Canaanite ... They [the Arab invaders of the seventh century AD] made
> Moslem converts of the natives, settled down as residents, and intermar-
> ried with them, with the result that all are now so completely Arabized
> that we cannot tell where the Canaanites leave off and the Arabs begin.
> The Jewish Kingdoms were only one of many periods in ancient Palestine.
> The extended kingdoms of David and Solomon, on which the Zionists
> base their territorial demands, endured for only about 73 years ...
> Then it fell apart ... [Even] if we allow independence to the entire life of
> the ancient Jewish kingdoms, from David's conquest of Canaan in 1000
> BC to the wiping out of Judah in 586 BC, we arrive at [only] a 414 year
> Jewish rule.
>
> (Beatty, 1957, pp. 45–46)

1.3   Jerusalem's Importance for Muslims, Christians and Jews

Jerusalem is undoubtedly the most significant religious city in the world because it is the most holy city in Christianity and Judaism, and the third holiest in Islam. This is why Jerusalem offers one of the tensest issues in the Israel/Arab conflict. For Muslims the name proposes peace and matches strongly to the Muslim concept of the sacred; a place where peace reigns and conflict is excluded. If we look at the history of Jerusalem we see that it is marked by conflict more than by peace.

The question arises: how did Jerusalem become so important in Islam and to Muslims? First, Jerusalem is the first Kiblah[4] to the Muslims before God commanded the Kiblah be changed to Mecca. Second, Jerusalem witnessed the life and works of the greatest prophets and messengers of God. In Islam, Mecca and Madinah are two sacred cities because of their relationship with the prophets Abraham, Ishmael and Mohammed. Similarly Jerusalem is associated with the prophets David, Solomon and Jesus. Third, in 620 AD the famous event of Isra[5] and Miraj[6] (Night Journey and Ascension) occurred when Mohammed was taken on a Buraq[7] from Mecca to Jerusalem and from there to the seven levels of heaven. This one-night journey creates a strong Muslim link with Jerusalem. Finally, in Jerusalem there is the Dome of the Rock, the earliest remaining Islamic monument, and the Al-Aqsa Mosque, which is associated with the Isra and Miraj (Ettinghausen and Grabar, 2003).

Jerusalem's role in the ministry of Jesus provides it with enormous Christian significance, apart from its place in the Old Testament. Christians see Jerusalem as the place of the gift of the spirit, of the birth of the church. For

Christians to be in Jerusalem is to be in their spiritual home. For Christians, Jerusalem is a tangible link with the salvation fulfilled through Jesus.

> Jerusalem is a holy place in Judaism mainly because of the destroyed temple. Jerusalem has been considered the central city of Judaism since the year 1005 BC when David conquered it and made it the capital of his kingdom. After that the temple was built there, destroyed, and then rebuilt, several times. The Romans destroyed the last of these temples and the only thing remaining from then until now are the Wailing Wall, the walls that used to surround the temple and now the holiest site for Jews in Jerusalem and the world. The second most important place is Hebron, where Abraham was buried, and the third most important place is Mt. Sinai, where Moses received the covenant.
>
> (Ettinghausen and Grabar, 2003, p. 135)

1.4 Demography in Israel/Palestine before 1948

> There have been two competing mythologies about Palestine circa 1880. The extremist Jewish mythology, long since abandoned, was that Palestine was 'a land without people, for a people without land'. (This phrase was actually coined by the British Lord Shaftesbury in his 1884 memoir.) The extremist Palestinian mythology, which has become more embedded with time, is that in 1880 there were a Palestinian people; some even say a Palestinian nation that was displaced by the Zionist invasion. The reality, as usual, lies somewhere in between.
>
> (Dershowitz, 2003, p. 23–25, his parentheses)

The demographic composition of Israel/Palestine has played a crucial role in shaping the area. From the beginning, population data were used to confirm or reject the particular claims raised by either side. Jewish claims were that Israel/Palestine was an empty land or had significantly few inhabitants, and thus its supreme argument for ownership is based on population. On the other hand, Arabs and Palestinian historians claim that a mainly Arab people have consistently inhabited Israel/Palestine. The main objective here is to examine changes in Israel/Palestine population before 1948 in light of the best available statistical data.

1.4.1 During the Ottoman Empire

The Ottoman Empire conquered Israel/Palestine in 1517 AD. It is difficult to find exact figures regarding the Israel/Palestine population during the Ottoman period for several reasons. First, Israel/Palestine was divided into districts that were connected to other provinces so there was no unique administrative district of Israel/Palestine. Second, Arabs and Jews alike avoided Turkish censuses, to evade military service and taxes. Third, groups

Table A.1 Population in Israel/Palestine by religion groups, 1st century to 1800 – rough estimates, thousands

Year	Jews	Christians	Muslims	Total[a]
First half 1st century CE	Majority	–	–	~ 2,500
5th century	Minority	Majority	–	> 1st century
End 12th century	Minority	Minority	Majority	> 225
14th century before Black Death	Minority	Minority	Majority	225
14th century after Black Death	Minority	Minority	Majority	150
1533–1539	5	6	145	157
1690–1691	2	11	219	232
1800	7	22	246	275

Source: Adapted from R. Bachi (1977).
[a] Including 'Others': Druzes, other small religious minorities

such as Bedouins, foreign residents, and illegal residents were not included in Turkish censuses. Finally, according to Justin McCarthy, the Turkish census tended to undercount women and children (McCarthy, 1990). Since the data were vague, different sources provide different estimates.

1.4.1.1   Before 1800

Looking at Table A.1 we find that the total population of Israel/Palestine is characterised by major changes in composition. The Jewish population in Israel/Palestine was a majority in the first half of the first century. During the Byzantine period, between the second and sixth centuries, the majority of the population were Christians. After the seventh century, with the rise of Islam and until the beginning of the British Mandate, Muslims formed the majority in Israel/Palestine. Between 1533 and 1539 the Muslims in Israel/Palestine numbered 145,000 and the Jews 5,000. During 1690 and 1691 around 94.4% of the total population in Israel/Palestine was Muslim. At the end of 1800, the total population of Israel/Palestine was estimated at 275,000, comprising about 246,000 (89.45%) Muslims, 22,000 (8%) Christians, and 7,000 (2.55%) Jews.

If we look at population size, we see a great decline after the fifth century, then minor growth ever since (see Table A.1).

1.4.1.2   Between 1860 and 1914

Table A.2 shows huge anomalies between different sources. Perhaps Zionists exaggerated the number of Jews and underestimated the number of Arabs; perhaps Arab historians undercounted Jews and overstated the number of Arabs. According to Bachi, the number of Arabs (whether

Table A.2 Comparison of different estimates of Arab population of Ottoman Palestine

	Bachi	Census	Rodinson	Ruppin	McCarthy	Beinin and Hajjar
1860					411,000	
1870			367,224			
1878						447,000
1893	489,000	414,648	469,000	600,000	553,000	
1912–1914			525,000		738,000	

Note: Constructed from data collected from http://www.mideastweb.org/palpop.htm.

Muslim or Christian) in Israel/Palestine in 1893 was 489,200; he gives the number of Jews as 42,900 (Bachi, 1977). However, according to Beinin and Hajjar (1989), of 462,465 in Israel/Palestine in 1878, 403,795 were Muslims (including Druze), 43,659 Christians, and 15,011 Jews. According to Karpat (1978), there were 371,959 Muslims, 42,689 Christians, and 9,000 Jews in 1893. The Turkish Census estimated the number of Arabs in 1893 as 414,648 (Beinin and Hajjar, 1989). However, Ruppin argues that there were around 689,275 in Israel/Palestine during 1893, of whom about 600,000 were Arabs and 80,000 Jews (Avneri, 1984). A study by McCarthy claims that there were 411,000 Arabs in Israel/Palestine in 1860, 738,000 in 1890, and 738,000 in 1914 (McCarthy, 1990). A study by Rodinson states that there were 367,224 Arabs in 1878, 469,000 in 1893, and 525,000 in 1914 (Rodinson, 1968). Rodinson also estimates the number of Jews as 7,000 in 1870, 10,000 in 1893, and 60,000 in 1914 (Rodinson, 1968). Fattah estimates the number of Jews in 1908 had risen to 80,000: 'when Sultan Abdul-Hamid II's rule collapsed, it was estimated that the Jewish population of Palestine had risen to 80,000, 3 times its number in 1882, when the first entry restrictions were imposed' (Fattah, 1999).

1.4.1.3   During the British Mandate between 1914 and 1948

After World War I, Britain gained control of Palestine and the League of Nations assigned Great Britain the mandate for Israel/Palestine. Britain divided the region in two, the Palestine Mandate west of the Jordan River, and the Emirate of Transjordan to its east. During the British Mandate there were two censuses taken, in 1922 and in 1931. Table A.3 shows that, according to estimates, the population in Israel/Palestine increased from 750,000 at the census of 1922 to 1,765,000 at the end of 1944. In this period the Muslim portion of the population increased from 589,000 to 1,061,000, although their proportion of the total population was falling (78.34% to 58.35%). In the same period the Jewish portion of the population increased from 84,000 to 554,000 and proportionally from 13% to 31% of the total.

Table A.3 Approximate population growth in Mandatory Palestine

Year	Source	Total	Muslims		Jews		Christians		Others	
			(No.)	(%)	(No.)	(%)	(No.)	(%)	(No.)	(%)
1922	Census	752,048	589,177	78.34	83,790	11.14	71,464	9.50	7,617	1.01
1931	Census	1,033,314	759,700	73.52	174,606	16.90	88,907	8.60	10,101	0.98
1937	Estimate	1,383,320	875,947	63.32	386,084	27.91	109,769	7.94	11,520	0.83
1945	Survey[1]	1,845,560	1,076,780	58.35	608,230	32.96	145,060	7.86	15,490	0.84
1947[2]	Projection	1,955,260	1,135,269	58.06	650,000	33.24	153,621	7.86	16370	0.84

[1] These widely quoted numbers are apparently based on official estimates and were not from a special survey.

[2] Figures for the Jewish population were estimated to include immigration. 650,000 is the accepted number. The estimate of 'Others' was based on average rates of increase in 1922–1945. The source http://www.palestineremembered.com/Acre/Maps/Story574.html gives 608,250 for 1945 as a revised survey figure, and this is generally accepted. However, Rodinson and others list the survey numbers as if they are for 1946 rather than 1945 (Rodinson, 1968).

Table A.4 Recorded immigration and emigration, Israel/Palestine, 1930–1939

Year	Immigration			Emigration			Net Immigration		
	Jews	Non-Jews	Total	Jews	Non-Jews	Total	Jews	Non-Jews	Total
1930	4,944	1,489	6,433	1,679	1,324	3,003	3,265	165	3,430
1931	4,075	1,458	5,533	666	680	1,346	3,409	778	4,187
1932	9,553	1,736	11,289	x[a]	x	X	9,553	1,736	11,289
1933	30,327	1,650	31,977	x	x	X	30,327	1,650	31,977
1934	42,359	1,784	44,143	x	x	X	42,359	1,784	44,143
1935	61,854	2,293	64,147	396	387	783	61,458	1,906	63,364
1936	29,727	1,944	31,671	773	405	1,178	28,954	1,539	30,493
1937	10,536	1,939	12,475	889	639	1,528	9,647	1,300	10,947
1938	12,868	2,395	15,263	1,095	716	1,811	11,773	1,679	13,452
1939	16,405	2,028	18,433	1,019	977	1,996	15,386	1,051	16,437
Total	222,648	18,716	241,364	6,517	5,128	11,645	216,131	13,588	229,719

Source: Adapted from data from the Esco Foundation (1947) from http://www.unu.edu/
unupress/unupbooks/80859e/80859E05.htm.
[a] 'x' indicates that emigration was not reported

Motivated by Zionism and encouraged by British sympathy, the Jewish population increased as a result of immigration particularly in the 1930s (see Table A.4). A net immigration of 216,131 Jews was recorded between 1930 and 1939. After Hitler's rise to power, there was organised illegal immigration to Israel/Palestine. Although two ships sank and two others were turned back by the British, 13 ships delivered more than 15,000 illegal immigrants before the outbreak of World War II in 1939. The majority emigrated from different places in Middle Europe. Illegal migration reached its climax in 1935 with the arrival of 61,854 refugees, then started to reduce as a result of the Arab revolution that flared in Israel/Palestine in 1936. In the period 1940–1948, 110,585 immigrants were transferred to Israel/Palestine with the help of the Haganah, the main body involved in illegal immigration. According to the Israel Central Bureau of statistics, the total number of Jewish immigrants between 1919 and 1948 was about 483,000. The immigrants of the 1930s brought with them a great deal of capital, as well as skills and experience in industry, science, banking, medicine, law and international commerce. With the mandate, British capital and technology were introduced to Israel/Palestine, and the Jewish immigration was accompanied by European capital and European technology. This led, by the 1930s, to a higher standard of living for Palestinian Arabs, compared with that of Arabs in surrounding countries.

There are several problems related to estimating Arab migration to Israel/Palestine. Arab immigration was unreported and unrecorded because most of it was illegal. According to all the reports of the period, Arab recorded immigration to Palestine was minimal, casual, and unquantifiable. For example,

British records in 1934 show only 1,784 non-Jews legally immigrated and around 3,000 came illegally.

1.5   *Conflicts between Arabs and Jews before 1948*

Two groups come into conflict when one group has interests and goals inimical to the goals and interests of the other group (Rubin, Pruitt and Kim, 1994). The conflict between the Arabs and Jews in the Middle East has taken different dimensions, such as Muslims versus Jews and Muslims and Arabs versus the West. During the Ottoman period, the first Zionist immigration to Israel/Palestine took place in 1880, but there were no direct conflicts during that period. At the end of the Ottoman period Arabs living in Israel/Palestine began to feel threatened by Jewish immigration, which was increasing each year. After World War I, the coming of the British and the Balfour Declaration intensified the conflict. Britain was allocated control on Jordan, Iraq and Israel/Palestine; Syria and Lebanon were given to France as mandate countries, based on the Sykes-Picot Agreement. Arabs felt that the British had betrayed them, since they expected Britain to fulfil its promise to create an independent Arab country or countries throughout the Middle East. Arabs inside Israel/Palestine opposed the British Mandate because of the Balfour Declaration and the continuous Jewish immigration that threatened their position in the country.

The conflict between Arabs and Jews started when both the Arabs and Jews began to develop national consciousness and began to desire self-determination and sovereignty. Some historians declare that the true start of the Arab–Israeli conflict was between 1920 and 1921, when a man named Amin Al-Husseini[8] began propaganda against Jews who purchased large tracts of land from absentee landowners and expelled the Arabs living in these areas (Rowley and Taylor, 2006a). In March 1920, the first Arab public disturbance took place in Jerusalem, and violence increased between Arabs and Jews. After a speech by Amin Al-Husseini on 4 April 1920, Arabs destroyed the Jewish Quarter of Jerusalem, beating anyone they could find. The riot lasted for four days, and five Jews and four Arabs were killed. These developments led to the founding of the Haganah,[9] a Jewish military organisation, on 15 June 1920. A new wave of violence took place, this time in Jaffa, on 1 May 1921, when two groups of Jews began fighting each other. Arabs believed that they were under attack, and fighting between Arabs and Jews erupted and went on for several days. The casualties were 48 Arabs and 47 Jews killed, and 219 people wounded (Farsoun, 1997).

On 15 August 1929, there was a major incident between Arabs and the Jews over the Wailing Wall. The accident occurred when several hundreds of Betar raised a Zionist flag over the Wailing Wall, shouting, 'the Wall is ours'. Arabs, hearing rumours that Betar members had attacked local residents and cursed the name of Mohammed, demonstrated on 16 August and marched to the Wall where pages from Jewish prayer books were burnt. The next day a Jew was killed. On 20 August, Haganah members offered to evacuate the Jews from Hebron, but the Jews refused, stating that they trusted the Arab notables to protect them. After three days, Arabs attacked them, angered by a rumour that Jews had killed two Arabs. The violence spread all over Israel/Palestine, although the worst killings happened in Hebron and Safad. In Hebron 64 Jewish men, women, and children were massacred, while many others were saved by hiding in their Arab neighbours' houses or taking shelter at the British Police station (Kimmerling and Migdal, 2003). The Jewish survivors were obliged to leave their properties, which were occupied by Arabs. The aftermath of the 1929 Arab–Jewish conflict was the death of 133 Jews and 116 Arabs; most of the Arabs were killed by British military action (Wasserstein, 2001). The British blamed Arabs for the violence, but noted that it was the result of Jews expelling cultivators after buying Arab land.

The main achievement of the 1929 conflict for the Arabs was the British decision to halt Jewish immigration. The Zionists used their access to members of the British Cabinet to pressure for a change to this ruling. The Palestinians, lacking this kind of influence on the British Cabinet, lost their case by default.

Zionists denied the existence of a problem by convincing themselves that Arabs would accept a Jewish state in Israel/Palestine because of the benefits that they would gain (Dowty, 2005). By the mid-1930s, both Arabs and Zionists looked forward to establishing a state in the area. David Ben-Gurion[10] said, 'We and they [Arabs] want the same thing. We both want Palestine' (Teveth, 1994). Hitler's rise to power in 1933 increased European Jewish immigration to Israel/Palestine, which heightened tensions between Arabs and Jews (Hajjar and Beinin, 1988). Pressure increased between both sides, especially after the Histadrut, the Jewish Labour Federation, started to besiege Jewish firms and farms that hired Arab labour (Bickerton and Pearson, 1986). During that period, newly arrived European Jews led in land purchases and Jewish settlement (see Table A.5). The Mufti Amin Al-Husseini established the Arab Higher Command, which called for general protest, and demanded the termination of Jewish immigration and immediate elections. The protest began by calling Arab workers to strike and boycott Jewish products. These actions turned into violence and Arab attacks began on railways, oil pipelines and Jewish settlements. In October 1936 the strike ended and a short-term peace between Arabs and Jews existed for approximately a year. Following the report by the Peel Commission[11] in September 1937, Arab violence against Jews renewed, and Jews responded more forcibly than before. British forces, with help from the Haganah and support from the neighbouring Arab regimes, crushed the Arab revolt in early 1939. They arrested or expelled the main Arab leaders, and left the Arabs inside Israel/Palestine without political leadership at a time when their future was decided (Khalaf 1991). The result of the 1936–1939 revolt was 5,000 Arabs dead, 15,000 wounded, and 5,600 imprisoned. The Jewish and British tolls were 415 and 200 killed, respectively. Although the British crushed the Arab revolt,

Table A.5 Areas purchased by the Jewish community

Year	Dunums^a
1930	19,365
1931	18,585
1932	18,893
1933	36,991
1934	62,114
1935	72,905

Source: Adapted from S. Graham Brown (1980).

[a] One Dunum equals approximately four acres

it did pressurise them to reverse their policy in support of a Jewish national home (Kimmerling and Migdal, 2003). They issued a White Paper[12] that limited future Jewish immigration and land purchases inside Israel/Palestine. Jewish immigration was limited to 75,000 persons within the next five years, and after that none would be admitted without Arab agreement; in addition Israel/Palestine would be granted its independence after ten years (Cattan, 1969). The Jewish replied to the White Paper by calling on the British to fulfil the promises of the Balfour Declaration, to open the gates of Israel/Palestine to immigration, and to establish a Jewish Commonwealth which could right the 'age-old wrong to the Jewish people' (Laqueur, 1968).

The 1936–1939 events received little attention at the time, but were a crucial stage in the confrontation between Arabs and Jews. After 30 years, the military correspondent of the Israeli daily newspaper *Ha'aretz* noted:

> with respect to the events of 1936, it seems to us that had they not happened in the manner and at the time in which they did in fact occur, it is doubtful that the Jewish community could have waged a war for independence eight years later. The Jewish community emerged from these dangerous 1936 events in a stronger position as a result of the strong support it received from the British government and army in Palestine.
>
> (El Kodsy and Lobel, 1970, p. 54)

1.6 Holocaust and partition

World War II and the Holocaust played an important role in shaping the future of Israel/Palestine. On 3 September 1939, in response to 1.8 million German troops invading Poland, Britain declared war on Germany. Immediately Jewish leaders expressed their loyalty to the British and their willingness to fight against Germany. In September 1939, David Ben-Gurion declared, 'We shall fight the war against Hitler as if there were no White Paper, and we shall fight the White Paper as if there were no war.' As there were some Arabs sympathetic to the Nazi cause, Arab reactions were less supportive of the British.

The Holocaust became a central part of Nazi activity. Hitler believed that Jews were responsible for Germany's defeat in World War I. At first he attempted to push Jews to leave Germany, but the majority did not leave because they had nowhere to go. Countries like the US, Australia and South American nations had restrictions on Jewish immigration. Nazi leadership decided on murdering the Jews. The Nazis employed several methods. One was obliging the victims to dig their own graves before they were shot and buried. Another way was locking the Jews in chambers and gassing them. Afterwards the bodies were burned until nothing remained but ashes. Rudolf Hoess, the architect and commandant of the largest death camp, described this mass killing:

> The 'Final Solution' of the Jewish question meant the complete extermination of all Jews in Europe. I was ordered to establish extermination facilities at Auschwitz in 6/1941. At that time, there were already in the General Government three other extermination camps: Belzek, Treblinka and Wolzek. These camps were under the Einsatzkommando of the Security Police and SD. I visited Treblinka to find out how they carried out their exterminations. The camp commandant at Treblinka told me that he had liquidated 80,000 in the course of one-half year. He was principally concerned with liquidating all the Jews from the Warsaw ghetto. He used monoxide gas, and I did not think that his methods were very efficient. So when I set up the extermination building at Auschwitz, I used Zyklon B, which was a crystallized prussic acid which we dropped into the death chamber from a small opening. It took from 3–15 minutes to kill the people in the death chamber, depending upon climatic conditions. We knew when the people were dead because their screaming stopped. We usually waited about one-half hour before we opened the doors and removed the bodies. After the bodies were removed our special Commandos took off the rings and extracted the gold from the teeth of the corpses.
>
> (Rudolf Hoess, quoted in Dowty, 2005, p. 2)

The Holocaust created greater sympathy throughout the Western world for the creation of a Jewish state (Dowty, 2005). The US president, Harry Truman, reflected the effect the Holocaust had on the Western world when he said,

> the organised brutality of the Nazis against the Jews in Germany was one of the most shocking crimes of all times. The plight of the victims who had survived the mad genocide of Hitler's Germany was a challenge to Western civilisation, and as a President I undertook to do something about it.
>
> (Truman, 1965, p. 1)

Western sympathy towards the Jews was reflected by generosity towards the Jews at the expense of Arabs living in Israel/Palestine; for example, Truman demanded in 1946 the right of entry of 100,000 Jewish immigrants into Israel/ Palestine while the US itself accepted only 4,767 displaced persons from Europe between December 1945 and October 1946 (Cattan, 1969).

After the Holocaust, the Zionists were convinced that if they had already established a Jewish state the Nazi first solution to deport its Jews would have worked and hundreds of thousands of lives would have been saved. The Zionists were keen to bring the remaining European Jews to Israel/ Palestine. The British after the Holocaust promised to support a Jewish state in Israel/Palestine, but later broke their promise and doubled their efforts to prevent illegal immigration. In response, the Zionists began using force against the British to drive them out of Israel/Palestine. Zionists bombed trains and killed British personnel. The British reacted by raiding the Jewish agency's premises and taking a huge number of documents, some of them highly sensitive. At the same time they arrested 2,500 Jews in Israel/Palestine. Irgun, a militant Zionist organisation, bombed the King David Hotel[13] in order to destroy the documents gathered by the British. On 22 July 1946, 15 to 20 Jews, dressed as Arab workers, packed explosives into milk containers and placed them in the basement of the hotel. The explosion killed 91: 28 British, 41 Arab, 17 Jewish, and 5 others. The Irgun made it clear that they had obtained approval from the Haganah Command and the Jewish Agency to bomb the hotel.

In Britain, newspapers started to insist that the government resolve the conflict and stop endangering the lives of British troops. In early 1947, the British dumped the Israel/Palestine problem in the lap of the United Nations (UN). The UN formed a United Nations Special Committee on Palestine (UNSCOP) to explore and resolve the Israel/Palestine problem. UNSCOP members recommended that the country should be divided between Arabs and Jews.

On 29 November 1947 the UN General Assembly adopted the partition plan (General Assembly Resolution 181, adopted by a vote of 33 to 13, with ten abstentions and one absentee), giving 55% of Israel/Palestine to the Jews and 44% to the Arabs[14] (Cattan, 1969; Dowty, 2005). The 1% left, Jerusalem and Bethlehem, were to become international zones according to the UN Resolution, with the United Nations itself as the administering authority (Bailey, 1990). The supra majority vote was corrupt and in no sense constituted a calculus of consent (Buchanan and Tullock, 1962). The US threatened many countries to vote in favour of the UN Resolution or face trade boycotts and/or the withdrawal of financial aid (Grose, 1988). Greece was the only country that withstood US pressure and voted against the UN partition resolution (Cattan, 1969). The President of the American University in Beirut, Dr. Stephen Penrose, criticised the US pressure:

> The political manoeuvring which led to the final acceptance of the United Nations General Assembly of the majority report of UNSCOP provides one of the blacker pages in the history of American international politics.

> There can be no question but that it was American pressure which brought the acceptance of the recommendation for partition of Palestine ... It was this effective American pressure for partition which is largely responsible for the terrific drop which American prestige took in all parts of the Arab and Muslim world.
>
> (Cattan, 1969, p. 12)

The Jews accepted the UN Resolution, while the Arabs rejected it. Violence between Arabs and Jews spread all over Israel/Palestine. The Zionist military forces were numerically smaller than the Arab military forces but better organised, trained and armed. Arabs inside Israel/Palestine depended on their neighbour countries to help them fight. However, each Arab country had a different agenda. King Abdullah, King of Jordan, held a secret meeting with the Jews to prevent the creation of a Palestinian state on the one hand, and to annex portions of the West Bank on the other. Syria wanted to take control of the northern part of Israel/Palestine, including Jewish and Arab areas. King Ibn Saud (King of Saudi Arabia) stated that he would not use oil as a weapon against the West as a result of any differences over Palestine (Cohen, 1986).

1.7   Historic peace plans

David Ben-Gurion said once: 'Why should the Arabs make peace? If I was an Arab leader I would never make terms with Israel. That is natural: we have taken their country ... Why should they accept that?' (Goldman, 1978).

All historic peace plans were based on territory, which has been more prominent in the Israel/Palestine conflict then in any conflict elsewhere (Herman and Newman, 2000). The notion of a single, bi-national state within which Jews and Arabs could live together was considered before 1948 as an academic conception, divorced from reality (Kelman, 1995). The four major peace plans that were suggested before 1948 were for one Jewish state, one Arab state, one binomial state, and two state partitions.

One Jewish State: The Zionists were asked to submit suggestions concerning Israel/Palestine to the Paris Peace Conference. On 3 February 1919, the Zionists presented a proposed single Jewish state that would include the land between the Mediterranean Sea and the Jordan River, in addition to Gaza and parts of Lebanon. A group of Jews from the US (anti-Zionists) offered an alternative proposal, refusing the Zionist demand to turn Israel/Palestine into a national home for the Jewish people. In their proposal they say,

> But we raise our voices in warning and protest against the demand of the Zionists for the reorganisation of the Jews as a national unit, to whom, now or in the future, territorial sovereignty in Palestine shall be committed. This demand not only misrepresents the trend of the history of the

Jews, who ceased to be a nation 2000 years ago, but involves the limitation and possible annulment of the larger claims of Jews for full citizenship and human rights in all lands in which those rights are not yet secure. For the very reason that the new era upon which the world is entering aims to establish government everywhere on principles of true democracy, we reject the Zionistic project of a 'national home for the Jewish people in Palestine'.

(Tekiner, Abed-Rabbo and Mezvinsky, 1988, p. 25)

The Zionists abandoned the One Jewish State plan when they recognised that they could not become a majority in all parts of Israel/Palestine.

One Arab State: From 1920 the Arabs and the Arab leaders called for a single Palestinian Arab state in Israel/Palestine. The Palestinian Arabs called for one single state in which Jews and other religious minorities would be second-class citizens. After World War II, the United Nations sent an Anglo-American Committee of Inquiry to explore conditions inside Israel/Palestine. The Arabs in Israel/Palestine submitted to this committee a report in which they rejected both partition and a bi-national state as resolutions to the conflict. The Arabs called for the creation of one Arab state that would assure the rights of Jewish minority. The report submitted to the commission stated,

The Palestinian State would be an Arab state not in any narrow racial sense, nor in the sense that non-Arabs should be placed in a position of inferiority, but because the form and policy of its government would be based on a recognition of two facts: first that the majority of the citizens are Arabs, and secondly that Palestine is part of the Arab world and has no future except through close cooperation with the other Arab states ... The idea of partition and the establishment of a Jewish state in a part of Palestine is inadmissible for the same reasons of principle as the idea of establishing a Jewish state in the whole country. If it is unjust to the Arabs to impose a Jewish state on the whole of Palestine, it is equally unjust to impose it in any part of the country ... There are also serious practical objections to the idea of a bi-national state which cannot exist unless there is a strong sense of unity and common interest overriding the differences between the two parties. Moreover, the point made in regard to the previous suggestion may be repeated here: this scheme would in no way satisfy the Zionists. It would simply encourage them to hope for more and improve their chances of obtaining it.

(MidEast Web, 1999, p. 12)

Binomial State: The President of the Hebrew University, Dr. Yehuda Magnes, and Martin Buber developed this idea. The Binomial state is based on the idea that the state would have Arab and Jewish cantons. This idea was submitted to the Anglo-American Committee; however the Arab states and Palestinian leaders rejected it.

Two State Partition Solution: To some, it is 'the only possible solution to
the Arab–Israeli conflict' (Harkabi, 1992; Leibowitz, 1992). The Partition
Solution was based on two possibilities: the partition of Israel/Palestine into
a new Jewish and a new Palestinian state, or partition between a Jewish state
and one or more of the existing nearby Arab states (Dowty, 2005). The Peel
Commission, established by the British after the eruption of the Arab Revolt
in 1936, presented this solution. In July 1937, the committee in its report
called for the partition of Israel/Palestine into two unequal states (with an
Arab state much larger than the Jewish state) and recommended the idea of
population transfer:

> Those areas, therefore, should be surveyed and an estimate made of the
> practical possibilities of irrigation and development as quickly as pos-
> sible. If, as a result, it is clear that a substantial amount of land could be
> made available for the re-settlement of Arabs living in the Jewish area,
> the most strenuous efforts should be made to obtain an agreement for
> the transfer of land and population. In view of the present antagonism
> between the races and of the manifest advantage to both of them for
> reducing the opportunities of future friction to the utmost, it is to be
> hoped that the Arab and the Jewish leaders might show the same high
> statesmanship as that of the Turks and the Greeks and make the same
> bold decision for the sake of peace.
>
> (MidEast Web, 1999, p. 7)

The Arabs rejected the partition and the Jews were split over it. The two
state partition solutions were re-presented by the UN through UN General
Assembly Resolution 181. The Jewish accepted the UN Resolution, but the
Arab neighbour countries preferred to break up the territories, given for the
establishment of a Palestinian state, between them rather than see the creation
of a Palestinian state.

1.8 Terrorism

There is a definition provided by The New Shorter Oxford English
Dictionary: 'the systematic employment of violence and intimidation to
coerce a government or *community into acceding to specific political demands*'
(my italics). With respect to this definition we could say that both the Arabs
and the Jews in Israel/Palestine used terrorism in their struggle for land before
1948, which violence was waged not on battlefields but in market places and
villages (Kapitan, 1997).

The Arabs used terrorism against the Jews only, while the Jews directed
terrorism against the Arabs and the British (Rowley and Taylor, 2006a). After
the end of World War II, there were three essential armed Zionist organisations in Israel/Palestine, operating against both Arab and British with the precise intention of forcing them out of Israel/Palestine. These three groups were

the Haganah, the Irgun and the Stern Group. Jewish settlers before the British Mandate, called 'Hashomer', formed the Haganah. The Haganah had more than 16,000 trained men with a membership of 60,000 Zionist Jews, while the Irgun had between 3,000 to 5,000 trained men. The Stern Gang, Fighters for the Freedom of Israel (Lohamei Herut Yisra'el-Lehi), was formed by an officer who left the Irgun, taking with him more than 300 militants. These groups damaged public installations, blew up government offices, attacked military stores, and shot, kidnapped, and murdered British soldiers and government officials (Cattan, 1969).

After the 1936 Arab Revolt, the British began arming and training Zionist settlers. The Irgun, between 1937 and 1939, killed over 300 Arab civilians as revenge for Arab attacks on Jews. They killed 77 Arab men, women and children in three weeks in 1937 by planting bombs in Arab marketplaces (Smith, 2001). David Ben-Gurion regarded this act as so heinous that he thought it likely to have been committed by Nazi agents (Segev, 2000). Haganah commandos attacked a Palestinian family near Tel Aviv, killing 12, including the mother and six children on 14 August 1947.

During World War II, while most of the Zionists sided with Britain against the Nazis, there was one small group, the Stern Gang, which continued attacks to drive the British out of Israel/Palestine. This group proposed an alliance with Fascist Italy or even Nazi Germany in order to achieve their goal. The Stern Gang with the Irgun group tried to kill the British High Commissioner, Sir Harold MacMichael, and Lady MacMichael in Jerusalem, but failed. In November 1944, the Stern Gang assassinated Lord Moyne, the British military governor in Egypt. After World War II, the Irgun and the Stern Gang began murdering soldiers and policeman, and damaging British installations. These groups were regarded as terrorists by the British and much of the international community. Ben-Gurion referred to the Irgun as Jewish Nazis and compared Begin, later elected the Prime Minister of Israel, to Hitler (Segev, 2000).

The three groups, the Haganah, the Irgun and the Stern Gang, decided to form a united Hebrew resistance movement in October 1945. Begin explains the struggle to expel the British from Israel/Palestine:

> Our enemies called us terrorists ... And yet we were not terrorists. The original Latin word 'terror' means fear. If I am not mistaken the term 'terror' became current in political terminology during the French Revolution. The revolutionaries began cutting off heads with the guillotine in order to instil fear. Thenceforward the word 'terror' came to define acts of revolutionaries or counter-revolutionaries, of fighters for freedom and oppressors. It all depends on who uses the term. It frequently happens that it is used by both sides in their mutual exchange of compliments. The historical and linguistic origins of the political term 'terror' prove it cannot be applied to a revolutionary war of liberation. A revolution may give birth to what we call 'terror' as happened in France. Terror may sometimes be its herald, as what happened in Russia. But the revolution itself is not

terror, and terror is not the revolution. A revolution, or a revolutionary war, does not aim at instilling fear. Its object is to overthrow a regime and to set up a new regime in its place. In a revolutionary war both sides use force. Tyranny is armed. Otherwise it would be liquidated overnight. Fighters for freedom must arm; otherwise they would be crushed over-night. Certainly the use of force also awakens fear. Tyrannous rulers begin to fear for their positions or their lives, or both. And consequently they begin to try to sow fear among those they rule. But the instilling of fear is not an aim in itself. The sole aim on the one side is the overthrow of armed tyranny; on the other it is the perpetuation of that tyranny.

(Begin, 1977, p. 25)

Arabs inside Israel/Palestine tried to oppose Jewish settlement, which led to Arab terrorism against Jews from the early years of Jewish immigration. At the beginning, especially before 1920, small groups of unorganised Arabs engaged in violence against Jews. After the Arab Revolt in 1920, the attacks on Jews became more organised and widespread. The Arabs became even more violent during the second Arab Revolt (between 1936 and 1939), when many incidents of anti-Jewish Arab violence occurred in Israel/Palestine. When the UN General Assembly adopted the UN Resolution for partition, terrorism between Arabs and Jews occurred with greater frequency and on a larger scale than ever before (Kapitan, 2004).

2.   The history of land settlement and cascading conflicts in the Middle East since 1948

2.1   Introduction

After the state of Israel was declared on 14 May 1948, five major wars ensued between Israel and the Arabs. In this chapter we will examine these major wars and analyse the results achieved in each. We will also explore two cases of refugees: Jewish refugees from Arab countries and Palestinian refugees from Israel/Palestine. In addition, we will consider the peace initiatives proposed to solve the Arab–Israeli conflict after 1948. Finally, we will analyse several cases of Palestinian and Jewish terrorism.

2.2   Arab and Israeli conflicts

No war should begin, or at least, no war should be begun, if people acted wisely, without first finding an answer to the question: what is to be attained by and in the war.

Karl Von Clausewitz

With the declaration of the state of Israel in 1948, a series of wars erupted between Israel and the Arab states. These included the 1948 Arab–Israeli war, the 1956 Suez/Sinai War, the Six Day War in 1967, the 1973 Yom Kippur War, and the 1982 Lebanon invasion.

2.2.1   1948 Arab–Israeli War (1948–1949)

Britain decided to hand over Israel/Palestine to the UN in 1947; consequently, the UN formed UNSCOP to explore and resolve the Israel/Palestine problem (Bailey, 1990; Hourani, 1991). On 29 November 1947, the General Assembly adopted the partition plan proposed by UNSCOP to split Israel/Palestine into three parts (a Jewish state, an Arab state, and a corpus spectrum under international jurisdiction for the city of Jerusalem) (Lewis, 1993). After the adoption of the UN Resolution, bloodshed and fighting between Jews and Arabs was widespread over Israel/Palestine. Between November 1947 and May 1948, Jewish forces were able to hold on to most of the territory allotted to the Jewish state, and even to overrun Arab areas (Dowty, 2005). By the time the British completed their withdrawal from Israel/Palestine, the Zionists had declared the state of Israel,[15] and the next day Arabs (Jordan, Egypt, Syria, Lebanon, Saudi Arabia, Iraq and the Arabs inside Israel/Palestine) declared war to prevent Jewish independence (Laqueur, 1968; Friedman, 1995). The Zionist military forces were numerically smaller than the Arab military forces but were well manned, trained and equipped, and Arab military forces were largely ineffective in the face of significant Israeli military dominance. The Zionist military forces within weeks occupied around 80% of the territory of Israel/Palestine (20,850 square kilometres out of 26, 323 square kilometres), except for the Gaza Strip, which was taken under Egyptian administration, the remainder was under Jordan's control (Hourani, 1991; Cattan, 1969). The result of this war was, first, that in addition to Jews winning their war of independence and securing the state of Israel, it created about three-quarters of a million refugee Palestinian Arabs (Bickerton and Klausner, 2001). This loss and the exile of these Palestinians is known in the Arabic world as 'al-Nakba', or 'The Cataclysm'. Second, 6,373 Jews and 5,000 to 15,000 Arabs were killed. Arabs inside Israel/Palestine wound up with less territory than they would have had if they had accepted partition. The Palestinian Diaspora began, as hundreds of thousands of Arabs fled the new nation of Israel and moved to neighbouring Arab nations[16] to live as refugees, awaiting the day they could return to their homeland.

The Arab countries signed armistice agreements with Israel in 1949, starting with Egypt (24 February), followed by Lebanon (23 March), Jordan (3 April) and Syria (20 July) (Cattan, 1969; Bailey, 1990). Iraq was the only country that did not sign an agreement with Israel, choosing instead to withdraw its troops and hand over its sector to Jordan's Arab Legion.

2.2.2   The 1956 Suez/Sinai War (29 October to 4 November 1956)

In 1952, an Egyptian revolutionary named Jamal Abdul Nasser was the major mover among young army officers who overthrew the corrupt Egyptian monarchy (Dowty, 2005; Minnis, 2001). Nasser became the president of Egypt and a key figure of Arab nationalism until his death in 1970.

On 19 July 1956 the US informed Egypt that it was cancelling a promised grant to build the Aswan High Dam, thus cancelling the loan from the World Bank for Reconstruction and Development, which was predicated on US support (Hiro, 2003). In response, an angry Nasser in an emotional speech on 26 July announced that he would nationalise the Suez Canal in order to pay the expenses of building the dam (Bickerton and Klausner, 2001). He also continued to buy fighter aircraft, bombers, and tanks from Soviet bloc countries. The British and French governments regarded the Canal as crucial to their navies and trade, and feared that Nasser might close the Canal against their ships, or use it as a bargaining tool (Minnis, 2001). Israel saw a chance to weaken an over-powerful and aggressive neighbouring state (Hourani, 1991).

Israel, France and Britain began planning an attack on Egypt, and France rushed arms to Israel (Bickerton and Pearson, 1986). On the afternoon of Monday 29 October, Israel attacked Egypt, dropping 400 paratroops at the eastern end of the Mitla Pass and initiating four land thrusts into Sinai (Bailey, 1990). The next day Britain and France issued an ultimatum to Egypt to withdraw from the Canal Zone. Egypt refused the ultimatum, which gave an excuse for British and French forces to attack the Canal. This action was not accepted by the two great powers, the US and the Soviet Union; the Soviet Union threatened to interfere on Egypt's behalf and the US pressured Britain,[17] France and Israel into agreeing to a ceasefire and eventual withdrawal from Egypt. The three forces were obliged to withdraw under the combined Soviet and American pressure, augmented by worldwide hostility and the danger of financial collapse (Hourani, 1991).

Although Egypt was defeated militarily,[18] Egyptians were the big winners politically. The Canal became more Egyptian than before, and Nasser's regime gained huge popular support over the Arab world (Morris, 2001).

2.2.3 *1967 Arab–Israeli War (6 days war from 5 to 10 June 1967)*

Although neither Israel nor the Arabs actually wanted war, a chain of events that began in mid-May 1967 made war inevitable (Dowty, 2005). In May and June 1967 there was a high level of tension between Israel and Syria. The Soviet Union forwarded information to Egypt about a heavy Israeli troop concentration on the Syrian border (Laqueur, 1968; Bickerton and Klausner, 2001). In response, Egypt put its armed forces on maximum alert and requested the withdrawal of UNEF (United Nations Emergency Forces)[19] from all Egyptian soil. Egyptian troops and tanks began to move towards Sinai in order to replace the withdrawn UNEF troops. When Egyptian troops reached the Gulf of Aqaba, Nasser announced the closing of the Gulf to Israeli vessels or any vessels carrying goods to Israel (Hourani, 1991). This act made war unavoidable; Nasser had not consciously considered that (Morris, 2001).

On 5 June, Israel launched a surprise attack on Egypt, destroying aircraft on the ground and putting runways out of action (Cattan, 1973). The attack was more successful than expected, destroying most of the Egyptian air force (over 300 out of 340 Egyptian aircraft) with few Israeli casualties. On the same day, Israel attacked Syrian and Jordanian airfields and destroyed a number of aircraft on the ground (Cattan, 1973). In six days, Israel conquered an area 3.5 times larger than Israel itself; it occupied Sinai (61,000 square kilometres), Jordan's West Bank and East Jerusalem (5,700 square kilometres), and the Golan Heights (1,200 square kilometres) (Morris, 2001). Israel hoped to convert this spectacular military triumph into political success by using the occupied areas as bargaining tokens for peace.

The outcome of this war for Israel was that, in addition to the conquest of vast stretches of Arab territory, the IDF (Israel Defence Forces) became militarily stronger than any combination of Arab states. The war also launched Israel's strategic joint venture with the US, richly arming the IDF with American weaponry (Oren, 2002). For the Arabs, the outcome was a humiliating loss with a huge number of casualties,[20] which led to the collapse of pan-Arabism and its replacement with Islamic extremist ideas on one side, and the rise of Palestinian nationalism on the other.

2.2.4   *1973 Arab–Israeli War (the October War 1973)*[21]

On 6 October 1973, on Yom Kippur, the Jewish Day of Atonement, probably the most important holiday of the Jewish year, President Sadat of Egypt and President Assad of Syria jointly launched a sudden attack against Israel (Rowley and Taylor, 2006b). At first the Syrian Forces occupied part of the Golan Heights while Egyptian forces crossed the Suez Canal and reached the Bar-Lev Line. However in the next few days, the IDF crossed the Canal and created a defensive position on the West Bank, and obliging the Syrian troops to move back towards Damascus. At the same time as the US was making large airlifts to Israel, the Soviet Union was making massive airlifts to Damascus and Cairo. The attacks ended in a ceasefire forced by the influence of the Super Powers, as neither the US nor the Soviet Union wished the war to escalate and perhaps drag them in.

October 1973 proved that Arabs could collaborate and that their forces could fight well when properly trained; it proved that Israel was not invincible (Bickerton and Klausner, 2001). The 1948, 1956, and 1967 wars had conditioned the Israelis to astonishing victories over the Arabs, and the 1973 war was considered a stinging slap in the face (Morris, 2001). This was the first war between the Arabs and Israel to be followed by political settlement; the outcome[22] of this war was much more balanced than that of the 1967 war.

2.2.5   *The 1982 Lebanon War*

After the 'Black September' incident in Jordan, the PLO (Palestinian Liberation Organisation) was forced to move to Lebanon, a decision that led to disaster for Lebanon.[23] Lebanon became the centre of the PLO's social, educational, economic, and military institutions, and soon Palestinians had created a virtual state within a state (Wenger and Denney, 1990). The relation between the Lebanese and Palestinians collapsed in 1975 and resulted in open warfare. Syrian forces entered Lebanon in 1976 to assist in fighting the PLO.

On 3 June, the Fatah group, a Palestinian militant group that is vigorously opposed to many of the principles of the PLO, attempted to assassinate Israel's ambassador in London (Bickerton and Pearson, 1986). Israel blamed the PLO and retaliated by bombing Palestinian refugee camps in Lebanon along with other PLO targets. The PLO responded in turn by shelling Galilee, the northern part of Israel/Palestine. On 6 June 1982, Israeli forces began invading Lebanon in an operation called 'Peace of the Galilee' under the command of Defence Minister Ariel Sharon. According to the plan, the Israeli forces were to advance no further than 40 kilometres inside Lebanon, marked by the Litani River, in order to create a security zone that would free northern Israel from rocket attacks.

Three Israeli divisions invaded Lebanon from all sides and reached their target in just four days, but were determined to drive the PLO out of Lebanon. Syrian forces inside Lebanon had strong Russian air defence that repelled Israeli air attacks on their positions; however, in a surprise attack, the Israeli air force destroyed 17 out of 19 batteries. Israeli troops pushed towards Beirut, where the PLO fought well and obliged the Israelis to stay outside the city. The Israeli forces besieging Beirut initiated random bombing to turn the public against the PLO, and precise bombing to kill top PLO leaders (Wright, 1983). A writer for *Time Magazine*, described the siege of Beirut:

All across West Beirut, hour after hour, came the shattering detonations in crowded city streets, the crump, crump, crump of exploding bombs and shells, and then, after the brilliant flashes of red, the rising clouds of destruction ... Twice last week the Israelis staged attacks on the besieged western areas of Beirut that in sheer destructive power, though not in casualties, wreaked devastation that stirred memories of the punishment inflicted on European cities during World War II and recalled the fate of Jericho, the enemy city that the ancient Israelites had laid waste.

(Smith, 1982, p. 85)

After 70 days of continuous Israeli bombardment of Beirut, the Lebanese leaders, who had up to that time supported the PLO, requested Yasser Arafat, the PLO leader, to leave Beirut to end the suffering of the city and its people. An agreement was reached whereby 8,000 PLO fighters, with their personal arms, were sent out of Lebanon towards Jordan, Syria, Yemen, Sudan, Greece and Tunisia (Cobban, 1984).

The 1982 war was estimated to have cost 20,000 lives, most of them civilians (Bickerton and Pearson, 1986). Syrian forces were obliged to withdraw from Beirut and large parts of Lebanese territory (Perthes, 1997). The PLO lost its military infrastructure in southern Lebanon, and moved towards Tunisia, which became the new PLO headquarters. Israel's most important achievement in the invasion was to drive the PLO forces away from its border (Dowty, 2005). The 1982 war led to the formation of Hezbollah, an Islamic resistance movement sponsored by Iran, which resisted Israel's continuing occupation of southern Lebanon.

2.2.6   The 2006 Lebanon War

This conflict[24] started in July 2006 when Hezbollah fighters crossed the Israeli border from Lebanon and kidnapped two soldiers. Israel reacted with massive raids, artillery fire, a ground invasion of southern Lebanon, and air and naval blockades. Hezbollah responded by launching rockets into northern Israel. The conflict resulted in over a thousand people killed (mostly Lebanese civilians), approximately one million Lebanese and 300,000 Israelis displaced, and a severely damaged Lebanese civil infrastructure.

In an effort to end this conflict, the United Nations Security Council issued UN Security Council Resolution 1701[25] on 11 August 2006. The Lebanese government accepted the resolution by the next day, and the Israeli government the day after.

2.3   *Refugees and the Israeli–Palestinian population*

On 28 July 1951, the United Nations Conference of Plenipotentiaries on the Status of Refugees and Stateless Persons defined a refugee as a person who

> owing to well-founded fear of being persecuted for reasons of race, religion, nationality, membership of a particular social group or political opinion, is outside the country of his nationality and is unable, or owing to such fear, is unwilling to avail himself of the protection of that country; or who, not having a nationality and being outside the country of his former habitual residence as a result of such events, is unable or, owing to such fear, is unwilling to return to it.

Since the end of World War II, there have been many large groups of refugees: 9 million Koreans, 8.5 million Hindus and Sikhs leaving Pakistan for India, 6.5 million Muslims leaving India for Pakistan, 700,000 Chinese refugees in Hong Kong; 13 million Germans from East Europe reaching West and East Germany, thousands of Turkish refugees from Bulgaria, and finally Palestinian and Jewish refugees (Laqueur, 1968). In all these cases a solution has been reached by the integration of the refugees into their host countries, except in the case of Palestinian refugees, whose integration was obstructed by the Arab host countries.

2.3.1   Palestinian refugees

The 1947 partition plan and 1948 war created a refugee problem (Laqueur, 1968), although there is ongoing debate between Israel and the Palestinians regarding the reason behind the creation of the problem. Defenders of Israel claim that the Palestinians left their home of their own free will at the request of Arab authorities (Laqueur, 1968). On the other hand, Arabs claim that the Zionist forces expelled them from their land (Said, 1994). Maybe the truth lies between the two, as Bickerton and Klausner suggest: 'Arab Palestinians fled in some cases of their own free will, in some cases through fear; in other cases they were expelled' (Bickerton and Klausner, 2001).

No one can say precisely how many Palestinians became refugees after the formation of the Jewish state (Kimmerling and Migdal, 2003). Arab estimations range between 900,000 and 1,000,000, while the Israeli estimation was 520,000 and the British 600,000 to 760,000 (Morris, 1987). According to UN statistics, the number of Palestinian Refugees was 656,000: 280,000 moved to the West Bank, 70,000 to Jordan, 100,000 to Lebanon, 4,000 to Iraq, 75,000 to Syria, 7,000 to Egypt and 190,000 to the Gaza Strip (Johnson, 1987).

The UN did not deal with the Palestinian refugees via its normal refugee machinery, but instead formed a new, separate agency, the United Nations Relief and Works Agency for Palestinian Refugees in the Near East (UNRWA), to provide shelter, food, medical care, dental care and education (Dowty, 2005). The UNRWA, from its beginning on 1 May 1950 until now, has been the main provider of basic services to registered Palestinian refugees in Jordan, Lebanon, Syria, the West Bank and the Gaza Strip. At the end of June 2005, 4,283,892 Palestinian refugees were registered with UNRWA, an increase of nearly 468.5% since 1950 (see Table A.6). In June 2005, 1,795,326 Palestinian refugees (41.9%) were registered in Jordan, 969,588 (22.6%) in the Gaza Strip, 690,988 (16.1%) in the West Bank, 426,919 (10%) in Syria and 401,071 (9.1%) in Lebanon.

Neither Arabs nor Israelis have had much success in finding a solution to the refugee problem. On the Arab side, the refugees are ignored or interned in camps, and apart from Jordan, have refused to grant citizenship to refugees (Lewis, 1995). According to the Arabs, the solution to the Palestinian refugee problem lies in the UN General Assembly Resolution 194 (paragraph 11), which resolves that:

> refugees wishing to return to their homes and live at peace with their neighbours should be permitted to do so at the earliest practicable date, and that compensation should be paid for the property of those choosing not to return and for loss of or damage to property which, under principles of international law or in equity, should be made good by the Governments or authorities responsible;Instructs the Conciliation Commission to facilitate the repatriation, resettlement and economic and social rehabilitation of the refugees and the payment of compensation,

Table A.6 Number of registered Palestinian refugees[a]

Field	1950	1960	1970	1980	1990	2000	2005
Jordan	506,200	613,743	506,038	716,372	929,097	1,570,192	1,795,326
Lebanon	127,600	136,561	175,958	226,554	302,049	376,472	401,071
Syria	82,194	115,043	158,717	209,362	280,731	383,199	426,919
West Bank[b]	–	–	272,692	324,035	414,298	583,009	690,988
Gaza Strip	198,227	255,542	311,814	367,995	496,339	824,622	969,588
Total	914,221[c]	1,120,889	1,425,219	1,844,318	2,422,514	3,737,494	4,283,892

[a] Figures are based on UNRWA registration records, which are updated continually. However, the number of registered refugees present in the Agency's area of operations is almost certainly less than the population recorded.
[b] Until 1967, the West Bank was administered as an integral part of the Jordan field.
[c] This total excludes 45,800 persons receiving relief in Israel, who were the responsibility of UNRWA until June 1952.

and to maintain close relations with the Director of the United Nations Relief for Palestine Refugees and, through him, with the appropriate organs and agencies of the United Nations.

(Cattan, 1973, p. 5)

Israelis argue that the Palestinians abandoned their properties voluntarily, so the international community should pay the compensation to the Palestinian Refugees in the Arab countries. In addition, the Israeli government is not prepared to allow the refugees to return; indeed, Ben-Gurion told the Cabinet on 16 June 1948 that Israel should 'prevent their return' (Bickerton and Pearson, 1986).

2.3.2   Jewish refugees

For hundreds of years Jews lived in Arab countries such as Algeria, Egypt, Lebanon, Libya, Morocco, Syria, Tunisia, Iran, Iraq and Yemen. In 1945 there were around 856,000 Jews living in various Arab states (see Table A.7). After the 1947 UN Resolution for the partition of Israel/Palestine, Arab countries vented their anger against Jews throughout the Middle East and North Africa. Even before the UN Resolution, Arab delegates warned that the partition of Israel/Palestine might endanger Jews in Arab lands. An Iraqi diplomat said at the time 'The masses in the Arab world cannot be restrained' (Friedman, 2003).

Following the partition, the immediate effect on the Jews in Arab lands ranged from rebellion against them in Yemen and Syria to the withdrawal of citizenship in Libya and the confiscation of their property in Iraq. In Egypt in 1956, Jews were declared enemies of the state. By 1957, over half a million had either left or been expelled from Arab lands (Bickerton and Klausner, 2001). Many of those looked for refuge in the new state of Israel, where they

Table A.7 Jewish population in Arab countries 1948–2001

	1948	1958	1968	1976	2001
Aden	8,000	800	0	0	0
Algeria	140,000	130,000	1,500	1,000	0
Egypt	75,000	40,000	1,000	400	100
Iraq	135,000	6,000	2,500	350	100
Lebanon	5,000	6,000	3,000	400	Less than 100
Libya	38,000	3,750	100	40	0
Morocco	265,000	200,000	50,000	18,000	5,230
Syria	30,000	5,000	4,000	4,500	100
Tunisia	105,000	80,000	10,000	7,000	1,000
Yemen	55,000	3,500	500	500	200
TOTAL	856,000	475,050	72,600	32,190	Approx. 7,500
	(Roumani	(AJY 58)	(AJY 69; Yemen:	(AJY 78)	(AJY 01; Leb.:
	83)		AJY 70)		AJY 88)

Source: Adapted from Roumani, Maurice. 'The Case of the Jews from Arab Countries:
A Neglected Issue'. WOJAC, 1983 after gathering data from *American Jewish Yearbook*: 1958,
1969, 1970, 1978, 1988, 2001. Philadelphia: The Jewish Publication Society of America.

were absorbed and became an essential part of the state (Gilbert, 2002). The
Jewish government achieved a permanent economic integration of refugees
within its small territory and provided homes, work and citizenship to all
Jewish refugees from Arab lands.

2.4   The peace proposals

Before the 1973 Arab–Israeli War, peace negotiations between the Arabs and
the Israelis were minimal. After the war, there was mutual interest in resolving
issues and reaching a signed peace agreement. Egypt was the first to sign an
agreement with Israel on 26 March 1979, followed by Jordan on 26 October
1994. There were numerous plans to settle the Israeli–Palestinian conflict,
most of them focusing on major issues such as Jerusalem, the right of return
for Palestinian refugees, borders and Israeli settlements.

1. **1967 United Nations Resolution 242**
2. **The 1978 Camp David Accords**
3. **The 1982 Reagan Plan**
4. **The Madrid Conference**
5. **The 1993 Oslo Declaration of Principles**
6. **The 1994 Cairo Agreement**
7. **Israel–Jordan Peace Treaty**
8. **The 1995 Oslo Interim Agreement**
9. **The Wye River Memorandum**
10. **The 1999 Sharm el Sheikh Memorandum**
11. **The 2000 Camp David Proposal**

12. **The 2001 Taba Talks**
13. **The 2002 Arab Peace Initiative**
14. **The 2003 Geneva Accord**
15. **The 2003 Roadmap for Peace**
16. **The 2003–2004 Sharon Disengagement Plan**

2.5   Terrorism

> Terrorism between Arabs and Jews, in both directions, has had a corrosive effect on the attitudes of average people toward each other, on their capacity to reject violence morally, on the low threshold of outrage that any decent society must maintain to be shocked by its own behaviour and to prevent itself from degenerating into brutality. As terrorism becomes normal, it becomes acceptable. It grows into routine.
>
> (David Shipler, quoted in Gambill, 1998, p. 7)

Terrorism is a tactic likely to be used when one party is weaker than the other (Munger, 2006). After the 1948 'Diaspora', Palestinians found themselves alienated from their land and weaker than the Jews, and terrorism was a way to approach their goal of a state. Supporters of the Palestinians see their acts of violence as the efforts of freedom fighters battling for their rights (Bickerton and Pearson, 1986). In the same way, supporters of Israel consider Israeli acts of violence as self-defence.

2.5.1   Palestinian terrorism

A number of Palestinian liberation movements developed in the 1950s with the objective of creating a Palestinian state and destroying Israel. The first organisation to be established was Fatah, in 1957, founded by a group of Palestinians outside Israel/Palestine. Fatah supported and conducted violent attacks against Israel and Israeli citizens in order to achieve its goal of creating a Palestinian state. Although established in the 50s it was not until 1965 that Fatah started carrying out violent attacks inside Israel/Palestine through its military arm, Al-Asifa (the storm) (Cobban, 1984; Alexander and Sinai, 1989). The PLO was founded on 2 June 1964 by the Arab League, to represent the Palestinian people. In 1969 Fatah managed to take control of the decision-making arm of the PLO and Arafat was appointed PLO chairman on 3 February 1969.

Following the 1967 Arab–Israeli war, the Popular Front for the Liberation of Palestine movement (PFLP) was established on 11 December 1967. The Popular Democratic Front for the Liberation of Palestine (PDFLP) was founded on 22 February 1969 followed by the Palestinian Islamic Jihad (PIJ) in the 1970s. The Islamic Resistance movement (HAMAS) was founded in 1988 after the first Palestinian Intifada (Palestinian uprising), with the goal of establishing an Islamic Palestinian state in place of Israel.

Throughout the years, these Palestinian movements employed several types of violence against civilians, such as plane hijackings, suicide bombings, shooting attacks and car bombings. At first, violence focused on the international arena, but now it is concentrated inside Israel/Palestine. In the following we will offer some examples as an overview of Palestinian terrorism.

After 1967, the scale of terrorism intensified when Palestinian movements began engaging in violent activities to broadcast their cause and force the Israeli government to free Palestinian prisoners. In mid-1968, the first airplane was hijacked: three members from PFLP hijacked an El Al airplane (Alexander and Sinai, 1989). The same group attempted to hijack five planes in September 1970, succeeding with four but failing to hijack the fifth, an El Al airliner with Israeli security personnel on board (Alexander and Sinai, 1989). The hijackers released their hostages in exchange for the release of Palestinian prisoners, and the four planes were blown up.

The most infamous terrorist act took place at the Munich Olympics. On the morning of 5 September 1972, eight Palestinian terrorists raided the apartment that housed the Israeli team in the Olympic Village, killing two and taking nine hostages. In return for their hostages, the attackers demanded the release of 234 Palestinians and non-Arabs in Israel/Palestine prisons, the release of two German terrorists, and safe passage to Egypt. After a day of unsuccessful negotiations, a skirmish between the German forces and the terrorists claimed the lives of all nine hostages, while the police captured three and killed five terrorists (Alexander and Sinai, 1989; Nasr, 1997; Minnis, 2001). It has been argued that Munich was a most significant terrorist attack: one that 'thrust the Palestinian crimes into the world spotlight, set the tone for decades of conflict in the Middle East, and launched a new era of international terrorism' (Reeve, 2001). One month after the Munich massacre, a Lufthansa plane on flight from Beirut to Ankara was hijacked; the hijackers released the plane after German authorities freed the Munich terrorists.

During the 26th anniversary of Israeli independence on 15 May 1974, three members of the Democratic Front for the Liberation of Palestine (DFLP), a group split from the PFLP, infiltrated from Lebanon by dressing as Israeli Defence Forces, and attacked a school in Ma'alot, an Israeli town near the Lebanese border. The attackers demanded the release of 23 Arabs and three non-Arabs jailed in Israel/Palestine. When negotiations broke down, an Israeli unit stormed the building killing all the terrorists, but not before the terrorists killed 27 and wounded 70 (Alexander and Sinai, 1989). Another massacre took place inside Israel/Palestine on the morning of 11 March 1978, when a unit of 11 members came by Zodiac boat from Lebanon, landing on a beach near Tel Aviv where they killed an American photographer and hijacked a bus on the coastal highway. The attackers drove to Tel Aviv, shooting at passing cars from the bus. When they approached a police blockade, the attackers left the bus and fired missiles, killing 38 and injuring 71 (Deeb, 2003).

The first suicide attack occurred on 6 July 1989 when a Palestinian on a Tel Aviv–Jerusalem bus, grabbed the steering wheel, causing the bus to crash, and killing 14 and wounding 30.

2.5.2   *Israeli terrorism*

Since the state of Israel was declared, Palestinians have faced ongoing terrorism from Israel. Throughout the years, Israel has eradicated hundreds of villages and thousands of homes. The three Zionist groups, the Haganah, the Irgun and the Stern Gang, have committed relentless ethnic cleansing, using torture, shooting, bombing and murder against the Palestinian people.

During 1948 the Haganah began an operation called 'Nahshon', planned to create a passage to Jerusalem through territories allotted to the Arab state under the partition plan (Krystall, 1998). The Irgun and Stern gang committed the Deir Yassin massacre as their contribution to the 'Nahshon' operation. Early in the morning of Friday 9 April 1948, members of these groups attacked Deir Yassin village, 5.5 km west of Jerusalem, and home to 750 Palestinian civilians. They killed between 100 and 254 people, most of them women, children and the elderly, according to different sources (Morris, 1987; Sharif and Nihad, 1987); there were claims of other atrocities during the attack, such as rape and mutilation (Bickerton and Pearson, 1986). This massacre was described by Jacques de Reynier, Chief Delegate of the International Red Cross:

> Three hundred persons were massacred ... without any military reason nor provocation of any kind, old men, women, children, newly-born were savagely assassinated with grenades and knives by Jewish troops of the Irgun, perfectly under the control and direction of their chiefs ... large knives most of which were still bloodstained ... Thereupon terror seized the Arabs and gave rise to movements of panic which were wholly out of proportion with the real danger. The exodus began and became nearly general.
>
> (Cattan, 1969, p. 16)

News of the attack spread quickly all over Israel/Palestine, and the Jews used vans with loudspeakers to broadcast messages in Arabic such as: 'Unless you leave your homes, the fate of Deir Yssin will be your fate' (Krystall, 1998). As a result of this massacre and other incidents against the Palestinians, the Palestinians fled from four major villages in the Jerusalem area: Lifta, Deir Yassin, Ein Karim and El-Maliha (Mattar, 1983).

During the 1982 Israel invasion of Lebanon, another massacre took place in Sabra and Shatila, two Palestinian camps in Lebanon. On 16 September 1982 after the assassination of Gemayel, the leader of the Phalangist group

(Lebanese Christian Militia), a group from the Phalange entered the camps armed with knives, hatchets and firearms under the observation of their Israeli allies, who had encircled the area (Shahid, 2002). The Phalangists moved through the camps, slitting throats, shooting, axing, and raping. Kapeliouk, an Israeli journalist who was one of the first to enter Sabra and Shatila after the massacre, described the scene:

> From the beginning, the massacre assumed huge proportions, according to those who escaped. Throughout those first hours, the Phalangist fighters killed hundreds of people. They shot at anything which moved in the alleys. Breaking down the doors of the houses, they liquidated entire families in the middle of their supper. Residents were killed in their beds, in pyjamas. In numerous apartments, one would find children of 3 or 4 years, also in pyjamas, wrapped in blood-soaked blankets. But, often, the killers were not content just to kill. In very many cases, the assailants cut off the limbs of their victims before killing them. They smashed the heads of infants and babies against the walls. Women, and even young girls, were raped before being assassinated with hatchets ... Sometimes, [the killers] left one single member of the family alive, killing the others before his eyes, so that this unfortunate could afterwards tell what he had seen and been through.
>
> (Cobban, 1984, p. 23)

In 36 hours the Phalange group massacred an estimated 700–800 Palestinian civilians (Dowty, 2005), although Kapeliouk puts the figure much higher, at 3,000 to 3,500 (Shahid, 2002). Israel denied involvement and placed the blame on the Phalangists. The UN issued a resolution condemning the massacre and the US president blamed Israel for the massacre (Shahid, 2002). Inside Israel/Palestine a huge demonstration of 400,000 people (about 10% of Israel's population) demanded the appointment of a governmental investigating commission (Dowty, 2005). The commission was established, and reached the conclusion that Israeli commanders bore indirect responsibility for the massacre. This inquiry led Sharon, the Defence Minister at that time, to lose his position; and Raful Eitan, the army Chief of Staff, was dismissed.

Since the 1970s, Israeli forces and the Mossad have assassinated several Palestinians in terrorist attacks.[26] Throughout the 70s the Mossad assassinated several Palestinians and Arabs who were thought to have connections with the Munich massacre, in an operation called 'Wrath of God'.[27] In this operation Ali Hassan Salmeh (the Red Prince), who was accused of being the man behind the Munich massacre, was blown up in his station wagon on 22 January 1979. In April 1988, the Mossad succeeded in murdering Arafat's deputy, Abu Jihad, after invading his highly guarded residence in Tunisia.

3. Proof of Proposition 4

With the specified utility functions the first order condition (6c) is reduced to

$$\frac{G_1 - G^a}{G_2 - G^b} = \frac{n_2 S_2}{n_1 S_1} \tag{7a'}$$

Since the amount of resources for investing in defence spending is given at G^*, the optimal allocation of G^* is given by:

$$G_1 = \frac{G^* n_2 S_2 - n_2 S_2 G^b + n_1 S_1 G^a}{n_1 S_1 + n_2 S_2} \tag{7b'}$$

$$G_2 = \frac{G^* n_1 S_1 + n_2 S_2 G^b - n_1 S_1 G^a}{n_1 S_1 + n_2 S_2} \tag{7c'}$$

We can simplify the above as

$$G_1 = \frac{n_2 S_2}{n_1 S_1 + n_2 S_2}(G^* - G^b) + \frac{n_1 S_1}{n_1 S_1 + n_2 S_2} G^a \tag{7d'}$$

Hence $G_1 = w_1(G^* - G^b) + G^a(1 - w_1)$ (7a)

where $w_1 = \dfrac{n_2 S_2}{n_1 S_1 + n_2 S_2}$ (7b)

Similarly, $G_2 = w_2(G^* - G^a) + G^b(1 - w_2)$ (7c)

where $w_2 = \dfrac{n_1 S_1}{n_1 S_1 + n_2 S_2}$ (7d) QED.

4. Thomas Saaty scale

Table A.8.1 The Saaty scale

Intensity of Importance	Definition	Explanation
8	Absolute Importance	The evidence favouring one policy over another is of the highest possible order of affirmation
6	Demonstrated Importance	A policy is strongly favoured and its dominance is demonstrated in practice
4	Essential or Strong Importance	Experience and judgement strongly favour one activity over another

Intensity of Importance	Definition	Explanation
2	Weakly Importance of first policy over the other	Experience and judgement slightly favour one activity over another
0	Equal Importance	Two policies contribute equally to the objective
−2	Weakly Less Importance of first policy over the other	Experience and judgement slightly favour second activity over the first
−4	Essential or Strong Less Relevant	Experience and judgement strongly disapproves of one activity over another
−6	Irrelevant	A policy is strongly disapproved and its dominance is demonstrated in practice
−8	Absolutely Irrelevant	The evidence disapproved of one policy over another is of the highest possible order
1,3,5,7 −1,−2,−5,−7	Intermediate values between the two adjacent judgements	When compromise is needed

Source: Adapted from Isard, W. (1998).

5. Some additional tables and notes for Israel/Palestine during the British Mandate and Ottoman period

Table A.8.2 Estimated population of Palestine 1870–1946, according to Rodinson

Year	Arabs	%	Jews	%	Total
1870	367,224	98	7,000	2	375,000
1893	469,000	98	10,000	2	497,000
1912	525,000	93	40,000	6	565,000
1920	542,000	90	61,000	10	603,000
1925	598,000	83	120,000	17	719,000
1930	763,000	82	165,000	18	928,000
1935	886,000	71	355,000	29	1,241,000
1940	1,014,000	69	463,000	31	1,478,000
1946	1,237,000	65	608,000	35	1,845,000

Source: The numbers in this table are estimates created and adapted from from Ben-Arieh (1975); Scholch (1985); Encyclopedia Britannica, (1911); Encyclopedia of Islam (1964); UN Document A/AC 14/32 (1947); McCarthy (1981); Karpat (1978); Farell (1984); Khalidi (1971); Abu Lughod (1971).
Note: Figures are rounded.

Table A.9 Population of Palestine, 1922–1942[a,b]

Year	Total	Muslims		Jews		Christians		Others	
		(No.)	*(%)*	*(No.)*	*(%)*	*(No.)*	*(%)*	*(No.)*	*(%)*
1922 Census	752,048	589,177	78.34	83,790	11.14	71,464	9.50	7,617	1.01
1931 Census	1,033,314	759,700	73.52	174,606	16.90	88,907	8.60	10,101	0.98
1931[c]	1,036,339	761,922	73.52	175,138	16.90	89,134	8 60	10,145	0.98
1932	1,073,827	778,803	72.52	192,137	17.90	92,520	8.61	10,367	0.97
1933	1,140,941	798,506	69.99	234,967	20.59	96,791	8.48	10,677	0.94
1934	1,210,554	814,379	67.27	282,975	23.38	102,407	8.46	10,793	0.89
1935	1,308,112	836,688	63.96	355,157	27.15	105,236	8.04	11,031	0.85
1936	1,366,692	862,730	63.13	384,078	28.10	108,506	7.94	11,378	0.83
1937	1,401,794	883,446	63.02	395,836	28.24	110,869	7.91	11,643	0.83
1938	1,435,285	900,250	62.72	411,222	28.65	111,974	7.80	11,839	0.83
1939	1,501,698	927,133	61.74	445,457	29.66	116,958	7.79	12,150	0.81
1940	1,544,530	947,846	61.37	463,535	30.01	120,587	7.81	12,562	0.81
1941	1,585,500	973,104	61.38	474,102	29.90	125,413	7.91	12,881	0.81
1942	1,620,005	995,292	61.44	484,408	29.90	127,184	7.85	13,121	0.81

Source: Adapted from the data of the Esco Foundation (1947) available from the webpage: www.unu.edu/unpress/unupbooks/80859e/80859E05.htm.

[a] Exclusive of members of His Majesty's Forces (Great Britain).
[b] Adapted from table, 'Estimated Population of Palestine', Statistical Abstract of Palestine 1943, p. 2.
[c] The figures for 1931 and following years are as of 31 December of each year.

Table A.10 Israel/Palestine: Arab/Jewish population (1914–1946)

Year	Jews	Arabs	Total	% of Jews to Total
1914	60,000	731,000	791,000	7.585%
1918	59,000	688,000	747,000	7.898%
1922	83,790	668,258	752,048	11.141%
1931	174,606	858,708	1,033,314	16.897%
1941	474,102	1,111,398	1,585,500	29.902%
1944	554,000	1,211,000	1,765,000	31.388%
1946	608,225	1,237,334	1,845,559	32.956%

Source: Adapted by year from:
1914: Justin McCarthy: The Population of Palestine, 1990
1922 and 1931: British Census: Census conducted by the British Mandate Government
1941: Esco Foundation, Palestine: A Study of Jewish, Arab, and British Policies Vol. 1, p. 46, Yale University Press, 1947
1944: Anglo-American Committee of Inquiry: Chapter IV: Population, 20 April 1946.
1946: United Nations, General Assembly, A/364, 'UNSCOP Report to the General Assembly', 3 September 1947

Table A.11 Jewish immigration during the British Mandate

Year	Number of Immigrants	Number of Illegal Immigrants	Total
1919	1806	-	1806
1920	8223	-	8223
1921	8294	-	8294
1922	8685	-	8685
1923	8093	-	8093
1924	12856	-	12856
1925	33801	-	33801
1926	13081	-	13081
1927	2713	-	2713
1928	2178	-	2178
1929	5249	-	5244
1930	4944	-	4944
1931	4075	-	4075
1932	9553	-	9553
1933	27682	2465	30327
1934	38244	4115	30147
1935	58050	3804	42359
1936	27910	1807	29717
1937	9855	681	10536
1938	11441	1427	12868
1939	16405	11156	27561
1940	4547	3851	8398
1941	3647	2239	5886
1942	2194	1539	3733
1943	8507	-	8507
1944	14464	-	14464
1945	12751	370	13121
1946	7850	9910	17760
1947	7290	14252	21542
1948	2109	15065	17174

Source: Adapted from the data available from: http://nakba.sis.gov.ps/english/settlements/
The%20Jewish%20Immigration.html.

Table A.12 Human and income poverty: Middle East and Arab countries

HDI Rank		Human Poverty Index (HPI-1)		Population below income poverty line (%)			HPI-1 rank minus income poverty rank
		Rank	Value (%)	$1 a day	$2 a day	National Poverty Line	
33	Kuwait						
35	Qatar	13	7.8	...	...	...	...
39	United Arab Emirates	17	8.4	...	...	...	...
58	Oman						
61	Saudi Arabia						
84	Turkey	22	9.2	3.4	18.7	27	−1
86	Jordan	11	6.9	<2	7	14.2	5
88	Lebanon	18	8.5				...
91	Tunisia	45	17.9	<2	6.6	7.6	27
94	Iran	30	12.9	<2	7.3	...	19
104	Algeria	51	21.5	<2	15.1	22.6	31
106	Occupied Palestinian Territories	9	6.6	...	...	...	...
108	Syrian Arabic Republic	31	13.6	...	...	...	...
112	Egypt	48	20	3.1	43.9	16.7	18
126	Morocco	68	33.4	<2	14.3	19	41
147	Sudan	69	34.4	...	...	...	...
153	Yemen	82	38	15.7	45.2	41.8	21

Source: Adapted from the Human Development Report 2007/2008 (United Nations Development Program) available at: http://hdr.undp.org/en/media/hdr_20072008_en_complete.pdf.

Table A.13 Armed conflicts in Middle East countries, 1963–1999[28]

Location	Reason for conflict	Opposition Organisation	Year	Intensity Level
Algeria	Government	Govt Takfir wa'l Hijra (Exile and Rédemption), MIA (Mouvement Islamique Armée Armed Islamic Movement), FIS (Front Islamique du Salut/ Islamic Salvation Front), GIA (Groupe islamique armé: Armed Islamic Group), GSPC (Groupe salafiste pour la prédicationet le combat: Salafist Group for Preaching and Combat)	1991–92	Minor
			1993–99	War
Algeria – Morocco	Territory (Common Border)		1963	Minor
Egypt	Government	Al-Gama'a al-Islamiyya (Islamic Association)	1993–98	Minor
Iran	Government	Mujahideen e Khalq	1979–80	Minor
			1981–82	War
			1986–88	Minor*
			1991–93	Minor*
			1997	Minor*
			1999	Minor*
	Territory (Kurdistan)	KDPI (Kurdish Democratic Party of Iran)	1966–68	Minor*[29]
			1979–80	War
			1981	Minor*
			1982	War
			1983–88	Minor*
			1990	Minor*
			1993	Minor*
			1996	Minor*
Iran	Territory (Arabistan)	APCO (Arab Political and Cultural Organisation)	1979–80	Minor
Iran – Iraq	Territory (Various)[30]		1974	Minor

Table A.13 (cont.)

Location	Reason for conflict	Opposition Organisation	Year	Intensity Level
Iraq	Government	Military faction	1980–88	War
Iraq-Kuwait[31]	Territory (Kuwait)	SCIRI (Supreme Council for the Islamic Revolution in Iraq)	1963	Minor
		KDP (Al-hizb al dimuqraati al-kurid: Kurdish Democratic Party of Iraq), PUK (Patriotic Union of Kurdistan)[32]	1982–84	Minor
			1987	Minor
			1991	War
			1992–96	Minor*[33]
		PUK (Patriotic Union of Kurdistan)	1961–63	War
			1964	Minor*
			1965–66	War
			1967–68	Minor*
			1969	War
			1970	Minor*
			1973	Minor*
			1974–75	War
			1976–87	Minor*
			1988	War
			1989–90	Minor*
			1991	War
			1992–93	Minor*
			1996	Minor*
			1990	Minor
			1991	War
Israel	Territory (Palestine)	Palestinian insurgents	1963–64	Minor*
		PLO (Munazamat tahir falastin: Palestine Liberation Organization) groups, Non-PLO groups[34]	1965–88	Minor*

Conflict	Parties / Type	Year	Type
	PFLP (Al-Jabna Al-Shabiyya li Tahrir Falastin: Popular Front for the Liberation of Palestine) PFLP-GC (PFLG-General Command), Fatah (Harakat Tahrir Falastin: Movement for the National Liberation of Palestine), Hezbollah (Party of God), PIJ (Al-Jihad al-Islami fi Filastin: Palestinian Islamic Jihad), PNA (Palestinian National Authority), Hamas (Harakat almuqawarna al-islamiyya: Islamic Resistance Movement), AMB(Kataeb al-Shaheed al-Aqsa: al-Aqsa Martyr's Brigade), Harakat Amal (Hope Movement)	1989	Minor*
Israel-Egypt	Territory (Suez/Sinai)	1967	War
		1969–70	Minor*[35]
		1973	War
Israel-Jordan	Territory (West Bank)	1967	War
Israel-Syria	Territory (Golan Heights)	1967	War
		1973	War
Lebanon	Various Organisations,[36] Syria, Israel	1975	Minor*
		1976	War
		1977–79	Minor*[37]
		1980–82	War
		1983–88	Minor*
		1989–90	War
	Lebanese Army (Aoun), Lebanese Forces, Syria		
Syria	Military faction	1966	Minor
	Muslim Brotherhood	1979–81	Minor
		1982	War
Turkey	Territory (Northern Cyprus) Devrimci sol (Revolutionary Left)	1974	War
		1991–92	Minor
Government	Territory (Kurdistan) PKK (Partiya karkeren Kurdistan: Kurdistan Worker's Party)	1984–86	Minor
		1987–91	Minor*
		1992–97	War
		1998-	Minor*

Table A.13 (cont.)

Location	Reason for conflict	Opposition Organisation	Year	Intensity Level
Morocco	Government	Military faction	1971	Minor
Morocco-Mauritania	Territory (Western Sahara)	Polisario (Frente popular de liberación de Saguia el Hamra y Rio de Oro: Popular Front for the Liberation of Saguia al Hamra and Rio de Oro)	1975–80	War
Tunisia	Government	Résistance armée tunisienne (Tunisian Armed Resistance)	1981–89	Minor*
Saudi Arabia	Government	Juhayman movement	1980	Minor
North Yemen[38]	Government	Royalists	1979	Minor
North Yemen – South Yemen	Government/Territory (common border)	National Democratic Front	1972–75	Minor
South Yemen	Territory (Aden/South Yemen)	United Kingdom vs. NLF (National Liberation Front), FLOSY (Front for the Liberation of South Yemen)	1965	Minor
			1966–67	War
Yemen	Government	Faction of Yemenite Socialist Party	1968–70	Minor
			1980–82	Minor*[39]
	Territory (South Yemen)	Democratic Republic of Yemen	1972	Minor
			1978–79	Minor
			1964–67	War
			1986	War
			1994	War
Muscat and Oman/Oman	Government	PFLOAG (Popular Front for the Liberation of the Occupied Arab Gulf), South Yemen	1972–75	Minor

Source: Adapted from the PRIO data set.

* Minor armed conflict: at least 25 battle-related deaths in that year and fewer than 1,000 battle-related deaths during the course of conflict.
Note: **War**: at least 1,000 battle-related deaths in that year. Names of the opposition organisations are given in the local language, if available, and in English. The latest version of this document can always be found at http://www.prio.no/cwp/armedconflict/ and http://www.ucdp.uu.se/research/UCDP/our_data1.htm.

Notes

1 The Second Caliph, 634–644 CE.
2 It ran in part: 'From the servant of Allah and the commander of the Faithful, Omar: The inhabitants of Jerusalem are granted security of life and property. Their churches and crosses shall be secure. This treaty applies to all people of the city. Their places of worship shall remain intact. These shall neither be taken over nor pulled down. People shall be quite free to follow their religion. They shall not be put to any trouble...'
3 The Balfour Declaration: 'His Majesty's Government view with favour the establishment in Palestine of a national home for the Jewish people, and will use their best endeavours to facilitate the achievement of this object, it being clearly understood that nothing shall be done which may prejudice the civil and religious rights of existing non-Jewish communities in Palestine, or the rights and political status enjoyed by Jews in any other country.'
4 The Kiblah is the direction that Muslims must face when praying to God.
5 Isra is an Arabic word that refers to the miraculous night journey from Mecca to Jerusalem.
6 Miraj is an Arabic word that refers to the ascension of Mohammed from Jerusalem to the Heavens.
7 The Buraq is an animal, white and long, larger than a donkey but smaller than a mule, who would place its hoof at a distance equal to the range of vision.
8 He was the Mufti of Jerusalem and supported by the British.
9 A Hebrew word meaning 'The Defence'.
10 David Ben-Gurion became prime minister of the state of Israel when it was founded in May 1948.
11 It is formally known as the Palestine Royal Commission. This commission recommended that Israel/Palestine should be divided into Arab and Jewish States.
12 The key provisions of the White Paper were: first, that it was not British policy that Israel/Palestine should become a Jewish or Arab state; second, that Jewish immigration would be limited and the transfer of land from Arabs to Jews restricted; third, that Britain foresaw after ten years an independent state in Israel/Palestine sharing government between Arabs and Jews.
13 King David Hotel housed the British military command in Israel/Palestine and was the headquarters of the British Criminal Investigation Division.
14 The countries that voted accepting the UN Resolution were: Australia, Belgium, Bolivia, Brazil, Byelorussia, Canada, Costa Rica, Czechoslovakia, Denmark, Dominican Republic, Ecuador, France, Guatemala, Haiti, Iceland, Liberia, Luxembourg, Netherlands, New Zealand, Nicaragua, Norway, Panama, Paraguay, Peru, Philippines, Poland, South Africa, Sweden, Ukraine, Uruguay, US, USSR, Venezuela. Those who refused: Afghanistan, Cuba, Egypt, Greece, India, Iran, Iraq, Lebanon, Pakistan, Saudi Arabia, Syria, Turkey, Yemen. Countries absent: Argentina, Chile, China, Colombia, El Salvador, Ethiopia, Honduras, Mexico, United Kingdom, Yugoslavia.
15 Establishment of Israel: 'accordingly we, members of the People's Council, representatives of the Jewish community of Eretz-Israel and of the Zionist movement, are here assembled on the day of the termination of the British mandate over Eretz-Israel and, by virtue of our natural and historic right and on the strength of the resolution of the United Nations General Assembly, hereby declare the establishment of a Jewish state in Eretz-Israel, to be known as the state of Israel.'
16 These countries are Lebanon, Egypt, Syria, and Jordan.
17 The US placed pressure on Britain when the US Federal Reserve Board undermined the pound–dollar exchange rate by selling large amounts of British pounds (Hiro, 2003).

18 Egypt: 1,650 killed, 4,900 wounded, and 6,185 taken prisoner. Israel: 189 killed, 899 wounded, and 4 taken prisoner. France: 10 killed and 33 wounded. Britain: 16 killed and 96 wounded.

19 These forces were placed in Sinai after the 1956 war.

20 The Arab casualties in the Six Day War were 21,000 killed, 45,000 wounded and 6,000 taken prisoner; the Jewish casualties were 779 killed, 2,563 wounded, and 15 prisoners.

21 This war is called the Yom Kippur War in Israel and the Ramadan War in the Arab world.

22 Israel casualties: 2,656 killed and 7,250 wounded, Egypt and Syria casualties: 8,528 killed and 19,540 wounded (Western analysis).

23 Several incidents led to 'Black September'. First, King Hussein, King of Jordan, survived assassination attempts by Palestinians in both June and September. Second, the Palestinians began new forms of military activities against Israel such as hijacking planes. Finally, a group of Palestinians succeeded in assassinating the Jordanian Prime Minister in Cairo in November 1971. All these events encouraged King Hussein to use his troops to crush the power of Palestinian military groups inside his country and massacre Palestinians in their camps (Bickerton and Pearson, 1986).

24 This war is known in Lebanon as the July War and in Israel as the Second Lebanon War.

25 The resolution demands: (a) full cessation of hostilities; (b) Israel to withdraw all of its forces from Lebanon in parallel with the Lebanese, and the United Nations Interim Force in Lebanon (UNIFIL) deploying throughout the south; (c) Hezbollah to be disarmed; (d) full control of Lebanon by the government of Lebanon; (e) no paramilitary forces, including (and implying) Hezbollah, south of the Litani River.

26 The full list of Palestinian leaders killed from the 70s is: Abdel Wael Zwaiter, Dr. Mahmoud Hamshari, Hussein Al-Bashir, Mohamad Yussef Al-Najjar, Kamal Adwan, Kamal Nasser, Zaiad Muchasi, Mohammad Boudia, Abu Jihad, Fathi Shaqaqi, Yahya Ayyash, Jamal Abdul Raziq, Massoud Ayyad, Jamal Mansour, Imad Abu Sneneh, Salah Sahade, Sheikh Ahmad Yassin, Abdel Aziz Rantisi, Adnan Al-Ghoul, and Imad Abbas.

27 This operation was authorised by Israeli Prime Minister Golda Meir in 1972 and lasted for more than 20 years (Reeve, 2001).

28 Table 3 demonstrates the incidence of armed conflict in Middle Eastern Countries during the period 1963–1999, classified according to intensity level and type of rebel and insurgent groups.

29 Possibly war in 1966–68.

30 Notably the Shatt-al-Arab, but also islands in the Strait of Hormuz as well as territory along their common land border. By 1982, the stated incompatibility had widened to include governmental power in addition to territorial dispute.

31 In 1991, Kuwait, supported by the Multinational Coalition comprising troops from Argentina, Australia, Bahrain, Bangladesh, Belgium, Canada, Czechoslovakia, Denmark, Egypt, France, Greece, Honduras, Italy, Morocco, Netherlands, Niger, Norway, Oman, Pakistan, Portugal, Qatar, Saudi Arabia, Senegal, Spain, Syria, United Arab Emirates, the United Kingdom and the United States.

32 Possibly war in the years 1966, 1970 and 1979–87.

33 Possibly war 1992.

34 For example, Hamas, Islamic Jihad, PFLP-GC, Hizbollah and al-Aqsa Martyrs Brigade. For the period after 1988 it has been possible to be more exact in the coding, and more precise information is thus given for these years.

35 Possibly war in 1970.

36 Some of the main groups include the Progressive Socialist Party/Lebanese National Movement, Phalangist militia (Lebanese Forces), Lebanese Front, PLO, Mourabitoun, Lebanese Army, Amal, Hezbollah, SLA (South Lebanese Army), LCP (Lebanese Communist Party), PFLP-GC (Popular Front for the Liberation of Palestine-General Command), SSNP (Syrian Socialist Nationalist Party), Lebanese National Resistance Front, Popular Nasserite Organization, Lebanese Ba'ath Party, Syria, Israel and Iran (Revolutionary Guard); all active during all or part of the conflict.
37 Possibly war in the years 1977–79 and 1983–84.
38 Supported by troops from Egypt 1962–70.
39 Possibly reached the cumulative intensity of 1,000 battle-related deaths in 1980–82.

References

Abadie, A. (2006). 'Poverty, Political Freedom and the Roots of Terrorism', *American Economic Review*, 96(2), pp. 50–56.

Abadie A and Gardeazabal, J. (2004). "The Economic Costs of Conflict: A Case Study of the Basque Country", *American Economic Review*, 93 (1), pp. 113–132.

Abadie, A. and Gardeazabal, J. (2005). '*Terrorism and the World Economy*', Harvard University, typescript.

Abadie, A. and Gardeazabal, J. (2008). 'Terrorism and the World Economy', *European Economic Review*, 52(1), pp. 1–27.

Abolfathi, F. (1978). 'Defence Expenditure in the Persian Gulf: Internal, Interstate, and International Factors in the Iraqi-Iranian Arms Race, 1950–1969', in W.L. Hollist (ed.), *Exploring Competitive Arms Processes*, pp. 99–129. New York: Marcel.

Abu-Lughod, J. (1971). *Cairo: 1001 Years of the City Victorious*. Princeton, NJ: Princeton University Press.

Addison, T. and Murshed, M. (2001). 'From Conflict to Reconstruction: Reviving the Social Contract', UNU/WIDER Discussion Paper No. 48, Helsinki: UNU/WIDER.

Ainslie, G. and Herrnstein, R. (1981). 'Preference Reversal and Delayed Reinforcement', *Animal Learning and Behaviour*, 91(1), pp. 476–482.

Albright, J. and Kunstel, M. (1990). *Their Promised Land*. New York: The Crown Publishing Group.

Alemanni, B. and Ornelas J.R.H. (2008). 'Behaviour and Effects of Equity Foreign Investors on Emerging Markets', Working Papers Series 159, Central Bank of Brazil, Research Department.

Alesina, A. and Perotti, R. (1996). 'Income Distribution, Political Instability and Investment', *European Economic Review*, 40(4), pp. 1203–1228.

Alexander, Y. and Sinai, J. (1989). *Terrorism: The PLO Connection*. New York: Crane Russak.

Ali, H. (2004). 'Essays in Economic Development and Conflicts', PhD dissertation, University of Texas.

American Jewish Yearbook, 1958, 1969, 1970, 1978, 1988, 2001. Philadelphia, PA: The Jewish Publication Society of America.

Angell, N. (1933). *The Great Illusion*. Harmondsworth: Penguin.

Arrow, K. and Kurz, M. (1970). *Public Investment, the Rate of Return, and Optimal Fiscal Policy*. Baltimore, MD: Johns Hopkins University Press.

Avneri, A. (1984). *The Claim of Dispossession: Jewish Land-settlement and the Arabs, 1878–1948*. The State University of New Jersey: Transaction Publishers.

Axelrod, R. (1990). 'The Concept of Stability in the Context of Conventional War in Europe', *Journal of Peace Research*, 27(3), pp. 247–254.

Azar, E., Jureidini, P. and McLaurin, R. (1978). 'Protracted Social Conflict: Theory and Practice in the Middle East', *Journal of Palestine Studies*, 8(1), pp. 41–60.

Bachi, R. (1977). *The Population of Israel*. Jerusalem: CICRED, World Population Year Series.

Baddely, M. (2005). *Armed Conflict, Economic Development and Financial Stability*. Cambridge: Cambridge Centre for Economic and Public Policy.

Bailey, S. (1990). *Four Arab-Israeli Wars and the Peace Process*. London: Macmillan.

Baliga, S. (2011). Conflict Games with Payoff Uncertainty. Mimeo, Northwestern University.

Baliga, S. and Sjöström, T. (2004). 'Arms Races and Negotiations', *Review of Economic Studies*, 17(1), pp. 129–163.

Baliga, S. and Sjöström, T. (2008). 'Strategic Ambiguity and Arms Proliferation', *Journal of Political Economy*, 116(4), pp. 1023–1057.

Baliga, S. and Sjöström, T. (2012). 'The Hobbesian Trap', in M. Garfinkel and S. Scaperdas (eds), *Oxford Handbook of the Economics of Peace*, Chapter 5, pp. 165–178. Oxford: Oxford University Press.

Baliga, S. and Sjöström, T. (2013a). 'The Strategy of Manipulating Conflict', *American Economic Review*, 102(6), pp. 2897–2922.

Baliga, S. and Sjöström, T. (2013b). 'Durable Cheap Talk Equilibria', in R. Harbaugh (ed.), *Advances in Applied Economics Communication Games*, Chapter 4, pp. 172–210. Amsterdam: Elsevier.

Baliga, S., Lucca, D. and Sjöström, T. (2013). 'Domestic Political Survival and International Conflict: Is Democracy Good for Peace?', *Review of Economic Studies*, 78(2), pp. 458–486.

Baltagi, B.H. (1995). *Econometric Analysis of Panel Data*. Chichester: John Wiley.

Banerjee, A.V. (1992). 'A Simple Model of Herd Behavior', *Quarterly Journal of Economics*, 107(3), pp. 797–818.

Bard, M. (2007). 'The Arab Boycott', Jewish Virtual Library'. Retrieved 5 May 2007, from Jewish Virtual Library online: http://www.jewishvirtuallibrary.org/jsource/History/Arab_boycott.html.

Baron, R. and Greenberg, J. (eds) (1990). *Behaviour in Organizations: Understanding and Managing the Human Side of Work*. New York: Allyn and Bacon.

Barro, R. (1990). 'Government Spending in a Model of Endogenous Growth', *Journal of Political Economy*, 98(1), pp. 103–125.

Barro, R. (1991). 'Economic Growth in a Cross Section of Countries', *Quarterly Journal of Economics*, 106(3), pp. 407–443.

Bartlett, J. (1968). *Familiar Quotations*. Edited by Emily Morison Beck. Boston, MA: Little, Brown and Co.

Bates, R. (2001). *Prosperity and Violence*. New York: Norton.

Beatty, I. (1957). *Arab and Jew in the Land of Canaan*. Chicago, IL: Henry Regnery Company.

Begin, M. (1977). *The Revolt: Story of the Irgun*. New York: Nash.

Beinin, J. and Hajjar, L. (1989). 'Palestine and the Arab-Israeli Conflict for beginners', in Z. Lockman and J. Beinin (eds), *Intifada: the Palestinian uprising Against the Israeli occupation*, pp. 101–112. Cambridge, MA: South End Press.

Bekaert, G. and Harvery, C.R. (2000). Foreign Speculators and Emerging Equity Markets, *Journal of Finance*, 55, 465–514.

Benabou, R. (1993). 'Workings of a City', *Quarterly Journal of Economics*, 108(3), pp. 619–652.

Ben-Arieh, Y. (1975). 'The Population of the Large Towns in Palestine During the First Eighty Years of the Nineteenth Century, According to Western Sources', in M. Ma'oz (ed.), *Studies on Palestine During the Ottoman Period*. Jerusalem: Magnus Press.

Benhabib, J. and Day, R. (1982). 'A Characterization of Erratic Dynamics in Overlapping Generations Model', *Journal of Economic Dynamics and Control*, 4(1), pp. 37–55.

Benhabib, J. and Rustichini, A. (1996). 'Social Conflict and Growth', *Journal of Economic Growth*, 1(1), pp. 125–142.

Benmelech, E. and Berrebi, C. (2006). '*Attack Assignments in Terror Organizations and the Productivity of Suicide Bombers.*' Harvard University, typescript.

Ben-Yehuda, H. and Mishali-Ram, M. (2006). 'Protracted Conflicts, Crises, and Ethnicity: The Arab-Israeli and India-Pakistan Conflicts, 1947–2005', *The Journal of Conflict Studies*, 26(1), pp. 75–100.

Berman, E. (2003). 'Hamas, Taliban, and the Jewish Underground: An Economists View of Radical Religious Militias.' UC San Diego, typescript.

Bernheim, D. (1994). 'A Theory of Conformity', *Journal of Political Economy*, 102(3), pp. 841–877.

Berrebi, C. (2003). 'Evidence about the Link Between Education, Poverty and Terrorism among Palestinians', Princeton University Industrial Relations Section Working Paper #477.

Bickerton, I. and Klausner, C. (2001). *A Concise History of the Arab-Israeli Conflict*. New York: Prentice Hall.

Bickerton, I. and Pearson, M. (1986). *The Arab-Israeli Conflict*. Melbourne: Longman Cheshire.

Bikhchandani, S., Hirshleifer, D. and Welsh, I. (1992). 'A Theory of Fads, Fashion, Custom, and Cultural Change as Informational Cascades', *Journal of Political Economy*, 100(5), pp. 992–1026.

Bikhchandani, S., and Sharma, S. (2000). 'Herd Behavior in Financial Markets', *IMF Staff Chapters,* 47(3), pp. 279–310.

Binswanger, H., Deininger, K. and Feder, G. (1993). 'Power, Distortions, Revolt, and Reform in Agricultural Land Relations', Latin America and the Caribbean Technical Department and the Agriculture and Rural Development Department, World Bank, Mimeo.

Blanchard, O.J. (1985). 'Debts, Deficits and Finite Horizons', *Journal of Political Economy*, 93(2), pp. 223–247.

Blavatsky, P. (2004). 'Contest Success Function with the Possibility of a Draw: Axiomatization', Working Paper, Institute for Empirical Research in Economics: University of Zurich, Switzerland.

Blomberg, B., Hess, G. and Orphanides, A. (2004). 'The Macroeconomic Consequences of Terrorism', *Journal of Monetary Economics*, 51(5), pp. 1007–1032.

Blomberg, B., Brock, S., Hess, G.D. and Weerapana, A. (2004). 'Economic Conditions and Terrorism', *European Journal of Political Economy*, 20(2), pp. 463–478.

Bloom, M.M. (2005). *Dying to Kill: The Global Phenomenon of Suicide Terror*. New York: Columbia University Press.

Boix, C. (2003). *Democracy and Redistribution*. New York: Cambridge University Press.

Bös, D. (1994). *Pricing and Price Regulation: An Economic Theory of Public Enterprise and Public Utilities*, Third edition. New York: Elsevier Science.

Boswell, T. and Dixon, W. (1990). 'Dependency and Rebellion: A Cross-National Analysis', *American Sociological Review*, LV: 540–559.

Bourguignon, F. and Morrison, C. (1998). 'Inequality and Development: The Role of Dualism', *Journal of Development Economics*, 57(2), pp. 233–257.

Boyce, J. (1996). *Economic Policy for Building Peace: The Lessons of El Salvador.* Boulder, CO and London: Lynne Rienner Publishers.

Boycko, M., Shleifer, A. and Vishny, R.W. (1996). 'A Theory of Privatisation', *Economic Journal*, 106(2), pp. 309–319.

Brander, J. and Spencer, B. (1983). 'Strategic Commitment with RandD: the Symmetric Case', *Bell Journal of Economics*, 14(1), pp. 225–235.

Brander, J. and Spencer, B. (1985). 'Export Subsidies and International Market Share Rivalry', *Journal of International Economics*, 18(1), pp. 83–100.

Brauer, J. and Van Tuyll, H. (2008). *Castles, Battles, and Bombs: How Economics Explains Military History.* Chicago, IL: The University of Chicago Press.

Brekke, T. (2009). *The Ethics of War in Asian Civilizations: A Comparative Perspective.* London: Routledge, ISBN 978-0415544375.

Bresnahan, T. (1982). 'Duopoly Models with Consistent Conjectures', *American Economic Review*, 71(3), 934–45.

Brockett, C. (1992). 'Measuring Political Violence and Land Inequality in Central America', *American Political Science Review*, 46(1), pp. 169–176.

Bruno, M., Ravallion, M. and Squire, L. (1995). 'Equity and Growth in Developing Countries: Old and New Perspectives on the Policy Issues', World Bank Working Papers in Macroeconomics and Growth No. 1563.

Buchanan, J. and Tullock, G. (1962). *The Calculus of Consent: Logical Foundations of Constitutional Democracy.* Ann Arbor, MI: University of Michigan Press.

Bueno de Mesquita, E. (2005b). 'The Quality of Terror', *American Journal of Political Science*, 49(3), pp. 515–530.

Bueno de Mesquita, E. (2007). 'Politics and the Suboptimal Provision of Counterterror', *International Organization*, 61(1), pp. 9–36.

Bueno de Mesquita, E. (2008). '*Terrorist Factions.*' University of Chicago, typescript.

Bureau of Verification and Compliance (2000). World Military Expenditures and Arm Transfers 1998. Fact sheet, 21 August, US Department of State, Washington, DC. Retrieved 25 August 2007, from FAS online: http://www.fas.org/man/docs/wmeat98/wmeat98fs.html.

Burn, D. (1961). *The Steel Industry, 1939–1959.* London: Cambridge University Press.

Burton, J.W. (1997). *Violence Explained: The Sources of Conflict, Violence and Crime and Their Provention.* Manchester and New York: Manchester University Press.

Buzan, B., and Herring, E. (1998). *The Arms Dynamic in World Politics.* Boulder, CO: Lynne Rienner Publishers.

Caparrelli, F., D'Arcangelis, A.M. and Cassuto, A. (2004). 'Herding in the Italian Stock Market: A Case of Behavioral Finance', *The Journal of Behavioral Finance*, 5(2), pp. 222–230.

Cattan, H. (1969). *Palestine, the Arabs and Israel.* London: Longmans, Green.

Cattan, H. (1973). *Palestine and International Law: The Legal Aspects of the Arab-Israeli Conflict.* London: Longman.

Chai, S.-K. (1993). 'An Organizational Economics Theory of Anti-Government Violence', *Comparative Politics*, 26(1), pp. 99–110.

Chang, E.C., Cheng, J.W. and Khorana, A. (2000). 'An Examination of Herd Behavior in Equity Markets: An International Perspective', *Journal of Banking and Finance*, 24(6), pp. 1651–1679.

Choucri, N. and North, R. (1975). *Nations in Conflict.* San Francisco, CA: Freeman.

Christie, W.G. and Huang, R.D. (1995). 'Following the Pied Piper: Do Individual Returns Herd around the Market?', *Financial Analysts Journal*, 51(1), pp. 31–37.

Cobban, H. (1984). *The Palestinian Liberation Organization: People, Power and Politics*. New York: Colombia University.

Cohen, J.S., Stevenson, R., Mintz, A. and Ward, M.D. (1996). 'Defense Expenditures and Economic Growth in Israel: The Indirect Link', *Journal of Peace Research*, 33(3), pp. 341–352.

Cohen, M. (1986). 'Pluralism and Theocrats: the Conflict between Religion and State in Israel', in N. Biggar, J.S. Scott, and W. Schweiker (eds), *Cities of Gods: Faith, Politics and Pluralism in Judaism, Christianity and Islam*, pp. 35–54. New York: Greenwood Press.

Collier, P. (2000b). 'Doing Well out of War: An Econometric Perspective', in M. Berdal and D.M. Malone (eds), *Greed and Grievance: Economic Agendas in Civil Wars*, pp. 91–112. Boulder, CO: Lynne Rienner.

Collier, P. and Hoeffler, A. (1998). 'On Economic Causes of Civil War', *Oxford Economic Papers*, 50(4), pp. 563–573.

Collier, P. and Hoeffler, A. (2000). 'Greed and Grievance in Civil Wars', Working Paper, World Bank WPS 2000–18.

Collier, P. and Hoeffler, A. (2002a). 'On the Incidence of Civil War in Africa', *Journal of Conflict Resolution*, 46(1), pp. 13–28.

Collier, P. and Hoeffler, A. (2002b). 'Greed and Grievance in Civil Wars', Working Paper, Centre for the Study of African Economies, Oxford. WPS 2002–01.

Conceição, P. and Ferreira, P. (2000). 'The Young Person's Guide to the Theil Index: Suggesting Intuitive Interpretations and Exploring Analytical Applications', UTIP Working Paper Number 14. Retrieved 27 August 2007, from University of Texas (Inequality Project) online: http://utip.gov.utexas.edu/abstract.html#UTIP14.

Cooper, R. and Haltiwanger, J. (1996). 'Evidence on Macroeconomic Complementarities', *Review of Economic and Statistics*, 78(1), pp. 78–93.

Cooper, R. and John, A. (1988). 'Coordinating Coordination Failures in Keynesian Models', *Quarterly Journal of Economics*, 103(3), pp. 441–463.

Cramer, C. (2003). 'Does Inequality Cause Conflict?', *Journal of International Development*, 15(4), pp. 397–412.

Dashwood, H. (2000). *Zimbabwe: The Political Economy of Transformation*. Toronto: University of Toronto.

Day, R.H. (1982). 'Irregular Growth Cycles', *American Economic Review*, 72(1), pp. 406–432.

Deeb, M. (2003). *Syria's Terrorist War on Lebanon and the Peace Process*. Houndmills: Palgrave Macmillan.

Deininger, K. and Squire, L. (1996). 'A New Data Set Measuring Income Inequality', *The World Bank Economic Review*, 10(3), pp. 565–591.

Deininger, K. and Squire, L. (1998). 'New Ways of Looking at Old Issues: Inequality and Growth', *Journal of Development Economics*, 57(2), pp. 259–287.

Dershowitz, A. (2003). *The Case for Israel*. Indianapolis, IN: John Wiley.

Deutsch, M. (1973). *The Resolution of Conflict: Constructive and Destructive Processes*. New Haven, CT: Yale University Press.

Diamond, P.A. (1982). 'Aggregate Demand Management in Search Equilibrium', *Journal of Political Economy*, 90(3), pp. 881–894.

Diehl, P.F. (1983). 'Arms Races and Escalation: A Closer Look', *Journal of Peace Research*, 20(3), pp. 205–212.

Diehl, P.F. and Crescenzi, M.J.C. (1998). 'Reconfiguring the Arms Race–War Debate', *Journal of Peace Research*, 35(1), pp. 111–118.

Diehl, P.F. and Goertz, G. (2000), *War and Peace in International Rivalry*. Ann Arbor, MI: University of Michigan Press.

Dixit, A. (1984). 'International Trade Policy for Oligopolistic Industries', *Economic Journal*, 94(1), pp. 1–16.

Dixit, A. and Grossman, G. (1986). 'Targeted Export Promotion with Several Oligopolistic Industries', *Journal of International Economics*, 21(2), pp. 233–249.

Dixit, A. and Londregan, J. (1994). 'The Determinants of Success of Special Interests in Redistributive Politics', mimeo, Princeton University.

Dixon, H. (1985). 'Strategic Investment with Competitive Product Markets', *Journal of Industrial Economics*, 33(2), pp. 483–500.

Dixon, H. (1986). 'Strategic Investment with Consistent Conjectures', *Oxford Economic Papers*, 38(1), pp. 111–128.

Donahue, J.D. (1998). *The Privatisation Decision: Public End, Private Means*. New York: Basic Books.

Dowty, A. (2005). *Israel/Palestine*. Cambridge: Polity Press.

Drakos, K. and Gofas, A. (2006b). 'In Search of the Average Transnational Terrorist Attack Venue', *Defence and Peace Economics*, 17(2), pp. 73–93.

Duff, E. and McCamant, J. (1976). *Violence and Repression in Latin America: A Quantitative and Historical Analysis*. New York: Collier MacMillan.

Dwan, R. and Holmqvist, C. (2005). *Patterns of Major Armed Conflicts*. Stockholm, Retrieved 6 November 2006, from Stockholm International Peace Research Institute online: http://www.sipri.org/contents/conflict/MAC_patterns.html.

Eaton, J. and Grossman, G. (1986). 'Optimal Trade and Industrial Policy under Oligopoly', *Quarterly Journal of Economics*, 101(2), pp. 383–406.

Eckstein, Z. and Tsiddon, D. (2004). 'Macroeconomic Consequences of Terror: Theory and the Case of Israel', *Journal of Monetary Economics*, 51(4), pp. 971–1002.

Edkins, J. (1996). 'Legality with a Vengeance: Famines and Humanitarian Relief in Complex mergencies', *Journal of International Studies*, 25(3), pp. 547–575.

Ehrlich, A., Gleick, P. and Conca, K. (2000). 'Resources and Environmental Degradation as Sources of Conflict', Paper presented at 50th Pugwash Conference on Science and World Affairs, Cambridge. Retrieved on 4 April, 2009 from: http://www.studentpugwash.org/uk/WG5.pdf.

Elbadawi, I. (1992). 'Civil Wars and Poverty: The Role of External Interventions, Political Right and Economic Growth', Development Research Group, World Bank, mimeo.

Elbadawi, I. (1999). 'Civil Wars and Poverty; the Role of External interventions, Political Rights and Economic Growth', mimeo, presented at the launch Workshop of the DECRG Research Project on 'Civil Conflicts, Crime and Violence', February, World Bank, Washington, DC.

Elbadawi, I. and Sambanis, N. (2002). 'Why are there so many Civil Wars in Africa? Understanding and Preventing Violent Conflict', *Journal of African Economies*, 9(3), pp. 244–269.

El Kodsy, A. and Lobel, E. (1970). *The Arab World and Israel: Two Essays*. New York: Monthly Review.

Encyclopædia Britannica (1911). In *Encyclopædia Britannica*. Retrieved 23 February 2007, from Encyclopædia Britannica Online: http://www.1911encyclopedia.org/Palestine.

Encyclopedia of Islam (1965). Vol. 2, C-G, Edited by B. Lewis, Ch. Pellat and J. Schacht. Assisted by J. Burton-Page, C. Dumont and V.L. Ménage. ISBN 90-04-07026-5.

Enders, W. (2010). *Applied Econometric Time Series*. Hoboken, NJ: John Wiley.

Enders, W. and Sandler, T. (1993). 'The Effectiveness of Anti-terrorism Policies: Vector-Auto-Regression-Intervention Analysis', *American Political Science Review*, 87(4), pp. 829–844.

Enders, W. and Sandler, T. (2002). 'Patterns of Transnational Terrorism, 1970–99: Alternative Time Series Estimates', *International Studies Quarterly*, 46(1), pp. 145–165.

Enders, W. and Sandler, T. (2006). *The Political Economy of Terrorism*. Cambridge: Cambridge University Press.

Enders, W., Parise, G. and Sandler, T. (1992). 'A Time-series Analysis of Trans-national Terrorism: Trends and Cycles', *Defense Economics*, 3(3), pp. 305–320.

Enders, W., Sandler, T. and Cauley J. (1990). 'UN Conventions, Technology, and Retaliation in the Fight Against Terrorism: An Econometric Evaluation', *Terrorism and Political Violence*, 2(1), pp. 83–105.

Ettinghausen, R. and Grabar, O. (2003). *The Art and Architecture of Islam*, pp. 650–1250. London: Yale University Press.

Farell, B. (1984). 'Review of Joan Peters: From Time Immemorial', *Journal of Palestine Studies*, 53(3), pp. 126–134.

Farsoun, S. (1997). *Palestine and Palestinians*. Oxford: Westview.

Fattah, H. (1999). Sultan Abdul-Hamid and the Zionist Colonization of Palestine: A Case Study from Jerusalem, Retrieved 15 January 2007, from Jerusalemites Online: http://www.jerusalemites.org/jerusalem/ottoman/1.htm.

Fearon, J.D. (1997). 'Signaling Foreign Policy Interests: Tying Hands versus Sinking Costs', *Journal of Conflict Resolution*, 41(1), pp. 68–90.

Fearon, J.D. (1995). 'Rationalist Explanations for War', *International Organization*, 49(3), pp. 379–414.

Fearon, J.D. (1994). 'Signaling vs. the Balance of Power and Interests', *Journal of Conflict Resolution*, 38(2), pp. 236–269.

Fearon, J.D. and Laitin, D. (2003). 'Ethnicity, Insurgency and Civil Wars', *American Political Science Review*, 97(1), pp. 75–90.

Feigenbaum, M.J. (1978). 'Quantitative Universality for a Class of Non-Linear Transformations', *Journal of Statistical Physics*, 19(1), pp. 25–31.

Folberg, J. and Taylor, A. (1984). *Mediation: A Comprehensive Guide to Resolving Conflicts without Litigation*. San Francisco, CA: Jossey-Bass Publishers.

Forbes, K.J. (2000). 'A Reassessment of the Relationship between Inequality and Growth', *American Economic Review*, 90 (4), 869–87.

Forsyth, D. (1990). *Group Dynamics*. Belmont, CA: Wadsworth Publishing.

Frey, S., Herbst, P. and Walter, A. (2007). '*Measuring Mutual Fund Herding – A Structural Approach*', Working Chapter, Tübingen University, Germany.

Friedman, S. (2003). '*Are Jews who Fled Arab Lands to Israel Refugees, too?*', New York Times. 10/11/03 Late Edition – Final, Section B, Page 11.

Friedman, T. (1995). *From Beirut to Jerusalem*. New York: Anchor.

Frot, E. and Santiso, J. (2009). '*Herding in Aid Allocation*', Working chapter, 279, OECD Development Centre, Geneva.

Gambill, G. (1998). 'The Balance of Terror: War by Other Means in the Contemporary Middle East', *Journal of Palestine Studies*, 28(1), pp. 51–66.

Gangopadhyay, P. (2005). 'Chaotic Discrimination and Non-Linear Dynamics', *American Journal of Applied Sciences*, 2(4), pp. 440–442.

Gangopadhyay, P. (2007). 'Irrationality, Non-equilibrium Conflict and Complex Dynamics', *Peace Economics, Peace Science and Public Policy*, 13(2), Article 3, pp. 1–15.

Gangopadhyay, P. and Chatterji, M. (2009). *Peace Science: Theory and Cases*, Chapter 4, pp. 123–145. London: Emerald.

Gangopadhyay, P. and Elkanj, N. (2009). 'Politics of defence Spending and Endogenous Inequality', *Peace Economics, Peace Science and Public Policy*, 15 (1), Article 1, pp. 1–12.

Gangopadhyay, P. and Gangopadhyay, R. (2008). 'Flexible Reservation Prices and Price Inflexibility', *Economic Modelling*, 25(3), pp. 499–511.

Gibler, D.M., Rider, T.J. and Hutchison, M.L. (2005). 'Taking Arms against a Sea of Troubles: Conventional Arms Races during Periods of Rivalry', *Journal of Peace Research*, 42(2), pp. 131–147.

Gil, M. (1997). *A History of Palestine, 634–1099*. Cambridge: Cambridge University Press.

Gilbert, M. (2002). *The Routledge Atlas of Arab-Israeli Conflict (Routledge Historical Atlases)*. Oxford: Routledge.

Glaser, C. (2000), 'The Causes and Consequences of Arms Races', *Annual Review of Political Science*, 3(2), pp. 251–276.

Gleditsch, N. (1967). 'Trends in World Airline Patterns', *Journal of Peace Research*, 4(3), pp. 366–408.

Goldman, N. (1978). *The Jewish Paradox*. New York: Grosset and Dunlap.

Graham-Brown, S. (1980). *Palestinians and their Society 1880–1946*. London: Quartet Books.

Grimmett, R. (2012). Conventional Arms Transfers to Developing Nations, 2004–2011, CRS Report for Congress, 24 August 2012.

Grinblatt, M., Titman, S. and Wermers, R. (1995). 'Momentum Investment Strategies, Portfolio Performance, and Herding: A Study of Mutual Fund Behaviour', *American Economic Review*, 85(4), 1088–1105.

Greene, W.H. (1997). *Econometric Analysis*. 3rd edition. New York: Prentice-Hall.

Grose, P. (1988). 'The President versus the Diplomats', in *The End of the Palestine Mandate*, ed. W. R. Louis and R. W. Stookey. Austin, TX: University of Texas.

Grossman, H.I. (1991). 'A General Equilibrium Model of Insurrections', *American Economic Review*, 81(4), pp. 912–921.

Gurr, T. (1970). *Why Men Rebel*. Princeton, NJ: Princeton University Press.

Hajjar, L. and Beinin, J. (1988). 'Palestine for Beginners', *Middle East Report*, 154(1), pp. 17–20.

Hardy, M. (1979). 'Economic Growth, Distributional Inequality, and Political Conflict in Industrial Societies', *Journal of Political and Military Sociology*, 7(2), pp. 209–227.

Harkabi, Y. (1992). *The Arab-Israeli Conflict on the Threshold of Negotiations*. Center of International Studies Monograph Series Number 3, Princeton University.

Havrilesky, T. (1980). 'The Discordance-Inequality Trade-off', *Journal of Public Choice*, 35(3), pp. 371–377.

Hayek, A.A. (1979). *Law, Legislation and Liberty*, vol. 3, the Political Order of Free People. Chicago, IL: Chicago University Press.

Hegre, H., Ellingsen, T., Gates, S. and Petter Gleditsch, N. (2001). 'Toward a Democratic Civil Peace? Democracy, Political Change, and Civil War, 1816–1992', *American Political Science Review*, 95(1), pp. 33–48.

Hensel, P.R. (1999). 'An Evolutionary approach to the Study of Interstate Rivalry', *Conflict Management and Peace Science*, 17(2), pp. 179–206.

Heo, U. and DeRouen, K. Jr. (1998). 'Military Expenditures, Technological Change, and Economic Growth in the East Asian NICs', *Journal of Politics*, 60(3), pp. 830–846.

Herman, D. and Newman, T. (2000). 'A Path Strewn with Thorns: Along the Difficult Road of Israel-Palestian Peace Making', in J. Darby and R. MacGinty (eds), *The Management of Peace Processes*, Chapter 3, pp. 107–153. Basingstoke: Palgrave Macmillan.

Hiro, D. (2003). *The Essential Middle East: A Comprehensive Guide*. New York: Carroll and Graf.

Hirsch, F. (1977). *Social Limits to Growth*. London: Routledge.

Hirshleifer, D. and Teoh, S.H. (2003). 'Herd Behaviour and Cascading in Capital Markets: A Review and Synthesis', *European Financial Management*, 9(1), pp. 25–66.

Hirshleifer, J. (1988). 'The Analytics of Continuing Conflict', *Synthese Journal*, 76(2), pp. 201–233.

Hirshleifer, J. (1989). 'Conflict and Rent-seeking Success Functions: Ratio vs. Difference Models of Relative Success', *Journal of Public Choice*, 63(1), pp. 101–112.

Hirshleifer, J. (1991). 'The Technology of Conflict as an Economic Activity', *AER Chapters and Proceedings*, 81, pp. 130–134.

Hirshleifer, J. (1994). 'The Dark Side of the Force', *Economic Inquiry*, 32(1), pp. 1–16.

Hirshleifer, J. (1995a). 'Anarchy and its Breakdown', *Journal of Political Economy*, 103(1), pp. 26–52.

Hirshleifer, J. (1995b). 'Theorizing about conflict', in K. Hartley and T. Sandler (eds), *Handbook of Defense Economics*, pp. 165–189. Amsterdam: Elsevier.

Hirshleifer, J. (2000). 'The Macro-technology of Conflict', *Journal of Conflict Resolution*, 44(6), pp. 773–792.

Holt, C. (1982). 'An Experimental Test of the Consistent-Conjectures Hypothesis', in A. Daughety (ed.), *Cournot Oligopoly Characterizations and Applications*, pp. 179–200. Cambridge: Cambridge University Press.

Homer-Dixon, T. (1994). *Environment, Scarcity and Violence*. Princeton, NJ: Princeton University Press.

Homer-Dixon, T. (1999). 'Environmental Scarcities and Violent Conflict: Evidence from Cases', *International Security*, 16(91), pp. 4–40.

Homer-Dixon, T. and Percival, V. (1997). Environmental Scarcity, State Capacity, and Civil Violence: The Case of Bihar, India, mimeo.

Hommes, C.H. (1991). 'Adaptive Learning and Roads to Chaos: The Case of the Cobweb', *Economics Letters*, 36(1), pp. 127–132.

Hommes, C.H. (1993). 'Periodic, Almost Periodic and Chaotic Behaviour in Hicks' Non-Linear Trade Cycle Model', *Economics Letters*, 41(5), pp. 391–397.

Hourani, A. (1991). *A History of the Arab Peoples*. Cambridge, MA: Belknap Press.

Hsiang, S.M., Meng, K.C. and Cane, M.A. (2015). 'Civil Conflicts are Associated with the Global Climate', *Nature*, 476: 438–441, 4.

Human Development Report, United Nations Development Programme (2007). Retrieved 20 May 2007, from United Nations Online: http://hdr.undp.org/en/media/hdr_20072008_en_complete.pdf.

Humphreys, M. (2003). 'Economics and Violent Conflict', retrieved 7 July 2007, from HPCR online: http://www.preventconflict.org/portal/economics.

Iannaccone, L.R. and Berman E. (2006). 'Religious Extremists: The Good, the Bad and the Deadly', *Public Choice*, 128(1–2), pp. 109–129.

Im, E.I., Cauley, J. and Sandler, T. (1987). 'Cycles and Substitutions in Terrorist Activities: A Spectral Approach', *Kyklos*, 40(2), pp. 238–255.

Isard, W. (1998). *Methods of Interregional and Regional Analysis*. Aldershot, Ashgate.

Isard, W. (2002). 'Developing Mutual Improvement Joint Actions: A Need for Interdisciplinary Research', *Peace Science, Peace Economics and Public Policy*, 89(1), pp. 1–30.

Isard, W. (2004). 'A Jordan/West Bank Development Proposal', *Peace Economics, Peace Science and Public Policy*, 10(2), pp. 36–55.

Isard, W. and Azis, I.J. (1999). 'A Cooperative Analysis Procedure for Use by Diplomats and Negotiators: With a Proposed Step for Resolving Conflict on the Korean Peninsula', *Peace Economics, Peace Science, and Public Policy*, 5(1), pp. 1–22.

Isard, W. and Chung, Y. (2000). 'A Proposal for North/South Korea Cooperation that Proved Effective: A Plea for More Multi-Analytic Approaches in Conflict Management', *Peace Economics, Peace Science and Public Policy*, 6(1), pp. 1–11.

Isard, W. and Hara, T. (2003a). 'The Old City of Jerusalem as a Tourist International Magnet: An Initial Proposal for a First Step Cooperation in the Middle East. Part II: Projection of Decrease in Hostilities and Terrorist Activity', *Peace Science, Peace Economics and Public Policy*, 9(1), pp. 1–9.

Isard, W. and Hara, T. (2003b). 'Some Theoretical Thoughts on Constructing a Poverty-Eliminating Social Accounts Bill of Goods', *Peace Science, Peace Economics and Public Policy*, 9(2), pp. 1–14.

Isard, W. and Moyersoen, J. (2003). 'A Preliminary Look at the Relevance of Psychology's Prospect Theory for Identifying Mutual Improvement Joint Actions', *Peace Economics, Public Policy and Peace Science*, 9(3), pp. 27–38.

Isard, W. and Smith, C. (1983). *Conflict Analysis and Practical Conflict Management Procedures*. Ithaca, New York: City and Regional Planning Department, Cornell.

Jalilian, H. et al. (2003). 'Creating the Conditions for International Business Expansion: The Impact of Regulation on Economic Growth in Developing Countries – A Cross-country Analysis', Centre on Competition and Regulation, Working Paper 54, IDPM, University of Manchester.

Jawett, B. (2012), Laws: Plato, Book IV, e-book, University of Adelaide,http://ebooks. adelaide.edu.au/p/plato/p71l/complete.html.

Jean, F. and Rufin, J. (1996). *Économie des guerres civiles*. Paris: Hachette.

Jensen, R.V. and Urban, R. (1984). 'Chaotic Price Behaviour in a Non-Linear Cobweb Model', *Economics Letters*, 15(2), pp. 235–240.

Jervis, R. (1976). *Perceptions and Misperceptions in International Politics*. Princeton, NJ: Princeton University Press.

Johansen, S. (1991). 'Estimation and Hypothesis Testing of Cointegrating Vectors in Gaussian Vector Autoregressive Models', *Econometrica*, 59(5), pp. 1551–1580.

Johansen, S., Mosconi R. and Nielsen, B. (2000). 'Cointegration Analysis in the Presence of Structural Breaks in the Deterministic Trend', *Econometric Journal*, 12(3), pp. 1–34.

Johnson, P. (1987). *A History of the Jews*. New York: Harper and Row.

Juselius, K. (2006). *The Cointegrated VAR Model: Methodology and Applications*. Oxford: Oxford University Press.

Kahneman, D. and Tversky, A. (1979). 'Prospect Theory: An Analysis of Decision under Risk', *Econometrica*, 47(3), pp. 263–291.

Kaldor, M. (1999). *New and Old Wars: Organized Violence in a Global Era.* Cambridge: Polity Press.

Kamien, M.I and Schwartz, N.L. (1983). 'Conjectural Variations', *Canadian Journal of Economics*, 16(2), pp. 191–211.

Kapitan, T. (1997). *Philosophical Perspectives on the Isaeli-Palestinian Conflict, Armonk.* New York: M.E. Sharpe.

Kapitan, T. (2004). 'Terrorism in the Arab-Israeli Conflict', *The Philosophical Issues*, 9(1), pp. 175–191.

Karpat, K. (1978). 'Ottoman Population Records and the Census of 1881/82–1893', *International Journal of Middle East Studies,* XCI(2), pp. 237–274.

Kay, J.A. and Thompson. D.J. (1986). 'Privatisation: A Policy in Search of a Rationale', *Economic Journal*, 96(1), pp. 18–32.

Keen, D. (1998). *The Economic Functions of Violence in Civil Wars*, Adelphi Paper 320 for the International Institute of Strategic Studies. Oxford: Oxford University Press.

Keen, D. (2000). 'Incentives and Disincentives for Violence', in M. Berdal and D.M. Malone (eds), *Greed and Grievance: Economic Agendas in Civil Wars*, Chapter 1, pp. 19–42. Boulder, CO: Lynne Rienner.

Kelley, C.P., Mohtadi, S., Cane, M.A., Seager, R. and Kushnir, Y. (2015). 'Climate change in the fertile crescent and implications of the recent Syrian drought', Proceeding of the National Academy of Sciences, 112: 3241–3246.

Kelman, H. (1995). 'Contributions of an Unofficial Conflict Resolution Effort to the Israeli-Palestinian Breakthrough', *Negotiation Journal*, 11(1), pp. 19–27.

Kennedy, P. (1983). 'Arms Races and the Causes of War, 1850–1945', in P. Kennedy (ed.), *Strategy and Diplomacy, 1870–1945*, pp. 165–177. London: Allen and Unwin.

Khalaf, I. (1991). *Politics in Palestine: Arab Factionalism and Social Disintegration 1939–1948.* Albany: State University of New York.

Khalidi, W. (1971). *From Heaven to Conquest: Readings in Zionism and the Palestine Problem until 1948.* Beirut: Institute for Palestine Studies.

Kikeri, S. and Nellis, J. (2001). 'Privatisation in Competitive Sectors: The Record so far', mimeo, World Bank, Washington (DC).

Kikeri, S., Nellis, J. and Shirley, M. (1992). *Privatisation: The Lessons of Experience.* Washington, DC: World Bank.

Kimmerling, B. and Migdal, J. (2003). *The Palestinian People: A History.* London: Harvard.

Knauss, R.L. (1988). 'Corporate Governance – A Moving Target', *The Michigan Law Review,* 79(9), pp. 478–500.

Konard, K. (2005). *Strategy in Contests.* Social Science Research Centre Berlin, WZB-Berlin.

Krueger, A.B. and Maleckova, J. (2003). 'Education, Poverty, and Terrorism: Is There a Causal Connection?', *Journal of Economic Perspectives*, 17(4), pp. 119–144.

Krystall, N. (1998). 'The De-Arabization of West Jerusalem 1947–50', *Journal of Palestine Studies*, 27(2), pp. 5–22.

Laitner, J. (1980). 'Rational Duopoly Equilibria', *Quarterly Journal of Economics*, 95(4), pp. 641–662.

Lakonishok, J., Shleifer, A. and Vishny, R.W. (1992). 'The Impact of Institutional Trading on Stock Prices', *Journal of Financial Economics*, 32(1), pp. 23–43.

Laqueur, W. (1968). *The Road to War 1967: The Origins of the Arab-Israel Conflict.* London: Weidenfeld and Nicolson.

Leibowitz, Y. (1992). *Judaism, Human Values, and the Jewish State*. Cambridge, MA: Harvard University Press.

Lewis, B. (1993). *The Arabs in History*. New York: Oxford.

Lewis, B. (1995). *The Middle East*. London: Weidenfeld and Nicolson.

Li, Q. and Schaub, D. (2004). 'Economic Globalization and Transnational Terrorist Incidents: A Pooled Time Series Cross Sectional Analysis', *Journal of Conflict Resolution*, 48(2), pp. 230–258.

Lichbach, M.I. (1987). 'Deterrence of Escalation? The Puzzle of Aggregate Studies of Repression and Dissent', *The Journal of Conflict Resolution*, 31(3), pp. 266–297.

Lindbeck, A. and Weibull, J. (1987). 'Balanced Budget Redistribution as the Outcome of Political Competition', *Public Choice*, 54(3), pp. 273–297.

Loewenstein, G. and Prelec, D. (1991). 'Negative Time Preference', *American Economic Review*, 81(2), pp. 347–352.

Londregan, J. and Poole, K. (1990). 'Poverty, the Coup Trap, and the Seizure of Executive Power', *World Politics*, XLII(2), pp. 151–183.

Lopez de Silanes, F. (1993). 'Determinants of Privatisation Prices', Harvard (mimeo).

Luce, R.F. (1959). *Individual Choice Behaviour: A Theoretical Analysis*. New York: John Wiley.

Luterbacher, U. (2004). 'Conflict and Irrevocable Decisions', *Peace Economics, Peace Science and Public Policy*, 10(3), pp. 1–14.

Machiavelli, N. (1961). *The Prince*. London: Penguin, Translated by George Bull.

Mack, A. (2002). 'Civil War: Academic Research and the Policy Community', *Journal of Peace Research*, 39(4), pp. 515–525.

Mansfeld, Y. (1999). 'Cycles of War, Terror, and Peace: Determinants and Management of Crisis and Recovery of the Israeli Tourism Industry', *Journal of Travel Research*, 38(1), pp. 30–36.

Maoz, Z. and Mor, B.D.(2002). *Bounded by Struggle: The Strategic Evolution of Enduring International Rivalry*. Ann Arbor, MI: University of Michigan Press.

Marshak, T. and Nelson, R. (1962). 'Flexibility, Uncertainty, and Economic Theory', *Metroeconomica*, 14(1), pp. 42–58.

Marshall, A. (1961). *Principles of Economics*. London: Macmillan and Co.

Martin, P. and Rogers, C.A. (1995). 'Industrial Location and Public Infrastructure', *Journal of International Economics*, 39(3), pp. 335–351.

Mattar, I. (1983). 'From Palestinian to Israeli: Jerusalem 1948–1982', *Journal of Palestine Studies*, 12(4), pp. 57–63.

May, R.M. (1976). 'Simple Mathematical Models with Very Complicated Dynamics', *Nature* 261(4), pp. 459–467.

Mazur, J. and Herrnstein, R. (1988). 'On the Functions Relating Delay, Reinforcer Value, and Behaviour', *Behavioural and Brain Sciences*, 11(7), pp. 690–691.

McAdam, D. (1982). *Political Process and the Development of Black Insurgency, 1930–1970*. Chicago, IL: University of Chicago Press.

McCarthy, J. (1981). 'The Population of Ottoman Syria and Iraq, 1878–1914', *Asian and African Studies*, 15(1), pp. 3–44.

McCarthy, J. (1990). *The Population of Palestine*. Institute for Palestine Studies Series. New York: Columbia University.

McGinnis, M.D. and Williams, J.T. (2001). *Compound Dilemmas: Democracy, Collective Action and Superpower Rivalry*. Ann Arbor, MI: University of Michigan Press.

Meldrum, A. (2000). 'Harare Dispatch: Good-Bye Mugabe vs. Zimbabwe', New Republic. Retrieved 17 April 2007, from New Republic Online: http://www.ucm.es/BUCM/compludoc/W/10001/00286583_7.htm.

MidEast Web, Population of Ottoman and Mandate Palestine (1999). Retrieved 6 February 2006, from MidEast Web online: http://www.mideastweb.org/palpop.htm.

Midlarsky, M. (1988). 'Rulers and the Ruled: Patterned Inequality and the Onset of Mass Political Violence', *American Political Science Review*, 52(4), pp. 491–509.

Minnis, I. (2001). *The Arab-Israeli Conflict*. Oxford: Heinemann.

Mintz, A. and Huang, C. (1991). 'Guns versus Butter: An Indirect Link', *American Journal of Political Science*, 35(3), pp. 738–757.

Mitchell, E. (1969). 'Some Econometrics of the Huk Rebellion', *American Political Science Review*, 63(6), pp. 1159–1171.

Montesquieu, C.-L. de (1979[1748]). *De l'Espirit des Lois*. Paris: Flammarion.

Moore, M. (2001). 'Political Underdevelopment: What Causes "Bad Governance"', Working Paper, Institute for Development Studies, Sussex.

Morgan, W. and Clark, T. (1973). 'The Causes of Racial Disorders: A Grievance-Level Explanation', *American Sociological Review*, 38(4), pp. 611–624.

Morgenthau, H. (1985). *Politics among Nations: The Struggle for Power and Peace*. 5th edn. New York: Knopf.

Morris, B. (1987). *The Birth of the Palestinian Refugee Problem, 1947–1949*. Cambridge: Cambridge University Press.

Morris, B. (2001). *Righteous Victims: A History of the Zionist-Arab Conflict, 1881–2001*. London: Vintage.

Morris, S. and Shin, H. (1998), Global Games: Theory and Applications, mimeo, Yale University.

Moyersoen, J. (2007). 'On Joint Local Satisficing Actions For Conflict Resolution: The Case of the Conflict in Nepal', *International Journal of Economic Research*, 4(2), pp. 135–170.

Mueller, W. (1989). 'Antitrust in a Planned Economy: Anachronism or an Essential Complement?', in J. Warren (ed.), *State, Society and Corporate Power*, Chapter 8, pp. 285–305. Oxford: Transaction.

Muller, E. and Seligson, M. (1987). 'Inequality and Insurgency', *American Political Science Review*, 52(4), pp. 425–451.

Muller, E.N. (1985). 'Income Inequality, Regime Repressiveness, and Political Violence', *American Sociological Review*, 50(1), pp. 47–61.

Munger, M. (2006). 'Preference Modification vs. Incentive Manipulation as Tools of Terrorist Recruitment: The Role of Culture', *Journal of Public Choice*, 128(2), pp. 131–146.

Murshed, M. and Mamoon, D. (2010). 'The Consequences of Not Loving Thy Neighbour as Thyself: Trade, Democracy and Military Expenditure Explanations Underlying India-Pakistan Rivalry', *Journal of Peace Research*, 52(1), 16–28.

Murshed, M. and Tadjoeddin, Z. (2009). 'Revisiting the Greed and Grievance Explanations for Violent Conflict', *Journal of International Development*, 21(1), pp. 87–111.

Mwanasali, M. (2000). 'The View from Below', in M. Berdal and D.M. Malone (eds), *Greed and Grievance: Economic Agendas in Civil Wars*, Chapter 5, pp. 137–153. Boulder, CO: Lynne Rienner.

Nafziger, W. and Auvinen, J. (1997). 'War, Hunger and Displacement: An Econometric invest/igation into the Sources of Humanitarian Emergencies', Working Papers No.142, Helsinki: UNU/WIDER.

Nasr, K. (1997). *Arab and Israeli Terrorism: The Causes and Effects of Political Violence, 1936–1993*. Jefferson, NC: McFarland.

Newman, P. (1961). 'Approaches to Stability Analysis', *Journal of Economics*, 28(1), pp. 12–29.

Nitzan, S. (1994). 'Modelling Rent Seeking Contests', *European Journal of Political Economy*, 10(1), pp. 41–60.

Olson, M. (1963). 'Rapid Growth as a Destabilizing Force', *Journal of Economic History*, 23(4), pp. 529–552.

Oneal, J. and Russett, B. (1999). 'Assessing the Liberal Peace with Alternative Specifications: Trade Still Reduces Conflict', *Journal of Peace Research*, 36(4), pp. 423–432.

Oren, M. (2002). *Six Days of War: June 1967 and the Making of the Modern Middle East*. Oxford: Oxford University Press.

Ornelas, J.R.H. and Alemanni, B. (2008). 'Herding Behaviour by Equity Foreign Investors on Emerging Markets', *Banco Central do Brasil Working Chapter*, No. 125.

Ostrom, V. (1987). *The Political Theory of Compound Republic*. University of Nebraska.

Pacific Institute, Information on the World's Freshwater Resources. Retrieved 8 June 2007, from Pacific Institute Online: http://www.worldwater.org/data.html.

Palley, T.I. (1995). 'Safety in Numbers: A Model of Managerial Herd Behavior', *Journal of Economic Behavior and Organization*, 28(4), pp. 443–445.

Paranzino, D. (1972). 'Inequality and Insurgency in Vietnam: A Further Re-analysis', *World Politics*, 24(4), pp. 565–578.

Pareto, V. (1966). Les Systèmes d'Economie Politique, in S.E. Finer (ed.), *Vilfredo Pareto Sociological Writings*. New York: Praeger.

Park, K. (1986). 'Re-examination of the Linkage between Income Inequality and Political Violence', *Journal of Political and Military Sociology*, 14(2), pp. 185–197.

Parvin, M. (1973). 'Economic Determinants of Political Unrest: An Econometric Approach', *Journal of Conflict Resolution*, 17(2), pp. 271–296.

Peretz, D. (1996). *The Arab-Israel Dispute*. New York: Facts on File.

Perry, M.K. (1982). 'Oligopoly and Consistent Conjectural Variations', *Bell Journal of Economics*, 13(1), 197–205.

Perthes, V. (1997). 'Syria's Involvement in Lebanon', *Middle East Report*, 203, 18.

Pondy, L. (1967). 'Organizational Conflict: Concepts and Models', *Administrative Science Quarterly*, 12(2), pp. 296–320.

Powell, B. (1982). *Contemporary Democracies: Participation, Stability and Violence*. Cambridge, MA: Harvard University Press.

Powell, R. (2007a). 'Allocating Defensive Resources Prior to Attack', University of California, Berkeley, typescript.

Powell, R. (2007c). 'Defending Against Terrorist Attacks with Limited Resources', *American Political Science Review*, 101(3), pp. 527–541.

Rattinger, H. (1975). 'Armaments, Détente and Bureaucracy: The Case of the Arms Race in Europe', *Journal of Conflict Resolution*, 19(4), pp. 571–595.

Ravallion, M. (1986). 'Testing market integration', *American Journal of Agricultural Economics*, 68, 102–109.

Ravallion, M. (1996). 'Famines and Economics', Policy Research Working Paper 1693 (Washington, DC, World Bank).

Reeve, S. (2001). *One Day in September: The Story of the 1972 Munich Olympics Massacre*. London: Faber and Faber.

Reich, B. (1996). *An Historical Encyclopedia of the Arab-Israel Conflict*. Oxford: Greenwood.

Reimann, C. (2005). 'Assessing the State-of-the-Art in Conflict Transformation', in D. Bloomfield, M. Fischer and B. Schmelzle (eds), *Berghof Handbook for Conflict Transformation, Berlin*. Retrieved 4 April 2009 from http://www.berghofhandbook. net/articles/reimann_handbook.pdf.

Rider, T.J. (2009). 'Understanding Arms Race Onset: Rivalry, Threat, and Territorial Competition', *Journal of Politics*, 71(2), pp. 693–703.

Rider, T.J., Findley, M.G. and Diehl, P.F. (2011). 'Just Part of the Game? Arms Race, Rivalry and War', *Journal of Peace Research*, 48(1), pp. 85–100.

Riker, W. (1964). *Federalism*. New York: Little, Brown.

Rodinson, M. (1968). *Israel and the Arabs*. New York: Penguin.

Rodrik, D. et al. (2002). 'Institutional Rule: The Primacy of Institutions over Geography and Integration in Economic Development', NBER Working aper No. 9305.

Ross, M. (2001). 'How Does Natural Resource Wealth Influence Civil War? Evidence from 13 Case Studies', Paper presented at the World Bank conference on Civil Wars and Post-Conflict Transition. Irvine, University of California, 18 May 2001.

Rothfels, H. (1941). 'Clausewitz', in E.M. Earle (ed.), *Makers of Modern Strategy*, Chapter 5. Princeton, NJ: Princeton University Press.

Roumani, M. (1983). *The Case of the Jews from Arab Countries: A Neglected Issue*. Tel Aviv: World Organization of Jews from Arab Countries (WOJAC).

Rowley, C. and Taylor, J. (2006a). 'The Israel and Palestine Land Settlement Problem: An Analytical History, 4000 B.C.E. – 1948 C.E', *Journal of Public Choice*, 128(1), pp. 41–75.

Rowley, C. and Taylor, J. (2006b). 'The Israel and Palestine Land Settlement Problem, 1948–2005: An Analytical history', *Journal of Public Choice*, 128(1), pp. 77–90.

Rubin, J., Pruitt, D. and Kim, S. (1994). *Social Conflict: Escalation, Stalemate and Settlement*. New York: McGraw-Hill.

Russo, A. (1972). 'Economic and Social Correlates of Government Control in South Vietnam', in I. Feierabend, R. Feierabend and T. Gurr (eds), *Anger, Violence, and Politics: Theories and Research*, Chapter 6, pp. 214–270. Englewood Cliffs, NJ: Prentice Hall.

Saari, D.G. (1996). 'The Ease of Generating Chaotic Behaviour in Economics', *Chaos, Solitions and Fractals*, 7(8), pp. 2267–2278.

Saaty, T. (1980). *The Analytic Hierarchy Process*. New York: McGraw Hill.

Said, E. (1994). *The Politics of Dispossession: The Struggle for Palestinian Self-Determination*. New York: Vintage.

Sambanis, N. (2002). 'What is a Civil War? Conceptual and Empirical Complexities of an Operation'. *Journal of Conflict Resolution*, 48(6), 814–858.

Sample, S.G. (1997). 'Arms Races and Dispute Escalation: Resolving the Debate', *Journal of Peace Research*, 34(1), pp. 7–22.

Sample, S.G. (1998). 'Military Buildups, War, and Realpolitik: A Multivariate Model', *Journal of Conflict Resolution*, 42(2), pp. 156–175.

Samuelson, P.A. (1954). 'The Transfer Problem and Transport Costs, II: Analysis of Effects of trade Impediments', *Economic Journal*, 64(4), pp. 264–289.

Sandler, T. and Lapan, H.E. (1988). 'The Calculus of Dissent: An Analysis of Terrorists Choice of Targets', *Snythese*, 76(2), pp. 245–261.

Scharfstein, D. and Stein, J. (1990). 'Herd Behaviour and Investment', *American Economic Review*, 80(4), pp. 465–479.

Schelling, T.C. (1966). *Arms and Influence*. New Haven, CT: Yale University Press.

Schmalensee, R. (1972). *The Economics of Advertising*. Amsterdam: North-Holland.

Schock, K. (1996). 'A Conjectural Model of Political Conflict: The Impact of Political Opportunities on the Relationship between Economic Inequality and Violent Political Conflict', *Journal of Conflict Resolution*, 30(1), pp. 98–133.

Scholch, A. (1985). 'The Demographic Development of Palestine 1850–1882', *International Journal of Middle East Studies*, 12(4), pp. 485–505.

Segev, T. (2000). *One Palestine, Complete: Jews and Arabs under the British Mandate*. London: Metropolitan Books.

Sen, A.K. (1976). 'Famines as failures of exchange entitlements', *Economic and Political Weekly*, 11(31–33), pp. 1273–1280.

Sen, A.K. (1981). *Poverty and Famines: An Essay on Entitlement and Deprivation*. Oxford: Clarendon Press.

Sen, A.K. (1984b). *Resources, Values and Development*, Oxford: Basil Blackwell.

Shahid, L. (2002). 'The Sabra and Shatila Massacres: Eye-Witness Reports', *Journal of Palestine Studies*, 32(1), pp. 36–58.

Shapiro, I. (1989). 'Gross Concepts in Political Arguments', Political Theory, 17(1), pp. 51–76.

Shapiro, J.N. and Siegel, D.A. (2007). 'Underfunding in Terrorist Organizations', *International Studies Quarterly*, 51(2), pp. 405–429.

Sharif, K. and Nihad, Z. (1987). *The Village of Deir Yassin*. Birzeit: Birzeit University.

Shirley, M.M and Walsh, P. (2001). 'Public Versus Private Ownership: The current state of the debate', mimeo, World Bank, Washington DC.

Shlaim, A. (2001). *The Iron Wall: Israel and the Arab World*. New York: Norton.

Sigelman, L. and Simpson, M. (1977). 'A Cross-National Test of the Linkage between Economic Inequality and Political Violence', *Journal of Conflict Resolution*, 21(1), pp. 105–128.

Siqueira, K. (2005). 'Political and Militant Wings within Dissident Movements and Organizations', *Journal of Conflict Resolution*, 49(2), pp. 218–236.

Skaperdas, S. (1996). 'Contest Success Functions', *Economic Theory*, 7, pp. 283–290.

Smith, A. (1993). *An Enquiry into the Nature and Causes of the Wealth of Nations*. Edited with an introduction and commentary by K. Sutherland. New York: Oxford University Press.

Smith, C. (2001). *Palestine and the Arab-Israeli Conflict*. New York: Palgrave Macmillan.

Smith, J.W. (1994). 'The World's Wasted Wealth II', Institute for Economic Democracy, pp. 224.

Smith, L. and Sorensen, P. (2000). 'Pathological Outcomes of Observational Learning', *Econometrica*, 68(2), pp. 371–398.

Smith, W. (1982). 'Beirut Goes up in Flames', *Time Magazine,* 120(7), retrieved 17 March 2006 from Time Magazine Online: http://www.time.com/time/magazine/article/0,9171,950719,00.html.

Spengler, J. (1971). *Indian Economic Thought*. New York: Duke University Press.

Spilerman, S. (1971). 'The Causes of Racial Disturbances: Tests of an Explanation', *American Sociological Review*, 36(3), pp. 427–442.

Stewart, F. (1998). 'The Root Causes of Conflict: Some Conclusions', Queen Elizabeth House, Working Paper no. 16.

Szymanski, S. (2003). 'The Economic Design of Sporting Contests', *Journal of Economic Literature*, 41(6), pp. 1137–1187.

Tan, L., Chiang, T.C., Mason, J.R. and Nelling, E. (2008). 'Herding Behavior in Chinese Stock Markets: An Examination of A and B Shares', *Pacific-Basin Finance Journal*, 16(1), pp. 61–77.

Tekiner, R., Abed-Rabbo, S. and Mezvinsky, N. (1988). *Anti-Zionism – Analytical Reflections*. New York: Amana Books.

Teveth, S. (1994). *Ben-Gurion and the Palestinian Arabs, from Peace to War*. Oxford: Oxford University Press.

Theil, H. (1972). *Decomposition Analysis*. Amsterdam: North-Holland.

Thompson, W.R. (1982). 'Phases of the Business Cycle and the Outbreak of War', *International Studies Quarterly*, 26(2), pp. 301–311.

Thompson, W.R. (2001b). 'Evolving toward an Evolutionary Perspective on World Politics and International Political Economy', in W. Thompson (ed.), *Evolutionary Interpretations of World Politics*. New York: Routledge.

Townsend, R.M. (1983). 'Forecasting the Forecasts of Others', *Journal of Political Economy*, 91(4), pp. 546–568.

Tripp, R. (1970). *The International Thesaurus of Quotations*. New York: Harper and Row.

Truman, H. (1965). *Memoirs, Vol. 2: Years of Trial and Hope*. New York: Signet.

Tullock, G. (1980). 'Efficient Rent Seeking', in J. Buchanan, R. Tollison, and M. Tullock (eds), *Toward a Theory of the Rent Seeking Society*, Chapter 1, pp. 3–15. College Station, TX: Texas A&M University Press.

Uchida, H. and Nakagawa, R. (2007). 'Herd Behavior in the Japanese Loan market: Evidence from Bank Panel Data', *Journal of Financial Intermediation*, 16(4), p. 555–583.

UN Document A/AC 14/32, AD HOC Committee on the Palestinian Question, 11 November 1947, Retrieved 16 November 2007 from United Nations Online: http://domino.un.org/UNISPAL.NSF/0080ef30efce525585256c38006eacae/ba8f82c57961b9fc85257306007096b8!OpenDocument.

Valeriano, B. (2013), *Becoming Rivals: The Process of Interstate Rivalry Development*. Oxford: Routledge.

Vasquez, J.A. (1993). *The War Puzzle*. Cambridge: Cambridge University Press.

Verbeek, M. (2008). *A Guide to Modern Econometrics* (3rd edition). Chichester: John Wiley.

Vining, A. and Boardman, A. (1993). 'Costs and Benefits through Bureaucratic Lenses: Examples of Highway Projects', *Journal of Policy Analysis and Management*, 12, pp. 532–555.

Vives, X. (2005). 'Complementarities and Games: New Developments', *Journal of Economic Literature*, XLIII(2), p. 437–479.

Waldauer, C. et al. (1996). 'Kautilya's Arthashastra: A Neglected Precursor to Classical Economics', *Indian Economic Review*, XXXI(1), pp. 101–108.

Wallace, M.D. (1979). 'Arms Races and Escalation: Some New Evidence', *Journal of Conflict Resolution*, 23(1), pp. 3–16.

Wallace, M.D. (1982). 'Armaments and Escalation: Two Competing Hypotheses', *International Studies Quarterly*, 26(1), pp. 37–56.

Wallensteen, P. and Sollenberg, M. (1997). 'Armed Conflicts, Conflict Termination and Peace Agreements, 1989–96', *Journal of Peace Research*, 34(3), pp. 339–358.

Wallensteen, P. and Sollenberg, M. (2005). 'Armed Conflict and its International Dimensions, 1946–2004', *Journal of Peace Research*, 42(5), pp. 623–635.

Ward, M.D. and Davis, D.R. (1992). 'Sizing up the Peace Dividend: Economic Growth and Military Spending in the United States, 1948–1996', *American Political Science Review*, 86(3), pp. 748–755.

Wasserstein, B. (2001). *Divided Jerusalem: The Struggle for the Holy City*. London: Yale.

Weede, E. (1980). 'Arms Races and Escalation: Some Persisting Doubts', *Journal of Conflict Resolution*, 24(2), pp. 285–287.

Weede, E. (1981). 'Income Inequality, Average Income, and Domestic Violence', *Journal of Conflict Resolution*, 35(4), pp. 639–654.

Weede, E. (1987). 'Some New Evidence on Correlates of Political Violence: Income Inequality, Regime Repressiveness, and Economic Development', *European Sociological Review*, 3(1), pp. 97–108.

Weiner, R.J. (2006). Do Birds of a Feather Flock Together? Speculator Herding on the World Oil Market. Discussion Chapter 06-31, Resources for the Future.

Welch, I. (1992). 'Sequential Sales, Learning and Cascades', *Journal of Finance*, 47(2), pp. 693–732.

Wells, H.G. (1961). *The Outline of History: Being a Plain History of Life and Mankind*. New York: Doubleday Garden City.

Welzer H.C. (2012). *Climate Wars: Why People will be Killed in the Twenty-First Century*. Cambridge: Polity Press.

Wenger, M. and Denney, J. (1990). 'Lebanon's Fifteen-Year War 1975–1990', *Middle East Report*, 162(1), pp. 23–25.

Wermers, R. (1999). 'Mutual Fund Herding and the Impact on Stock Prices', *Journal of Finance, 54(2)*, pp. 581–622.

Wickham-Crowley, T. (1992). *Guerrillas and Revolution in Latin America: A Comparative Study of Insurgents and Regimes Since 1956*. Princeton, NJ: Princeton University Press.

Wittman, D. (1989). 'Why Democracies Produce Efficient Results', *Journal of Political Economy*, 97(6), pp. 1395–1424.

Wright, C. (1983). 'The Israeli War Machine in Lebanon', *Journal of Palestine Studies*, 12(2), 38–53.

Yaari, M. (1965). 'Uncertain Lifetime, Life Insurance, and the Theory of the Consumer', *Review of Economic Studies*, 32(1), pp. 137–150.

Yarrow, G. (1986). 'Privatisation in Theory and Practice', in E. Bailey (ed.), *The Political Economy of Privatisation and Deregulation*, Chapter 6, pp. 295–345. London: Edward Elgar.

Zinnes, D.A. et al. (1978). Arms and Aid: A Differential Game Analysis, in W.L. Hollist *(ed.)*, *Exploring Competitive Arms Processes*, pp. 17–38. New York: Marcel Dekker.

Zuk, G. (1985). 'National Growth and International Conflict: A Revaluation of Choucri and North's Thesis', *The Journal of Politics*, 47(3), pp. 269–281.

Index

Taylor & Francis eBooks

Helping you to choose the right eBooks for your Library

Add Routledge titles to your library's digital collection today. Taylor and Francis ebooks contains over 50,000 titles in the Humanities, Social Sciences, Behavioural Sciences, Built Environment and Law.

Choose from a range of subject packages or create your own!

Benefits for you
- » Free MARC records
- » COUNTER-compliant usage statistics
- » Flexible purchase and pricing options
- » All titles DRM-free.

Benefits for your user
- » Off-site, anytime access via Athens or referring URL
- » Print or copy pages or chapters
- » Full content search
- » Bookmark, highlight and annotate text
- » Access to thousands of pages of quality research at the click of a button.

> REQUEST YOUR **FREE** INSTITUTIONAL TRIAL TODAY
>
> **Free Trials Available**
> We offer free trials to qualifying academic, corporate and government customers.

eCollections – Choose from over 30 subject eCollections, including:

Archaeology	Language Learning
Architecture	Law
Asian Studies	Literature
Business & Management	Media & Communication
Classical Studies	Middle East Studies
Construction	Music
Creative & Media Arts	Philosophy
Criminology & Criminal Justice	Planning
Economics	Politics
Education	Psychology & Mental Health
Energy	Religion
Engineering	Security
English Language & Linguistics	Social Work
Environment & Sustainability	Sociology
Geography	Sport
Health Studies	Theatre & Performance
History	Tourism, Hospitality & Events

For more information, pricing enquiries or to order a free trial, please contact your local sales team:
www.tandfebooks.com/page/sales

Routledge
Taylor & Francis Group

The home of
Routledge books

www.tandfebooks.com

For Product Safety Concerns and Information please contact our EU
representative GPSR@taylorandfrancis.com
Taylor & Francis Verlag GmbH, Kaufingerstraße 24, 80331 München, Germany

www.ingramcontent.com/pod-product-compliance
Ingram Content Group UK Ltd.
Pitfield, Milton Keynes, MK11 3LW, UK
UKHW021013180425
457613UK00020B/919